Hybrid Soft Computing Techniques for Machine Learning and Optimization

Nikhil Kumar Marriwala
University Institute of Engineering and Technology, Kurukshetra University, Kurukshetra, India

Shruti Jain
Jaypee University of Information Technology, Solan, India

Vinod Kumar Shukla
Amity University, Dubai, UAE

Dinesh Kumar
Electrical and Computer System Engineering, RMIT University, Melbourne, Australia

IGI Global
Scientific Publishing
Publishing Tomorrow's Research Today

Vice President of Editorial	Melissa Wagner
Managing Editor of Acquisitions	Mikaela Felty
Managing Editor of Book Development	Jocelynn Hessler
Production Manager	Mike Brehm
Cover Design	Phillip Shickler

Published in the United States of America by
IGI Global Scientific Publishing
701 East Chocolate Avenue
Hershey, PA, 17033, USA
Tel: 717-533-8845
Fax: 717-533-8661
Website: https://www.igi-global.com E-mail: cust@igi-global.com

Library of Congress Cataloging-in-Publication Data

LCCN: 2024051848 (CIP Data Pending)
ISBN13: 9798369368640
Isbn13Softcover: 9798369368688
EISBN13: 9798369368657

British Cataloguing in Publication Data
A Cataloguing in Publication record for this book is available from the British Library.

Table of Contents

Detailed Table of Contents

to overcome these limitations by enabling real-time, continuous monitoring and automated analysis of the signals. This chapter will explore the importance of IoT and Machine learning in biomedical signal processing, highlighting their roles, challenges, and future direction.

User and Entity Behavior Analytics (UEBA) is a critical component of modern cybersecurity strategies aimed at detecting and mitigating security threats within enterprise environments. The system is designed to enhance security through the analysis of user and entity actions. The architecture encompasses data collection and integration techniques, feature extraction, deep learning models, detecting and analyzing.Data collection strategies acquire statistics from quite a few sources, such as system logs, network site visitors, and application logs, resulting in a comprehensive dataset for analysis Feature extraction transforms uncooked facts right into a meaningful representation, for reading a deep modelling can locate patterns in person conduct and entity conduct. Long-term and brief- term reminiscence (LSTM) and convolutional LSTM (ConvLSTM) fashions are used to investigate temporal, spatial, and temporal dependence, respectively.

This speeds up training and can lead to more stable convergence. This helps the optimization process to overcome small local minimal and converge faster. Instead of using a fixed learning rate, learning rate schedules adaptively change the learning rate during training. Techniques like learning rate decay, step decay, or cosine annealing can help improve convergence. These methods often converge faster and are less sensitive to manual tuning of learning rates. Proper weight initialization techniques, such as His initialization or Xavier initialization, can significantly speed up convergence and reduce the likelihood of getting stuck in poor local minima. Batch normalization normalizes activations within a layer, making training more stable and enabling the use of higher learning rates. It can accelerate training and improve the final model's performance. The choice of optimization methods and their configurations should be tailored to the specific task and dataset, emphasizing the need for careful experimentation and hyper parameter tuning.

The system aims to empower farmers by providing insights into the diverse range of crops suitable for their specific land. The work focuses on developing a system that predicts the optimal crop priority, considering various factors such as land characteristics, soil conditions, and climate data. By understanding the intricate relationships between different crop types, farmers can make informed decisions to maximize yield quality. The absence of a robust system for identifying cropping patterns results in random crop choices, leading to yield fluctuations. This prioritization minimizes losses due to suboptimal crop combinations. The proposed system is designed to assist both individual farmers and agricultural departments by incorporating machine learning algorithms that explore the data gathered from the agricultural department to perform an exploratory analysis. This approach allows for a more informed and effective decision-making process in smart agriculture.

The paper presents a comprehensive overview of recent advancements in the field of sickle-shaped cells in the blood leading to a disease commonly known as Sickle Cell anaemia. Machine learning techniques, including classification and clustering algorithms, are employed to analyze complex datasets derived from blood samples, genetic markers, and clinical records. By leveraging these approaches, researchers aim to develop accurate and efficient diagnostic tools capable of identifying individuals with sickle cell anaemia with high sensitivity and specificity. Furthermore, machine learning models facilitate the integration of diverse data sources, enabling a holistic understanding of disease pathophysiology and progression. Challenges such as data heterogeneity, class imbalance, and model interpretability are addressed through innovative algorithmic designs and validation strategies.

The emergence of wearable devices for health monitoring has revolutionized personal healthcare, enabling continuous tracking of vital signs and physical activity in real time. These devices empower individuals to proactively manage their health, leading to early detection of potential issues and improved overall well-being. However, challenges such as data privacy concerns and integration with existing healthcare systems must be addressed to maximize their benefits. This paper provides a comprehensive overview of wearable health monitoring devices, highlighting their transformative impact on personal healthcare and discussing potential solutions to address existing challenges.

People across the globe are actively participating in online groups due to excessive usage of social media as channel of communication and data exchange. Also, due to social media platforms such as Instagram, Facebook social communication has seen a considerable increase. Social media's emergence has revolutionized how people talk to one another and engage with the world. However, there is mounting apprehension regarding the potential repercussions of social networking sites on mental welfare. This paper examines the effect of social networking sites on mental health from a social informatics perspective. Drawing on theories and concepts from social informatics, this paper explores the social, cultural, and technological factors that influence the connection between social networks consumption and psychological health. The paper discusses the possible risks and benefits of social media usage and offers commendations for designing social media platforms that promote psychological health and wellbeing.

Healthcare proves transformed through the IoT and ML combination because this union enables proactive and personalized medical care. The research investigates ML integration possibilities with IoT-connected devices to strengthen data acquisition while operating more efficiently and running predictions and improving patient involvement. The paper addresses obstacles related to using standard centralized data learning systems on distributed Internet of Things information while presenting potential solutions. This document presents details about how ML performs analysis of healthcare data which includes both genetic sequences and wearable sensor information and medical pictures and electronic health records. The paper addresses both ethical considerations and legal aspects that stem from ML applications in healthcare settings. Healthcare benefits from IoT and ML developments to enhance both patient health results and operational resource utilization toward a future streaming medical system.

The healthcare has been substantially revolutionized as a result of the introduction of remote patient monitoring (RPM) technologies. These technologies have made it feasible to continually monitor the health state of patients outside of traditional clinical settings. Wearables, smartphone applications, and cloud-based systems are just examples of the kind of technologies that are used by RPM in order to give healthcare practitioners with real-time data collecting and transmission. The analysis of this data enables medical professionals to detect potential health issues at an earlier stage, take the necessary steps to address them, and develop tailored treatment programs that will improve patient outcomes while simultaneously reducing costs. Integration of artificial intelligence results in improved data interpretation, which in turn enables predictive analytics and proactive treatment of chronic diseases.

Preface

The rapid advancements of machine learning (ML) and artificial intelligence (AI) has created a need for more intelligent and adaptive computational techniques. Conventional methods tend to find it difficult to handle intricate, nonlinear, and high-dimensional problems. To counter these issues, hybrid soft computing methods have evolved as a strong paradigm that fuses several computational intelligence approaches, taking advantage of their strengths and avoiding their limitations.

This book, Hybrid Soft Computing Techniques for Machine Learning and Optimization, offers an in-depth discussion of hybrid approaches that combine fuzzy logic, neural networks, evolutionary algorithms, swarm intelligence, and other soft computing methods. These approaches improve the efficiency, accuracy, and flexibility of ML models and optimize intricate decision-making processes in different fields, such as healthcare, finance, engineering, and data science. Optimized responses emerge from multiple technological combinations that advance healthcare while supporting agricultural systems as well as finance security operations. The main goal of this book is to close the gap between theory and practice. It deals with basic concepts, recent developments, and applications of hybrid soft computing methods. Researchers, practitioners, and students will gain insights into designing intelligent systems that can manage uncertainty, imprecision, and dynamic conditions effectively.

The book delivers extensive knowledge of hybrid soft computing through a systematic structure from theories to practical applications with strategic section organization. Research chapters of the book contain extensive testing work which demonstrates modern transformation methods for computational intelligence systems. We hope that the book is of use to researchers, engineers, and amateurs keen on understanding the changing scene of hybrid soft computing and its revolutionary contribution to contemporary AI applications. All researchers along with professionals together with contributors have our deepest gratitude for their advanced insights. Students and practitioners together with academic researchers find guidance in this book for their study of hybrid soft computing applications for machine learning and optimization.

The content of this book demonstrates the extraordinary capabilities that computational paradigms achieve when working together to improve decision processes and learning operations.

With artificial intelligence (AI) and machine learning (ML) transforming industries, there has never been a greater need for more intelligent, responsive, and effective computational approaches. Conventional ML methods, though potent, tend to be weak with sophisticated real-world problems involving uncertainty, imprecision, and non-linearity.

Hybrid Soft Computing Methods for Machine Learning and Optimization is a timely and thorough investigation of how these paradigms of soft computing can be synergistically integrated to make machine learning models more powerful. The book examines hybrid methods that combine the advantages of several approaches to achieve more effective optimization and decision-making mechanisms. This multidisciplinary methodology has far-reaching implications for applications from healthcare and finance to robotics and big data analysis.

The authors have made a superb effort at discussing both theoretical background and pragmatic usage of hybrid soft computing. The book succeeds in bridging the gap between industry practice and academic research and becomes an ideal read for professionals, students, and researchers. With the advancement of AI, hybrid soft computing methods will become more and more crucial in designing intelligent and flexible systems. This book is a must-read for anyone looking to remain at the forefront of the constantly expanding machine learning and optimization domain.

Nikhil Kumar Marriwala
University Institute of Engineering and Technology, Kurukshetra University, India

Shruti Jain
Jaypee University of Information Technology, India

Vinod Kumar Shukla
Amity University, Dubai, UAE

Dinesh Kumar
Electrical and Computer System Engineering, RMIT University, Melbourne, Australia

Acknowledgement

It gives us immense pleasure to express our deepest gratitude to everyone who played a role in the successful completion of this book, Hybrid Soft Computing Techniques for Machine Learning and Optimization.

We extend our heartfelt appreciation to all the chapter authors for their sincere, timely, and enthusiastic support. Your contributions brought together diverse insights, case studies, and innovative research that transformed this book into a meaningful and valuable resource.

We are equally thankful to the executive board members of IGI Global for their kind approval and unwavering trust in our editorial vision. A very special note of thanks goes to Mrs. Jocelynn Hessler, Director of Book Development at IGI Global Scientific Publishing, for her constant encouragement, guidance, and thoughtful suggestions that helped us shape this project with clarity and excellence.

We wish to acknowledge our institutions for their continuous encouragement and support. We are incredibly grateful to our colleagues, friends, and families, whose love, support, and motivation carried us through every challenge during the creation of this book. Our heartfelt thanks also go to the reviewers, who graciously provided timely feedback and constructive critique, elevating the academic rigor and quality of the work.

We are especially thankful to all our co-authors, whose tireless contributions and collaborative spirit helped craft a cohesive and compelling volume. Your insightful findings and interdisciplinary perspectives have added immense depth and clarity across all chapters.

A sincere word of appreciation goes out to our academic institutions, which provided us with the necessary facilities, research infrastructure, and intellectual freedom to pursue this endeavor. The momentum behind this work was made possible by the steadfast support of our mentors, research collaborators, and students, who constantly inspired and challenged us to push boundaries.

We also wish to acknowledge that there may be many individuals whose names we may have unintentionally missed — to all of you, please accept our sincere thanks. Your presence and support have been vital to this journey.

With gratitude,

— *The Editors*

Chapter 1
Fundamentals of IoT and Machine Learning

Rajeshwari Sissodia
https://orcid.org/0000-0002-9978-0187
Galgotias University, India

ManMohan Singh Rauthan
Hemwati Nandan Bhaguna Garhwal University, India

Varun Barthwal
https://orcid.org/0000-0002-5289-9471
Hemwati Nandan Bhaguna Garheal University, India

Vinay Dwivedi
https://orcid.org/0009-0007-7502-3222
Galgotias University, India

ABSTRACT

The convergence of the Internet of Things (IoT) and Machine Learning (ML) is reshaping industries by enabling smarter, data-driven decision-making and operational efficiencies. This chapter delves into the foundational principles of IoT, illustrating how interconnected devices generate vast amounts of real-time data. It then explores the role of ML algorithms in analyzing this data to uncover patterns, optimize processes, and enhance automation. The chapter discusses emerging trends such as the adoption of 5G networks for improved connectivity, federated learning for decentralized data processing, and the expanding role of artificial intelligence in predictive analytics and automation. Additionally, it highlights the importance of continuous learning and adaptation in these rapidly evolving fields, as well as the potential for groundbreaking innovations in both everyday applications and industrial operations. By addressing both opportunities and challenges, this chapter

DOI: 10.4018/979-8-3693-6864-0.ch001

provides a comprehensive understanding of how IoT and ML are shaping the future of technology and society.

1. INTRODUCTION TO IOT AND MACHINE LEARNING

The rapid evolution of digital technology has led to the proliferation of interconnected devices and intelligent systems, shaping the modern world in unprecedented ways. Two of the most influential and complementary technologies driving this transformation are the Internet of Things (IoT) and Machine Learning (ML). Individually, both IoT and ML have revolutionized various industries, but their integration holds even greater promise, enabling more intelligent, autonomous, and efficient systems.

The Internet of Things (IoT) refers to a network of physical devices embedded with sensors, software, and connectivity that enables them to collect, exchange, and process data in real time. These devices, ranging from everyday household appliances to industrial machinery and smart city infrastructure, generate vast amounts of data that, when analyzed effectively, can lead to improved decision-making, automation, and efficiency. However, managing and deriving meaningful insights from such large-scale data streams presents significant challenges.

This is where Machine Learning (ML) comes into play. ML, a subset of artificial intelligence (AI), enables computers to learn from data and make predictions or decisions without explicit programming. By applying ML algorithms to IoT-generated data, organizations can uncover hidden patterns, predict outcomes, optimize performance, and automate responses with minimal human intervention. This synergy between IoT and ML enhances various sectors, including healthcare, manufacturing, transportation, agriculture, and smart cities.

The integration of IoT and ML is transforming industries by enabling predictive maintenance in manufacturing, personalized healthcare monitoring, real-time traffic optimization in smart cities, and intelligent supply chain management, among many other applications. However, this convergence also brings challenges such as data privacy concerns, cybersecurity risks, scalability issues, and the need for robust infrastructure.

This chapter aims to provide a comprehensive understanding of the foundational principles of IoT and ML, their individual significance, and the vast potential unlocked through their integration. It will explore real-world applications, emerging trends, and the challenges associated with adopting these technologies. By doing so, it highlights the crucial role IoT and ML play in shaping the future of digital transformation and innovation.

1.1 Understanding IoT

The Internet of Things (IoT) is a transformative concept that describes a vast network of interconnected devices capable of communicating and sharing data over the internet. These devices span a wide array of categories, from everyday household items, such as smart thermostats and refrigerators, to complex industrial machinery and infrastructure systems. The core principle of IoT is to enable seamless interaction between these devices, allowing them to collect and exchange information, which can lead to enhanced efficiency, improved quality of life, and innovative applications across various sectors.

Key concepts within IoT include connectivity, which ensures that devices can transmit and receive data reliably over the internet. This connectivity relies on various communication protocols, enabling devices to interact regardless of manufacturer or platform. Another crucial concept is interoperability, which refers to the ability of different devices and systems to communicate and work together effectively. This is often achieved through standardized protocols that facilitate data exchange and integration. Furthermore, IoT relies heavily on data collection and analysis, as devices continuously gather valuable information about their environment, user behavior, and operational status. This data can then be processed and analyzed to derive actionable insights, allowing for more informed decision-making and automation of processes.

The evolution of IoT has been marked by several significant milestones. It traces its roots back to the early days of the internet, where the idea of connecting devices was first explored. In the 1960s and 1980s, the development of ARPANET laid the groundwork for networked communication. However, it wasn't until 1999 that the term "Internet of Things" was coined by Kevin Ashton, who envisioned a future where everyday objects could connect to the internet and communicate autonomously. The following years witnessed rapid advancements in wireless technologies and sensor capabilities, leading to a proliferation of IoT applications across various industries. Today, we are witnessing an explosion of IoT devices, driven by the convergence of advancements in artificial intelligence, cloud computing, and the rollout of 5G technology, which enables faster data processing and real-time analytics.

1.2 Overview of Machine Learning

Machine Learning (ML) is a pivotal subset of artificial intelligence that focuses on enabling systems to learn from data, recognize patterns, and make decisions with minimal human intervention. At its core, ML empowers devices and applications to improve their performance over time by learning from past experiences and adapting to new information. The significance of ML lies in its ability to automate processes, thereby enhancing efficiency and reducing the need for manual input. This capability is crucial in a world inundated with data, where human analysis alone would be insufficient to derive meaningful insights.

One of the most impactful applications of ML is in predictive analytics, where algorithms analyze historical data to identify trends and forecast future outcomes. This has profound implications across various fields, including finance—where it can predict market trends—healthcare—by anticipating patient outcomes—and marketing—by forecasting consumer behavior. The history of ML reveals its gradual evolution from simple algorithms to sophisticated models capable of handling complex tasks. In the early decades, particularly from the 1950s to the 1980s, researchers focused on foundational theories and algorithms, including decision trees, linear regression, and early neural networks. The 1990s brought about the introduction of more advanced techniques such as support vector machines and ensemble methods, which improved the accuracy and reliability of predictions.

The advent of big data and enhanced computational power in the 2000s significantly accelerated the development of ML. These advancements enabled the training of complex models that could process vast datasets, leading to breakthroughs in various applications. In recent years, the emergence of deep learning—a subfield of ML that employs multi-layered neural networks—has revolutionized the field, allowing for remarkable progress in image and speech recognition technologies. As a result, ML has found widespread adoption across diverse industries, shaping the future of technology and driving innovation.

1.3 Intersection of IoT and Machine Learning

The intersection of IoT and Machine Learning creates powerful synergies that significantly enhance the capabilities of both domains. When ML is integrated into IoT systems, organizations can leverage the vast amounts of data generated by connected devices to achieve intelligent decision-making and automation. For example, in industrial settings, predictive maintenance becomes possible through the analysis of data from machinery. ML algorithms can detect patterns that indicate potential failures, allowing organizations to proactively service equipment before breakdowns occur. This not only minimizes downtime but also optimizes maintenance schedules, ultimately saving costs and improving operational efficiency.

Moreover, ML excels in anomaly detection, which is crucial for ensuring the security and reliability of IoT systems. By continuously analyzing data streams from devices, ML algorithms can identify unusual patterns or behaviors that may indicate security breaches or system failures. For instance, in smart home environments, ML can monitor energy usage patterns to detect abnormal behavior that might signal a potential security threat or malfunction. Additionally, in smart cities, traffic management systems utilize ML to analyze data from various sensors, optimizing traffic flow and reducing congestion, thereby enhancing urban mobility and sustainability.

Personalization is another area where the integration of ML into IoT shines brightly. In consumer applications, IoT devices can gather data about user preferences and behavior. ML algorithms can then analyze this data to deliver tailored experiences, such as personalized recommendations for products or services. For instance, a smart thermostat can learn a user's schedule and preferences, adjusting heating and cooling settings to enhance comfort while optimizing energy consumption.

Numerous real-world examples illustrate the transformative benefits of integrating IoT and ML. In agriculture, IoT sensors monitor soil conditions, weather data, and crop health, while ML analyzes this information to optimize irrigation practices and improve crop yields. In the healthcare sector, wearable devices track patient data, such as heart rate and activity levels. ML algorithms can then process this data to provide personalized health recommendations and detect potential health issues early, improving patient outcomes. Similarly, in smart cities, IoT sensors collect data on traffic patterns and environmental conditions, and ML analyzes this data to implement real-time adjustments, enhancing public safety and resource management.

Overall, the exploration of IoT and ML not only highlights their individual significance but also underscores their interconnections, paving the way for innovative applications that can fundamentally reshape industries and improve the quality of life.

Khan and Alghamdi (2019) investigate a wide array of IoT applications designed to enhance urban living through smart city initiatives. They delve into specific use cases, such as smart transportation systems that improve traffic management, waste management technologies that optimize resource use, and environmental monitoring systems that track air quality. Their analysis illustrates how these applications not only enhance operational efficiency but also promote sustainability, thereby improving the quality of life for urban residents. The authors provide real-world case studies, showcasing successful implementations in cities around the globe, which serve as benchmarks for future developments.

Zhou and Yang (2020) present a comprehensive survey on the utilization of machine learning techniques within IoT ecosystems. They categorize these techniques based on their operational frameworks, including supervised, unsupervised, and reinforcement learning methods. The authors emphasize the role of machine learning in improving IoT functionalities, such as data analysis, anomaly detection, and predictive maintenance. By examining existing literature, they identify best practices and highlight the strengths and weaknesses of various approaches, offering insights into which methods are most effective for specific IoT applications.

Saha and Saha (2020) focus on the critical issue of data security within IoT environments. Their review outlines the multifaceted security challenges that IoT systems encounter, including vulnerabilities to cyberattacks and the risk of data breaches. The authors propose a range of mitigation strategies, such as implementing robust encryption techniques, secure authentication protocols, and regular security assessments. They stress the importance of developing a comprehensive security framework to protect sensitive data and ensure the integrity of IoT systems, thereby fostering user trust and system reliability.

Patel and Shah (2021) analyze the convergence of artificial intelligence and IoT, emphasizing the transformative potential of this integration across various sectors, including healthcare, agriculture, and manufacturing. They discuss specific applications, such as AI-driven predictive analytics in healthcare that improve patient outcomes and smart agriculture solutions that enhance crop yields. The authors also address challenges related to data privacy, ethical considerations, and system interoperability, advocating for standardized protocols to facilitate seamless integration and maximize the benefits of AI in IoT.

Gupta and Jha (2021) provide a systematic review of machine learning applications in healthcare, focusing on areas like remote patient monitoring and predictive analytics. They assess how machine learning algorithms can analyze health data to identify patterns and predict potential health issues, ultimately leading to more personalized care. The authors examine various case studies to illustrate successful implementations and highlight areas where further research is needed, particularly in improving algorithm accuracy and ensuring data privacy.

Bertin and Ciarallo (2022) examine the role of edge computing in enhancing IoT system performance. They explain how processing data closer to the source can reduce latency and bandwidth consumption, making IoT systems more efficient. The authors review various edge computing architectures and their applications in sectors such as healthcare and manufacturing. They conclude that edge computing is essential for real-time data processing and analysis, which is increasingly important for applications requiring immediate responses, such as autonomous vehicles and smart manufacturing systems.

Singh and Kumar (2022) highlight the challenges associated with IoT data analytics, particularly the vast volume of data generated by connected devices. Their review addresses issues such as data quality, integration complexities, and the need for real-time processing. The authors explore various analytical techniques and frameworks that can be employed to overcome these challenges, emphasizing the importance of robust data management strategies and the implementation of machine learning models that can handle high-velocity data streams.

Dey and Chakraborty (2023) review the application of IoT technologies in agriculture, focusing on innovations like precision farming and smart irrigation systems. They discuss how IoT devices collect and analyze data on soil conditions, crop health, and weather patterns to optimize farming practices. The authors present case studies that illustrate the positive impact of these technologies on agricultural productivity, resource efficiency, and sustainability, advocating for further research to enhance the scalability of IoT solutions in farming.

Liu and Zhang (2023) explore machine learning techniques specifically designed for optimizing energy management in smart grids. They review various algorithms used for demand forecasting, load balancing, and resource allocation. The authors emphasize the potential for machine learning to improve energy efficiency and reduce costs for consumers. They provide case studies showcasing successful implementations and discuss the importance of integrating these algorithms into existing energy infrastructure.

Nashat and Abu-Mahfouz (2023) discuss the intersection of IoT and big data analytics, focusing on the challenges and opportunities presented by large datasets generated by IoT devices. Their review highlights analytics techniques, including real-time data processing and predictive modeling, that can be employed to extract meaningful insights from IoT data. The authors emphasize the need for advanced analytical frameworks that can handle the complexity and scale of big data in IoT applications.

Kumar and Gupta (2023) highlight recent advances in machine learning specifically tailored for IoT applications. They explore novel algorithms and frameworks that improve the efficiency and effectiveness of IoT systems, including techniques for data fusion and real-time decision-making. The authors discuss the implications of these advancements for various sectors, emphasizing the potential for enhanced automation and intelligence in IoT systems.

Fernandez and Gonzalez (2024) examine the role of IoT in smart transportation systems, reviewing applications such as smart traffic management, vehicle-to-everything (V2X) communication, and public transportation optimization. They discuss how IoT technologies can reduce congestion, improve safety, and enhance the overall efficiency of transportation networks. The authors present case studies that demonstrate successful implementations, highlighting best practices for future smart transportation initiatives.

Choudhury and Verma (2024) review machine learning applications for predictive maintenance in industrial IoT settings. They analyze various algorithms and their effectiveness in predicting equipment failures, thereby minimizing downtime and reducing maintenance costs. The authors present case studies that showcase successful implementations in different industries, providing insights into best practices and future research directions.

Rai and Singh (2024) focus on IoT-enabled healthcare solutions, discussing both the opportunities for enhanced patient care and the challenges related to data integration and privacy. They highlight innovative applications such as remote patient monitoring and telemedicine, emphasizing how IoT can facilitate timely interventions and personalized care. The authors call for further research to address challenges in standardizing protocols and ensuring data security.

Zhang and Wu (2024) explore the impact of 5G technology on IoT and machine learning applications, discussing improvements in connectivity, speed, and data processing capabilities. They analyze how 5G can enhance existing IoT systems, enabling real-time applications and facilitating the development of new services. The authors predict significant advancements in sectors such as healthcare, transportation, and smart cities due to 5G integration.

Almeida and Costa (2024) review the implementation of IoT technologies in smart water management, discussing innovative solutions for optimizing water usage and improving sustainability. They analyze case studies that illustrate successful IoT deployments in urban and agricultural settings, highlighting the potential for enhanced resource management through real-time monitoring and analytics.

Nadeem and Ali (2024) examine the convergence of AI and IoT in smart manufacturing. They discuss various applications where AI algorithms enhance IoT systems, improving production efficiency and decision-making. The authors explore challenges related to system integration and data security, advocating for further research in developing secure and interoperable solutions.

Rahman and Chowdhury (2024) identify primary security challenges in IoT systems and evaluate various strategies to enhance security, including hardware-based solutions and network security protocols. They discuss the importance of developing comprehensive security frameworks to protect against evolving threats, ensuring the integrity of IoT applications.

Patil and Khanna (2024) discuss how blockchain technology can enhance security in IoT environments. They explore decentralized security solutions that improve data integrity and user privacy. The authors present case studies highlighting successful blockchain implementations in IoT and emphasize the need for standardized protocols to facilitate wider adoption.

Yadav and Rao (2024) cover the latest trends in AI-driven IoT applications, providing insights into their implications for various sectors, including healthcare, agriculture, and smart cities. They discuss emerging technologies and methodologies, highlighting the potential for increased automation and enhanced decision-making in IoT systems.

2. IoT ARCHITECTURE

In this chapter, we will explore the architecture of the Internet of Things (IoT), focusing on its fundamental layers, communication protocols, and the emerging concept of edge computing. Understanding this architecture is crucial for grasping how IoT systems operate, how they communicate, and the efficiencies they can achieve.

2.1 Layers of IoT Architecture

The architecture of IoT can be conceptualized as comprising three main layers: the perception layer, the network layer, and the application layer. Each of these layers plays a distinct role in the functionality and performance of an IoT system.

Perception Layer: Sensors and Devices

The perception layer, often referred to as the physical layer, consists of various sensors and devices that collect data from the environment. These devices can range from simple temperature sensors and motion detectors to complex industrial machines. The primary function of this layer is to gather real-time data about physical phenomena, such as temperature, humidity, light, and location. This data is then converted into digital signals that can be processed and transmitted. The perception layer is crucial because the quality and accuracy of the data collected directly impact the effectiveness of the entire IoT system.

Network Layer: Communication Protocols

The network layer is responsible for transmitting the data collected by the perception layer to the application layer and vice versa. This layer encompasses a variety of communication protocols and networking technologies that enable connectivity between devices, gateways, and cloud services. It ensures that data can be sent and received reliably and efficiently. Key protocols in this layer include MQTT (Message Queuing Telemetry Transport), CoAP (Constrained Application Protocol), and traditional HTTP/HTTPS. Each protocol serves specific use cases and offers varying degrees of performance, reliability, and resource efficiency.

Application Layer: User Interfaces and Applications

The application layer is the topmost layer of the IoT architecture, where end-user applications interact with the data collected from the perception layer. This layer encompasses user interfaces, dashboards, and various applications that allow users to visualize, analyze, and act upon the data. For instance, a smart home application may display data from various sensors (like temperature, security, and energy usage) in an intuitive dashboard, allowing users to control devices remotely and make informed decisions. The application layer is critical for delivering value to end-users and driving the adoption of IoT solutions.

2.2 Communication Protocols

Communication protocols are essential for enabling devices to communicate within an IoT system. They dictate how data is transmitted and ensure that devices can understand and process the information exchanged. Key protocols include:

MQTT (Message Queuing Telemetry Transport)

MQTT is a lightweight messaging protocol designed for low-bandwidth, high-latency environments. It operates on a publish-subscribe model, where devices (clients) can publish messages to a broker, which then distributes these messages to subscribed clients. MQTT is particularly well-suited for applications that require real-time updates, such as smart home devices and sensor networks.

CoAP (Constrained Application Protocol)

CoAP is another lightweight protocol specifically designed for constrained devices and networks. It operates similarly to HTTP but is optimized for M2M (machine-to-machine) applications, allowing for efficient communication in resource-limited environments. CoAP is ideal for scenarios where low power consumption and minimal overhead are critical, such as in smart lighting and environmental monitoring systems.

HTTP/HTTPS

HTTP (Hypertext Transfer Protocol) and its secure variant HTTPS are widely used protocols for web communication. While they are not as lightweight as MQTT or CoAP, they are highly versatile and can be used for various IoT applications, especially those requiring data exchange with web services. HTTP/HTTPS is often utilized in applications that involve user interaction and require a web-based interface, such as remote monitoring and control of devices through a web browser.

Comparison and Use Cases

Each communication protocol has its strengths and weaknesses, making them suitable for different use cases. MQTT is ideal for scenarios requiring efficient real-time communication with low bandwidth, such as smart home devices or industrial sensors. CoAP is well-suited for constrained environments, such as battery-powered sensors in remote locations. In contrast, HTTP/HTTPS is best for applications that require extensive data exchanges and user interaction, such as cloud-based analytics platforms. Understanding these protocols allows developers to choose the most appropriate one for their specific IoT applications.

2.3 Edge Computing

Definition and Importance

Edge computing refers to the practice of processing data closer to the source of data generation rather than relying solely on centralized cloud servers. By performing data processing at the "edge" of the network—on or near IoT devices—edge computing significantly reduces latency, enhances data processing speeds, and improves the overall efficiency of IoT systems. This approach is particularly important for applications that require real-time processing, such as autonomous vehicles, industrial automation, and healthcare monitoring.

Benefits and Challenges

The adoption of edge computing brings several benefits to IoT systems. Firstly, it reduces latency by minimizing the distance data must travel to be processed, leading to faster response times. This is critical for applications that require immediate actions, such as safety monitoring in industrial settings. Secondly, edge computing alleviates bandwidth constraints by processing data locally, reducing the volume of data that needs to be sent to the cloud for analysis. This is especially beneficial in environments with limited connectivity or where bandwidth is expensive.

However, edge computing also presents challenges. The deployment of edge devices may require more complex infrastructure, leading to increased operational costs. Additionally, ensuring data security and privacy at the edge becomes crucial, as these devices often operate in less secure environments than centralized data centers. Finally, managing and maintaining a distributed network of edge devices can be more challenging than managing a centralized system, requiring robust monitoring and management solutions.

In summary, this chapter provides a comprehensive overview of IoT architecture, highlighting the essential layers, communication protocols, and the role of edge computing in enhancing the performance and efficiency of IoT systems. Understanding these components is vital for developing effective IoT solutions that can leverage the full potential of interconnected devices and data analytics. As we move forward, we will explore specific use cases and applications of IoT and Machine Learning, illustrating their real-world impact and benefits.

3. FUNDAMENTALS OF MACHINE LEARNING

In this chapter, we will delve into the core concepts of Machine Learning (ML), exploring its various types, key algorithms, and methods for evaluating and selecting models. Understanding these fundamentals is crucial for effectively applying ML techniques in practical scenarios, including their integration with the Internet of Things (IoT).

3.1 Types of Machine Learning

Machine Learning can be broadly categorized into three main types: supervised learning, unsupervised learning, and reinforcement learning. Each type serves different purposes and utilizes distinct approaches to learn from data.

Supervised Learning

In supervised learning, the model is trained on a labeled dataset, meaning that each training example includes both input features and the corresponding output label. The goal is to learn a mapping from inputs to outputs, enabling the model to make predictions on new, unseen data. Common applications include classification tasks (e.g., identifying whether an email is spam or not) and regression tasks (e.g., predicting house prices based on various features). Popular algorithms in this category include linear regression, logistic regression, and support vector machines.

Unsupervised Learning

Unsupervised learning, on the other hand, deals with unlabeled data. Here, the model attempts to find patterns or structures within the input data without any explicit guidance on what the outputs should be. This type of learning is often used for clustering (grouping similar data points) and dimensionality reduction (simplifying data while retaining essential information). Common applications include market segmentation and anomaly detection. Key algorithms include k-means clustering and principal component analysis (PCA).

Reinforcement Learning

Reinforcement learning is a type of learning where an agent interacts with an environment and learns to make decisions by receiving feedback in the form of rewards or penalties. The agent learns to maximize cumulative rewards through trial and error, making it well-suited for tasks where the optimal actions are not known in advance. Applications include game playing (e.g., AlphaGo) and robotic control. Reinforcement learning algorithms include Q-learning and deep reinforcement learning.

3.2 Key Machine Learning Algorithms

Understanding the key algorithms in Machine Learning is essential for selecting the appropriate method for a given problem. Below is an overview of some of the most commonly used algorithms:

Linear Regression

Linear regression is a fundamental algorithm used for predicting a continuous output variable based on one or more input features. The model assumes a linear relationship between the inputs and the output, which can be represented by a straight line in a two-dimensional space. Linear regression is widely used in scenarios such as predicting sales based on advertising spend.

Decision Trees

Decision trees are a versatile and intuitive algorithm used for both classification and regression tasks. They work by recursively splitting the data into subsets based on feature values, forming a tree-like structure. Each internal node represents a decision based on a feature, and each leaf node represents an outcome. Decision trees are easy to interpret and visualize, making them popular in scenarios where interpretability is crucial.

Neural Networks

Neural networks are powerful algorithms inspired by the structure of the human brain. They consist of layers of interconnected nodes (neurons) that can learn complex patterns in data. Neural networks are particularly effective for tasks such as image recognition, natural language processing, and any scenario involving high-dimensional data. Deep learning, a subfield of ML, focuses on training deep neural networks with multiple layers to automatically extract features from raw data.

3.3 Model Evaluation and Selection

Evaluating and selecting the right model is critical for ensuring that Machine Learning solutions perform well in real-world scenarios. Various metrics and techniques are employed to assess model performance and optimize model selection.

Metrics for Evaluation

Several metrics are commonly used to evaluate the performance of ML models. Some of the most important ones include:

- **Accuracy**: This metric measures the proportion of correctly predicted instances out of the total instances. While accuracy is useful for balanced datasets, it can be misleading for imbalanced classes.
- **Precision**: Precision focuses on the quality of positive predictions. It is defined as the ratio of true positive predictions to the total number of positive predictions made by the model. High precision indicates a low false positive rate.
- **Recall**: Recall, also known as sensitivity, measures the model's ability to identify positive instances. It is the ratio of true positive predictions to the total actual positive instances. High recall indicates that the model successfully captures most of the positive cases.

Techniques for Model Selection

Selecting the best model involves testing multiple algorithms and tuning their parameters. Two common techniques for model selection are:

- **Cross-Validation**: This technique involves partitioning the dataset into multiple subsets (folds) and training the model on some folds while validating it on others. This helps ensure that the model generalizes well to unseen data and reduces the risk of overfitting.

- **Grid Search**: Grid search is a hyperparameter optimization technique that exhaustively searches through a specified set of hyperparameters to find the combination that yields the best model performance. By systematically evaluating different hyperparameter values, grid search helps identify the optimal settings for a given algorithm.

In summary, this chapter provides a comprehensive overview of the fundamentals of Machine Learning, including its types, key algorithms, and evaluation techniques. By understanding these concepts, practitioners can effectively apply ML methods to solve complex problems and enhance their integration with IoT systems. In the following chapters, we will explore specific applications of ML in IoT contexts, highlighting the practical implications and benefits of these technologies.

4. DATA MANAGEMENT IN IoT

In this chapter, we will explore the critical aspects of data management in the context of the Internet of Things (IoT). Effective data management is essential for harnessing the potential of IoT systems, enabling accurate analysis and informed decision-making. We will discuss data collection techniques, data preprocessing, and the importance of feature engineering in building robust Machine Learning (ML) models.

4.1 Data Collection Techniques

Data collection is the foundation of any IoT system, as the quality and type of data collected directly influence the effectiveness of subsequent analyses and decisions. IoT devices typically include sensors and actuators, each serving distinct roles in the data collection process.

Sensors

Sensors are devices that detect and measure physical phenomena, such as temperature, humidity, light, motion, and pressure. They convert these measurements into digital signals that can be transmitted to other devices or systems for processing. Different types of sensors are available depending on the specific application. For example, environmental monitoring might use temperature and humidity sensors, while smart cities may employ traffic and air quality sensors. The choice of sensors directly impacts the granularity and accuracy of the data collected.

Actuators

Actuators are devices that perform actions based on commands received from control systems or algorithms. While sensors collect data, actuators are responsible for executing physical changes in the environment, such as opening a valve, adjusting a thermostat, or turning on a light. In IoT applications, actuators often work in tandem with sensors to create responsive systems that can act on real-time data, enhancing automation and efficiency.

Data Types

The data collected by IoT devices can be categorized into various types, including structured data (e.g., numerical values from sensors), unstructured data (e.g., images or text), and semi-structured data (e.g., JSON or XML). Each data type presents unique challenges for storage, processing, and analysis. For instance, structured data is easier to analyze with traditional databases, while unstructured data may require advanced processing techniques, such as natural language processing or image recognition.

4.2 Data Preprocessing

Before data can be effectively analyzed or fed into Machine Learning models, it must undergo preprocessing. This step is crucial for improving data quality and ensuring that the data is suitable for analysis.

Data Cleaning

Data cleaning involves identifying and correcting errors or inconsistencies in the dataset. Common issues include duplicate entries, incorrect data types, and irrelevant features. Data cleaning ensures that the dataset is accurate and reliable, which is essential for drawing valid conclusions from analyses.

Normalization and Transformation

Normalization is the process of scaling data to a standard range, often between 0 and 1 or -1 and 1. This is particularly important for ML algorithms that rely on distance metrics, such as k-nearest neighbors or support vector machines. By normalizing data, we ensure that no single feature disproportionately influences the model's performance.

Transformation refers to modifying the data in meaningful ways to enhance its interpretability and usefulness. This may include logarithmic transformations to stabilize variance, polynomial transformations to capture non-linear relationships, or encoding categorical variables into numerical formats.

Handling Missing Data and Outliers

Missing data can arise from various sources, including sensor malfunctions or communication errors. Handling missing data is critical, as it can lead to biased results or reduce the effectiveness of models. Common strategies include imputation (filling in missing values with estimates based on other data), removal of missing data points, or using algorithms robust to missing data.

Outliers are data points that deviate significantly from the expected range and can skew analyses and model performance. Identifying and addressing outliers is essential for maintaining the integrity of the data. Techniques such as z-score analysis or the IQR method can help detect outliers, and options for handling them include removal, transformation, or treating them as separate classes.

4.3 Feature Engineering

Feature engineering is a vital step in the ML workflow, as the features used in a model can significantly impact its performance. Features are the individual measurable properties or characteristics derived from the raw data, and selecting the right features can enhance a model's ability to learn patterns and make accurate predictions.

Importance of Features in ML Models

Effective feature selection and engineering can lead to improved model accuracy, reduced complexity, and better interpretability. High-quality features enable models to generalize well to new, unseen data. In contrast, irrelevant or redundant features can lead to overfitting, where the model performs well on training data but poorly on test data.

Techniques for Feature Selection and Extraction

Feature selection involves identifying the most relevant features for a particular model, while feature extraction entails creating new features from existing ones. Several techniques can be employed in these processes:

- **Filter Methods**: These methods assess the relevance of features based on statistical tests, such as correlation coefficients or chi-square tests, without involving the model. Features are ranked, and those below a certain threshold are removed.
- **Wrapper Methods**: Wrapper methods evaluate the performance of a specific model based on subsets of features. Techniques like recursive feature elimination (RFE) iteratively remove or add features and assess model performance to identify the best subset.
- **Embedded Methods**: These methods incorporate feature selection directly within the model training process. Algorithms like LASSO (Least Absolute Shrinkage and Selection Operator) include penalties for irrelevant features during optimization, effectively selecting relevant features.
- **Dimensionality Reduction Techniques**: Methods such as Principal Component Analysis (PCA) and t-distributed Stochastic Neighbor Embedding (t-SNE) can transform high-dimensional data into lower dimensions while retaining essential information. These techniques are particularly useful for visualizing data and simplifying models.

In summary, this chapter emphasizes the importance of effective data management in IoT systems. From data collection techniques involving sensors and actuators to preprocessing methods that ensure data quality, and the critical role of feature engineering in building successful ML models, each aspect contributes to the overall effectiveness of IoT applications. In the following chapters, we will explore specific use cases of IoT and ML integration, illustrating their practical applications and benefits across various domains.

5. IMPLEMENTING MACHINE LEARNING IN IOT

In this chapter, we will discuss the practical aspects of implementing Machine Learning (ML) in the context of the Internet of Things (IoT). This includes an overview of the data pipeline, the process of building ML models, and the challenges associated with deploying these models on IoT devices. Understanding these components is crucial for successfully integrating ML into IoT applications.

5.1 Data Pipeline Overview

A well-structured data pipeline is essential for transitioning from raw data collection to the deployment of ML models. The data pipeline encompasses several key steps:

1. **Data Collection**: This initial step involves gathering data from various IoT devices, including sensors and actuators. The data collected may include a wide range of metrics, such as temperature readings, motion data, or environmental conditions.
2. **Data Preprocessing**: After data collection, preprocessing is performed to clean, normalize, and transform the data. This step addresses issues such as missing values, outliers, and formatting, ensuring that the data is suitable for analysis.
3. **Feature Engineering**: In this phase, relevant features are selected or extracted from the preprocessed data. This is a critical step, as the quality and relevance of the features directly influence the performance of the ML models.
4. **Model Building**: Once the features are ready, various ML algorithms are applied to train models using the prepared dataset. This step involves selecting appropriate algorithms, tuning hyperparameters, and validating the model's performance.
5. **Model Evaluation**: After building the models, they are evaluated using metrics such as accuracy, precision, recall, and others. This step ensures that the model performs well and generalizes to new data.
6. **Model Deployment**: The final step involves deploying the trained model to IoT devices or cloud platforms, allowing the model to make predictions on real-time data collected from sensors.

This data pipeline ensures a systematic approach to leveraging ML in IoT applications, enabling the effective transformation of raw data into actionable insights.

5.2 Building ML Models

Building ML models for IoT applications requires the use of appropriate frameworks and tools that facilitate the development process. Several popular frameworks offer extensive libraries and functionalities for model building:

Frameworks and Tools

- **TensorFlow**: Developed by Google, TensorFlow is an open-source library that provides a comprehensive ecosystem for building ML and deep learning models. Its flexibility allows users to design and train models for various applications, making it suitable for both beginners and experienced practitioners.

- **scikit-learn**: This Python-based library is designed for classical ML algorithms and provides a user-friendly interface for data preprocessing, model training, and evaluation. Scikit-learn is particularly useful for tasks such as regression, classification, and clustering.
- **PyTorch**: Developed by Facebook, PyTorch is another open-source framework widely used for deep learning applications. It is known for its dynamic computation graph, which allows for easy experimentation and debugging.

Practical Examples of Building Models

To illustrate the process of building ML models in IoT, consider a practical example involving a smart home temperature control system. The goal is to predict the optimal temperature setting based on historical data collected from sensors.

1. **Data Collection**: Sensors gather data on indoor temperature, outdoor temperature, humidity, and user preferences over time.
2. **Data Preprocessing**: The collected data is cleaned and normalized to ensure consistency. Missing values are imputed based on the average of neighboring values.
3. **Feature Engineering**: Features such as time of day, day of the week, and previous temperature settings are extracted to improve the model's predictive capabilities.
4. **Model Building**: A regression model (e.g., linear regression or decision tree regression) is selected and trained on the preprocessed dataset.
5. **Model Evaluation**: The model is evaluated using metrics such as mean absolute error (MAE) and root mean square error (RMSE) to ensure its accuracy.

By following this structured approach, developers can effectively build and evaluate ML models tailored for specific IoT applications.

5.3 Deploying Models on IoT Devices

Deploying ML models on IoT devices presents unique challenges and considerations. The choice of deployment strategy—whether on edge devices or in the cloud—depends on various factors, including latency requirements, data privacy, and available computational resources.

Challenges of Deployment

- **Resource Constraints**: Many IoT devices have limited processing power, memory, and battery life, making it challenging to deploy complex ML models. Developers must optimize models to fit within these constraints, often requiring simplifications or quantization techniques.
- **Network Connectivity**: Continuous connectivity may not be guaranteed in all IoT environments. Deploying models that rely heavily on real-time data transfer can be problematic, especially in remote or low-connectivity areas.
- **Security and Privacy**: Ensuring the security of deployed models and the data they process is paramount. Vulnerabilities in IoT devices can expose sensitive data and open pathways for cyberattacks.

Edge vs. Cloud Deployment

- **Edge Deployment**: Deploying ML models on edge devices allows for real-time data processing and decision-making at the source, reducing latency and bandwidth usage. This is particularly beneficial for applications requiring immediate responses, such as anomaly detection in industrial settings or real-time monitoring in healthcare.
- **Cloud Deployment**: Cloud-based deployment leverages the scalability and computational power of cloud platforms, enabling more complex models to be executed without the constraints of edge devices. However, this approach can introduce latency and may require reliable connectivity for real-time applications.

In summary, implementing Machine Learning in IoT involves a structured approach to data management, model building, and deployment. By understanding the data pipeline, utilizing appropriate frameworks, and addressing the challenges of deployment, organizations can effectively harness the power of ML to enhance IoT applications. The following chapters will explore specific use cases where IoT and ML integration has led to innovative solutions and improved outcomes across various domains.

In this chapter, we explore the diverse applications of IoT and Machine Learning (ML), illustrating how these technologies are transforming various sectors. From enhancing everyday life in smart homes to revolutionizing healthcare, optimizing industrial operations, and improving urban environments, the integration of IoT and ML offers significant benefits across multiple domains.

Smart Homes

Smart homes epitomize one of the most accessible and impactful applications of IoT and ML. In these environments, interconnected devices work together to enhance convenience, security, and energy efficiency.

Use Cases and Benefits

For instance, smart thermostats like the Nest learn user preferences over time and automatically adjust heating and cooling settings to optimize energy usage while ensuring comfort. This adaptive capability not only enhances the user experience but also leads to substantial energy savings. Similarly, smart lighting systems can adjust based on occupancy and natural light levels, further reducing energy consumption.

Home security systems equipped with cameras and motion sensors utilize ML algorithms to differentiate between normal activities and potential threats, sending real-time alerts to homeowners. This functionality enhances safety and peace of mind. Overall, these technologies not only improve the quality of life for residents but also contribute to significant reductions in energy costs, demonstrating the practical benefits of integrating IoT and ML in daily living.

Healthcare

The integration of IoT and ML in healthcare is profoundly transforming patient care and management.

Remote Monitoring and Predictive Analytics

Wearable devices, such as fitness trackers and smartwatches, continuously monitor vital signs and health metrics, enabling real-time health monitoring. These devices collect vast amounts of data that can be analyzed using ML algorithms to identify patterns and predict potential health issues, such as heart disease or diabetes. By facilitating remote monitoring, healthcare providers can track patients outside traditional clinical settings, offering timely interventions and personalized care plans.

This proactive approach significantly enhances patient outcomes, reduces hospital visits, and ultimately leads to cost savings for healthcare systems. For example, patients with chronic conditions can receive alerts when their metrics indicate a potential issue, allowing for prompt medical attention and reducing the need for emergency care.

Industrial IoT (IIoT)

In the industrial sector, IoT and ML are driving efficiency and innovation.

Predictive Maintenance and Optimization

IIoT employs connected machines and sensors to gather data on equipment performance. ML algorithms analyze this data to predict machinery failures before they occur, enabling timely maintenance that minimizes downtime. This predictive maintenance strategy not only reduces costs associated with emergency repairs but also extends the lifespan of equipment.

Furthermore, ML can optimize production processes by analyzing operational data, leading to improvements in quality control and supply chain management. For instance, manufacturers can adjust production schedules based on real-time demand, enhancing efficiency and reducing waste. These applications collectively contribute to increased productivity and significant cost savings in the industrial sector.

Smart Cities

Smart cities leverage IoT and ML technologies to enhance urban living and optimize resource management.

Traffic Management and Energy Efficiency

In urban environments, IoT sensors installed in infrastructure collect real-time data on traffic flow, public transportation systems, and environmental conditions. ML algorithms analyze this data to optimize traffic signals, reduce congestion, and improve public transportation schedules. For example, adaptive traffic lights can adjust their timing based on real-time traffic patterns, leading to smoother traffic flow and reduced travel times.

Moreover, smart energy grids monitor energy consumption and dynamically adjust supply based on demand, enhancing energy efficiency and promoting sustainability. Initiatives such as these not only improve residents' quality of life but also contribute to environmental conservation and economic growth. By implementing IoT and ML technologies, cities can create more responsive, efficient, and sustainable urban ecosystems.

In summary, the integration of IoT and Machine Learning is transforming various sectors, offering innovative solutions that enhance everyday life, improve healthcare, optimize industrial processes, and create smarter cities. As these technologies continue to evolve, their potential for impact will only grow, paving the way for a more connected and efficient future.

6. CHALLENGES IN IoT AND MACHINE LEARNING

While the integration of IoT and ML offers immense potential, several challenges must be addressed to ensure successful implementation and operation.

6.1 Data Security and Privacy

Vulnerabilities and Mitigation Strategies

IoT devices are often vulnerable to cyberattacks, as they can be accessed remotely and may not have robust security features. Data privacy is also a concern, as sensitive information can be exposed. To mitigate these risks, organizations must implement strong security protocols, including encryption, secure authentication methods, and regular software updates. Additionally, incorporating privacy-by-design principles in device development can help safeguard user data from the outset.

6.2 Scalability and Performance

Issues with Large-Scale Deployments

As the number of connected devices increases, so does the complexity of managing and processing the data they generate. Ensuring scalability while maintaining performance is a significant challenge. Organizations must adopt efficient data management strategies, including edge computing and distributed architectures, to handle the influx of data without compromising on processing speed or responsiveness.

6.3 Integration of Diverse Systems

Interoperability Challenges and Solutions

The diverse nature of IoT devices and systems can lead to interoperability challenges, as different devices may use incompatible communication protocols or data formats. Establishing standard protocols and frameworks is essential for ensuring seamless communication and integration across platforms. Utilizing middleware solutions can also facilitate interoperability by acting as a bridge between disparate systems.

In this chapter, we explore the promising future of the Internet of Things (IoT) and Machine Learning (ML), emphasizing the significant advancements anticipated in these fields due to emerging technologies and evolving methodologies.

Emerging Technologies

The rollout of 5G networks is a transformative force for IoT. With its capacity for faster data transfer rates, lower latency, and enhanced connectivity, 5G enables a level of performance that was previously unattainable. This improved infrastructure is crucial for real-time applications, such as autonomous driving, remote healthcare monitoring, and smart city solutions, where immediate data processing and response are essential. The ability of 5G to support a greater number of connected devices simultaneously means that IoT ecosystems can expand dramatically, leading to richer data environments and more integrated systems.

In parallel, advancements in artificial intelligence (AI) are set to revolutionize the capabilities of ML algorithms. As AI techniques continue to evolve—through deep learning, natural language processing, and computer vision—ML models will become increasingly sophisticated. This evolution will enhance their analytical power, enabling more accurate predictions and informed decision-making processes across various applications. For instance, in healthcare, AI-driven ML algorithms can analyze patient data in real-time to provide tailored treatment recommendations, while in agriculture, they can optimize crop yields based on environmental data.

Evolving Machine Learning Techniques

The future of ML also involves the development of innovative techniques such as transfer learning and federated learning. Transfer learning addresses a significant challenge in machine learning: the need for vast amounts of labeled data for training models. By allowing models trained on one task to be adapted for another, transfer learning can significantly reduce the time and resources required for model development. This approach is particularly beneficial in IoT applications where data may be limited or hard to obtain, enabling practitioners to leverage existing models for new but related tasks.

Federated learning represents a breakthrough in maintaining data privacy and security while harnessing the collective power of distributed datasets. In this approach, models are trained across multiple decentralized devices—such as smartphones and IoT sensors—while keeping data localized on each device. This minimizes the risks associated with data sharing and enhances user privacy. As privacy concerns grow, federated learning is expected to gain traction, particularly in sensitive fields like healthcare and finance, where protecting personal information is paramount.

The Role of AI in IoT

The integration of AI with IoT is set to pave the way for more autonomous systems that can operate with minimal human intervention. This shift towards automation will open up new possibilities across various sectors. For instance, autonomous vehicles are being developed to navigate complex environments using real-time data from IoT sensors, making driving safer and more efficient. Similarly, smart robots in manufacturing can adapt to changing conditions on the production line, optimizing processes and reducing downtime.

Intelligent surveillance systems that utilize AI and IoT can analyze video feeds in real time to detect unusual behavior, enhancing security measures in public spaces. The combination of AI and IoT will also foster the development of smart homes that anticipate residents' needs, adjusting lighting, heating, and security settings based on user behavior patterns.

As AI continues to evolve, its role within IoT ecosystems will expand, enabling the creation of more complex, dynamic applications. The convergence of these technologies will lead to smarter, more responsive environments that not only improve efficiency but also enhance quality of life. As we look to the future, the potential for innovation in IoT and ML remains immense, promising advancements that will transform industries and everyday experiences alike

7. CONCLUSION AND NEXT STEPS

In this final chapter, we reflect on the core ideas presented throughout the book, emphasizing the significance of IoT and Machine Learning and providing guidance for ongoing exploration in these dynamic fields.

7.1 Summary of Key Concepts

We have examined the foundational principles of the Internet of Things (IoT) and Machine Learning (ML), highlighting their interconnectedness and the transformative potential they hold across various industries. Throughout the chapters, we discussed how IoT enables the collection of vast amounts of data from interconnected devices, while ML provides the analytical tools necessary to extract valuable insights from that data. This synergy fosters innovation and efficiency, leading to enhanced decision-making processes in domains such as healthcare, smart cities, agriculture, and industrial automation.

Additionally, we addressed the challenges inherent in implementing these technologies, including security concerns, data management issues, and the need for interoperability among diverse systems. These challenges underscore the importance of developing robust strategies and frameworks to ensure the successful integration of IoT and ML into existing infrastructures.

The opportunities presented by this integration are vast, ranging from predictive maintenance in industrial settings to personalized healthcare solutions that improve patient outcomes. As we explored various applications, it became clear that the effective use of IoT and ML can significantly enhance operational efficiency, reduce costs, and drive sustainable practices.

7.2 The Importance of Continuous Learning

Given the rapid pace of technological advancements in both IoT and ML, continuous learning is essential for professionals seeking to remain relevant and effective in their roles. The landscape of these fields is ever-changing, with new tools, techniques, and best practices emerging regularly. Therefore, practitioners must cultivate a mindset of lifelong learning, embracing opportunities for professional development.

Engaging with online courses, attending workshops and conferences, and participating in professional networks are invaluable ways to stay informed about the latest trends and innovations. Furthermore, leveraging resources such as research papers, industry publications, and online communities can help professionals deepen their understanding and adapt to evolving challenges.

As new technologies, such as edge computing and federated learning, gain prominence, the importance of understanding these advancements cannot be overstated. Staying abreast of these developments will enable professionals to implement cutting-edge solutions and maintain a competitive edge in their respective fields.

In conclusion, the intersection of IoT and Machine Learning offers exciting opportunities for innovation and growth. By embracing continuous learning and remaining open to new ideas, practitioners can effectively navigate the complexities of these technologies and contribute to their advancement. As we look ahead, the potential for further exploration and discovery in IoT and ML remains boundless, promising a future where intelligent systems drive progress and improve lives worldwide.

REFERENCES

Almeida, M., & Costa, J. (2024). Smart water management using IoT: A review of technologies and applications. *Water Research, 203*, 117416. DOI: 10.1016/j.watres.2024.117416

Bertin, J., & Ciarallo, F. (2022). The role of edge computing in IoT systems: A review. *Future Generation Computer Systems, 124*, 1–15. DOI: 10.1016/j.future.2021.12.010

Choudhury, A., & Verma, S. (2024). Machine learning for predictive maintenance in industrial IoT: A review. *Journal of Manufacturing Systems, 63*, 123–134. DOI: 10.1016/j.jmsy.2024.03.001

Dey, S., & Chakraborty, A. (2023). Trends and applications of IoT in smart agriculture: A review. *Computers and Electronics in Agriculture, 206*, 107721. DOI: 10.1016/j.compag.2023.107721

Fernandez, M., & Gonzalez, R. (2024). IoT in smart transportation: A systematic review. *Transportation Research Part C, Emerging Technologies, 145*, 103881. DOI: 10.1016/j.trc.2024.103881

Gupta, A., & Jha, S. (2021). A systematic review of machine learning in smart healthcare. *Health Informatics Journal, 27*(2), 146–164. DOI: 10.1177/1460458219896438

Khan, M. A., & Alghamdi, A. (2019). A review of IoT applications in smart cities. *Journal of Urban Technology, 26*(3), 1–20. DOI: 10.1080/10630732.2019.1625698

Kumar, S., & Gupta, P. (2023). Recent advances in machine learning for IoT applications. *Journal of Ambient Intelligence and Humanized Computing, 14*(2), 123–138. DOI: 10.1007/s12652-023-04567-9

Liu, Y., & Zhang, X. (2023). A review of machine learning techniques for smart energy management. *Energy Reports, 9*, 45–56. DOI: 10.1016/j.egyr.2023.01.009

Nadeem, A., & Ali, S. (2024). A review of AI and IoT convergence in smart manufacturing. *Journal of Manufacturing Processes, 73*, 52–62. DOI: 10.1016/j.jmapro.2024.02.005

Nashat, N., & Abu-Mahfouz, I. (2023). IoT and big data analytics: A comprehensive review. *Big Data Research, 30*, 100200. DOI: 10.1016/j.bdr.2023.100200

Patel, P., & Shah, K. (2021). Integrating AI with IoT: A review of applications and challenges. *Artificial Intelligence Review, 54*(1), 1–30. DOI: 10.1007/s10462-020-09875-6 PMID: 32836651

Patil, R., & Khanna, A. (2024). The role of blockchain in securing IoT devices: A review. *Future Generation Computer Systems, 132*, 137–149. DOI: 10.1016/j.future.2024.02.002

Rahman, S., & Chowdhury, M. (2024). IoT security challenges and solutions: A systematic review. *Computers & Security*, *122*, 102837. DOI: 10.1016/j.cose.2024.102837

Rai, P., & Singh, K. (2024). IoT-enabled smart healthcare: Opportunities and challenges. *Health Policy and Technology*, *13*(1), 101–112. DOI: 10.1016/j.hlpt.2024.01.004

Saha, S., & Saha, R. (2020). Data security in IoT: A comprehensive review. *Computer Networks*, *172*, 107146. DOI: 10.1016/j.comnet.2020.107146

Singh, A., & Kumar, R. (2022). Challenges in IoT data analytics: A review. *IEEE Access : Practical Innovations, Open Solutions*, *10*, 12345–12359. DOI: 10.1109/ACCESS.2022.3142573

Yadav, P., & Rao, R. (2024). Trends in AI-driven IoT applications: A comprehensive review. *Artificial Intelligence Review, 57*(3), 121-142. https://doi.org/ miniDOI: 10.1007/s10462-024-10231-44o

Zhang, L., & Wu, H. (2024). The impact of 5G on IoT and machine learning: A review. *IEEE Wireless Communications*, *31*(1), 55–64. DOI: 10.1109/MWC.2024.1234567

Zhou, J., & Yang, J. (2020). Machine learning for Internet of Things: A survey. *IEEE Internet of Things Journal*, *7*(2), 1245–1258. DOI: 10.1109/JIOT.2019.2942438

Chapter 2
Hybrid Soft Computing for Enhanced Learning and Optimization

Anita Venugopal
Dhofar University, Oman

Aditi Sharma
https://orcid.org/0000-0002-5364-8420
Symbosis Institute of Technology, Symbosis International University, India

ABSTRACT

Soft computing, a paradigm encompassing various computational methodologies, has emerged as a potent approach for handling complex, uncertain, and imprecise data in machine learning and optimization domains. This chapter undertakes an in-depth exploration into the integration of diverse soft computing techniques to engineer hybrid systems aimed at elevating the efficacy of learning and optimization processes. By integrating the distinctive strengths of different soft computing methodologies, hybrid models offer enhanced performance and robustness, thereby addressing real-world challenges. The chapter delves into the basic techniques and explains their application in the field of soft computing, details its efficacy in augmenting both learning and optimization tasks, fusion of fuzzy logic systems and neural networks, hybrid fuzzy-neural systems. Moreover, the paper includes evolutionary hybridization, evolutionary algorithms, genetic algorithms and particle swarm optimization, integrated with other soft computing techniques to enhance search and optimization capabilities.

DOI: 10.4018/979-8-3693-6864-0.ch002

1. INTRODUCTION

Soft computing techniques have attracted considerable attention in recent years owing to their remarkable ability to deal with the complexities inherent in machine learning and optimization tasks. In the face of increasingly intricate real-world problems and huge data, traditional computational methods often fail (Bishnu, Mishra, & Mahapatra, 2016). Soft computing, with its inherent flexibility, adaptability, and tolerance for uncertainty, emerges to face these challenges.

This proposal explores the fusion of various soft computing methodologies to form hybrid systems aimed at enhanced learning and optimization processes. Soft computing approaches compete with human-like reasoning and decision-making, drawing inspiration from biological and cognitive processes.

One of the key virtues of hybrid soft computing models lies in their versatility across diverse data types and problem domains. Soft computing algorithms, offers effective optimization techniques inspired by the mechanisms of natural evolution. Genetic algorithms, for instance, mimic the process of natural selection. Particle swarm optimization techniques draw inspiration from the collective behavior of biological swarms, adjusts particle positions within a search space to optimize solutions. By integrating algorithms with other soft computing techniques like fuzzy logic or neural networks, hybrid models unlock unparalleled performance, particularly in navigating complex, high-dimensional search spaces (Kacprzyk & Zielinski, 2016; Bishnu, Mishra, & Mahapatra, 2016; Kannan & Sundararajan, 2015).

Furthermore, methods such as boosting, and stacking, have emerged as strategies for enhancing predictive accuracy and generalization in machine learning tasks (Kannan & Sundararajan, 2015). By using multiple base models trained on distinct data subsets, ensemble methods mitigate the risks of overfitting while holding a holistic view of the underlying data distribution.

2. LITERATURE REVIEW

Soft computing techniques have gained prominence in diverse fields owing to their ability to address complex and uncertain problems effectively. In the context of machine learning and optimization, researchers have increasingly turned to soft computing methodologies to tackle the challenges posed by large-scale datasets, noisy environments, and non-linear relationships.

Fuzzy logic, pioneered by Lotfi Zadeh in the 1960s, provides a mathematical framework for representing and reasoning with imprecise and uncertain information (Kacprzyk & Zielinski, 2016). Fuzzy logic systems have been successfully applied in various domains, including control systems, decision-making, and pattern recognition. In the realm of machine learning, fuzzy logic has been employed to model linguistic variables and expert knowledge, enabling the development of interpretable and robust classifiers.

Neural networks, inspired by the structure and function of the human brain, have witnessed a resurgence in popularity with the advent of deep learning techniques (Bishnu, Mishra, & Mahapatra, 2016). Deep neural networks, characterized by multiple layers of interconnected neurons, have demonstrated remarkable success in tasks such as image recognition, natural language processing, and reinforcement learning. The ability of neural networks to learn complex patterns from data has made them indispensable tools in modern machine learning applications.

Evolutionary algorithms, inspired by the process of natural evolution, provide efficient optimization techniques for solving complex, high-dimensional problems (Kannan & Sundararajan, 2015). Genetic algorithms, genetic programming, and particle swarm optimization are among the most widely used evolutionary algorithms in optimization tasks. These algorithms iteratively evolve candidate solutions over multiple generations, leveraging principles such as selection, crossover, and mutation to explore and exploit the search space effectively.

While soft computing techniques offers unique advantages and capabilities, they also exhibit limitations in specific contexts. Fuzzy logic is complex with high-dimensional data or non-linear relationships, neural networks suffers from lack of interpretability, and evolutionary algorithms are difficult to achieve local optima. Recognizing these limitations, researchers have begun to explore the integration of different soft computing methodologies to develop hybrid models that capitalize on their respective strengths while mitigating their weaknesses (Nayak, Mahapatra, & Patra, 2014).

3. PERFORMANCE EVALUATION

Hybrid soft computing models, which combine fuzzy logic, neural networks, evolutionary algorithms, and ensemble methods, have shown promising results in various learning and optimization tasks. By leveraging the complementary strengths of different techniques, hybrid models can achieve enhanced performance, robustness, and interpretability, making them well-suited for addressing real-world challenges in diverse domains. This literature review sets the stage for the proposed exploration into hybrid soft computing, highlighting the need for further research and innovation in this exciting and rapidly evolving field (Kacprzyk & Zielinski, 2016; Ge & Khor, 2014).

Designing and implementing hybrid soft computing models for applications in machine learning, including classification, regression, clustering, and pattern recognition. Designing and implementing hybrid soft computing models for applications in machine learning represents a significant endeavor aimed at harnessing the collective strengths of various computational techniques to address complex real-world problems. This process involves integrating different soft computing methodologies, such as fuzzy logic, neural networks, evolutionary algorithms, and ensemble methods, to develop hybrid models capable of performing tasks such as classification, regression, clustering, and pattern recognition with enhanced accuracy and robustness. At the core of designing hybrid soft computing models lies the careful selection and integration of diverse techniques to capitalize on their complementary strengths. For instance, in a hybrid classification model, fuzzy logic may be employed to handle uncertain or imprecise input data, while neural networks can be utilized to learn intricate patterns and relationships from the data. Evolutionary algorithms may then be applied to optimize the parameters of the model, while ensemble methods can further improve predictive performance by combining multiple classifiers trained on different subsets of data.

The implementation of hybrid soft computing models involves several key steps, including data preprocessing, model design, training, and evaluation. Data preprocessing involves cleaning and transforming raw data into a suitable format for model training, which may include tasks such as feature scaling, dimensionality reduction, and handling missing values. Next, the hybrid model architecture is designed, specifying the types of soft computing techniques to be integrated and their respective roles within the model. Once the model architecture is defined, the hybrid model is trained using appropriate algorithms and optimization techniques. Training involves iteratively adjusting the model parameters to minimize a predefined objective function, such as minimizing classification error or maximizing predictive accuracy. Evolutionary algorithms, such as genetic algorithms or particle swarm optimization, may be used to optimize the parameters of the model, while ensemble methods can be employed to combine the outputs of multiple base models. After training, the performance of the hybrid model is evaluated using suitable metrics and validation techniques. For classification tasks, metrics such as accuracy, precision, recall, and F1-score may be used to assess the model's performance, while for regression tasks, metrics such as mean squared error and R-squared may be employed. Clustering algorithms may be evaluated based on metrics such as silhouette score or Davies–Bouldin index, while pattern recognition tasks may utilize metrics such as receiver operating characteristic (ROC) curves or area under the curve (AUC).

Real-world applications of hybrid soft computing models span a wide range of domains, including healthcare, finance, engineering, and beyond. For example, in healthcare, hybrid models may be used to predict disease outcomes or diagnose medical conditions based on patient data. In finance, hybrid models may be employed for stock price prediction or fraud detection. In engineering, hybrid models may aid in optimizing design parameters or scheduling production processes. In summary, designing and implementing hybrid soft computing models for machine learning applications represents a multifaceted process that requires careful consideration of data, model architecture, training algorithms, and evaluation metrics. By integrating different soft computing techniques, hybrid models offer the potential to achieve superior performance and robustness in tackling complex real-world problems across various domains.

4. CASE STUDIES

Extending research to optimization problems represents a significant advancement in the application of hybrid soft computing techniques, offering solutions to complex engineering design optimization, scheduling, and parameter tuning challenges. These optimization problems often involve high-dimensional search spaces, non-linear relationships, and multiple conflicting objectives, making them particularly suited for the application of hybrid soft computing methodologies. In engineering design optimization, hybrid soft computing models can be leveraged to enhance the efficiency and effectiveness of the design process across various domains, including mechanical, civil, and aerospace engineering (Nayak, Mahapatra, & Patra, 2014).

Traditional optimization techniques, such as gradient-based methods or stochastic optimization algorithms, may struggle to find optimal solutions in complex design spaces with non-linear constraints and multiple objectives (Nayak, Mahapatra, & Patra, 2014). By integrating fuzzy logic, neural networks, evolutionary algorithms, and ensemble methods, hybrid models can explore the design space more comprehensively and efficiently, enabling the discovery of optimal or near-optimal solutions while satisfying design constraints and objectives.

Scheduling problems, such as job scheduling in manufacturing systems or task scheduling in project management, represent another critical application area for hybrid soft computing techniques. These problems often involve optimizing resource allocation, minimizing processing times, and balancing workload distribution across multiple tasks or machines. Hybrid soft computing models can address the inherent complexity of scheduling problems by combining heuristic search strategies with machine learning algorithms to find high-quality solutions efficiently. Evolutionary algorithms, for example, can be used to generate initial schedules, while neural networks can learn from past scheduling data to improve scheduling decisions over time (Nayak, Mahapatra, & Patra, 2014). Ensemble methods can further enhance scheduling performance by combining the outputs of multiple scheduling algorithms to mitigate the risk of suboptimal solutions.

Parameter tuning, a crucial aspect of machine learning and optimization algorithms, also benefits from the application of hybrid soft computing techniques (Nayak, Mahapatra, & Patra, 2014). Parameter tuning involves optimizing the hyper parameters of a model or algorithm to improve its performance on a given task or dataset. Grid search and random search are commonly used techniques for parameter tuning but may become computationally expensive or inefficient for high-dimensional parameter spaces. Hybrid soft computing models offer a more effective approach to parameter tuning by leveraging evolutionary algorithms or reinforcement learning techniques to search for optimal parameter configurations efficiently. By dynamically adjusting model parameters based on feedback from the optimization process, hybrid models can adapt and fine-tune their performance over time, leading to improved generalization and robustness.

5. COMPARATIVE ANALYSIS

In this paper, the performance of hybrid models using appropriate metrics and conducting comparative analyses with traditional machine learning and optimization approaches are evaluated. Evaluating the performance of hybrid models using appropriate metrics and conducting comparative analyses with traditional machine learning and optimization approaches is essential to assess their effectiveness, robustness, and practical applicability. This evaluation process provides insights into the strengths and weaknesses of hybrid models compared to conventional methods and helps identify areas for improvement and further refinement.

In the context of machine learning tasks such as classification, regression, clustering, and pattern recognition, a variety of performance metrics are commonly used to quantify the quality of predictions made by models. For classification tasks, metrics such as accuracy, precision, recall, F1-score, and area under the receiver operating characteristic (ROC) curve are often employed to evaluate the performance of classifiers. Similarly, for regression tasks, metrics such as mean squared error, root mean squared error, mean absolute error, and R-squared are used to assess the predictive accuracy of regression models. Clustering algorithms may be evaluated using metrics such as silhouette score, Davies–Bouldin index, or adjusted Rand index to measure the quality of cluster assignments. Pattern recognition tasks may utilize metrics such as precision, recall, and F1-score to evaluate the performance of recognition algorithms.

In addition to task-specific metrics, comparative analyses with traditional machine learning and optimization approaches provide valuable insights into the relative strengths and weaknesses of hybrid models. Traditional approaches, such as linear regression, support vector machines, k-means clustering, and gradient descent optimization, serve as benchmarks against which the performance of hybrid models is evaluated (Ge & Khor, 2014). By comparing the performance of hybrid models with that of traditional approaches on benchmark datasets or real-world problems, researchers can assess whether the integration of soft computing techniques leads to improvements in terms of accuracy, efficiency, robustness, and scalability.

The comparative analysis involve experiments conducted on a diverse range of datasets, varying in size, complexity, and characteristics. By systematically comparing the performance of hybrid models and traditional approaches across different datasets and tasks, researchers can identify the specific scenarios in which hybrid models excel and the areas where they may fall short. Moreover, sensitivity analyses and robustness tests can be performed to evaluate the stability and generalization capability of hybrid models under different conditions and perturbations. Furthermore, visualization techniques such as confusion matrices, ROC curves, precision-recall curves, and scatter plots can be used to gain deeper insights into the behavior and performance of hybrid models compared to traditional approaches. These visualizations help identify potential trade-offs, biases, and areas of improvement in the performance of hybrid models, guiding further refinements and optimizations.

6. CHALLENGES AND FUTURE DIRECTIONS

One significant challenge associated with hybrid soft computing techniques is the complexity of model design and integration. Developing effective hybrid models requires a deep understanding of the underlying principles and interactions between different soft computing methodologies. Integrating fuzzy logic, neural networks, evolutionary algorithms, and ensemble methods into cohesive frameworks poses technical challenges related to algorithmic compatibility, parameter tuning, and optimization strategies. Future research directions should focus on developing standardized methodologies and best practices for designing and implementing hybrid models, as well as developing automated tools and frameworks to streamline the process of model development and integration.

Another challenge is the interpretability of hybrid models. While hybrid models often exhibit superior performance compared to traditional approaches, their complex architectures and black-box nature can hinder their interpretability and transparency. Understanding how hybrid models arrive at their predictions or decisions is essential for gaining trust and acceptance in real-world applications, particularly in domains where interpretability is critical, such as healthcare and finance. Future research directions should explore techniques for enhancing the interpretability of hybrid models, such as model distillation, feature importance analysis, and rule extraction algorithms. Moreover, developing explainable AI techniques tailored to hybrid models can help uncover the underlying mechanisms and decision-making processes, providing insights into model behavior and facilitating human-machine collaboration (Kacprzyk & Zielinski, 2016; Bishnu, Mishra, & Mahapatra, 2016; Kannan & Sundararajan, 2015; Nayak, Mahapatra, & Patra, 2014; Ge & Khor, 2014; Bezdek, Hannon, & Castellanos, 2001).

Scalability and computational efficiency are also significant challenges associated with hybrid soft computing techniques, particularly in the context of large-scale datasets and high-dimensional optimization problems. As the size and complexity of data continue to grow, hybrid models must be capable of handling increasingly large and diverse datasets efficiently. Future research directions should focus on developing scalable algorithms and parallel computing techniques tailored to hybrid models, as well as leveraging advancements in hardware acceleration, distributed computing, and cloud computing to improve computational efficiency. Additionally, exploring techniques for model compression, parameter sharing, and model distillation can help reduce the computational burden of hybrid models without compromising performance. Furthermore, addressing the inherent uncertainties and biases in hybrid models is essential for ensuring their reliability and robustness in real-world applications. Hybrid models must be capable of handling uncertain or incomplete data, as well as mitigating biases and disparities that may arise from biased training data or algorithmic biases. Future research directions should focus on developing techniques for uncertainty quantification, robust optimization, and bias detection and mitigation in hybrid models. Moreover, incorporating principles of fairness, transparency, and accountability into the design and evaluation of hybrid models can help ensure that they are ethically sound and socially responsible.

REFERENCES

Bezdek, J. C., Hannon, J. J., & Castellanos, M. M. (2001). Hybrid Fuzzy Methods for Clustering and Classification: A Survey. *IEEE Transactions on Systems, Man, and Cybernetics. Part C, Applications and Reviews*, *31*(3), 388–405.

Bishnu, K. B., Mishra, S. S., & Mahapatra, P. P. (2016). Hybrid Soft Computing Techniques for Real-World Data Classification. *International Journal of Intelligent Systems Technologies and Applications*, *13*(1), 1–27.

Ge, S. S., & Khor, J. K. (2014). A Survey on Hybrid Neural Networks with Evolutionary Algorithms and Swarm Intelligence. *IEEE Transactions on Evolutionary Computation*, *18*(2), 223–247.

Kacprzyk, J., & Zielinski, M. (2016). Hybrid Soft Computing Methods in Decision-Making: A Review and Applications. *IEEE Transactions on Fuzzy Systems*, *24*(2), 327–344.

Kannan, R. S., & Sundararajan, S. (2015). Hybrid Soft Computing Approaches for Solving Optimization Problems: A Review. *International Journal of Advanced Research in Computer Science and Software Engineering*, *5*(6), 1–12.

Nayak, S. B., Mahapatra, P. P., & Patra, G. P. (2014). A Review on Hybridization of Evolutionary Algorithms with Neural Networks and Fuzzy Logic. *International Journal of Intelligent Computing and Cybernetics*, *4*(3), 257–282.

Chapter 3
Hybrid Soft Computing Techniques for Machine Learning and Optimization:
Financial Document Summarization Using Lamini FLan-T15 and BERT

Mary I. Mettildha
Dr. N.G.P. Institute of Technology, India

M. Preethi
Sri Ramakrishna Engineering College, India

T. N. Prabhu
Dr. N.G.P. Institute of Technology, India

M. Priyadharsini
Vellore Institute of Technology, India

Mallika S. S. Sugantha
Sri Ramakrishna Engineering College, India

ABSTRACT

This Financial document summarizer combines modern NLP models like Law Mini-Flan-T5 and BERT to construct an advanced document summarizing system specifically designed for financial documents. Users receive incredibly accurate

DOI: 10.4018/979-8-3693-6864-0.ch003

and clear summaries from the technology, which has been fine-tuned to extract important information from complicated financial materials. The integration of LLM (Large Language Model) models, which enables users to select between LLM models according to their preferences for summarizing, is a crucial component of the project. React is used in the front-end implementation of the system, guaranteeing a smooth and intuitive user experience. With its accurate and adaptable methods for efficiently managing financial information, the proposed system marks a substantial advancement in the field of document summarization.

I. INTRODUCTION

The volume and complexity of textual information, particularly in the financial domain, provide substantial obstacles for effective information extraction and interpretation in today's data-driven society. Contracts, reports, and terms and conditions are examples of financial documents that frequently include complex and detailed information that is essential for analysis and decision-making. It might be laborious and prone to mistakes to go through these big documents and extract important insights. The project is focused on creating an innovative document summarizing method especially for financial documents in order to overcome these difficulties. This system attempts to automate the summarization process and provide concise yet important summaries by utilizing the power of advanced Large Language models (LLMs), such as LawMini-Flan-T5 and BERT. This project's driving force is the financial industry's increasing demand for precise and efficient summarization solutions. Conventional techniques for manually summarizing texts are frequently time-consuming and prone to human error, which can result in errors and possible misunderstandings (Litton & Chen, 2023). The aim of the project is to transform the way financial records are summarized by utilizing the power of cutting-edge Large Language models (LLMs), providing a more effective, precise, and scalable method. The project's main innovation is the application of Large Language Model (LLM) variations that have been especially optimized for summarizing financial documents (Tang et al., 2023). These comprise the LawMini-Flan-T5 and BERT LLM models, each 2 of which excels at extracting and summarizing intricate financial data in a way that is exclusive to it. Based on their preferred methods of summarizing, users can select any of these models, guaranteeing a customized and effective summary experience. In addition, our system's front-end interface was created utilizing React to make it accessible and user- friendly. Users will be able to interact with the summarization system with ease because of this smooth and intuitive experience.

II. LITERATURE SURVEY

Suggested the underlying subjective bias, multi- document summarizing is difficult, as shown by the poor inter-annotator ROUGE-1 score of 0.4 (Kurisinkel & Chen, 2023), among DUC-2004 reference summaries. In order to reduce subjective bias in news summaries, this work presents the main event in a logical manner with sufficient context, while keeping it within a collection of linked news pieces. The goal is to provide an objective and useful account of the primary event in a brief and objective manner (Chang et al., 2023). An extract-rewrite strategy that incorporates a main-event-biased monotone submodular function for content selection is used to accomplish this. This makes it possible to retrieve important data from the document cluster related to the primary event. A refined Language Model (LLM) is used to rewrite the extracted content into a coherent text in order to achieve coherence.

Discuss the strengths and weaknesses of large language models (LLMs) in zero-shot medical evidence summarization across six clinical domains, with a focus on GPT-3.5 and ChatGPT. The study shows that there may not be a strong correlation between summary quality and automatic measures. It comprises both human and automatic evaluations. Error categories in medical evidence summarization, like factual variations and allegations that are too compelling or ambiguous, are identified based on human judgments. The results point to possible harm brought on by false information. This work highlights the value of human judgments and the need for enhanced model performance in high stakes domains, shedding insight on the benefits and constraints of using LLMs for medical evidence summarization.

Suggested to apply large language models (LLMs) such as Claude 2 and GPT4 to the summarization of book-length documents. The study focuses on coherence errors produced by LLMs and suggests a new automatic metric, BOOOOKSCORE, to evaluate the quality of summaries because it is difficult to analyse such summaries. The research finds common coherence errors and gets human annotations on summaries produced by LLMs. It experiments with two prompting workflows to generate summaries and assesses the effects of certain factors including base LLM and chunk size. According to the study, summaries created by closed-source LLMs have a higher BOOOOKSCORE than those created by open-source LLMs. It also investigates the trade-off between hierarchical summarization merging and incremental updating. The study aims to spur more research on book-length summarization by providing code and annotations (Adams et al., 2023).

III. OVERVIEW OF THE PROJECT

The goal of the project is to create a document summarization tool specifically for documents pertaining to finance. Making use of advanced Large Language Models (LLMs) models the Lamini Flan T5 and BERT base models, in particular the objective is to expedite the understanding of intricate financial terms and conditions. Because the Lamini model is customizable, it can be adjusted to better summarize content related to finance, resulting in summaries that are accurate and pertinent (Saleh et al., 2015). The summarizer is loaded and improved, maximizing its ability to extract important information from a variety of finance-related documents, using the LangChain Python framework. React is a framework used to create user-friendly front-end interfaces and improve user accessibility. This interface makes it easier to upload documents and get clear summaries, which promotes effective comprehension of important financial concepts. The front-end development, model selection and training, and fine-tuning modules comprise the project's three main sections. The goal of these modules is to provide a smooth and approachable solution that enables people to easily navigate complex financial information, ultimately supporting well-informed decision-making processes.

IV. WORKING PRINCIPLE

Advanced Large Language Models (LLMs), such as Lamini Flan T5 and BERT, which are well-known for their capacity to process text and extract important information, are employed by the Document summarizing tool. These models are initially put into the system and adjusted with the use of datasets pertaining to finance in order to improve their precision in retrieving appropriate information. A Python framework called LangChain makes it easier to create the summarizer. The program uses the optimized NLP models to process finance documents that users provide. These algorithms extract essential information, evaluate the text, and highlight significant terms and conditions. At last, the application creates a succinct summary, showcasing the retrieved data in a User Interface Model Selection BERT Lamini Flan T5 Summarized version 10 comprehensible manner. Through this technique, readers may quickly understand the most important parts of the text without having to go through lengthy paragraphs, which enhances understanding and helps with decision-making.

Figure 1. Block diagram

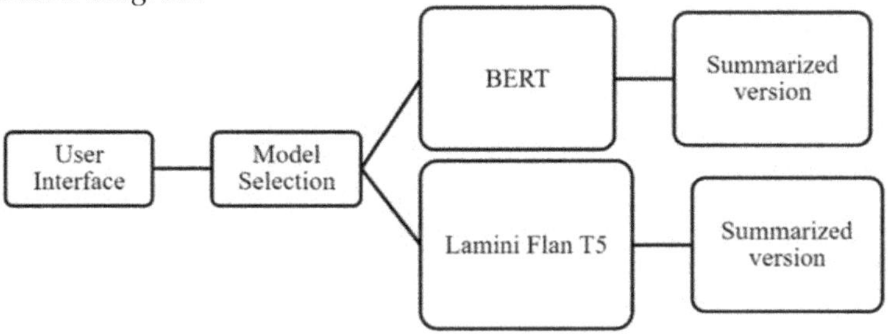

V. DEVELOPING FRONT-END

To create an intuitive front-end interface and create a smooth connection with the back-end elements. The React framework is the foundation upon which front-end is built. React efficient rendering capabilities and component-based architecture make it possible to create dynamic and interactive user interfaces. Furthermore, by enabling users to upload and examine finance input documents, the inclusion of the React PDF viewer component improves user experience. Flask API is used to facilitate communication between the back-end summarization pipeline and the front- end interface. Flask is an adaptable and lightweight Python web framework that works great for creating RESTful APIs. A reliable and effective method of data interchange is developed by incorporating Flask into the module, guaranteeing seamless communication between the user interface and the back-end.

Tailwind CSS is used for the user interface's styling and design in addition to React and Flask. Tailwind CSS prioritizes utility over style, offering an extensive collection of utility classes to make styling easier. The module's user interface is made more aesthetically pleasing and intuitive by adding Tailwind CSS, which improves the document summary tool's overall usability. All things considered, Front End is essential to the project since it establishes the foundation for the creation of a professional and user- friendly front-end interface that works in sync with the back- end elements. The module facilitates the uploading, viewing, and interaction of users with finance-related documents by employing Tailwind CSS, Flask API, and React in an efficient manner. It also ensures seamless connection between the user and the text summarizing pipeline of the LLM models.

Figure 2. Front-end react application

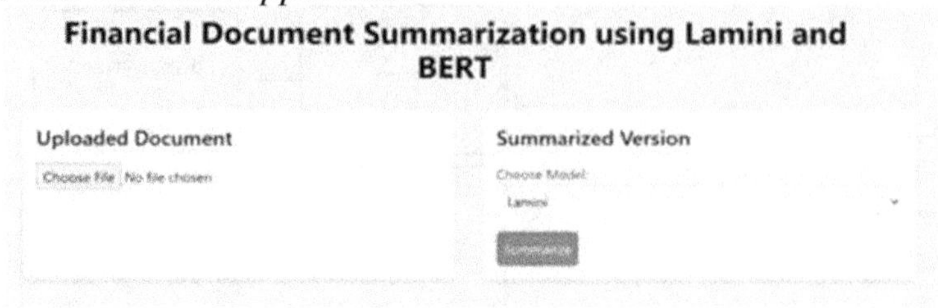

VI. MODEL SELECTION: LAMINI FLAN T5

The Lamini Flan T5 248M parameters model was selected for the project using an extensive selection procedure. Its exceptional performance on a range of downstream NLP tasks and user-oriented instructions influenced this decision. This model, with a reasonable size of 248M parameters, balances efficiency and quality. It is also compactable with LangChain Framework. After a comprehensive evaluation procedure, it is determined to be one of the best option for financial document summarizing tasks. The Lamini Flan T5 248M model plays a significant role in the project's architecture. Known for its outstanding results in both human and automatic assessments on a variety of NLP tasks, this model is an improved version of the Flan- T5 base model. With 248 million parameters, its guarantees maximum efficiency without sacrificing quality. Its smooth integration with the Langchain framework is significant since it makes operations inside the project's ecosystem more efficient. This methodology, which meets the unique requirements of financial document summary by utilizing an effective pipeline for summarization, is an example of its adaptability and effectiveness in practical applications.

Figure 3. Summarization using LaMini Flan T5

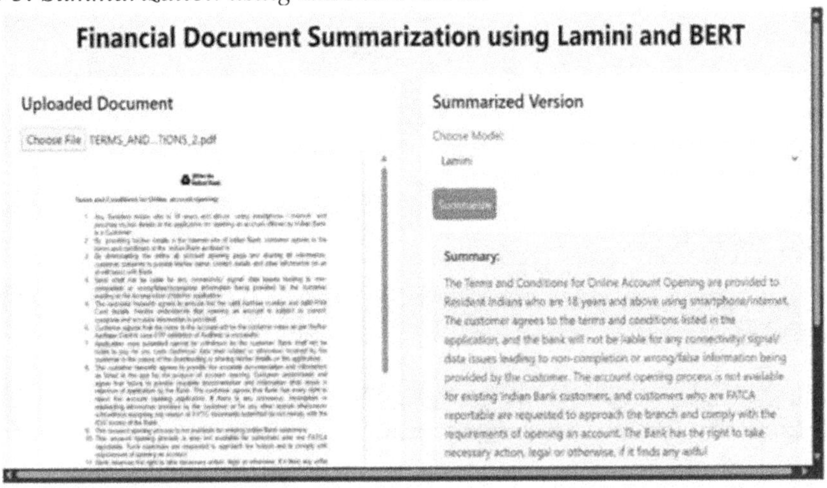

VII. MODEL SELECTION: BERT

The After a thorough model selection procedure, the BERT (Bidirectional Encoder Representations from Transformers) model is chosen by the project. BERT's proven track record of success in Large Language model (LLM) activities serves as the foundation for this choice. BERT's transformer-based design and bidirectional architecture enable it to capture complex linguistic nuances and context relationships, which makes it especially useful for jobs involving document summary. Additional evidence of the model's robustness and dependability comes from its thorough pre-training on large-scale corpora and broad adoption.

The project is to use BERT to achieve high-quality document summarizing outcomes that satisfy the demanding requirements of the finance industry. The project's architecture is based on the BERT model, which provides unmatched performance in NLP tasks. Well-known for its two-way approach to language representation learning, BERT is excellent at extracting context from both previous and next tokens in a text. BERT is able to produce financial document summaries that are more precise and pertinent to the context because to this bidirectional comprehension. In addition, BERT's transformer-based architecture ensures scalability and performance by facilitating the effective processing of big document datasets. By means of its incorporation into the project structure, BERT represents a potent instrument for the extraction of significant insights and data from financial documents, thus augmenting decision-making procedures and optimizing the efficiency of information retrieval.

Figure 4. Summarization using BERT

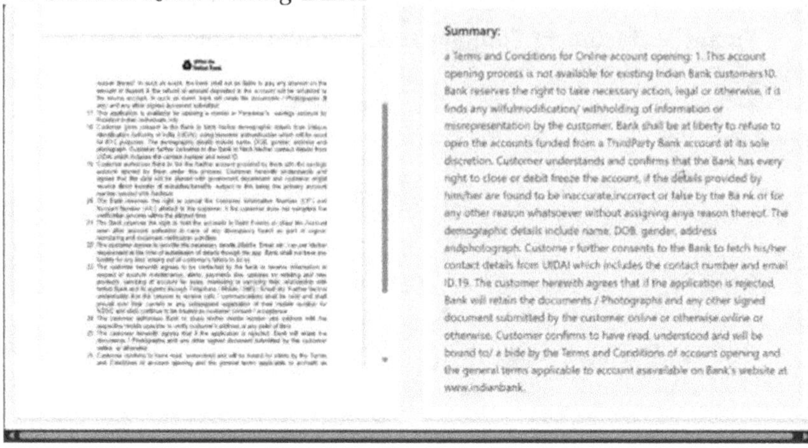

VIII. FINE TUNING

In order to guarantee optimal performance and accuracy when summarizing documents connected to assets, the third module concentrates on optimizing the text summarization tool. This module is crucial for fine-tuning the model's parameters and maximizing its potential in light of the particular demands of the financial industry. Analyzing the integrated NLP models' performance and pinpointing areas for development is the first step in the fine-tuning process. This could entail modifying the model architecture to incorporate domain-specific features, refining training methods, or altering hyperparameters. To increase the model's performance, iterative fine-tuning techniques are used once problem areas have been discovered. This involves attentively observing the model's performance metrics while training it on a representative collection of financial documents. The model's resilience and generalization may be enhanced by applying strategies like regularization, data augmentation, and hyper-parameter tuning.

Precise testing and validation processes are carried out during the fine-tuning phase to evaluate the text summarizing tool's effectiveness and dependability. To make sure that generated summaries meet user expectations, this may include comparing their quality to human annotations or ground truth summaries. Moreover, efforts are undertaken to maximize the summarization process's computing effectiveness, guaranteeing that the tool can manage massive amounts of documents quickly and effectively. By the end of the module, the text summary tool has become highly accurate and efficient, and it is ready to give users succinct and understandable summaries of papers pertaining to finance. The tool's ability to adjust to changing user needs and maintain its ability to produce dependable results over time is guaranteed by the iterative fine-tuning process.

IX. RESULTS

The comparison indicates significant variations in accuracy in the assessment of document summarizing models, specifically Lamini and BERT. Lamini's accuracy scores for Rouge-2 and Rouge-1 were 6.24% and 0.86%, respectively, suggesting a lesser degree of overlap between the generated summaries and the reference summaries. In comparison, BERT demonstrated a greater degree of accuracy, scoring 8.24% for Rouge-2 and 0.26% for Rouge-1(Liu, 2019). This indicates that BERT may provide summaries that significantly overlap with the reference summaries. This difference indicates that BERT performs better than Lamini in summarizing the source documents accurately and producing summaries that are similar to the reference summaries. Thus, BERT outperforms Lamini in the financial arena when it comes to accuracy when it comes to document summary

Figure 5. Accuracy of LaMini and BERT

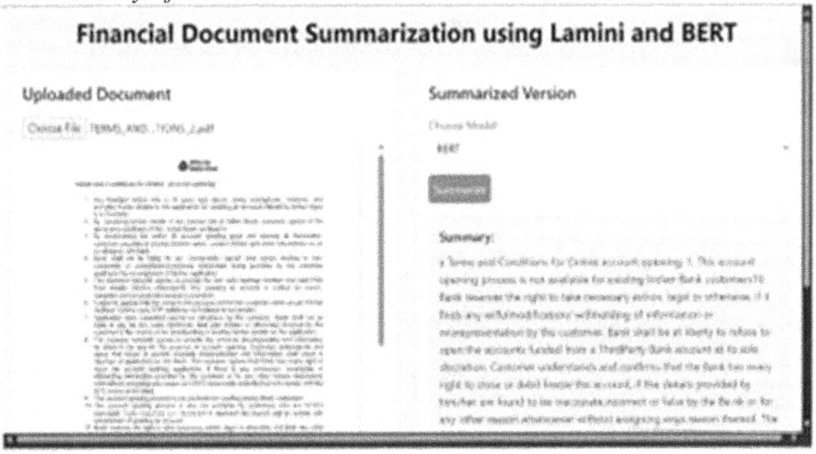

X. CONCLUSION

The Financial Document Summarization Project is a major advancement in applying cutting-edge natural language processing (NLP) techniques to real-world financial document analysis problems. The project's automation of the summary process has greatly improved financial information accessibility by enabling users to rapidly extract the most important information from lengthy documents without requiring manual inspection. Further improving model parameters and fine-tuning techniques can improve summarization models' accuracy and functionality.

REFERENCES

Adams, G., Fabbri, A. R., Ladhak, F., Lehman, E., & Elhadad, N. (2023, December). From sparse to dense: GPT-4 summarization with chain of density prompting. In Proceedings of the Conference on Empirical Methods in Natural Language Processing. Conference on Empirical Methods in Natural Language Processing (Vol. 2023, No. 4th New Frontier Summarization Workshop, p. 68).

Alguliev, R. M., Aliguliyev, R. M., & Isazade, N. R. (2013). Multiple documents summarization based on evolutionary optimization algorithm. *Expert Systems with Applications*, *40*(5), 1675–1689. DOI: 10.1016/j.eswa.2012.09.014

Cao, S., & Wang, L. (2023). Awesome: Gpu memory-constrained long document summarization using memory mechanism and global salient content. arXiv preprint arXiv:2305.14806.

Carew, H. T., Zhang, W., & Rea, T. D. (2007). Chronic health conditions and survival after out-of-hospital ventricular fibrillation cardiac arrest. *Heart (British Cardiac Society)*, *93*(6), 728–731. DOI: 10.1136/hrt.2006.103895 PMID: 17309904

Chang, K. K., Cramer, M., Soni, S., & Bamman, D. (2023). Speak, memory: An archaeology of books known to chatgpt/gpt-4. arXiv preprint arXiv:2305.00118. DOI: 10.18653/v1/2023.emnlp-main.453

Chang, Y., Lo, K., Goyal, T., & Iyyer, M. (2023). Booookscore: A systematic exploration of book-length summarization in the era of llms. arXiv preprint arXiv:2310.00785.

Erdem, E., Kuyu, M., Yagcioglu, S., Frank, A., Parcalabescu, L., Plank, B., Babii, A., Turuta, O., Erdem, A., Calixto, I., Lloret, E., Apostol, E.-S., Truică, C.-O., Šandrih, B., Martinčić-Ipšić, S., Berend, G., Gatt, A., & Korvel, G. (2022). Neural natural language generation: A survey on multilinguality, multimodality, controllability and learning. *Journal of Artificial Intelligence Research*, *73*, 1131–1207. DOI: 10.1613/jair.1.12918

Kurisinkel, L. J., & Chen, N. F. (2023). LLM Based Multi-Document Summarization Exploiting Main-Event Biased Monotone Submodular Content Extraction. arXiv preprint arXiv:2310.03414.

Liu, Y. (2019). Fine-tune BERT for extractive summarization. arXiv preprint arXiv:1903.10318.

Liu, Y., Iter, D., Xu, Y., Wang, S., Xu, R., & Zhu, C. (2023). G-eval: Nlg evaluation using gpt-4 with better human alignment. arXiv preprint arXiv:2303.16634. DOI: 10.18653/v1/2023.emnlp-main.153

Saleh, H. H., Kadhim, N. J., & Bara'a, A. A. (2015). A genetic based optimization model for extractive multi-document text summarization. *Iraqi Journal of Science*, •••, 1489–1498.

Tang, L., Sun, Z., Idnay, B., Nestor, J. G., Soroush, A., Elias, P. A., Xu, Z., Ding, Y., Durrett, G., Rousseau, J. F., Weng, C., & Peng, Y. (2023). Evaluating large language models on medical evidence summarization. *NPJ Digital Medicine*, *6*(1), 158. DOI: 10.1038/s41746-023-00896-7 PMID: 37620423

Wang, Q., Li, B., Xiao, T., Zhu, J., Li, C., Wong, D. F., & Chao, L. S. (2019). Learning deep transformer models for machine translation. arXiv preprint arXiv:1906.01787. DOI: 10.18653/v1/P19-1176

Chapter 4
A Novel Approach for Early Detection of Type 2 Diabetes With Advanced ML Algorithms Based on SFS and PCA

Mohd Firoz Warsi
Greater Noida Institute of Technology, Greater Noida, India

Shiv Narain Gupta
Greater Noida Institute of Technology, Greater Noida, India

Jitendra Mohan
Jaypee Institute of Information Technology, Noida, India

Dhiraj Gupta
Greater Noida Institute of Technology, Greater Noida, India

ABSTRACT

Premature recognition of diabetes is crucial to prevent severe complications. This study focuses on detecting and classifying type 2 diabetes in patients using machine learning (ML) models to identify the best model for predicting diabetes risk. Eight ML models were analyzed: random forest classifier (rfc), XGB booster classifier, bagging classifier, adaboost classifier, voting classifier (hard voting), LGBM classifier, catboost classifier, and decision tree (DT). The study used a Kaggle-based Pima Indian dataset with 768 patient records, including variables like the number of pregnancies, blood glucose concentration, insulin levels, skin thickness, blood

DOI: 10.4018/979-8-3693-6864-0.ch004

pressure, BMI, age, diabetes pedigree function, and outcome (diabetic or not). Results show that the rfc and xgboost classifiers perform best without PCA. After applying PCA, the rfc classifier's accuracy improved, outperforming other models. The rfc and xgboost models initially achieved 92% accuracy. Post-PCA, the rfc model's accuracy increased to 97%. Thus, using ML models for early diabetes detection is promising.

1. INTRODUCTION

Diabetes mellitus, a long-term metabolic disease marked by large amount of blood sugar levels, has become one of the foremost public health issues of the 21st century. Among its various forms, type 2 diabetes mellitus (T2DM) constitutes the majority of diabetes cases globally, representing a considerable burden on healthcare systems and individuals alike. The prevalence of T2DM has been progressively rising over the previous few decades, attributed to factors such as sedentary lifestyles, unhealthy dietary habits, and an ageing population. Consequently, there has been an urgent need for effective strategies for early detection, management, and prevention of T2DM to mitigate its adverse health outcomes and socioeconomic implications. Adults are at high risk for diabetes. Presently, the Western Pacific area has the biggest number of patients worldwide (Li et al., 2023; Kalyankar, Poojara & Dharwadkar 2017; Anand & Shakti, 2015; *Pan American Health Organization*, 2024).

Traditional diagnostic approaches for T2DM have relied on clinical criteria, including fasting plasma glucose levels, oral glucose tolerance tests, and glycated haemoglobin (HbA1c) measurements (Kalyankar et al., 2017; Anand & Shakti, 2015). While these diagnostic methods are widely used and clinically validated, they may not always capture subtle variations in disease progression or risk factors, leading to delayed diagnosis or misclassification. Moreover, conventional diagnostic approaches are often invasive, time-consuming, and require specialised laboratory infrastructure, posing challenges, particularly in resource-limited settings and routine clinical practice. In some recent years, the convergence of healthcare system and technology has flagged the way for advanced solutions to tackle the challenges associated with T2DM diagnosis and management. One such technological advancement that holds great promise is the application of machine learning (ML) algorithms and artificial intelligence (AI) techniques in healthcare. ML algorithms, particularly those based on supervised learning, have shown remarkable efficacy in leveraging large-scale clinical data to develop predictive models for disease detection and risk stratification. By analysing diverse data types such as electronic health records (EHRs), medical imaging, genomic profiles, and wearable sensor data, ML algorithms can extract complex patterns and relationships that may not be readily apparent to human experts

(*IDF Diabetes Atlas*, 2024; El-Attar et al., 2022). Amidst the burgeoning interest in ML-based approaches for healthcare applications, one fundamental challenge lies in the effective utilisation of high-dimensional data while avoiding the curse of dimensionality. High-dimensional datasets, characterised by a large number of features or variables, can pose computational challenges and increase the risk of overfitting, thereby compromising the generalizability and interpretability of ML models. To address this challenge, dimensionality reduction techniques play a pivotal role in extracting relevant information from the data while reducing its complexity (Mohamed & Kumar, 2022; Philip et al., 2022).

One powerful technique in machine learning, extensively used for dimensionality reduction with feature extraction, is PCA (principal component analysis). PCA enables the transformation of correlated variables into linearly uncorrelated components, known as principal components, thereby reducing the dimensionality of the data while preserving as much variance as possible. PCA makes machine learning models more useful and easy to understand by keeping only the most important features and getting rid of variables that aren't needed or cause a lot of noise (Susana et al., 2022). It also makes computations faster and lowers the risk of overfitting. Against this backdrop, the automatic detection of T2DM using ML and PCA represents a promising avenue for improving early diagnosis, risk prediction, and personalised management of the disease. ML models can learn complex patterns that show when T2DM starts or gets worse by combining different clinical, demographic, biochemical, and lifestyle-related factors. This lets for timely and targeted interventions. Furthermore, by incorporating PCA as a pre-processing step, the dimensionality of the feature space can be reduced without significant loss of information, enhancing the scalability and generalizability of the predictive models across heterogeneous patient populations and healthcare settings (Zhou et al., 2020). The aims this works is to provide a detailed outline of the present state-of-the-art in automatic detection of T2DM using ML and PCA techniques. The work will cover various aspects, including the epidemiology and clinical characteristics of T2DM, the role of ML in healthcare, the principles and applications of PCA in feature extraction, and the existing literature on ML-based approaches for T2DM detection. Furthermore, the work will explore the challenges and opportunities in implementing ML and PCA algorithms in real-world clinical settings, including data acquisition, model development, validation, and deployment. Additionally, the work will highlight emerging trends, future directions, and potential implications for clinical practice, public health policy, and biomedical research.

The remaining of this work is structured as follows: Section 2 will present a comprehensive review of the existing literature on ML-based approaches for T2DM detection, including studies utilising PCA for dimensionality reduction. Section 3 will delve into the principles and applications of ML in healthcare, with a focus on supervised learning algorithms and their potential for T2DM detection with the proposed methodology. It will explore the fundamentals of PCA, its role in feature extraction, its applications in healthcare analytics, and all data pre-processing techniques. Section 4 will present the trained model's training and evaluation, as well as the results. Section 4 will delve into the challenges and opportunities associated with implementing ML and PCA algorithms in clinical practice, addressing issues such as data privacy, model interpretability, and regulatory considerations. Finally, Section 5 will end with an outline of the most important results, what they mean for future research, and suggestions for how to make the field of automatic detection of T2DM using ML and PCA techniques even better (Care, 2018).

2. RELATED WORK

Various studies have employed machine learning (ML) for diabetes detection using the Pima Indian dataset, which has 9 attributes and 768 patients (Aggarwal & Pandey, 2023; Diwani & Sam, 2014; Zou et al., 2018; Alam et al., 2019). For instance, in Kushwaha et al. (2022), a model was developed using cross-validation with six different ML models to predict diabetes through non-invasive methods. The XGBoost classifier achieved the highest performance with a cross-validation score of 0.9013, while the SVM model had the lowest performance at 61.17%. In another study Padierna et al. (2020), a non-invasive approach was proposed for analyzing features extracted from tomographic images, using SVM as the ML classifier, achieving a sensitivity of 91% and a cross-validation accuracy of 92.64%. Similarly, Ganie and Malik (2022) introduced a novel ML-based structure for early prediction of type 2 diabetes, employing various techniques, with the decision tree (DT) model attaining the highest results with an accuracy of 0.9941, a precision of 0.99, a recall of 95.83% with a specificity of 99.11%, and an F1-score of 99.15%.

Likewise, Khanam and Foo (2021) utilized ML algorithms and neural networks (NNs) for diabetes prediction, including DT, random forest (RF), logistic regression (LR), Naïve Bayes (NB), K-nearest neighbours (KNN), and SVM, finding that LR and SVM algorithms performed best in terms of accuracy. Wei et al. (2022) focused on predicting blood insulin levels using an ML model, achieving 80% accuracy. In Pramanik and Bandyopadhyay (2023), DT and random tree (RT) models were used to create a classifier capable of detecting diabetes based on collected data. Given the increasing prevalence of diabetes as a leading cause of death, Theerthagiri et al. (2022) explored numerous ML algorithms such as NB, DT, KNN and multi-layer perceptron (MP) to identify the best classifier for use in healthcare settings to enhance decision-making. Additionally, Pal et al. (2022), investigated various supervised learning techniques to improve the accuracy of diabetes prediction. Warsi,

Khanam, et al. (2022) examined several ML techniques with PCA application for the detection of cancer and to improve the accuracy ANN is used with PCA dimension reduction technique.

3. PROPOSED METHODOLOGY

This section outlines the procedures and materials employed in current study, presented as follows:

(A). Description of the dataset.
(B). Description of EDA technique for the visualisation and exploration of data.
(C). Description of feature elimination method (sfs)
(D). Description of ML models used in this work and PCA

The model development and our projected procedure is clearly shown in the Figure 1.

Figure 1. Proposed methodology model

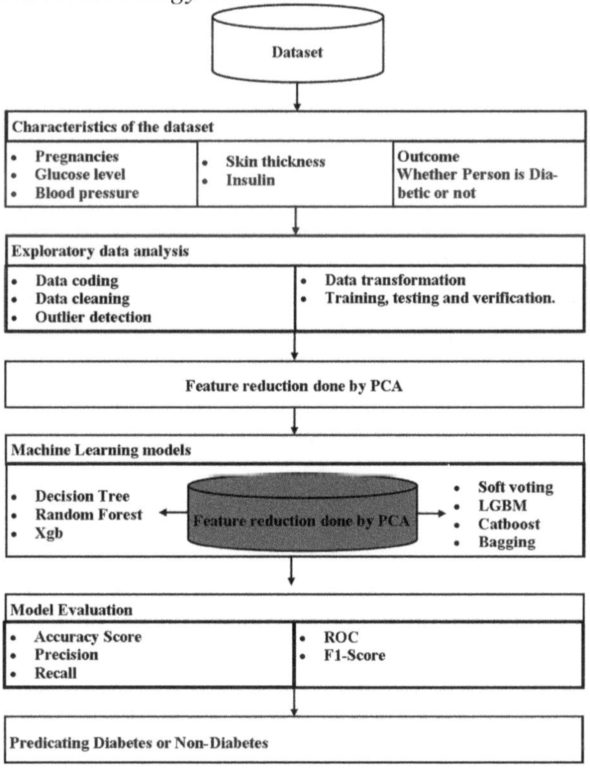

(A). Description of the dataset

This section begins with loading the dataset from Kaggle, which contains 768 patient records and 9 attributes (number of pregnancies in women, skin fold thickness, blood glucose level, diastolic blood pressure, insulin level, body mass index, family history of diabetes, age, and diabetes diagnosis (yes/no)). The dataset was loaded using the pandas library and the read_csv() function, as illustrated in Figure 2.

Figure 2. Description of the dataset

```
 #   Column                    Non-Null Count  Dtype
---  ------                    --------------  -----
 0   Pregnancies               768 non-null    int64
 1   Glucose                   768 non-null    int64
 2   BloodPressure             768 non-null    int64
 3   SkinThickness             768 non-null    int64
 4   Insulin                   768 non-null    int64
 5   BMI                       768 non-null    float64
 6   DiabetesPedigreeFunction  768 non-null    float64
 7   Age                       768 non-null    int64
 8   Outcome                   768 non-null    int64
dtypes: float64(2), int64(7)
memory usage: 54.1 KB
```

a. Missing values

Missing values in a dataset can significantly impact the quality and reliability of analyses and conclusions drawn from the data. They occur when no data is stored for a particular variable in a particular observation. This data does not have any missing values as it is clear from the Figure 3.

Figure 3. Missing values

```
Pregnancies                 0
Glucose                     0
BloodPressure               0
SkinThickness               0
Insulin                     0
BMI                         0
DiabetesPedigreeFunction    0
Age                         0
Outcome                     0
dtype: int64
```

b. Statistical value

Statistical values play a crucial role in dataset analysis, especially in the context of classification tasks such as predicting diabetes. The mean and standard deviation provide insights into the central tendency and dispersion of numerical features related to diabetes, such as blood glucose levels, insulin levels, BMI, etc. Understanding the distribution of these features can help identify potential patterns and relationships with the target variable (diabetes) and guide feature selection and engineering. statistical values provide valuable insights into the characteristics of the dataset and play a crucial role in building accurate and robust classification models for predicting diabetes. By leveraging these statistical measures effectively, researchers and data scientists can identify relevant predictors, address data challenges, and develop models that generalize well to unseen data. The important statistical values are shown in the Figure 4.

Figure 4. Statistic of the dataset

	Pregnancies	Glucose	BloodPressure	SkinThickness	Insulin	BMI	DiabetesPedigreeFunction	Age	Outcome
0	6	148	72	35	0	33.6	0.627	50	1
1	1	85	66	29	0	26.6	0.351	31	0
2	8	183	64	0	0	23.3	0.672	32	1
3	1	89	66	23	94	28.1	0.167	21	0

c. Class imbalance

Class imbalance is a common issue encountered in datasets for classification tasks, including the prediction of diabetes. Class imbalance occurs when one class (in this case, diabetic or non-diabetic individuals) is significantly more prevalent than the other in the dataset. In the context of diabetes classification, the imbalance typically arises because the prevalence of diabetes in the population is lower compared to the non-diabetic population. A count plot is a type of categorical plot that displays the counts of observations in each category of a categorical variable. In the context of classification of diabetes using a dataset, a count plot can provide valuable insights into the distribution of certain categorical features related to diabetes. Here statics of diabetic and non-diabetic values are shown in Figure 5.

Figure 5. Count plot

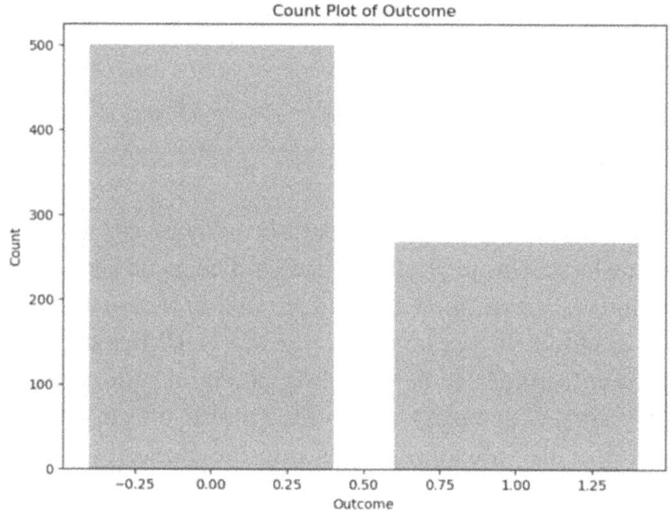

(B). Description of EDA technique for the visualisation and exploration of data

a. Correlation heat map

One crucial task in using ML models for diabetes detection and classification is analyzing the relationships among variables in the dataset through data analysis methods and software tools. For this purpose, we utilized Python to get the dataset, compute the correlation matrix, and conduct the correlation analysis. It's important to note that correlation amid two variables does not certainly indicate a connecting relationship; correlation merely shows the strength and direction of a linear relationship. In this study, we employed correlation analyses to explore the associations between variables. Correlation coefficients values from -1 to 1, where -1 shows a negative correlation, 1 shows a positive correlation, and 0 signifies no linear relationship. Understanding these correlations is crucial for interpreting the strength and direction of relationships between variables. Figure 6 illustrates that most characteristics have low correlation values, generally below 0.5. However, notable exceptions include the relationship between age and pregnancies, where the number of pregnancies increases with age up to a certain point. Another important correlation is between glucose and insulin levels, where higher glucose levels are linked to an increased likelihood of diabetes. Additionally, there's a association between body fat percentage and BMI, with higher BMI indicating a higher fat percentage.

Figure 6. Correlation heat map

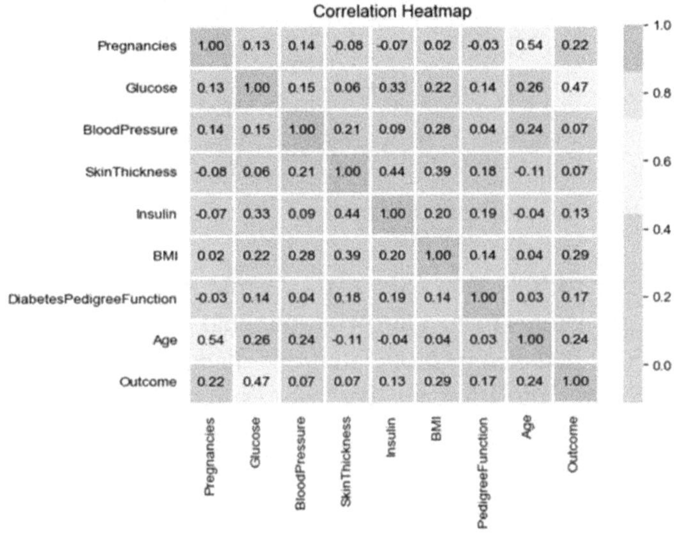

b. Synthetic Minority Over-Sampling Technique

SMOTE (Synthetic Minority Over-Sampling Technique) is a popular data intensification technique used to address class imbalance in datasets, particularly in the context of classification tasks such as predicting diabetes. Class imbalance occurs when one class (e.g., diabetic individuals) is significantly underrepresented compared to another class (e.g., non-diabetic individuals) in the dataset. SMOTE aims to balance the distribution of classes by generating synthetic samples of the minority class, thereby improving the performance of classification models. Figure 7 shows the status of outcome data after applying SMOTE (Chawla et al., 2002).

Figure 7. Data balance after SMOTE

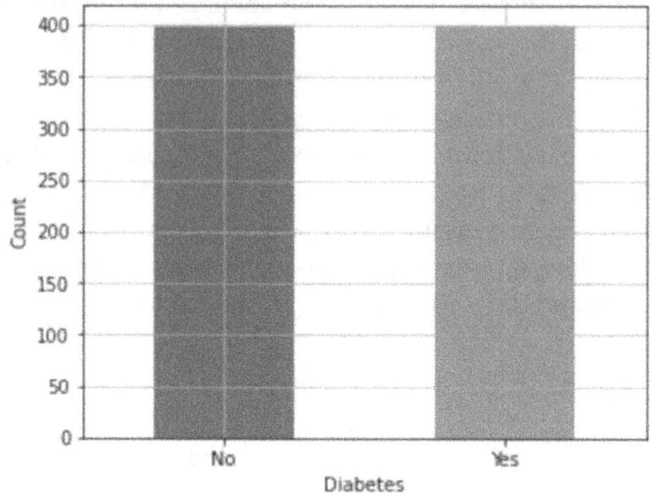

c. Description of feature elimination method

Sequential Forward Selection (SFS) is a feature selection technique used to identify a subset of features from a larger set that maximizes the performance of a classification model. In the context of classifying diabetes using a dataset, SFS can be applied to select the most informative features that are relevant for accurately predicting diabetes status. SFS starts with an empty set of selected features and iteratively adds features one at a time based on their individual performance. The process begins by evaluating the performance of the classification model using each individual feature separately. The feature that results in the highest improvement in model performance, as measured by a predefined evaluation metric (e.g., accuracy, F1-score, AUC-ROC), is selected and added to the set of selected features (Cotter et al., 1999). Figure 8 and 9 shows the selected feature with their accuracy values after applying SFS technique. So there are 4 best features (glucose, insulin, BMI, Age) taken for the classification.

Figure 8. Accuracy of the feature with SFS

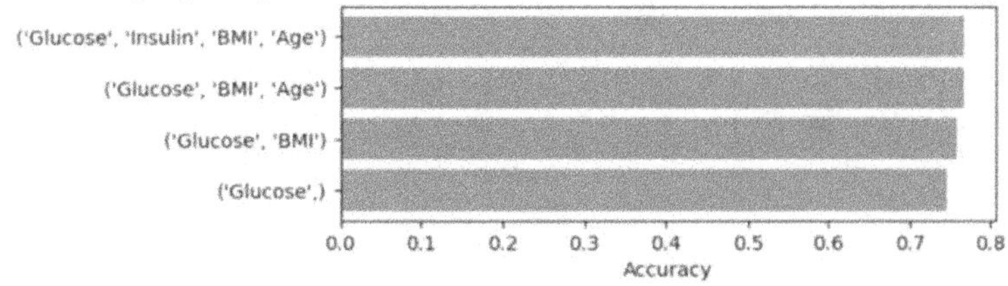

Figure 9. Best average score of features with SFS

	feature_idx	cv_scores	avg_score	feature_names
1	(1,)	[0.7077922077922078, 0.7077922077922078, 0.766...	0.747475	(Glucose,)
2	(1, 5)	[0.7727272727272727, 0.7337662337662337, 0.766...	0.759121	(Glucose, BMI)
3	(1, 5, 7)	[0.7727272727272727, 0.7337662337662337, 0.740...	0.768305	(Glucose, BMI, Age)
4	(1, 4, 5, 7)	[0.7662337662337663, 0.7337662337662337, 0.753...	0.768296	(Glucose, Insulin, BMI, Age)

(C). Description of ML models used in this work and PCA

a. Decision tree classifier

A decision tree classifier is a widely used machine learning algorithm for regression as well as classification tasks. It works by recursively dividing the feature space into smaller subsets based on input feature values, resulting in a tree-like structure of decision rules. Let's denote:

- X as the input features vector.
- *Y* as the output class variable.

For classification, a decision tree seeks to find a series of decision rules that minimize impurity within each subset, aiming to maximize the homogeneity of the target variable within each partition. The decision tree algorithm builds the tree by selecting the best feature to split the data at each node, based on a chosen criterion, often measures like Gini impurity or information gain (entropy). The decision rules are learned from the data, and the procedure lasts recursively until a ending criterion is met, such as attainment of a maximum tree depth, having a minimum number of samples per leaf, or when further splits fail to improve the purity significantly

(Warsi, Chauhan, et al., 2022; Gupta et al., 2023). Here's a simplified equation to represent the decision tree classifier:

$$f(X) = \sum_{m=1}^{M} c_m : I(x \in R_m) \tag{1}$$

Where

- (X) is the predicted output.
- M is the number of terminal nodes or leafs.
- c_m is the class label assigned to the mth leaf.
- R_m is the mth region, which is defined by a set of conditions on the input features.
- $(x \in R_m)$ is an indicator function that outputs 1 if the input X falls within the region R, and 0 otherwise.

The decision tree effectively partitions the feature space into regions $R1$, $R2$---- R_M where each region corresponds to a leaf node in the tree. The class assigned to a new data point X is determined by which leaf node the point falls into after traversing the decision tree based on the learned decision rules.

b. Random forest classifier

Random Forest is a collaborative training method that bodies many decision trees during training and produces a final output based on the majority vote (for classification) or the average prediction (for regression) of the individual trees. It combines the predictions of multiple decision trees to improve generalization and robustness over a single tree. In a Random Forest classifier:

- X represents the input features vector.
- Y represents the output class variable.

Here's an equation to represent the Random Forest classifier:

$$f(X) = \frac{1}{N} \sum_{i=1}^{N} T_i(X) \tag{2}$$

Where

- $(X)$is the predicted output.
- N is the number of decision trees in the forest.

- $T_i(X)$is the prediction of the ith decision tree

Each decision tree in the forest is constructed with a subcategory of the training data (bootstrap sampling) and an arbitrary features subset at each node (feature bagging). This randomness helps to decor relate the individual trees, making them different from each other and reducing the risk of over fitting (Warsi, Chauhan, et al., 2022).

To do an estimation for a new data point *X*, the Random Forest sums the predictions of all the individual decision trees. For classification tasks, it returns the class that receives the most votes from the individual trees, while for regression tasks, it returns the average prediction across all trees (Gupta et al., 2023; Warsi et al., 2019).

c. XGBOOST classifier

XG Boost (Extreme Gradient Boosting) is a radical application of gradient boosting algorithm, which is known for its high performance and efficiency in handling structured data. It has become a widely used algorithm in machine learning models and real-world applications due to its scalability, speed, and effectiveness. XG Boost builds a group of weak learners (typically decision trees) sequentially, with each new learner correcting errors made by the existing ensemble. The algorithm minimizes a loss function by adding new weak learners in a greedy manner (Chen & Guestrin, 2016).

d. ADABOOST classifier

AdaBoost, short for Adaptive Boosting, is a powerful collaborative training method that adds the outcomes of many weak learners to create a strong classifier. It was proposed by Yoav Freund and Robert Schapire in 1996 and has since become one of the most widespread and extensively used algorithms in the field of machine learning. AdaBoost works by sequentially training a series of weak learners, typically decision trees with only a few nodes (stumps), on different subsets of the training data. A weak learner model performs somewhat better than random guessing. In each iteration, the algorithm focuses on the instances that were misclassified by the previous weak learners, assigning them higher weights to ensure that subsequent learners pay more attention to these instances (Hu et al., 2008).

e. Bagging classifier

Bagging, short for Bootstrap Aggregating, is an ensemble learning technique that improves the results of machine learning models by joining the outcomes of different base learners. It was introduced by Leo Breiman in 1996 as a method to reduce variance and prevent overfitting in predictive models. Bagging works by training different base learners independently on different subsets of the training data and then combining their predictions through a weighted average (for regression) or voting (for classification) (Breiman, 1996).

Advantages of Bagging:

- Reduces variance and prevents overfitting.
- Improves model robustness and generalization performance.
- Can be parallelized to speed up training.
- Works well with a variety of base learners and data types

f. Voting classifier

A voting classifier is a kind of ensemble learning classifier that syndicates the outcomes of different individual classifiers to make a last prediction. There are mostly two types of voting classifiers: soft voting and hard voting.

i. **Hard Voting Classifier**: In a hard voting classifier, the ultimate prediction is based on the votes having majority of the individual classifiers. Each classifier in the ensemble gets one vote, and the section with the greatest votes is chosen as the ultimate prediction.
ii. **Soft Voting Classifier**: In a soft voting classifier, the final prediction is based on the average probability of each class predicted by the individual classifiers. Each classifier assigns a probability to each class, and the section with the highest average probability across all classifiers is chosen as the final prediction (Mienye & Sun, 2022).

g. LGBM classifier

Light GBM (Light Gradient Boosting Machine) is a powerful gradient boosting framework developed by Microsoft. It is designed for efficiency, scalability, and high performance in handling large-scale datasets. Light GBM belongs to the family of gradient boosting machines, which are collective learning methods used for regression and classification tasks. Gradient boosting makes a collaboration of weak learners (typically decision trees) sequentially, where each succeeding learner corrects the errors of its predecessor. Light GBM is a highly efficient, scalable, and accurate gradient boosting framework suitable for a wide range of machine learning tasks, especially those involving large-scale datasets. Its innovative algorithms and optimizations mark it as a worthy tool for both researchers and practitioners in the field of machine learning and data science (Ke et al., 2017).

h. CATBOOST classifier

CatBoost is a state-of-the-art gradient boosting library developed by Yandex. It's particularly known for its robust handling of categorical features and its high predictive accuracy. CatBoost, like other gradient boosting frameworks, builds a collaboration of weak learners (decision trees) sequentially, where each tree modifies the errors of its precursor. It minimizes a differentiable loss function by adding new trees in a greedy fashion. Cat Boost is highly efficient and scalable, making it suitable for large-scale datasets with millions of instances and features. It employs advanced algorithms and data structures to optimize memory usage and computation time. Additionally, CatBoost provides support for parallel and GPU training, further improving its efficiency (Prokhorenkova et al., 2018).

i. Principal Component Analysis (PCA)

Principal Component Analysis (PCA) technique is broadly applied for dimensionality reduction in data science and machine learning. It works by changing the current features into a new set of orthogonal components called principal components, which gets the maximum variance in the data. PCA can be used for dimensionality reduction by picking a subset of the principal components that has most of the variance in the data. The method has the following steps (1) dataset normalization; (2) covariance matrix calculation (3) obtain eigenvalues and eigenvectors (4) projection matrix construction with vectors; and (5) transformation to get the reduced dataset (Gupta et al., 2023).

4. RESULTS

First of all, we applied SMOTE, RFE and PCA on our dataset consisted of 768 patients with 9 predictors for training and testing. After balancing the data (SMOTE), and choosing the right features we go for splitting the dataset (70% and 30% were used for training and testing), then we proceeded with training and prediction. The aim was to predict and categorize patients with type 2 diabetes using ML methods and pick the outperformed classification model to calculate the risk of diabetes. To train and test classifiers like RFC, DT, XGBOOST, ADABOOST, VOTING, BAGGING, CATBOOST and LGBM models we used different algorithm on our dataset. To calculate the result of the classification models Metrics such as the accuracy, precision F1-score, and recall are used. It can be seen from Table 1 that accuracy for xgboost and bagging classifier is very good 92% before applying PCA. But after the application of PCA, RFC has outperformed getting accuracy of 97%.

Table 1. The value of performance parameters in this research

Classifier	Accuracy before PCA				Accuracy after PCA			
Parameters	Precision	Recall	F1-score	Accuracy	Precision	Recall	F1-score	Accuracy
DT	0.92	0.95	0.93	0.91	0.91	0.93	0.92	0.90
RF	0.85	0.86	0.85	0.81	0.96	0.99	0.98	0.97
XGB	0.92	0.96	0.94	0.92	0.77	0.92	0.84	0.77
ADABOOST	0.81	0.89	0.85	0.79	0.84	0.83	0.83	0.78
BAGGING	0.92	0.95	0.94	0.92	0.91	0.93	0.92	0.90
VOTING	0.90	0.98	0.94	0.92	0.84	0.96	0.90	0.86
LGBM	0.91	0.95	0.93	0.91	0.88	0.90	0.89	0.85
CATBOOST	0.85	0.85	0.85	0.80	0.82	0.86	0.84	0.78

Performance parameter to evaluate the model is described in detail:

a. Accuracy

When the number of accurate predictions is divided by the total number of input samples or predictions made, accuracy is defined. This experiment is made possible by the Artificial Neural Network's 99.81% maximum accuracy performance. Decision trees have an accuracy of 91%, which is significantly closer to an ANN.

$$Accuracy = \frac{True\ Positive + True\ Negative}{(True\ Positive + False\ Positive) + (True\ Negative + False\ Positive)} \quad (3)$$

b. Precision

The precision definition is the percentage of real positive numbers among the total number of positive numbers that the classifier predicts. The greatest precision values of AAN in this experiment are 0.98.

$$Precision = \frac{True\ Positive}{True\ Positive + False\ Positive} \quad (4)$$

c. Recall

Recall is the ratio of accurately projected positive numbers to the total number of examples that are truly positive. It is also known as sensitivity or true positive rate. The greatest recall values of ANN in this experiment are 0.97.

$$Recall = \frac{True\ Positive}{True\ Positive + False\ Negative} \tag{5}$$

d. F1-score

It is also known as F-measures or F1-score. It is used to calculate test accuracy as well as to determine the proportion.

$$F - Measure = \frac{2 * \text{Precision} * \text{Recall}}{\text{Precision} + \text{Recall}} \tag{6}$$

e. Receiver Operating Characteristic (ROC)

This curve is also used to depict the performance of RFC classifier and shown in Figure 10. The ROC curve shows a graph plot that illustrates the outcome of a binary classification model across various thresholds. It is widely used in machine learning and diagnostic medicine to evaluate the trade-off between false positive rate (1-specificity) and true positive rate (sensitivity). ROC curve is a valuable tool for evaluating and comparing the outcomes of binary classification models. It provides insights into the trade-off between sensitivity and specificity and helps in understanding the discriminative ability of the classifier across different threshold values.

Figure 10. ROC curve of RFC after applying PCA

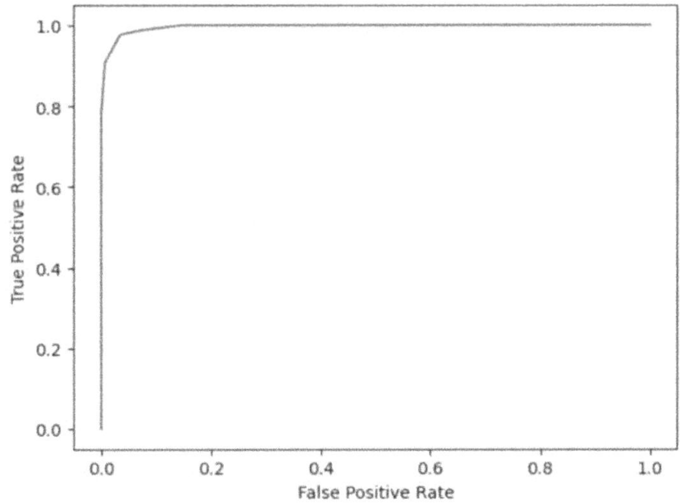

More ever a bar chart is also applied to clear the difference in performance of different classifiers before PCA and after application of PCA.

f. Comparison with other research

In this methodology we have used different machine learning and according to the study our work outperforms without and with PCA with RFC classifier with current dataset respectively illustrated in Figures 11 and 12, respectively. Table 2 shows a comparison of our work with other existed ML techniques.

Figure 11. Comparative analysis of different ML technique before application of PCA

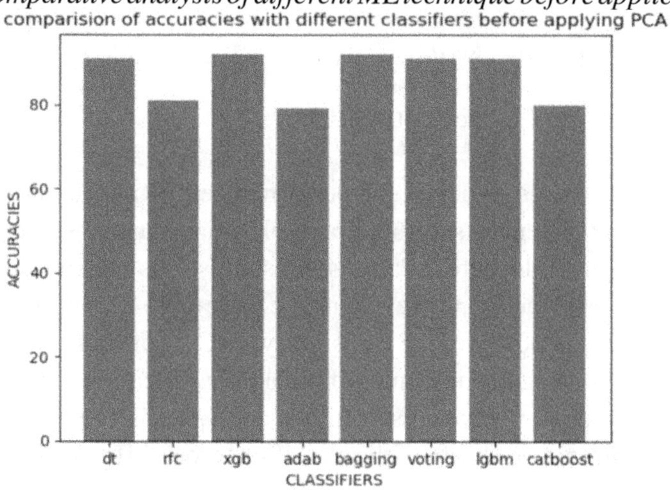

Figure 12. Comparative analysis of different ML technique after application of PCA

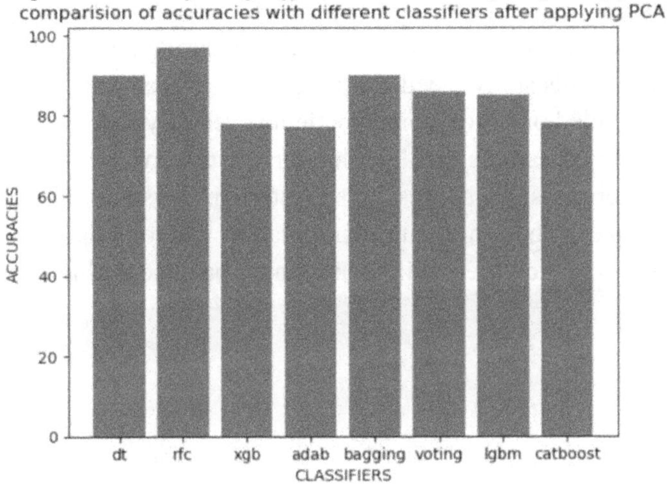

Table 2. Result analysis with recent researches

References	Method	Accuracy
Carlos Padierna et al. (2020)	SVM	92.64%
Kushwaha, S (2022)	XGBOOST	90%
Wei, H (2022)	DT	80%
Theerthagiri, P (2022)	MLP	80%
Proposed Methodology	Ensemble classifiers with RFC	97%

5. CONCLUSION

In conclusion, the exploration of a novel approach for the early detection of type 2 diabetes, leveraging advanced classification algorithms, sequence forward selection (SFS), and Principal Component Analysis (PCA) for feature reduction, holds significant promise in improving diagnosis and intervention strategies. Through the integration of SFS and PCA, the proposed method not only identifies relevant features but also mitigates the curse of dimensionality, enhancing the efficiency and effectiveness of the classification process. the proposed approach represents a important development in the field of diabetes detection, offering a systematic and data-driven methodology for early diagnosis. By leveraging the synergistic benefits of advanced classification algorithms, sequence forward selection, and PCA, this novel approach holds the potential to revolutionize early intervention strategies, finally leading to enhanced patient performances and healthcare delivery in the management of type 2 diabetes. This study faced challenges due to the specific composition of the dataset. It included only 768 female patients over 21 years old with indigenous heritage. This limited sample size can hinder the effectiveness of detection and classification algorithms. To address this limitation, the study employed SMOTE and PCA techniques. These are data manipulation methods that can increase the number of samples in a dataset while maintaining balance within the data.

REFERENCES

Aggarwal, S., & Pandey, K. (2023). Early identification of PCOS with commonly known diseases: Obesity, diabetes, high blood pressure and heart disease using machine learning techniques. *Expert Systems with Applications*, *217*, 119532.

Alam, T. M., Iqbal, M. A., Ali, Y., Wahab, A., Ijaz, S., Baig, T. I., Hussain, A., Malik, M. A., Raza, M. M., & Ibrar, S. (2019). A model for early prediction of diabetes. *Informatics in Medicine Unlocked*, *16*, 100204.

Anand, A., & Shakti, D. (2015). Prediction of diabetes based on personal lifestyle indicators. *2015 1st International Conference on Next Generation Computing Technologies (NGCT)*, 673–676.

Breiman, L. (1996). Bagging predictors. *Machine Learning*, *24*, 123–140.

Care, D. (2018). Care in Diabetesd2018. *Diabetes Care*, *41*(1), S137–S143.

Chawla, N. V., Bowyer, K. W., Hall, L. O., & Kegelmeyer, W. P. (2002). SMOTE: Synthetic minority over-sampling technique. *Journal of Artificial Intelligence Research*, *16*, 321–357.

Chen, T., & Guestrin, C. (2016). Xgboost: A scalable tree boosting system. *Proceedings of the 22nd Acm Sigkdd International Conference on Knowledge Discovery and Data Mining*, 785–794.

Cotter, S. F., Rao, B. D., Kreutz-Delgado, K., & Adler, J. (1999). Forward sequential algorithms for best basis selection. *IEE Proceedings. Vision Image and Signal Processing*, *146*(5), 235. DOI: 10.1049/ip-vis:19990445

Diwani, S. A., & Sam, A. (2014). Diabetes forecasting using supervised learning techniques. *Adv Comput Sci an Int J*, *3*, 10–18.

El-Attar, N. E., Moustafa, B. M., & Awad, W. A. (2022). Deep Learning Model to Detect Diabetes Mellitus Based on DNA Sequence. *Intelligent Automation & Soft Computing*, *31*(1). (El-Attar et al., 2022)

Ganie, S. M., & Malik, M. B. (2022). An ensemble machine learning approach for predicting type-II diabetes mellitus based on lifestyle indicators. *Healthcare Analytics*, *2*, 100092. DOI: 10.1016/j.health.2022.100092

Gupta, S. N., & Warsi, M. F. (2023). A technical analysis of skin cancer classification techniques with machine learning algorithms. Econophysics, Sociophysics & Other Multidisciplinary Sciences Journal (ESMS], 12(2), 34-39.

Hu, W., Hu, W., & Maybank, S. (2008). Adaboost-based algorithm for network intrusion detection. *IEEE Transactions on Systems, Man, and Cybernetics. Part B, Cybernetics, 38*(2), 577–583. DOI: 10.1109/TSMCB.2007.914695 PMID: 18348941

IDF Diabetes Atlas. (2024). Copyright © IDF Diabetes Atlas 2024. All Rights Reserved. https://diabetesatlas.org/

Kalyankar, G. D., Poojara, S. R., & Dharwadkar, N. V. (2017). Predictive analysis of diabetic patient data using machine learning and Hadoop. 2017 International Conference on I-SMAC (IoT in Social, Mobile, Analytics and Cloud) (I-SMAC).

Ke, G., Meng, Q., Finley, T., Wang, T., Chen, W., Ma, W., Ye, Q., & Liu, T.-Y. (2017). Lightgbm: A highly efficient gradient boosting decision tree. *Advances in Neural Information Processing Systems*, 30.

Khanam, J. J., & Foo, S. Y. (2021). A comparison of machine learning algorithms for diabetes prediction. *ICT Express*, *7*(4), 432–439. DOI: 10.1016/j.icte.2021.02.004

Kushwaha, S., Srivastava, R., Jain, R., Sagar, V., Aggarwal, A. K., Bhadada, S. K., & Khanna, P. (2022). Harnessing machine learning models for non-invasive pre-diabetes screening in children and adolescents. *Computer Methods and Programs in Biomedicine*, *226*, 107180. DOI: 10.1016/j.cmpb.2022.107180 PMID: 36279639

Li, Z., Han, D., Qi, T., Deng, J., Li, L., Gao, C., Gao, W., Chen, H., Zhang, L., & Chen, W. (2023). Hemoglobin A1c in type 2 diabetes mellitus patients with preserved ejection fraction is an independent predictor of left ventricular myocardial deformation and tissue abnormalities. *BMC Cardiovascular Disorders*, *23*(1), 49. DOI: 10.1186/s12872-023-03082-5 PMID: 36698087

Mienye, I. D., & Sun, Y. (2022). A Survey of Ensemble Learning: Concepts, Algorithms, Applications, and Prospects. *IEEE Access : Practical Innovations, Open Solutions*, *10*, 99129–99149. DOI: 10.1109/ACCESS.2022.3207287

Mohamed, A. T., & Kumar, S. (2022). Deep Learning Based Process Analytics Model for Predicting Type 2 Diabetes Mellitus. *Computer Systems Science and Engineering*, *40*(1).

Padierna, L. C., Amador-Medina, L. F., Murillo-Ortiz, B. O., & Villaseñor-Mora, C. (2020). Classification method of peripheral arterial disease in patients with type 2 diabetes mellitus by infrared thermography and machine learning. *Infrared Physics & Technology*, *111*, 103531. DOI: 10.1016/j.infrared.2020.103531

Pan American Health Organization. (2024, June 14). https://www.paho.org/en

Pal, S., Mishra, N., Bhushan, M., Kholiya, P. S., Rana, M., & Negi, A. (2022). Deep learning techniques for prediction and diagnosis of diabetes mellitus. *2022 International Mobile and Embedded Technology Conference (MECON)*, 588–593. DOI: 10.1109/MECON53876.2022.9752176

Philip, N. Y., Razaak, M., Chang, J., O'Kane, M., & Pierscionek, B. K. (2022). A data analytics suite for exploratory predictive, and visual analysis of type 2 diabetes. *IEEE Access : Practical Innovations, Open Solutions, 10*, 13460–13471. DOI: 10.1109/ACCESS.2022.3146884

Pramanik, S., & Bandyopadhyay, S. K. (2023). Identifying Disease and Diagnosis in Females Using Machine Learning. In *Encyclopedia of Data Science and Machine Learning* (pp. 3120–3143). IGI Global.

Prokhorenkova, L., Gusev, G., Vorobev, A., Dorogush, A. V., & Gulin, A. (2018). CatBoost: Unbiased boosting with categorical features. *Advances in Neural Information Processing Systems*, •••, 31.

Susana, E., Ramli, K., Murfi, H., & Apriantoro, N. H. (2022). Non-invasive classification of blood glucose level for early detection diabetes based on photoplethysmography signal. *Information (Basel), 13*(2), 59. DOI: 10.3390/info13020059

Theerthagiri, P., Ruby, A. U., & Vidya, J. (2022). Diagnosis and classification of the diabetes using machine learning algorithms. *SN Computer Science, 4*(1), 72. DOI: 10.1007/s42979-022-01485-3

Warsi, M. F., Chauhan, U., Gupta, S. N., & Tiwari, P. (2022). A comparative analysis of melanoma detection methods based on computer aided diagnose system. *Materials Today: Proceedings, 57*, 1962–1968. DOI: 10.1016/j.matpr.2021.10.137

Warsi, M. F., Khanam, R., Chauhan, U., & Kamya, S. (2022). Melanoma classification by 3D colour-texture feature and neural network with improved computational complexity using PCA. *International Journal of Medical Engineering and Informatics, 14*(4), 369–378. DOI: 10.1504/IJMEI.2022.123929

Warsi, M. F., Khanam, R., Kamya, S., & Suárez-Araujo, C. P. (2019). An efficient 3D color-texture feature and neural network technique for melanoma detection. *Informatics in Medicine Unlocked, 17*, 100176. DOI: 10.1016/j.imu.2019.100176

Wei, H., Sun, J., Shan, W., Xiao, W., Wang, B., Ma, X., Hu, W., Wang, X., & Xia, Y. (2022). Environmental chemical exposure dynamics and machine learning-based prediction of diabetes mellitus. *The Science of the Total Environment, 806*, 150674. DOI: 10.1016/j.scitotenv.2021.150674 PMID: 34597539

Zhou, H., Myrzashova, R., & Zheng, R. (2020). Diabetes prediction model based on an enhanced deep neural network. *EURASIP Journal on Wireless Communications and Networking*, *2020*(1), 1–13. DOI: 10.1186/s13638-020-01765-7

Zou, Q., Qu, K., Luo, Y., Yin, D., Ju, Y., & Tang, H. (2018). Predicting diabetes mellitus with machine learning techniques. *Frontiers in Genetics*, *9*, 515. DOI: 10.3389/fgene.2018.00515 PMID: 30459809

Chapter 5

Integration of IoT and Machine Learning in Biomedical Signal Processing

Hina Bansal
https://orcid.org/0000-0003-1683-1581
Amity University, Noida, India

Yash Nautiyal
Amity Institute of Biotechnology, Amity University, Noida, India

Ayush Gujar
Amity Institute of Biotechnology, Amity University, Noida, India

ABSTRACT

Biomedical signal processing is a critical domain in health care, providing us insights into physiological processes and enabling diagnosis, treatment, and monitoring applications. Biomedical signals, such as Electrocardiograms (ECG) and electroencephalograms (EEG) contain a huge amount of information about the health status of an individual. Tradition methods of signal processing often rely on manual or semi-automated techniques, which can be time-consuming and vulnerable to errors. The Internet of Things (IoT) and Machine Learning (ML) have revolutionized this field, providing us with unprecedented capabilities in data acquisition and analysis. Integration of ML and IoT offers a transformative approach to overcome these limitations by enabling real-time, continuous monitoring and automated analysis of the signals. This chapter will explore the importance of IoT and Machine learning in biomedical signal processing, highlighting their roles,

DOI: 10.4018/979-8-3693-6864-0.ch005

challenges, and future direction.

INTRODUCTION

Animals comprise complex units and subunits that perform specific physiological roles in a body. The human body has multiple systems including the nervous system, cardiovascular system, and musculoskeletal system. The cardiovascular system includes supplying blood to the pulmonary system for oxygenation and delivering nutrients all over the body including the subsystems of organs, vessels, and cells. Physiological functions are usually dynamic processes with control mechanisms that accept inputs in different forms ranging from physical, chemical such as neurotransmitters, or electrical stimuli. They often produce distinct signals that point to their presence and/or function in the different biological processes that occur within a living organism. Such signals may be in the form of electrical potentials, ion currents, hormone levels, neurotransmitter levels, pressure differentials, and thermal gradients. In conclusion, most of the physiological processes consist of highly coordinated dynamics and feedback, which are imprinted with alarm signals and can be electrical, chemical, mechanical, or thermal (Rangayyan & Krishnan, 2024).

These are signals produced by the human body that carry information from inside the body and may be a result of an external stimulus or as an outcome of the natural functioning of the body's organs. Such signals can be grouped based on the kind of physical characteristics that are genetically determined to appear in response to specific stimuli. Useful biological signals in clinical contexts often include:

- Bioelectrical impulses originating from electricity occurring in between the cell's membrane.
- Bioacoustics signals (Hadjileontiadis et al., 2006; Inan et al., 2015), acquiring sound produced due to mechanical or fluid movement in organs.
- Pressure, flow, motion, and other tissue displacement signals which are biomechanical (Criée et al., 2011; Fortino & Giampà, 2010; Korostynska et al., 2007).
- Certain changes in biochemical (Waddell & Bates, 1969; Ring et al., 2010) that is likely to show pH levels and concentrations of chemicals.
- Body temperature (Sund-Levander & Grodzinsky, 2013; Rose et al., 2015), Heat that is an index of metabolic processes within the body.

BIOELECTRICAL SIGNALS

Overview of Electroencephalography (EEG) and Brain Activity

One of the most well-known diagnostic techniques applied to assess various brain states, including epilepsy, is electroencephalography (EEG). It is helpful when one is investigating sleep disorders as well as determining the nature and location of the kind of electrical activity in the brain during an epileptic attack. Now, let's consider the fact that EEG signals, or brain waves, are a window into brain activity since they reveal electrical activity. In a more invasive method, Electrocorticography (ECoG) involves the implantation of electrodes on the exposed cortex of the brain. In comparison to the conventional EEG, this procedure makes it possible for more specific recordings.

Structure of the Human Brain

Several main parts of the human brain can be defined. The biggest lobe is the cerebral lobe and it has four parts referred to as the cerebral hemisphere. It consists of two hemispheres which are connected through a bundle of nerve fibers known as the corpus callosum.

The outermost layer of the cerebrum is known as the cerebral cortex which is evolved ridges and gyri of grey matter containing neuron cell bodies. The parts of the cortex that are divided by sulci, and grouped in gyri enable a larger surface. Below the grey matter, the cortex is on the cerebral white matter and consists of myelinated fibers that transmit messages between neurons. Embedded at the lowest part of the brain is the brainstem, which includes the midbrain pons, and medulla oblongata. The brainstem is the lower end of the brain and is attached to the spinal cord and is responsible for basic bodily functions such as breathing and heart rate. Separated from the cerebral hemispheres and the brainstem is the thalamus which serves as a relay centre and acts as a filter to incoming signals to other areas of the brain (Figure 1).

Figure 1. Structure of brain

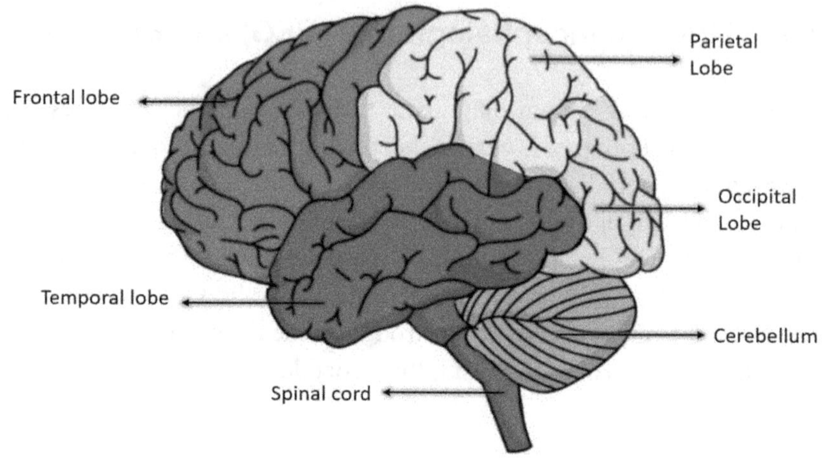

Certain EEG techniques include:

Needle Electrodes – This type of electrodes can penetrate deep tissues and capture signals from deeper structures in the brain. This is placed on the head and is passed through the skull into the brain tissues.

Naso-pharyngeal Electrodes – These electrodes are placed in the nasopharynx to provide a recording of electrical activity at the base of the brain.

Electrocorticogram (ECoG) – A direct cortical recording approach where electrode grids are positioned on the outer layer of the brain to record activity from the cerebral cortex.

Intracerebral Electrodes – This refers to electrodes that are positioned within the brain matter itself. Permit the recording of electrical signals obtained from deep structures. Require neurosurgical implantation.

EEG Rhythms or Frequency Bands

The brain exhibits electrical activity that has some rhythm, and this is measured and divided into bands based on frequency. Delta band is between 0.5-4 Hertz (Hz) and is most dominant in sleep but it is very helpful in other sleep functions. Theta is associated with creativity, formation of memories as well as relaxation and is observed in the range of 4-8 hertz. Alpha waves are in the range of 8 to 13Hz which means wakefulness but relaxation, lower during stress or concentration. Lastly, there are the beta waves that range from 13-30 Hz and they are associated with active thinking, concentration and external attention. Each of the mentioned frequencies has some purpose for cognition and physical well-being.

Event-Related Potentials (ERPs)

Event-related or evoked potentials (ERPs) can be described as the electrical brain activity which is directly elicited by a specific sensory cognitive or motor event. SSEPs are usually assessed with electroencephalography or electromyography and are generated in response to external stimuli such as light, sound, or electric impulses.

ERPs are oscillatory, short, and have very small amplitudes and therefore are not easily discernible from the background EEG with the naked eye. They give data on the processes involved in the functioning of the human brain and various cognitive functions.

Types of ERPs:

Short latency ERPs - These are the initial responses to the stimulus and are influenced greatly by the physical properties of the stimulus and manifest themselves soon after the stimulus is presented. They are the raw and direct representation of the outer happening in the consciousness of the character.

Longer-latency ERPs – In addition, these later waves also depend upon the context and the relevance of the stimulus. They give information about higher-order cognitive processes and how decision-making takes place about the event in question and its importance.

UNDERSTANDING ELECTROCARDIOGRAM (ECG) AND HEART FUNCTION

The electrocardiogram (ECG) is a basic clinical tool that can be used to evaluate the electrical involvement of the heart. Placement of electrodes involves positioning them on the arms, legs, and chest regions. Every single pulsation of the heart generates an electrical signal that stimulates the heart tissues to coordinate rhythm and rate and to cause contraction of cardiac muscle to facilitate the pumping of blood. Heart attack is one common condition that ECG is usually employed to evaluate.

An EG is more invasive than an ECG, as electrodes are directly placed on the heart. This signal is used by certain implanted devices such as defibrillators and pacemakers.

The heart is a crucial organ in the circulatory system of the human body in charge of pumping blood around the body (Figure 2). Blood circulation is the transportation of blood to and from all organs, limbs, and tissues to supply them with oxygen, nutrients, and other requirements while at the same time supplying other waste products and toxins.

The heart has two synchronized pumping circuits:

- Pulmonary Circulation: Pump, oxygen from the body, blood goes to the right atrium, then the right ventricle, and lungs to get rid of carbon dioxide and bring in oxygen.

Oxygenated blood then flows to the left atrium.

- Systemic Circulation: The left ventricle then contracts after receiving blood from the left atrium and pumps blood with high pressure to all the tissues of the body to enable them to receive nutrients and oxygen. Hence deoxygenated blood with wastes then circulates back to the right atrium.

Figure 2. Structure of heart

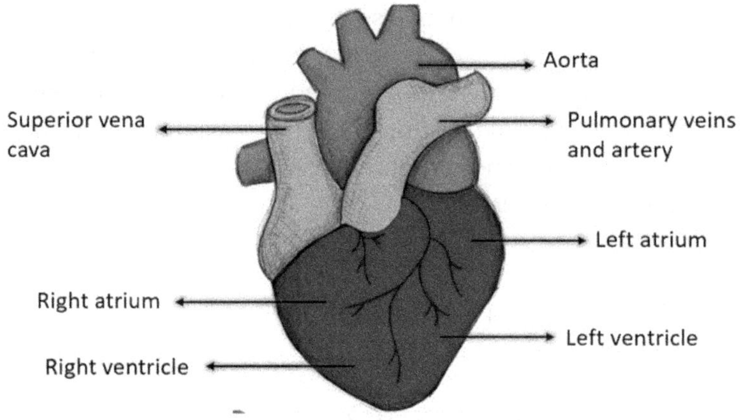

Contraction and relaxation occur in each heart chamber which is supplied with the electrical signals to prompt the muscle contraction at the desired time in the cardiac cycle.

The electrical conduction system has main components:

The sinoatrial (SA) node is located in the right atrium just above the AV node; it retains the ability to spontaneously depolarize and go through the entire cycle repeatedly without any external trigger.

The Atrioventricular (AV) node also keeps a check on the transfer of blood before the ventricles contract. It receives signals from the SA node and it controls heartbeats. The impulse from the AV node is transmitted by the His-Purkinje system to the ventricles, which, to pump blood into the pulmonary and systemic circulation, contract.

Understanding ECG Signals

P-wave: The final stage of electrical activity in the atria is called atrial depolarization and it causes atrial contraction.
QRS complex: An action potential that renders the ventricles of the heart capable of contraction.
T-wave: The time taken to restore the resting membrane potential following contraction is referred to as ventricular repolarization during relaxation.

Electromyogram (EMG)

Skeletal muscles are mapped by an EMG to record electrical activity in them. It is used to determine changes associated with muscle disease and nerve supply disruption. There are two main types:

1. Surface EMG – Electrodes positioned on the skin to monitor muscle's response.
2. Intramuscular EMG – These involve additional insertion of the needle electrodes in muscles to obtain finer details.

Electroneurogram (ENG)

An ENG measures electrical activity traveling along the lengths of nerves. It is required in the assessment of nerve conduction velocity for diagnosing injured nerves and nerve diseases. There are two main methods:

1. Fine needles are then placed on the nerves.
2. External skin surface electrodes, also known as telemetry electrodes.

The amplitude of the ENG is usually in the range of 10 μV and can fluctuate with small differences. It is imperative to define essential parameters such as high amplifier gain and an extensive bandwidth. By applying current to the two nerves and measuring activity at distal sites, conduction velocity may be calculated.

Electrooculogram (EOG)

The EOG is used to evaluate the potential of the retina to determine eye movements (Figure 3). As the polarized eye rotates the voltage changes since the electrical field is dependent on the orientation of the polarizing eye. EOGs are useful for examining sleep disorders and REM necessary to diagnose pathologies, such as sleep apnoea. Other signs and symptoms that EOGs help to detect include nystagmus which is an involuntary eye movement that is a symptom of balance disorders. It also has use in virtual reality where it can give a natural motion for eye tracking.

Figure 3. Structure of an eye

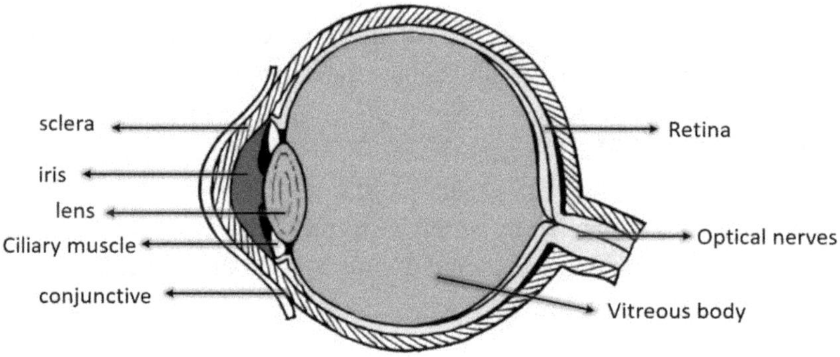

It is recommended to use both horizontal and vertical eye movements where vertical eye movements are recorded by eyelid electrodes. Horizontal movements are done by electrodes placed at the canthi bones. EOGs reflect the discharges that control the eye's movements that help maintain gaze stability and shifts in attention voluntarily.

TECHNIQUES OF BIOPROCESS SIGNALLING

The Fourier Transform

The Fourier Transform is a method that performs the transformation of a signal from time domain to the frequency domain. This helps in determining the various frequency bands contained in the signal under analysis.

In the time domain, a signal is plotted in terms of time as the independent variable and how the signal varies over time as the dependent variable. Some of the questions that can be posed within the time domain are "At what time did a particular event, in the signal, happen?"

On the other hand, the frequency domain representation represents the signal as a function of frequency, that is, it illustrates the amount of the signal that is contained in each of the frequencies within a given frequency spectrum. Some of the questions that can be answered by the frequency domain are; "what is the periodicity of the fluctuations in the signal?"

The Fourier Transform acts as the mediator between these two domains by permitting the conversion of the time signal into sinusoids of varying frequencies. This frequency spectrum is another way of expressing the same signal in such a way that more characteristics and information of the signal may be observed and extracted than by just observing it in the time domain.

It is possible that by gaining insights into both time-varying and frequency-varying signals, one could obtain a more comprehensive view of the signals important for a wide range of applications, ranging from biomedical to telecommunications. The Fourier Transform enables this dual perspective in an inherently rigorous but easy-to-understand mathematical structure that does not necessarily require advanced AI.

Discrete Fourier Transform (DFT)

The Fast Fourier Transform (FFT) applies the Discrete Fourier Transform (DFT) when it is used for practical applications employing digital signals. It simply replaces a finite sequence of N samples of a signal at equally spaced intervals of time to a sequence of N samples at equally spaced intervals of frequency.

Fast Fourier Transform (FFT)

The FFT is a fast method of calculating the DFT and its inverse, which makes it popular in many applications. When compared to directly evaluating the DFT definition which comes with a complexity of O(N2), the FFT comes out as a genius with a complexity of only O(N log N). This speedup is accomplished using Fourier symmetries and properties of periodicity in the definition of the DFT. Cooley–Tukey is the most popular FFT algorithm because it works by breaking down a DFT of size N into smaller DFTs iteratively.

This makes the FFT feasible for operations in real-time or large datasets of signals that need to be analysed. It has been huge over science and engineering specialties that involve analysis of spectrums of signals.

Filtration

Several techniques involve image filtering, which is a process of altering or improving an image by adjusting the pixel values. It is the kind of processing that proves useful in enhancing quality, filtering out noise, and noting down significant characteristics. Two primary strategies of filtration affect either the spatial or the frequency domain.

Space-Domain Methods

Any processing that manipulates the pixel intensities themselves falls under the category of space filtering. Various filter types exist:

A. **Low-pass filters** eliminate high frequencies, such as edges and noise, but maintain low-frequency content. It is normally used in removing high-frequency details such as ragged edges or removing noise. Averaging filters replace each pixel with the average of the neighbourhood's centre and thus remove noises while at the same time smearing edges. Gaussian filters convolve the image using Gaussian functions making them smoother and more realistic blurs than averaging.

B. **High-pass filters** have the opposite effect of low-pass filters; they allow high frequencies to pass through while restricting lows. An application aims to make specific features stand out and enhance the resolution of images. By applying the Laplacian filter, it highlights regions where there are sharp variations in intensity, thus enhancing edges. Sobel filters calculate the intensity differences and thereby find boundaries.

C. **Median Filter** is this type of filter, noise is efficiently eliminated without having a significant negative impact on edges. For each pixel, there is a new value which is the median of the neighbours' pixel values. It performs well in terms of resisting outliers for images with speckled noise. It was suggested that median filtering should suppress noise while preserving edges for a clearer interpretation of the image.

D. **High-boost filters** also reproduce high frequencies but sustain general brightness. Image enhancement and the need to see greater detail are some of the factors that spur the use of sharpening. Increasing requires adding the original image with a high-passed copy of the image to emphasize high-frequency features without changing the overall image brightness.

Frequency Domain Methods

Transforms such as the discrete Fourier transform are used for representing images that can be manipulated in the frequency domain.

a) **Low-pass frequency** domain filters allow low frequencies but eliminate high frequencies, which is beneficial for averting and refreshing. An ideal cutoff filter can pose the danger of introducing ringing artifacts. Moving from Butterworth filters is done more gradually to minimize artifacts.
b) **High-pass** equivalents, on the other hand, give high frequencies for sharpening and feature extraction while denying lows. Discontinuity and trade-offs between ideal step cutoff and more gradual Gaussian roll-off transitions impact artifacts similarly.
c) **Passive filters**, which include band-pass filters, allow the flow of signals within specific bands of frequencies. Perfect specimens meet the defined band perfectly. Smoothing transitions are incorporated into Butterworth versions to decrease artifacts and improve particular aspects.

WAVELET

Wavelets are a powerful mathematical tool used in signal processing and image analysis for analysing localized variations of power within a time series. Unlike traditional Fourier analysis, which provides frequency information without localization in time, wavelet analysis allows for both time and frequency localization, making it particularly useful for non-stationary signals.

A wavelet is a small wave-like oscillation that is localized in time and space. The wavelet transform involves breaking a signal down into shifted and scaled versions of the original (or mother) wavelet.

Types of Wavelet Transforms

- **Continuous Wavelet Transform (CWT)**:

- **Purpose**: Provides a highly redundant representation of the signal by scaling and shifting the mother wavelet continuously.
- **Applications**: Analyzing signals with high time resolution for transient or non-stationary features.
- **Discrete Wavelet Transform (DWT)**:
- **Purpose**: Provides a non-redundant, efficient representation of the signal using discrete scaling and translation.
- **Applications**: Data compression, noise reduction, and feature extraction.

Wavelets enable analysis in both time and frequency domains that are not possible using Fourier transforms which only analyse in frequency. Due to this unique property, wavelets are ideal for signal analysis which is non-stationary.

A wavelet works based on analysing a signal into shifted and scaled versions of a certain wavelet or mother wavelet. In CWT, data is represented by shifting and scaling the mother wavelet over a continuous range of parameters resulting in a highly redundant representation. The other method is more efficient and is called the discrete wavelet transform where the decomposition uses discrete parameters. DWT can be used effectively for data compression and reduction of the noise.

Wavelets have several advantages such as time and frequency localization, multiresolution decomposition for examination of the signals in different scales, and orthogonality permitting invertible transform. Some of the common wavelet functions include Haar wavelet which has a step function profile and is well suited for piecewise constant signals, Daubechies wavelets with good time-frequency localization that make it preferred for JPEG2000 compression, symlets which is a variant of the Daubechies wavelets with increased symmetry, and the coiflets which is well suited for smoothness through vanishing moments.

Major applications of wavelets in signal and image processing include:

Noise Detection – A methodology of dividing a signal into wavelet coefficients and then applying a threshold to estimate noises in it. This is effective for ECG signals especially when the length of the analysed segment is unknown and hence has to be estimated.

Compression – Since coefficients with insignificant values are discarded, quantization and encoding only important coefficients is possible. JPEG2000 uses this to achieve higher compression ratio than JPEG since it detects regions with no important information and reduces the number of code values in those areas.

Feature Extraction for Classification – The properties of the wavelet transform at different time frequencies make it suitable for extracting features that help in the classification of EEG, ECG and other signals.

Image Processing – edge detection, texture analysis and image fusion all use wavelet transforms to extract features from images needed for analysis. Wavelets enhance medical images.

USE OF ML/IOT

Introduction to IoT (Internet of Things)

• The Internet of Things is defined as a collection of tangible objects with integrated Internet, sensors, computers and communication technologies for the purpose of connecting, capturing and sharing information through the internet. IoT allows objects and devices to be controlled and used by using existing network infrastructures (Gubbi et al., 2013).

Role of IoT in Healthcare

- **Remote Monitoring**: From clinics, constant patient monitoring is made possible through IoT devices that give real-time information on things such blood pressure, pulse rate, etc. Thus, treatment is promptly given where needed (Islam et al., 2015).
- **Data Collection and Analysis**: This means that IoT devices are capable of gathering a significant amount of health data from patients that can be summed up and analyzed to provide diagnoses on health complications. It can also help doctors in arriving at diagnostic and treatment decisions that are relevant to patients' conditions (Istepanian & Woodward, 2016).
- **Improved Patient Care**: IoT applies specially and individually provided health care since patient records could be analyzed to formulate the best treatment plan. IoT devices also enable patient to monitor and manage their health condition using available tools they possess (Kourou et al., 2015).

Introduction to ML (Machine Learning)

- **Definition**: Artificial intelligence or AI can be described as the branch of computer science that deals with automating tasks and having machines perform operations on their own without prior instructions. This is achieved through the development of statistical models from the data, which can be used to make either a prediction or a decision. As previously mentioned, there are several applications of ML in the healthcare sector (Litjens et al., 2017).

Personalized medicine, automated image analysis, predictive analytics, and diagnostic tools are some types of examples of machine learning in the healthcare industry (Rajpurkar et al., 2017).

Role of ML in Healthcare

- **Diagnostic Tools**: Machine learning can also assess different kinds of medical records such as images, ECG, EEG, and other biological data for cancer, neurological disorders, and arrhythmias (Jiang et al., 2017).
- **Predictive Analytics**: ML models can be used on patients' data to be able to do early intervention and predict outcomes, disease progression, and complications of chronic ailments (Dey et al., 2018).
- **Personalized Medicine**: Considering someone's genetic predisposition, their ability to lead a certain lifestyle, and how they are likely to react to certain treatments, ML can predict what therapy and medication will be best for this person (Dey et al., 2018).

INTERNET OF THINGS (IOT) IN BIOMEDICAL SIGNAL PROCESSING

The Internet of Things (IoT) represents a technological revolution, where everyday objects are connected to the Internet, enabling them to send and receive data. In the healthcare sector, this interconnected network helps in continuous monitoring and data collection, leading to enhanced patient care, streamlined clinical operations, and innovative medical research.

By integrating IoT with biomedical signal processing, the healthcare system can collect real-time data from various sensors, analyze it, and provide timely intervention which helps in improving patient outcomes (Aledhari et al., 2022).

Biomedical signal processing involves the acquisition, analysis, and interpretation of physiological signals such as electrocardiograms (ECGs), electroencephalograms (EEGs), and Electromyograms (EMGs). These signals provide critical information about the functional status of various biological systems and are crucial for diagnosis and treating various medical conditions. Using IoT in biomedical signal processing signifies a new era of healthcare characterized by continuous monitoring, remote diagnostics, and personalized medicine.

COMPONENTS OF AN IOT SYSTEM

The architecture of IoT in biomedical signal processing comprises several interconnected components that work together to capture, transmit, and analyze physiological data (Figure 4). These components include sensors, communication networks, data storage systems, and data processors. Each of these components plays a vital role in ensuring seamless integration and operation of the IoT ecosystem in healthcare (Panja et al., 2022).

Sensor and Actuators

Sensors are the fundamental building block of the IoT in biomedical signal processing. They are responsible for detecting and measuring physiological parameters. Various types of sensors are used in healthcare, including:

- **Electrocardiogram (ECG) Sensor**:

These sensors are used to measure the electrical activity of the heart by detecting voltage differences on the skin surface. The electrical signals are recorded using electrodes, which pick up depolarization and repolarization of the heart cells (Sattar & Chhabra, 2023).

Holter Monitors and Wearable ECG devices can be used to record the ECG signals. Holter Monitor is a portable device that continuously collects the ECG data, and can be worn for a long time (typically 24-48 hours. Wearable ECG devices are integrated into smartwatches and patches for continuous and real-time heart monitoring.

These modern ECG sensors can achieve clinical-grade accuracy, often within the range of ± 2 bpm for heart rate detection and with a signal-to-noise ratio (SNR) of about 60 dB (Li et al., 2023).

- **Electroencephalogram (EEG) Sensor:**

These sensors measure the electrical activity in the brain by detecting the voltage fluctuations resulting from ionic current flows within neurons. Conventional standard EEG caps, which consist of multiple electrodes placed on the scalp to cover frontal, temporal, parietal, and occipital lobes are used to record these signals. Nowadays, wearable EEG headbands, which are simplified devices with fewer electrodes, typically placed on the forehead or across the scalp are also used (Tyagi et al., 2012).

EEG sensors offer high temporal resolution, capturing brain wave frequencies from 0.1 Hz to 100 Hz with an amplitude range typically around 0.1 – 100 μV. The accuracy depends on the electrode placement and contrast quality, with advanced algorithms used to filter out noise and artifacts.

- **Electromyogram (EMG) Sensor**:

EMG sensors measure the electrical activity produced by skeletal muscles during contractions. It detects the voltage change caused by muscle fiber depolarization. Intramuscular EMG sensor or Surface EMG sensor can be used to measure this voltage change. Intramuscular EMG sensors contain invasive needles that are inserted directly into the muscle tissue to measure deeper muscle activity whereas surface EMG sensors contain non-invasive electrodes placed directly over the target muscle (Kamavuako, 2022).

Surface EMG sensors provide an SNR of 20-30 dB and can detect muscle activity within an amplitude range of 5-500 μV. Intramuscular EMG offers higher accuracy for deep muscle analysis but is more invasive and less commonly used in everyday applications.

- **Temperature Sensor**:

Temperature sensors measure the body temperature by detecting changes in physical properties like resistance (thermistors) or infrared radiation (infrared sensors). Thermistors are typically placed on the skin or embedded in wearable devices. They measure the temperature change by measuring the resistance changes.

- **Pulse Oximeter:**

A pulse oximeter measures the oxygen saturation (SpO2) and heart rate by analyzing the light absorption characteristic of oxygenated and deoxygenated hemoglobin. It typically uses two wavelengths of light (red and infrared) to differentiate between the two forms of haemoglobin. Most common type of pulse oximeters are Finger pulse oximeters and wearable pulse oximeters. Finger pulse oximeters are clip-on devices for the finger, providing quick and easy measurements whereas wearable pulse oximeters are integrated into wristbands, smartwatches, or patches for continuous monitoring. They have high accuracy with an error margin of ±2% in the case of blood oxygen saturation level and ±2 bpm in the case of pulse rate (Pupim et al., 2013). Factors like skin pigmentation, ambient light, and motion can affect the reading, but advanced algorithms are used to remove these issues.

- **Glucose Sensor:**

Glucose Sensors measure blood glucose levels through electrochemical reactions or optical methods. Electrochemical methods detect glucose via enzymatic reactions that produce electrical signals proportional to glucose concentration. Optical sensors use light absorption or scattering properties to detect glucose levels.

Electrochemical sensors are often implanted under the skin or worn as adhesive patches on the arm or abdomen (Oliver et al., 2009). Optical sensors are non-invasive and are placed on the skin or are integrated into wearables like smartwatches. Electrochemical sensors typically have an error margin of $\pm 10\%$ whereas non-invasive optical sensors have a broader error margin of $\pm$ 20%.

COMMUNICATION NETWORKS

The communication network is the backbone of IoT architecture, enabling the data transfer between sensors, devices and data processing units. Various communication technologies are employed, including:

- **Wireless Personal Area Networks (WPANs):**

Technologies such as Bluetooth, and Zigbee provide short-range communication between sensors and local devices such as smartphones or gateways. It can be used to connect fitness trackers and wearable health devices to smartphones (Frenzel, 2018). It can also enable communication between multiple health devices within a home setting. They are energy efficient and suitable for battery-operated devices.

- **Wireless Local Area Networks (WLANs):**

Technologies such as Wi-Fi can facilitate data transfer within healthcare facilities, supporting higher data transfer rates over longer distances than WPANs. It provides high data transfer rates over and also provides broad coverage (Garg, 2007).

- **Cellular Networks:**

Technologies such as 4G LTE, and 5G enable long-range communication for remote patient monitoring and telemedicine. It has high bandwidth, low latency, and extensive coverage which are crucial for real-time applications (Javaid et al., 2023).

- **Low Power Wide Area Networks (LPWANs):**

Technologies such as LoRaWAN, and NB-IoT provide long-range communication with minimal power consumption, ideal for rural and remote healthcare applications. It allows long-range communication with low power requirements and is cost-effective for wide-area deployment **(Chilamkurthy et al., 2022)**.

Data Acquisition and Transmission

Data Acquisition involves collecting raw physiological data from sensors and converting it into digital form. The process includes signal conditioning, amplification, filtering and analog to digital conversion. Once digitized, data is transmitted to the central processing unit via communication networks.

Data Storage Systems

The vast amount of data generated by IoT devices requires robust data storage solutions. Cloud computing platforms are commonly used to store and manage biomedical data due to their scalability, reliability, and accessibility (Banimfreg, 2023). Cloud storage enables healthcare providers to access patient data from anywhere, facilitating remote consultation and telemedicine.

Data Processing Units

Data processing units, including edge and cloud computing systems, are responsible for analyzing acquired data. In the case of edge computing, data is processed near the source (e.g., on local devices), reducing latency and bandwidth usage. Cloud computing on the other hand offers extensive computational resources for complex data analysis and machine learning applications.

Figure 4. Components of IoT system

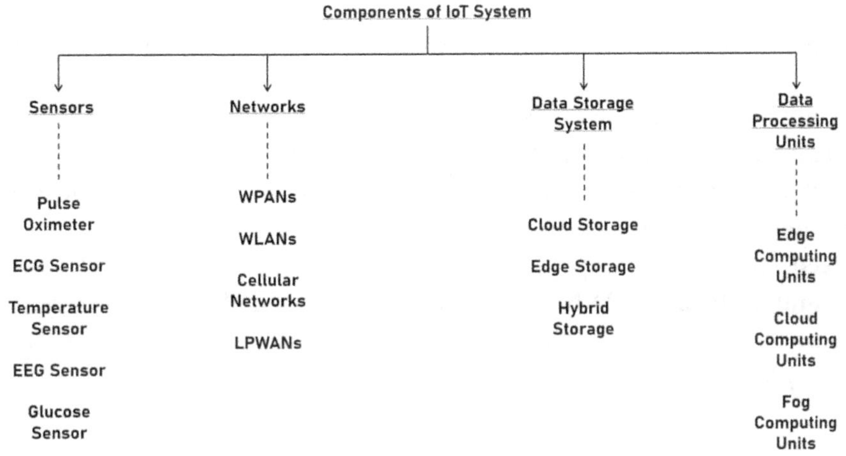

ALGORITHMS USED IN IOT-BASED BIOMEDICAL SIGNAL PROCESSING

Various algorithms are employed in IoT-based biomedical signal processing to ensure accurate data acquisition, transmission, storage, and analysis. These algorithms include:

- **Signal Processing Algorithms**
- **Filtering Algorithms:** Techniques such as Finite Impulse Response (FIR) and Infinite Impulse Response (IIR) filters are used to remove noise and artifacts from biomedical signals ensuring the accuracy of the data (An & Stylios, 2020).
- **Wavelet Transform:** The wavelet transform is used for multi-resolution analysis of biomedical signals. It decomposes signals into different frequency components, aiding in the identification of specific patterns or anomalies.
- **Fourier Transform:** The Fourier Transform converts time-domain signals into frequency-domain representations, helping in the analysis of periodic components in biomedical signals.

Machine Learning Algorithms

- **Supervised Learning:** Algorithms such as Support Vector Machines (SVM), Decision Trees, and Neural Networks are used to classify biomedical signals and predict health outcomes based on labelled training data.
- **Unsupervised Learning:** Clustering algorithms like K-means and Hierarchical clustering identify patterns and group similar biomedical signals without predefined labels.
- **Deep Learning:** Convolutional Neural Networks (CNNs) and Recurrent Neural Networks (RNNs) are employed for complex pattern recognition tasks, such as image-based diagnosis and time series analysis of physiological signals.

Data Fusion Algorithm

- **Kalman Filter:** This algorithm combines data from multiple sensors to provide a more accurate estimation of physiological parameters, reducing the measurement noise and uncertainty (Assa & Janabi-Sharifi, 2015).
- **Bayesians Networks:** Bayesians Networks Model the probabilistic relationships between different physiological signals, enhancing the interpretation and diagnosis of complex medical conditions.

Architecture in IoT Biomedical Signal Processing

- **Centralized Architecture**

In a centralized architecture, all data collected from IoT devices is transmitted to a central server or a cloud platform for processing and analysis (Hamdan et al., 2020). The architecture benefits from the extensive computational resources of the cloud but may suffer from latency of bandwidth issues.

- **Decentralized (Edge) Architecture**

In a decentralized architecture, data processing occurs at edge of the network, near the data source. Edge device analyse the data locally, reducing latency and bandwidth requirements (Nguyen et al., 2024). This architecture is suitable for real time applications, such as emergency response system.

- **Hybrid Architecture**

A hybrid architecture combines both centralized and decentralized architecture approaches. Initial data processing is performed at edge to enable real time decision making, while more complex analysis and long-term data storage are handled by the centralized server. This architecture balances the latency, bandwidth and computational resource utilization.

MACHINE LEARNING IN BIOMEDICAL SIGNAL PROCESSING

Machine Learning (ML) has revolutionized many fields, including biomedical signal processing. Biomedical signals, such as electrocardiograms (ECG), electroencephalograms (EEG), and electromyograms (EMG), contains important information about physiological processes and states. The analysis and interpretation of these signals are crucial for diagnosing diseases, monitoring health conditions, and guiding treatment plans. Traditional methods of analysing biomedical signals often involve manual and heuristic-based approaches, which can be time-consuming, error-prone, and limited in scope. Machine learning, with its ability to automatically learn patterns and make predictions from large datasets, offers a powerful alternative (Vashishth et al., 2024).

Machine learning in biomedical signal processing involves several steps, including data acquisition, preprocessing, feature extraction, feature selection, model training, and validation. This detailed examination begins with an overview of common machine learning algorithms used in biomedical signal processing, followed by a discussion on feature extraction and selection.

Common Machine Learning Algorithms Used in Biomedical Signal Processing

- Support Vector Machines (SVM)

Support Vector Machines are supervised learning models used for classification and regression tasks. They are particularly effective in high-dimensional spaces and are robust against overfitting (Frank, 2024a).

SVM aims to find the optimal hyperplane that maximises the margin between different classes in the feature space. The data point that lies closet to the hyperplane are called support vectors, which are important for defining they hyperplane's position and orientation.

Applications in Biomedical Signal Processing

ECG Classification

SVMs are used to classify heartbeats into normal and abnormal classes, helping in the detection of arrythmias. They classify heartbeats into different types such as normal, premature ventricular contractions (PVCs) and other arrythmias (Khazaee & Ebrahimzadeh, 2013). This is achieved by training the SVM on features extracted from ECG signals, such as RR intervals, P-wave duration and QRS complex characteristics.

EEG Analysis:

SVMs help in distinguishing between different mental states, such as relaxation, concentration, and stress based on EEG patterns. Features such as spectral power in difference frequency bands (alpha, beta, gamma) and coherence between different EEG channels are extracted. The SVM then learns to differentiate these states by finding the optimal hyperplane that separates the feature vectors corresponding to each mental state.

- Convolutional Neural Networks (CNN)

Convolutional Neural Networks are a class of deep learning algorithm, specifically suited for processing grid like data, such as images and time series signals. CNNs are highly effective in capturing spatial hierarchies in data through convolutional layers (Yamashita et al., 2018).

CNNs consist of multiple layers, including convolutional layer, pooling layers and fully connected layers. Convolutional layers apply filters to the input data to extract local features, while the pooling layer reduces the dimensionality, retaining the most significant figures.

Applications in Biomedical Signal Processing

ECG Analysis

CNN automatically extract features from raw ECG signals. This involves convolutional layers that apply filters to detect local patterns, such as the shape of the P wave, QRS complex, and T wave (Ansari et al., 2023). The hierarchical nature of CNNs allows them to learn increasingly complex representations, which are then used to classify different types of cardiac arrhythmias.

Medical Imaging

CNNs process medical images to detect anomalies such as tumours. Convolutional layers capture spatial features like edges and textures, while deeper layers combine these features to recognize complex structures. Pooling layers reduce the dimensionality, making the network more computationally efficient and less prone to overfitting (Mall et al., 2023).

- Recurrent Neural Networks (RNN)

Recurrent Neural Networks are designed to handle sequential data by maintaining a memory of previous inputs. This makes RNN suitable for tasks involving time series data **(Petsagkourakis et al., 2019)**.

RNNs have loop that allow information to be passed from one step of the network to the next. This ability to maintain state makes them powerful for modelling sequences.

Applications in Biomedical Signal Processing

Seizure Detection

RNNs analyse EEG signals to detect epileptic seizures. By maintaining a memory of previous inputs, RNN captures temporal dependencies and pattern that are indicative of seizure events (Samee et al., 2022). For instance, abnormal bursts of high frequency oscillations in EEG signals can be detected by RNN to predict the onset of seizure.

Speech Recognition

RNNs can be used to recognize and interpret speech patterns in patients with speech impairments. This involves converting speech signals into text, enabling better communication aids. RNNs model the sequential nature of speech, capturing temporal dependencies that are crucial for understanding spoken language.

- **Long Short-Term Memory (LSTM) Networks**

Long Short-Term Memory (LSTM) networks are a type of RNN designed to overcome the limitations of traditional RNNs, such as the vanishing gradient problem. LSTMs can learn long-term dependencies in sequential data (Frank, 2024b).

LSTMs use memory cells with gates that control the flow of information, enabling the network to retain or forget information over long sequences.

Applications in Biomedical Signal Processing

Heart Rate Predicition

LSTMs predict future heart rate trends by analysing historical heart rate data. They learn long-term dependencies, capturing patterns over extended periods. This can be crucial for early detection of conditions like arrhythmias or for managing chronic heart diseases.

Activity Recognition

LSTMs process data from wearable sensors to recognize physical activities, such as walking, running, or sitting. They can also detect abnormal movements that might indicate falls or other health issues. The ability to remember long sequences of sensor data makes LSTMs particularly effective in this domain.

- **Random Forest**

Random Forest is an ensemble learning method that constructs multiple decision trees during training and outputs the mode of the classes for classification tasks or the mean prediction for regression tasks.

By averaging the results of multiple decision trees, Random Forest reduces the risk of overfitting and improves generalization (Liu et al., 2012).

Applications in Biomedical Signal Processing

Gene Expression Analysis

Random Forests classify genes based on expression levels, which helps in diagnosing diseases like cancer. By constructing multiple decision trees, Random Forests aggregate their predictions to enhance accuracy and robustness. This ensemble method can handle the high-dimensional nature of gene expression data and identify the most informative genes (Lu et al., 2024).

ECG Signal Classification

Random Forests analyse ECG signal features to detect various heart conditions. Features like heart rate variability, QRS complex duration, and ST-segment elevation are used to train the model. The ensemble approach reduces overfitting and improves generalization, making it effective for clinical applications.

- **K-Nearest Neighbour (KNN)**

K-Nearest Neighbours (KNN) is a simple, non-parametric algorithm used for classification and regression. It makes predictions based on the majority class or average value of the k-nearest neighbours in the feature space. KNN assigns the class of a new data point based on the most common class among its k-nearest neighbours.

Applications in Biomedical Signal Processing

Activity Recognition

KNN classifies different physical activities based on data from wearable sensors. Features like acceleration, gyroscope readings, and heart rate are used to determine activities such as walking, running, or cycling. KNN's simplicity makes it suitable for real-time applications with smaller datasets (Mohsen et al., 2021).

EEG Signal Classification

KNN is used to detect mental states or neurological conditions based on EEG signals. Features like power spectral density and coherence between EEG channels are used to classify states like relaxation, concentration, or drowsiness (Bablani et al., 2018).

INTEGRATION OF IOT AND MACHINE LEARNING IN BIOMEDICAL SIGNAL PROCESSING

The integration of the Internet of Things (IoT) and Machine Learning (ML) in biomedical signal processing represents a significant advancement in the healthcare domain. IoT devices, equipped with various sensors, collect vast amounts of real-time biomedical data, while ML algorithms analyse and interpret these data to extract meaningful insights (Figure 5). This combination enhances patient monitoring, diagnostics, and personalized medicine, leading to improved healthcare outcomes.

End-to-End Systems

- **IoT Devices and Sensors**

  Wearable Sensors: These include smartwatches, fitness bands, and medical patches that monitor physiological parameters such as heart rate, body temperature, and activity levels. Wearable sensors are typically equipped with photoplethysmography (PPG) sensors to detect heart rate and accelerometers to monitor movement and orientation.

  Implantable Sensors: Devices like glucose sensors for diabetes management and cardiac monitors for heart disease are implanted within the body. These sensors continuously monitor specific health conditions and transmit data to external devices.

- **Data Transmission**

  Bluetooth: Ideal for short-range communication, Bluetooth is commonly used between wearable devices and smartphones or other hub devices. Bluetooth Low Energy (BLE) is favoured in healthcare for its low power consumption and high data rate.

  Wi-Fi: Suitable for longer-range data transmission, Wi-Fi is used in home monitoring systems to connect to healthcare provider servers, offering higher data rates but higher power consumption.

  Cellular Networks: Essential for continuous, long-distance data transmission in remote patient monitoring systems, cellular networks support real-time data transmission and alerts, with 4G LTE and 5G providing high-speed, low-latency connectivity.

- **Cloud Based Storage and Processing**

  Data Storage: Scalable cloud databases are used to store large volumes of biomedical data, handling both structured data (e.g., patient demographics, lab results) and unstructured data (e.g., ECG waveforms, EEG signals).

  Computational Resources: Cloud platforms (e.g., AWS, Google Cloud, Microsoft Azure) provide computational power for running complex ML algorithms. Virtual Machines (VMs), GPU instances, and serverless computing services are utilized to accelerate data processing and model training.

  Data Security and Privacy: Implementing encryption, access controls, and data anonymization techniques to protect patient privacy and comply with regulations. Techniques such as data masking, pseudonymization, and anonymization of personal identifiers are employed.

- **Machine Learning Models**

Supervised Learning: Training models using labelled biomedical data to predict outcomes like disease diagnosis or patient risk stratification. Key algorithms include:

- **Support Vector Machines (SVM):** Effective for binary classification tasks, such as detecting arrhythmias from ECG signals. SVMs find the optimal hyperplane that maximizes the margin between different classes.
- **Convolutional Neural Networks (CNN):** Suited for analysing medical images and time-series data. CNNs automatically learn features from raw data, making them ideal for classifying cardiac events in ECG signals or detecting tumours in medical images.
- **Long Short-Term Memory Networks (LSTMs):** Specialized RNNs designed to handle long-term dependencies in sequential data, useful for predicting time-series data such as heart rate trends or epileptic seizures.

Unsupervised Learning: Identifying patterns and anomalies in unlabelled data using techniques like clustering and dimensionality reduction:

- **K-Means Clustering:** Groups similar data points based on feature similarity, useful for identifying patient subgroups or disease clusters.
- **Principal Component Analysis (PCA):** Reduces dimensionality while preserving variance, aiding in data visualization and feature selection.

Figure 5. End to end biomedical system architecture

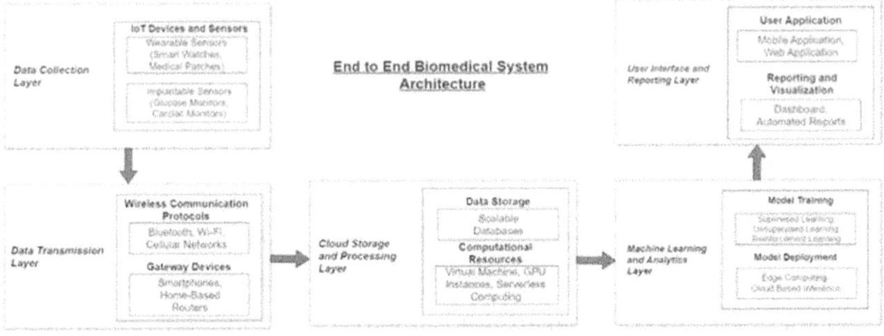

CASE STUDIES ON ROLE OF IOT AND MACHINE LEARNING IN BIOMEDICAL SIGNAL PROCESSING

Case Study 1: Remote Patient Monitoring for Diabetes using IoT and ML

Overview

Diabetes is a chronic disease characterized by high levels of blood glucose due to the body's inability to produce or effectively use insulin. Managing diabetes requires regular monitoring of blood glucose levels, adherence to medication, dietary adjustments, and physical activity. The integration of IoT and machine learning (ML) technologies has led to the development of sophisticated remote patient monitoring systems that provide continuous, real-time insights and personalized care for diabetes patients (Vashist, 2019).

System Components

Wearable Glucose Monitors

Continuous glucose monitors (CGMs) are wearable devices that measure glucose levels in the interstitial fluid just under the skin. CGMs provide real-time data on glucose levels, typically updated every five minutes. These devices use small sensors inserted under the skin to measure glucose levels continuously and transmit this data wirelessly to a receiver or a smartphone.

Data Acquisition and Transmission

Data from CGMs, along with other health parameters such as physical activity (measured by accelerometers in smartwatches or fitness trackers), dietary intake (logged via mobile apps), and insulin administration (recorded via smart insulin pens or apps), are collected. IoT protocols such as Bluetooth, Wi-Fi, and cellular networks facilitate seamless data transmission to a central cloud-based platform.

Cloud-Based Analytics

The cloud platform serves as the repository for all collected data and hosts the analytics engine. Machine learning algorithms deployed in the cloud process the incoming data to identify trends, detect anomalies, and make predictions. The platform is designed to handle large volumes of data, ensuring scalability and reliability.

Real-Time Alerts and Recommendations

ML models, such as decision trees, neural networks, and ensemble methods, analyse the data to generate real-time alerts and personalized recommendations. For instance, if the system predicts an impending hypoglycaemic event based on the patient's current glucose trend and historical data, it sends an immediate alert to the patient and their healthcare provider. Recommendations might include adjusting insulin dosage, modifying dietary intake, or altering physical activity levels.

Data Preprocessing Techniques

Preprocessing

Raw glucose data collected from CGMs often contains noise and artifacts due to various factors such as sensor calibration errors, movement artifacts, and environmental conditions. Preprocessing steps include filtering out noise using techniques like moving averages, median filtering, and normalization to ensure the data is clean and reliable for further analysis (Veerapandian & Karuppiah, 2021).

Feature Extraction

Relevant features are extracted from the pre-processed data to capture essential aspects of glucose dynamics. These features may include:

- Mean glucose level
- Glucose variability (standard deviation)
- Time-in-range (percentage of time glucose levels are within the target range)
- Frequency and duration of hypoglycaemic and hyperglycaemic events
- Trends and patterns over different times of the day

Machine Learning Models

Various ML models are employed to analyse the extracted features and predict future glucose levels or classify current glucose states (Contreras & Vehi, 2018). Commonly used models include:

- **Support Vector Machines (SVMs)**: Effective for binary classification tasks such as detecting hypoglycaemia or hyperglycaemia.

- **Long Short-Term Memory (LSTM) Networks**: A type of recurrent neural network (RNN) that is particularly suited for time-series prediction, making it ideal for forecasting future glucose levels.
- **Random Forests**: An ensemble learning method that combines multiple decision trees to improve classification accuracy and reduce overfitting.
- **Gradient Boosting Machines (GBMs)**: Another ensemble technique that builds models sequentially to correct errors made by previous models.

REAL WORLD IMPACT

Improved Glycaemic Control

Continuous monitoring and personalized recommendations help patients maintain better glycaemic control, reducing the risk of complications such as diabetic ketoacidosis, retinopathy, neuropathy, and cardiovascular diseases. Studies have shown that CGM use leads to significant reductions in HbA1c levels (a long-term marker of blood glucose control) and improved time-in-range.

Enhanced Patient Engagement

Real-time feedback and personalized care plans increase patient engagement and adherence to treatment. Patients are more likely to follow recommendations when they see immediate benefits and understand the rationale behind them. Mobile apps and user-friendly interfaces further enhance patient engagement by making it easy to track and manage their condition.

Reduced Healthcare Costs

By preventing complications and reducing hospitalizations and emergency room visits, remote monitoring systems lower healthcare costs for both patients and providers. Proactive management of diabetes leads to fewer acute events and less need for intensive medical interventions.

CASE STUDY 2: IOT AND MACHINE LEARNING IN CARDIAC REHABILITATION

Overview

Cardiac rehabilitation is a structured program of exercise and education designed to help patients recover from cardiovascular events such as heart attacks, surgeries, or procedures like angioplasty. The goal is to improve cardiovascular health, reduce the risk of future heart problems, and enhance overall quality of life. The integration of IoT and machine learning technologies enables continuous monitoring and personalized rehabilitation programs, significantly improving patient outcomes and reducing the risk of recurrent events (Ambinder, 2020).

SYSTEM COMPONENTS

Wearable Heart Rate Monitors

Wearable devices such as heart rate monitors, smartwatches, and fitness trackers collect real-time cardiac data. These devices are equipped with sensors to measure heart rate, physical activity, and other vital signs. These devices provide continuous monitoring and transmit data wirelessly to a central server.

Data Acquisition and Transmission

Data from wearable devices, including heart rate, physical activity (steps, distance, intensity), and other vital signs (e.g., blood oxygen levels), are collected and transmitted to a cloud-based platform via IoT protocols. The data transmission can occur through Bluetooth, Wi-Fi, or cellular networks, ensuring seamless and real-time data flow.

Cloud-Based Analytics

The cloud platform serves as the repository for all collected data and hosts the analytics engine. Machine learning algorithms deployed in the cloud process the incoming data to assess the patient's progress, detect anomalies, and provide personalized rehabilitation plans. The platform ensures scalability and can handle large volumes of data from multiple patients simultaneously.

Personalized Exercise Programs

ML models, such as regression models, clustering algorithms, and neural networks, analyse the data to generate personalized exercise programs tailored to the patient's specific needs and recovery goals. Real-time feedback is provided to patients during their rehabilitation exercises, ensuring they perform the activities correctly and safely.

DATA PROCESSING TECHNIQUES

Preprocessing

The raw heart rate and activity data are pre-processed to remove noise and artifacts. This includes filtering to eliminate high-frequency noise and normalization to ensure data consistency. Techniques like moving averages and median filtering are used to smooth the data and enhance its quality.

Feature Extraction

Relevant features are extracted from the pre-processed data to capture essential aspects of cardiac health and recovery. These features include:

- Heart rate variability (HRV): Measures the variation in time between heartbeats, indicating autonomic nervous system function.
- Exercise intensity: Calculated based on heart rate response to physical activity.
- Recovery rate: Assesses how quickly the heart rate returns to baseline after exercise.
- Physical activity metrics: Steps, distance, duration, and intensity of exercises performed.

Machine Learning Models

Various ML models are employed to analyse the extracted features and provide insights into the patient's recovery progress and future risk. Commonly used models include:

- **Random Forests**: An ensemble learning method that combines multiple decision trees to improve classification accuracy and reduce overfitting. Used to classify different stages of recovery and predict patient outcomes.
- **k-Means Clustering**: A clustering algorithm used to group patients with similar recovery patterns, enabling personalized rehabilitation programs.
- **Support Vector Machines (SVMs)**: Effective for classification tasks such as detecting abnormal heart rate patterns or predicting adverse events.
- **Neural Networks**: Particularly useful for complex pattern recognition and prediction tasks, such as forecasting future cardiac events based on historical data.

REAL TIME MONITORING

The ML algorithms provide real-time monitoring and feedback, allowing patients to adjust their activities based on their current condition. For example, if the system detects that a patient's heart rate is too high during exercise, it can provide immediate feedback to slow down or take a break. Alerts are generated if any abnormalities are detected, such as arrhythmias or significant deviations from expected recovery patterns.

REAL WORLD IMPACT

Enhanced Recovery

Personalized rehabilitation programs improve the effectiveness of cardiac rehabilitation, leading to faster and more complete recovery (Maddison et al., 2019). Tailored exercise plans and real-time feedback ensure that patients perform activities that are appropriate for their specific condition and recovery stage.

Continuous Monitoring

Continuous monitoring allows for early detection of potential issues, enabling timely interventions and reducing the risk of recurrent cardiovascular events. Patients are continuously monitored, even outside of clinical settings, ensuring comprehensive care.

Patient Engagement

Real-time feedback and personalized programs increase patient engagement and adherence to rehabilitation exercises. Patients are more likely to follow their rehabilitation plan when they receive immediate, relevant feedback and understand the impact of their actions on their recovery.

CHALLENGES AND SOLUTIONS

Data Privacy and Security

- **Challenge**: While connected healthcare IoT devices gather and share a significant quantity of detailed patient information, they are a prime target for hackers. Ensuring the security of this information from hacking and break-ins is crucial in sustaining the privacy of patients and trust in the health care systems. (Dwivedi et al., 2019).
- **Solution**: Administrative measures such as the use of encryption and authentication protocols can protect information during transit and storage. Other measures include security audit and compliance with health care data regulations helps to protect information. (Saranya & Rajasekaran, 2020).

Interoperability and Standardization

- **Challenge**: The healthcare IoT environment consists of numerous IoT devices and systems, which operate with different proprietary and nonstandardized communication interfaces and exchange information in incompatible formats. This masks the data structure, and there is no smooth transfer and integration of data, which affects patient care. (Bashir & Gill, 2016).
- **Solution**: Interoperability between devices means that there must be a decision of the standards and formats of communication protocols between devices. The solutions to the development of middleware solutions can be used to address gaps within technologies. Other programs also seek to encourage best practices across the sector that can enhance the exchange of information. (Polonelli et al., 2020).

Power Consumption and Battery Life

- **Challenge**: Wearable devices and sensors are IoT devices that may have a low power capacity to support the proposed requirements. Continuous monitoring of the battery level by the user and replacing the battery or recharging as often as possible lowers the overall user compliance. (Harb, 2018).

- **Solution**: This way, the hardware and software are optimized for energy efficiency, and this helps to improve the battery life. Energy scavenging schemes also convert energy from the likes of body heat and movement into power. Sustainable battery types can provide better energy density for the power requirements of various healthcare IoT applications. (Johnson et al., 2016).

Data Quality and Quantity

- **Challenge**: The machine learning models need large and clean datasets to train and test in order to generalize on the identified patterns. However, there are challenges inherent in health care data which include; data being incomplete, noisy data and data from unconnected, isolated systems. (Jha et al., 2016).
- **Solution**: Several measures can be taken to overcome quality issues; these include strict data collection procedures and methods for data preparation. It is easier to bring together bigger initial training sets when there are standards for open data, sharing arrangements, and common repositories. (Ribeiro et al., 2016).

Model Interpretability and Explainability

- **Challenge**: Some of the biomedical data processing algorithms require a high level of complexity due to the nature of decision making involved, which may cause healthcare professionals to distrust the software applications. (Lundberg & Lee, 2017).
- **Solution**: when feasible, it is beneficial to adopt models that are easier to decipher and understand. For more complex models, techniques like SHAP (SHapley Additive exPlanations) and LIME (Local Interpretable Model-agnostic Explanations) can provide insights into model predictions. (McKinney Jr, 2018).

Ethical and Regulatory Considerations

- **Challenge**: Technological advancements cause ethic and regulatory concerns with issues like privacy, consent, and the possibility of bias. Policies are complex at the moment which makes it hard to meet the set standards. (Mittelstadt et al., 2016).
- **Solution**: Healthcare companies' commitment to data protection and continuous reassessment reduce risks and adapt to new standards where necessary, Adhering to ethical guidelines and regulations, such as the GDPR and

HIPAA, is essential. Conducting thorough ethical reviews and incorporating fairness and bias mitigation techniques in ML models can address ethical concerns. Ongoing dialogue with regulatory bodies ensures that IoT and ML solutions comply with evolving regulations (Dey et al., 2018).

CONCLUSION

Summary of Key Points

- **Integration of IoT and ML in Healthcare**: IoT devices help enforce constant tracking and monitoring of patient data in healthcare since all devices are interlinked. This improves diagnostics, individualizing treatment, and outcomes, while also offering directions for future research.
- **Challenges Addressed**: Throughout this chapter, we have discussed various challenges such as, some of the issues which have been mentioned include data privacy, which is a critical issue in the current world, system integration, power consumption, and data quality. Solutions entail node encryption, usage of standard protocols, efficient equipment, and secure links and pipelines.
- **Benefits and Potential**: IoT provides early disease identification and screening through constant supervision, hence lower costs due to tele-consultancy, and enhanced patient satisfaction. This leads to increased efficiency, prevention of acute occurrences and improved overall health care delivery.

Impact on Future Healthcare

- **Transformative Potential**: IoT monitoring in long-term care must be ongoing; otherwise, the effectiveness of the interventions is drastically reduced. Real-time information enables predictive analysis and diagnosis, turning healthcare systems from treatable conditions to preventable ones.
- **Enhanced Patient Care**: Real time accurate data make diagnosis times faster and offer care that is adapted to the patient's physiological and medical history. This enhances health standards and longevity, especially for individuals with chronic illnesses.
- **Efficiency and Cost-Effectiveness**: Elimination of the middlemen and remote overseeing decreases the expenses as fewer visits to the hospitals are needed. Conservation of scarce resources and improvements in the use of resources in the provision of health care services.

Potential for Innovation and Research Opportunities

- **Ongoing Research and Development**: The field of IoT and ML in healthcare is growing rapidly, Sensors, data analysis and devices having increased growth rate with the focus on enhancing performance and dependability, along with the issues of ethical dilemma. Future research will likely focus on improving the accuracy, reliability, and functionality of these technologies.
- **Interdisciplinary Collaboration**: interdisciplinary teamwork by engineers, physicians, computer scientists, and ethicists to advance the field and safeguard ethical application.
- **Emerging Technologies and Applications**: Biosensors, wearables, and edge computing are identified as promising technologies that will improve performance. The advancements have helped to integrate explainable techniques and the preservation of privacy as some of the significant considerations. These innovations will enable more accurate and comprehensive monitoring of physiological parameters, facilitating early detection of diseases and personalized treatment.

REFERENCES

Aledhari, M., Razzak, R., Qolomany, B., Al-Fuqaha, A., & Saeed, F. (2022). Biomedical IoT: Enabling Technologies, Architectural Elements, Challenges, and Future Directions. *IEEE Access : Practical Innovations, Open Solutions*, *10*, 31306–31339. DOI: 10.1109/ACCESS.2022.3159235 PMID: 35441062

Ambinder, M. D. (2020). IoT and Machine Learning for Remote Monitoring and Management of Heart Disease. *The Journal of Cardiovascular Medicine*, *21*(4), 265–272.

An, X. (2020, March 7). K Stylios G. Comparison of Motion Artefact Reduction Methods and the Implementation of Adaptive Motion Artefact Reduction in Wearable Electrocardiogram Monitoring. *Sensors (Basel)*, *20*(5), 1468. DOI: 10.3390/s20051468 PMID: 32155984

Ansari, Y., Mourad, O., Qaraqe, K., & Serpedin, E. (2023, September 15). Deep learning for ECG Arrhythmia detection and classification: An overview of progress for period 2017-2023. *Frontiers in Physiology*, *14*, 1246746. DOI: 10.3389/fphys.2023.1246746 PMID: 37791347

Assa, A., & Janabi-Sharifi, F. (2015). A Kalman Filter-Based Framework for Enhanced Sensor Fusion. *IEEE Sensors Journal*, *15*(6), 1–1. DOI: 10.1109/JSEN.2014.2388153

Bablani, A., Edla, D., & Dodia, S. (2018). Classification of EEG Data using k-Nearest Neighbor approach for Concealed Information Test. *Procedia Computer Science*, *143*, 242–249. DOI: 10.1016/j.procs.2018.10.392

Bashir, A., & Gill, H. (2016). Managing Interoperability in IoT. *Procedia Computer Science*, *91*, 449–456.

Bayan, H. (2023). A comprehensive review and conceptual framework for cloud computing adoption in bioinformatics, Healthcare Analytics, Volume 3. 100190, ISSN 2772-4425, https://doi.org/DOI: 10.1016/j.health.2023.100190

Chilamkurthy, N., Pandey, O., Ghosh, A., Cenkeramaddi, L. R., & Dai, H.-N. (2022). Low-Power Wide-Area Networks: A Broad Overview of Its Different Aspects. *IEEE Access : Practical Innovations, Open Solutions*, *10*, 1–1. DOI: 10.1109/ACCESS.2022.3196182

Contreras, I., & Vehi, J. (2018). Artificial Intelligence for Diabetes Management and Decision Support: Literature Review. *Journal of Medical Internet Research*, *20*(5), e10775. DOI: 10.2196/10775 PMID: 29848472

Criée, C., Sorichter, S., Smith, H., Kardos, P., Merget, R., Heise, D., Berdel, D., Köhler, D., Magnussen, H., Marek, W., Mitfessel, H., Rasche, K., Rolke, M., Worth, H., & Jörres, R. A. (2011). Body plethysmography—Its principles and clinical use. [PubMed] [CrossRef] [Google Scholar]. *Respiratory Medicine*, *105*(7), 959–971. DOI: 10.1016/j.rmed.2011.02.006 PMID: 21356587

Dey, N., Hassanien, A. E., Bhatt, C., Ashour, A., & Satapathy, S. C. (Eds.). (2018). *Internet of things and big data analytics toward next-generation intelligence* (Vol. 35). Springer.

Dwivedi, A. D., Srivastava, G., Dhar, S., & Singh, R. (2019). A Decentralized Privacy-Preserving Healthcare Blockchain for IoT. *Sensors (Basel)*, *19*(2), 326. DOI: 10.3390/s19020326 PMID: 30650612

Baum, K., Mantel, S., Schmidt, E., & Speith, T. (2022). From responsibility to reason-giving explainable artificial intelligence. *Philosophy & Technology*, *35*(1), 12.

Fortino, G., & Giampà, V. PPG-based methods for non invasive and continuous blood pressure measurement: An overview and development issues in body sensor networks; *Proceedings of the 2010 IEEE International Workshop on Medical Measurements and Applications*; Ottawa, ON, Canada. 30 April–1 May 2010; pp. 10–13. [Google Scholar] DOI: 10.1109/MEMEA.2010.5480201

Frank, L. (2024). Support Vector Machines (SVMs).

Frank, L. (2024). Long Short-Term Memory (LSTM). *Networks*.

Gubbi, J., Buyya, R., Marusic, S., & Palaniswami, M. (2013). Internet of Things (IoT): A Vision, Architectural Elements, and Future Directions. *Future Generation Computer Systems*, *29*(7), 1645–1660. DOI: 10.1016/j.future.2013.01.010

Hadjileontiadis, L. J., Rekanos, I. T., & Panas, S. M. Wiley Encyclopedia of Biomedical Engineering. John Wiley Sons, Inc.; Hoboken, NJ, USA: 2006. Bioacoustic signals. [Google Scholar]

Hamdan, S., Ayyash, M., & Almajali, S. (2020). Edge-Computing Architectures for Internet of Things Applications: A Survey. *Sensors (Basel)*, *20*(22), 6441. DOI: 10.3390/s20226441 PMID: 33187267

Harb, H. (2018). Energy Harvesting for IoT Nodes: Past, Present, and Future. *Renewable Energy*, *128*, 641–654.

Inan, O. T., Migeotte, P. F., Park, K. S., Etemadi, M., Tavakolian, K., Casanella, R., Zanetti, J., Tank, J., Funtova, I., Prisk, G. K., & Di Rienzo, M. (2015). Ballistocardiography and seismocardiography: A review of recent advances. [PubMed] [CrossRef] [Google Scholar]. *IEEE Journal of Biomedical and Health Informatics*, *19*(4), 1414–1427. DOI: 10.1109/JBHI.2014.2361732 PMID: 25312966

Dey, N., Ashour, A. S., & Borra, S. (2018). Internet of Things and Big Data Analytics Toward Next-Generation Intelligence. Springer.

Rose, K., Eldridge, S., & Chapin, L. (2015). The Internet of Things: An Overview. Internet Society. Retrieved from Internet Society.

Islam, S. M. R., Kwak, D., Kabir, M. H., Hossain, M., & Kwak, K. S. (2015). The Internet of Things for Health Care: A Comprehensive Survey. *IEEE Access : Practical Innovations, Open Solutions*, *3*, 678–708. DOI: 10.1109/ACCESS.2015.2437951

Istepanian, R. S., & Woodward, B. (2016). m-Health: Fundamentals and Applications. John Wiley & Sons.

Javaid, M., Haleem, A., Singh, R. P., & Suman, R. 5G technology for healthcare: Features, serviceable pillars, and applications, Intelligent Pharmacy, Volume 1, Issue 1, 2023, Pages 2-10, ISSN 2949-866X, https://doi.org/DOI: 10.1016/j.ipha.2023.04.001

Jha, S., Topol, E. J., & Adashi, E. Y. (2016). Precision Medicine: Time to Advance the Science. *The New England Journal of Medicine*, *376*(2), 119–126.

Jiang, F., Jiang, Y., Zhi, H., Dong, Y., Li, H., Ma, S., Wang, Y., Dong, Q., Shen, H., & Wang, Y. (2017). Artificial Intelligence in Healthcare: Past, Present and Future. *Stroke and Vascular Neurology*, *2*(4), 230–243. DOI: 10.1136/svn-2017-000101 PMID: 29507784

Johnson, A. E. W., Pollard, T. J., Shen, L., Lehman, L. W. H., Feng, M., Ghassemi, M., Moody, B., Szolovits, P., Anthony Celi, L., & Mark, R. G. (2016). MIMIC-III, a Freely Accessible Critical Care Database. *Scientific Data*, *3*(1), 160035. DOI: 10.1038/sdata.2016.35 PMID: 27219127

Kamavuako, E. N. (2022, October 19). On the Applications of EMG Sensors and Signals. *Sensors (Basel)*, *22*(20), 7966. DOI: 10.3390/s22207966 PMID: 36298317

Khazaee, A., & Ebrahimzadeh, A. (2013). Heart Arrhythmia Detection using support vector machines. *Intelligent Automation & Soft Computing*, *19*(1), 1–9. Advance online publication. DOI: 10.1080/10798587.2013.771456

Korostynska, O., Arshak, K., Gill, E., & Arshak, A. (2007). Materials and techniques for in vivo pH monitoring. [CrossRef] [Google Scholar]. *IEEE Sensors Journal*, *8*(1), 20–28. DOI: 10.1109/JSEN.2007.912522

Kourou, K., Exarchos, T. P., Exarchos, K. P., Karamouzis, M. V., & Fotiadis, D. I. (2015). Machine Learning Applications in Cancer Prognosis and Prediction. *Computational and Structural Biotechnology Journal*, *13*, 8–17. DOI: 10.1016/j.csbj.2014.11.005 PMID: 25750696

Li, X., Song, Y., Wang, H., Su, X., Wang, M., Li, J., Ren, Z., Zhong, D., & Huang, Z. Evaluation of measurement accuracy of wearable devices for heart rate variability, iScience, Volume 26, Issue 11, 2023, 108128, ISSN 2589-0042, https://doi.org/ DOI: 10.1016/j.isci.2023.108128

Litjens, G., Kooi, T., Bejnordi, B. E., Setio, A. A. A., Ciompi, F., Ghafoorian, M., & van Ginneken, B. (2017). A Survey on Deep Learning in Medical Image Analysis. *Medical Image Analysis*, *42*, 60–88. DOI: 10.1016/j.media.2017.07.005 PMID: 28778026

Liu, Y., Wang, Y., & Zhang, J. (2012). New Machine Learning Algorithm. *Lecture Notes in Computer Science*, *7473*, 246–252. DOI: 10.1007/978-3-642-34062-8_32

Louis, E. Frenzel, Chapter 9 - Networking: Wired and Wireless: All Devices Talking to One Another, Editor(s): Louis E. Frenzel, Electronics Explained (Second Edition), Newnes, 2018, Pages 217-242, ISBN 9780128116418, https://doi.org/DOI: 10.1016/B978-0-12-811641-8.00009-6

Lu, M., Yin, R., & Chen, X. S. (2024). Ensemble methods of rank-based trees for single sample classification with gene expression profiles. *Journal of Translational Medicine*, *22*(1), 140. DOI: 10.1186/s12967-024-04940-2 PMID: 38321494

Lundberg, S. M., & Lee, S.-I. (2017). A Unified Approach to Interpreting Model Predictions. *Advances in Neural Information Processing Systems*, *30*, 4765–4774.

Maddison, R., Rawstorn, J. C., Stewart, R. A., Benatar, J., Whittaker, R., Rolleston, A., Jiang, Y., Gao, L., Moodie, M., Warren, I., Meads, A., & Gant, N. (2019). Effects and costs of real-time cardiac telerehabilitation: Randomised controlled non-inferiority trial. *Heart (British Cardiac Society)*, *105*(2), 122–129. DOI: 10.1136/heartjnl-2018-313189 PMID: 30150328

Mall, P. K., Singh, P. K., Srivastav, S., Narayan, V., Paprzycki, M., Jaworska, T., & Ganzha, M. (2023). A comprehensive review of deep neural networks for medical image processing: Recent developments and future opportunities, Healthcare Analytics, Volume 4, 100216, ISSN 2772-4425, https://doi.org/DOI: 10.1016/j.health.2023.100216

Mittelstadt, B. D., Allo, P., Taddeo, M., Wachter, S., & Floridi, L. (2016). The Ethics of Algorithms: Mapping the Debate. *Big Data & Society*, *3*(2), 2053951716679679. DOI: 10.1177/2053951716679679

Rajpurkar, P., Hannun, A. Y., Haghpanahi, M., Bourn, C., & Ng, A. Y. (2017). Cardiologist-level arrhythmia detection with convolutional neural networks. arXiv preprint arXiv:1707.01836.

Ribeiro, M. T., Singh, S., & Guestrin, C. (2016, August). " Why should i trust you?" Explaining the predictions of any classifier. In Proceedings of the 22nd ACM SIGKDD international conference on knowledge discovery and data mining (pp. 1135-1144).

Mohsen, Saeed & Elkaseer, Ahmed & Scholz, Steffen. (2021). Human Activity Recognition Using K-Nearest Neighbor Machine Learning Algorithm. .DOI: 10.1007/978-981-16-6128-0_29

Nguyen, T., Nguyen, H., & Gia, T. N. (2024). Exploring the integration of edge computing and blockchain IoT: Principles, architectures, security, and applications, Journal of Network and Computer Applications, Volume 226, 103884, ISSN 1084-8045, https://doi.org/DOI: 10.1016/j.jnca.2024.103884

Oliver, N., Toumazou, C., Cass, T., & Johnston, D. (2009). Glucose Sensors: A Review of Current and Emerging Technology. *Diabetic Medicine*, *26*(3), 197–210. DOI: 10.1111/j.1464-5491.2008.02642.x PMID: 19317813

Panja, A. K., Mukherjee, A., & Dey, N. (2022). Chapter 1 - Introduction, Editor(s): Ayan Kumar Panja, Amartya Mukherjee, Nilanjan Dey, In Primers in Biomedical Imaging Devices and Systems, Biomedical Sensors and Smart Sensing, Academic Press, Pages 1-14, ISBN 9780128228562, https://doi.org/DOI: 10.1016/B978-0-12-822856-2.00006-X

Petsagkourakis, P., Orson Sandoval, I., Bradford, E., Zhang, D., & del Rio-Chanona, E. A. (2019). Reinforcement Learning for Batch-to-Batch Bioprocess Optimisation, Editor(s): Anton A. Kiss, Edwin Zondervan, Richard Lakerveld, Leyla Özkan, Computer Aided Chemical Engineering, Elsevier, Volume 46, Pages 919-924, ISSN 1570-7946, ISBN 9780128186343, https://doi.org/DOI: 10.1016/B978-0-12-818634-3.50154-5

Polonelli, T., Cucchi, F., Amorim, M. S., & Stanacevic, M. (2020). Low-Power IoT Sensors for Smart Healthcare: Design and Optimization. *IEEE Sensors Journal, 20*(11), 5592–5601.

Pupim, D. & Filho, L. & Takeshita, W. & Iwaki, L. (2013). Evaluation of accuracy of portable fingertip pulse oximeter, as compared to that of a hospital oximeter with digital sensor. Indian journal of dental research: official publication of Indian Society for Dental Research. 24. 542-6. . DOI: 10.4103/0970-9290.123362

Rangayyan, R. M., & Krishnan, S. (2024). *Biomedical signal analysis*. John Wiley & Sons.

Ring, E., McEvoy, H., Jung, A., Zuber, J., & Machin, G. (2010). New standards for devices used for the measurement of human body temperature. *Journal of Medical Engineering & Technology, 34*(4), 249–253. DOI: 10.3109/03091901003663836 PMID: 20397848

Samee, N. A., Mahmoud, N. F., Aldhahri, E. A., Rafiq, A., Muthanna, M. S. A., & Ahmad, I. (2022, November 22). RNN and BiLSTM Fusion for Accurate Automatic Epileptic Seizure Diagnosis Using EEG Signals. *Life (Basel, Switzerland), 12*(12), 1946. DOI: 10.3390/life12121946 PMID: 36556313

Saranya, S., & Rajasekaran, S. (2020). IoT Healthcare Data Management in Cloud using Interoperability and Standardization Issues: A Survey. *Journal of King Saud University. Computer and Information Sciences*.

Sattar, Y., & Chhabra, L. (2024 Jan). Electrocardiogram. In *StatPearls*. StatPearls Publishing., Available from https://www.ncbi.nlm.nih.gov/books/NBK549803/

Sund-Levander, M., & Grodzinsky, E. (2013). Assessment of body temperature measurement options. *British Journal of Nursing (Mark Allen Publishing), 22*(16), 942–950. DOI: 10.12968/bjon.2013.22.16.942 PMID: 24037397

Tyagi, A., Semwal, S., & Shah, G. (2012). A review of EEG sensors used for data acquisition. [IJCA]. *Jisuanji Yingyong*, •••, 13–17.

Vashishth, T. K., Sharma, V., Sharma, K. K., Kumar, B., Chaudhary, S., & Panwar, R. (2024). Enhancing biomedical signal processing with machine learning: A comprehensive review. Digital Transformation in Healthcare, 5.

Vashist, S. K. (2019). Continuous Glucose Monitoring Systems: A Review. *Diagnostics (Basel), 9*(1), 6. PMID: 30626128

Veerapandian, M., & Karuppiah, A. (2021). IoT-based Continuous Glucose Monitoring System: A Review. *Journal of Diabetes Science and Technology*, *15*(5), 1073–1082.

Vijay, K. Garg, CHAPTER 1 - An Overview of Wireless Systems, Editor(s): Vijay K. Garg, In The Morgan Kaufmann Series in Networking, Wireless Communications & Networking, Morgan Kaufmann, 2007, Pages 1-21, ISSN 18759351, ISBN 9780123735805, https://doi.org/DOI: 10.1016/B978-012373580-5/50035-1

Waddell, W. J., & Bates, R. G. (1969). Intracellular pH. [PubMed] [CrossRef] [Google Scholar]. *Physiological Reviews*, *49*(2), 285–329. DOI: 10.1152/physrev.1969.49.2.285 PMID: 4889321

Yamashita, R., Nishio, M., Do, R. K. G., & Togashi, K. (2018). Convolutional neural networks: An overview and application in radiology. *Insights Into Imaging*, *9*(4), 611–629. DOI: 10.1007/s13244-018-0639-9 PMID: 29934920

Chapter 6
Deep Learning for Analyzing User and Entity Behaviors:
Techniques and Applications

Rasmita Kumari Mohanty
https://orcid.org/0000-0002-5828-5649
VNR Vignana Jyothi Institute of Engineering and Technology, India

ABSTRACT

User and Entity Behavior Analytics (UEBA) is a critical component of modern cybersecurity strategies aimed at detecting and mitigating security threats within enterprise environments. The system is designed to enhance security through the analysis of user and entity actions. The architecture encompasses data collection and integration techniques, feature extraction, deep learning models, detecting and analyzing.Data collection strategies acquire statistics from quite a few sources, such as system logs, network site visitors, and application logs, resulting in a comprehensive dataset for analysis Feature extraction transforms uncooked facts right into a meaningful representation, for reading a deep modelling can locate patterns in person conduct and entity conduct. Long-term and brief- term reminiscence (LSTM) and convolutional LSTM (ConvLSTM) fashions are used to investigate temporal, spatial, and temporal dependence, respectively.

DOI: 10.4018/979-8-3693-6864-0.ch006

1. INTRODUCTION

In the modern-day quickly changing technological scene, the growing sophistication of cyber threats dreams robust and advanced cybersecurity answers. User and Entity Behaviour Analytics (UEBA) is a crucial issue in modern-day cybersecurity, helping to choose out and mitigate threats in organizational environments. UEBA uses deep learning strategies to analyse and interpret person and entity behaviours, offering a proactive and dynamic method to improving cybersecurity.

This observe investigates the mixture of deep mastering fashions with UEBA, giving an entire shape that consists of information accumulating, characteristic extraction, and superior detection algorithms. The emphasis is on the usage of LSTM and ConvLSTM fashions to discover temporal and spatiotemporal relationships, ensuring a greater nuanced statistic of individual behaviour.

The format is based totally on success statistics accumulating strategies that aggregate facts from an entire lot of assets, at the side of tool logs, network web site visitors, and application logs. The stated MBS is tested closer to the CERT dataset, illustrating its potential to reinforce safety in city massive records contexts with the aid of tackling the insider's chance. Feature extraction strategies convert raw statistics into sizable representations, allowing deep studying fashions to select out patterns in individual and entity behaviour.

The technique segment describes the multi-mind-set Anomaly Detection System (MBS), including a complete evaluation of its components. MBS makes use of three important models the motion function model, the motion collection model, and the placement feature model to analyse person information and find out aberrant insider behaviour.

The machine trains deep analysing models for anomaly detection and the use of historical data classified with the resource of UEBA. This deep analysing approach includes the use of LSTM, ConvLSTM, and Multi-Layer Perceptron (MLP) to have a look at log entries and stumble on probably suspicious behaviours. It emphasizes the importance of understanding data collection techniques, integration, and pre-processing, touching on challenges such as data diversity and privacy.

Furthermore, it highlights the significance of feature extraction methods, including both traditional statistical techniques and advanced deep learning approaches, in improving anomaly detection accuracy. The abstract also underscores the increasing role of deep learning models like LSTM and ConvLSTM networks in UEBA, particularly in analysing temporal and spatial dependencies within user and entity behaviour data.

Moreover, the abstract suggests the exploration of real-world use cases and case studies to demonstrate the practical applications and benefits of UEBA in threat detection and incident response. It also calls attention to scalability, versatility, and future research directions in UEBA, including challenges like explainability of deep learning models and regulatory compliance.

Additionally, it proposes conducting a comparative analysis of available UEBA solutions to provide insights into their features, performance metrics, and deployment options. Overall, by addressing these areas, researchers and practitioners can deepen their understanding of UEBA principles and techniques, ultimately enhancing cybersecurity defences in enterprise environments.

In essence, this observation contributes to the increasing discipline of cybersecurity with the useful resource of offering a sturdy UEBA framework supplemented with deep gaining knowledge of fashions. The combination of innovative methodologies and fashions has the capacity to significantly decorate cybersecurity via proactively figuring out and decreasing threats in organization environments.

1.1 Objective

To effectively utilize User and Entity Behavior Analytics (UEBA) in modern cybersecurity strategies, focusing on enhancing security through advanced analysis techniques and deep learning models.

- **Enhance Security:** Implement UEBA to strengthen cybersecurity measures within enterprise environments. Utilize deep learning models to detect and mitigate security threats effectively.
- **Comprehensive Data Collection:** Develop robust data collection strategies to gather statistics from diverse sources such as system logs, network traffic, and application logs. Ensure the acquisition of comprehensive datasets for thorough analysis.
- **Feature Extraction:** Implement feature extraction techniques to transform raw data into meaningful representations. Optimize feature extraction processes to facilitate deep modelling for identifying patterns in user and entity behavior.
- **Utilization of Deep Learning Models:** Explore the application of Long Short-Term Memory (LSTM) and Convolutional LSTM (ConvLSTM) models for analysing temporal, spatial, and temporal dependencies in user and entity behavior. Leverage deep learning models to detect irregularities and anomalies, enabling immediate corrective actions.
- **Rapid Threat Identification:** Deploy UEBA solutions to quickly identify insider threats, anomalies, and potential vulnerabilities. Utilize multi-layer perceptron (MLP) and other advanced techniques for efficient threat detection and analysis.

- **Versatility, Scalability, and Flexibility:** Highlight the versatility, scalability, and flexibility of UEBA systems in adapting to evolving cybersecurity threats. Emphasize UEBA's role as an essential asset for protecting critical data and ensuring the stability of organizational assets.

By focusing on these objectives, we aim to leverage UEBA effectively within cybersecurity strategies, thereby enhancing security measures and safeguarding organizational assets against emerging threats.

1.2 Some of the Existing Models

1. **Splunk Enterprise Security**: Splunk is a widely used platform for security information and event management (SIEM). Splunk Enterprise Security offers UEBA capabilities along with other security features. It collects and correlates data from various sources to detect and respond to security threats, including insider threats and anomalies.
2. **IBM QRadar:** IBM QRadar is another prominent SIEM solution that incorporates UEBA functionality. It provides real-time monitoring, threat detection, and incident response capabilities by analysing user and entity behaviour across the enterprise network.
3. **Cisco Stealth watch:** Cisco Stealth watch is a network traffic analysis solution that utilizes machine learning and behavioural modelling to identify threats and anomalies in network traffic. It offers UEBA features to detect suspicious activities and potential security breaches.
4. **Exabeam Security Management Platform:** Exabeam offers a comprehensive security management platform that includes UEBA capabilities. It analyses user and entity behaviour to detect insider threats, compromised accounts, and other security risks.
5. **Securonix Security Analytics Platform:** Securonix provides a security analytics platform with advanced UEBA functionality. It employs machine learning algorithms to detect anomalous behaviour and potential security incidents across various data sources.

1.3 Drawbacks of the Existing System

- **Complexity and Resource Intensiveness:** Many of these platforms, can be complex to set up and maintain. They often require significant resources in terms of expertise, time, and infrastructure, which can pose challenges for smaller organizations or those with limited budgets.

- **High Cost of Ownership:** The cost associated with licensing, implementation, and ongoing maintenance of these UEBA solutions can be prohibitive for some organizations. This high cost of ownership may make it difficult for smaller businesses to adopt and fully utilize these platforms, limiting their effectiveness in democratizing cybersecurity capabilities.
- **False Positives and Alert Fatigue:** UEBA solutions, despite their advanced analytics capabilities, are still prone to generating false positives and contributing to alert fatigue. This occurs when the system generates too many alerts, many of which are not actionable or relevant, leading to overwhelmed security teams and potentially missing real threats amidst the noise.
- **Integration and Compatibility Challenges:** Integrating UEBA solutions with existing cybersecurity infrastructure and workflows can be challenging. Compatibility issues with legacy systems, data silos, and disparate data formats may hinder the seamless operation of these platforms, reducing their overall effectiveness in providing holistic threat detection and response capabilities.

2. LITERATURE SURVEY

Many researchers, whose contribution has been instrumental in the foundation of the threat modelling practice, have been looking into the specific domains of the problem that have been pinpointed and working to fill up those gaps. For instance, while STRIDE, PASTA, and attack tree approaches are highlighted other advanced approaches are discovered, however, a combined methodology that pulls them from where they are good is created from them. Therefore, this framework investigates creating a platform for the improvement of the strengths of general threat modelling approaches while at the same time discarding their weaknesses - which in turn enhances the method for threat modelling in the real world.

Oyatee Datta highlights the use of unsupervised learning techniques (Datta et al., 2021) for correct detection of threats in User and Entity Behaviour Analytics (UEBA) structures. He specialises in employing state-of-the-art analytics methodologies to evaluate user and object interest in business company environments to swiftly understand and keep away from vulnerabilities.

Jagreet Kaur addresses the merging of UEBA with log analytics techniques (Kaur et al., 2022). It is vital to analyse how analysing logs would likely decorate risk detection in UEBA structures by way of Figuring out extraordinary person behaviour and capability protection troubles interior employer networks.

User Activity Analysis for Identifying hacked User Accounts (Jurišić et al., 2023) delves further into consumer behaviour assessment practices to spot hacked person accounts. It addresses problems such as differentiating between normal and suspicious behaviour and delves into answers like rule- based tally absolutely structures and device learning. It examines their overall performance and recommends future study paths using reviews and case research, providing an entire evaluation of the sector's present-day situation and feasible advances.

Florian Skopik illustrates using behaviour-based totally anomaly detection approaches to look at log information from physical manage of get entry to systems (Skopik et al., 2023). It reviews tactics for identifying aberrant styles in man or woman behaviour interior such systems to improve safety with the aid of detecting possible threats or breaches. Pavel Slipenchuk and Anna V propose a top-level view of UEBA strategies for fraud detection in online banking structures (Slipenchuk & Epishkina, 2019). It seems at numerous realistic mind and tactics for monitoring person behaviour and Figuring out fraudulent hobby to enhance online banking protection.

The research work explores the use of unsupervised deep learning to spot deviations in logbooks (Bursic et al., 2020), with the goal to pinpoint odd patterns in lack of labelled training data. Using deep learning algorithms, it spots usual behaviour patterns and flags deviations as potential abnormalities, allowing for early identification of safety hazards. Another work investigates how UEBA might improve company security through evaluating behaviours that reveal security risks (Shashanka et al., 2016). It uses ML to generate baselines and identify abnormalities, allowing for proactive risk mitigation. It optimises defences by noticing insider threats and enables proactive actions, assisting organisations eradicate cyber enemies.

The paper (Pandhurnekar et al., 2023) presents a proposed method for threat detection using user behaviour analysis, authored by Viplav Pandhurnekar, Anish Iyyappan, and Sampada Wazalwar. The method outlines an approach to detect security threats by analysing user behaviour patterns, aiming to enhance cybersecurity measures. The paper likely discusses the methodology, implementation, and potential impact of the proposed approach on improving threat detection mechanisms.

The paper (Calvo et al., 2023) authored by Albert Calvo, Santiago Escuder, and Jordi Guijarro introduces a data-driven approach for analysing risk exposure in enterprise security. The paper likely details methods and algorithms for assessing and mitigating security risks within organizational settings. It may also discuss the application of data analytics techniques to enhance risk management strategies in cybersecurity.

The paper (Yousef & Jazzar, 2021) authored by Yousef, Rasheed, and M. Jazzar investigates the effectiveness of user and entity behaviour analytics (UEBA) in mitigating insider threats. The study likely presents empirical research or a theoretical analysis on the efficacy of UEBA systems in preventing insider attacks. It may include discussions on UEBA methodologies, case studies, and recommendations for improving insider threat prevention strategies.

The survey by Pavel Slipenchuk and Anna V. Epishkina explores practical methods of User and Entity Behaviour Analytics (UEBA) for detecting fraud in online banking systems. The paper likely provides an overview of various UEBA techniques tailored specifically for identifying fraudulent activities in online banking environments. It may include insights into behavioural patterns, machine learning algorithms, and real-world applications aimed at enhancing fraud detection and prevention strategies in the digital banking sector.

Benson O. Odongo is predicted to offer studies on Security Information and Event Management (SIEM) the usage of deep mastering strategies (Odongo, 2022). Its information the appearance, deployment, and evaluation of a SIEM system that use deep getting to know to evaluate security records. He shares insights on employing deep getting to know in cybersecurity and SIEM structures.

The computer host-focused consumer chance detection machine that employs a self-organizing map (Hoglund et al., 2000) maximum likely represents a machine for figuring out abnormalities in man or woman behaviour on pc hosts. Its maximum probable gives a way based totally completely on the self- organizing map, a kind of synthetic neural community, for analysing user hobby patterns and detecting deviations that advocate possible protection problems or anomalous behaviour. It is anticipated to cover the machine's layout, deployment, and evaluation, emphasising its efficacy in improving host-primarily based safety capabilities.

The paper (Tang et al., 2017) authored by B. Tang, Q. Hu, and D. Lin addresses the issue of reducing false positives in user-to-entity first-access alerts within user behaviour analytics (UBA) systems. The study likely proposes techniques or algorithms aimed at improving the accuracy of alert generation in UBA systems. The research may involve investigating the factors contributing to false positives, such as anomalous behaviours or system noise, and proposing novel methodologies to mitigate these inaccuracies. Potential approaches might include refining anomaly detection algorithms, enhancing feature selection techniques, or incorporating contextual information to better differentiate genuine threats from benign activities.

M. Landauer and F. Skopik employ a set of records for UEBA in cloud-based settings (Landauer et al., 2022), intending to improve systems for recognising anomalies. It tackles the demand for strong safeguards in dynamic cloud environments. The set of files covers a wide range of log data that reflects the extensive variety of cloud systems, allowing for further cybersecurity study. This work helps to evaluate anomaly detection methods, identify dangers, and enhance privacy of systems in the cloud.

3. FUNCTIONAL REQUIREMENTS

- **Data Collection:** The system should collect data from various sources such as system logs, network traffic, and application logs.
- **Data Preprocessing:** It should preprocess collected data, handling missing values, normalizing data, and performing feature engineering.
- **Behaviour Modelling:** The system should develop models to analyse user and entity behaviours, including pattern recognition and anomaly detection.
- **Threat Detection:** It should detect potential security threats based on analysed behaviour data, such as insider threats, compromised accounts, or unusual activities.
- **Alert Generation:** The system should generate alerts or notifications for detected threats, providing actionable insights to security teams.
- **User Interface:** It should provide a user-friendly interface for security analysts to interact with the system, view alerts, and investigate detected threats.

3.1 Non-Functional Requirements

- **Security:** The system must securely handle all data, ensuring confidentiality, integrity, and availability (CIA).
- **Reporting:** It should generate reports and metrics to assess the effectiveness of the UEBA solution in improving cybersecurity posture.
- **Reliability:** The system must perform reliably with minimal downtime.
- **Usability:** The user interface should be intuitive and user-friendly, allowing users to perform all functions without extensive training.
- **Scalability:** The system should be scalable to handle large volumes of data and adapt to evolving cyber security threats.
- **Maintainability**: The system should be easy to maintain and upgrade, with clear documentation for future enhancements.
- **Integration:** It should integrate with existing security infrastructure and tools, such as SIEM (Security Information and Event Management) systems or endpoint security solutions.
- **Data Integrity:** The system must ensure data integrity, especially when adding or deleting information.
- **Compliance:** The system should comply with relevant regulations and standards, such as GDPR (General Data Protection Regulation) or HIPAA (Health Insurance Portability and Accountability Act), ensuring data privacy and security.

- **Customization:** The system should allow for customization of detection algorithms, thresholds, and alerting rules to meet specific organizational requirements.

4. PROPOSED SYSTEM

The approach focuses on using deep analytical techniques to analyse consumer data to find unexpected insider activity. We present the Multi-perspective Anomaly Detection System (MBS) and give a thorough description of each of its parts.

Figure 1. MBS workflow

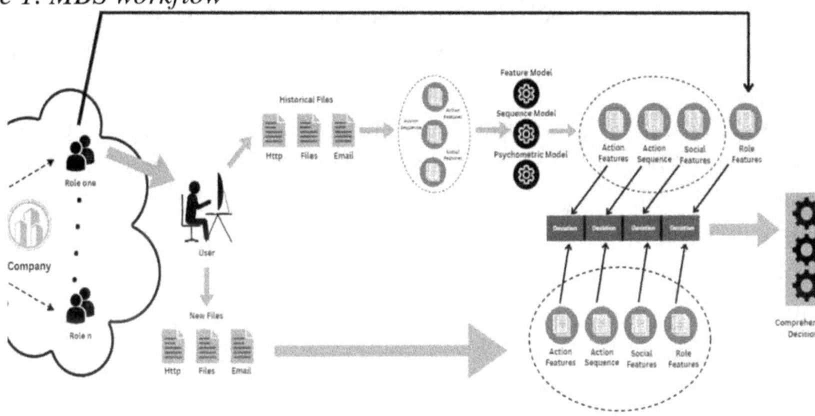

The action feature model, action sequence model, and role feature model are the three main models that center the MBS workflow. As seen in the illustration, these models serve as the framework for the MBS system. People work in groups according to their roles (financial analyst, software engineer, etc.), with the idea that people in the same group generally do similar tasks. By separating out role-specific behaviours and data, this classification makes it easier to spot abnormalities.

Workers in the finance department, for example, frequcntly do tasks like interacting with clients and evaluating financial data. A departure from their customary duties, including gaining illegal access to private financial records or moving substantial quantities of money to accounts they are not familiar with, could set up alarms that need to be investigated further. A concerted attempt to falsify financial data may be indicated if the person accesses backend databases without authorization and is a member of a financial software development team.

Training algorithms and extracting traits for individual users both heavily rely on historical data. Three primary types comprise these data, which are usually sourced from within the organization:

1. **User and Entity Behaviour Analysis (UEBA):** It involves analysing:
    1. Actions performed by users and operational data on individual computers.
    2. Logs from servers and internal systems.
    3. Organizational structure data along with logs of significant events and disciplinary actions.
2. Feature Types:
    1. **Action Features:** Numerical attributes that show a user's everyday actions over time, such as a day or a week. These functions, which are unique to each user's position, include activities such as login attempts, downloading or accessing files, accessing the network during off-hours or outside of typical work patterns, sending emails, and so on.
    2. **Action Sequence:** Sequential data that summarizes the steps taken by a user over time. All user activity is recorded and arranged chronologically to do this. The product is a series of operations such as "log on, web browsing, connect USB drive, disconnect USB drive, send email, log out".
    3. **Role Features:** Statistical characteristics that indicate the shared work attributes of all users in the same group (e.g., average action features of all Sales members).
    4. **Deep Learning Strategy:** The MBS analyses log entries (login/logout, network traffic, file access, file download) and looks for potentially suspicious behaviour using a variety of deep learning approaches. Observable changes in these logs, such as significant increases in failed login attempts, accessing sensitive or restricted areas of the network, running unusual or unauthorized programs or scripts, accessing the network during off- hours or outside of typical work patterns, may indicate anomalous activities that could lead to data exfiltration.

The primary techniques used in MBS are well known prediction algorithms that are commonly applied in natural language processing (NLP) and computer vision. MBS presents an innovative deep learning-based anomaly detection method along with a special combination of these algorithms, which includes the first known application of convLSTM for insider anomaly detection.

4.1 Long Short-Term Memory (LSTM) technique holds considerable Favor in supervised learning, notably in domains like Natural Language Processing, Gesture and Speech Recognition. Because of its ability to infer forthcoming states from a series of inputs, it is a prevalent choice for diverse regression projects. By utilizing LSTMs, MBS understands typical action sequences and predicts user behaviour by delving into past data. Through comparing actual and anticipated sequences, deviations are discerned, unveiling anomalies in the process.

4.2 ConvLSTM, an upgraded version of LSTM introduced in 2015, has demonstrated impressive efficacy in video frame sequence prediction. The technique combines the ability of convolutional neural networks (CNNs) to record localized characteristics with the predictive power of long short-term memory (LSTMs). MBS leverages ConvLSTMs for two objectives: • Like action sequences, daily behavioural patterns can be used to anticipate outcomes by leveraging LSTMs and reflecting an individual's work routines. • Using CNNs, ConvLSTMs can identify possible relationships between various activity features that are chosen to comprehend user behaviour.

4.3 MLP In the final component of MBS, the comprehensive decision model relies on Multi-Layer Perceptron (MLPs) to aggregate results from diverse deep learning models, facilitating anomaly detection. The MLP is one type of neural network that's commonly utilized to address non-linear problems. Like a classification problem, MBS determines the associations between features using an MLP that has been trained on previous data. The MLP determines if anomalous behaviours are present based on aberrations in action sequences, action features, and role attributes.

5. TESTCASES

The User and Entity Behaviour Analysis utilized synthetic data generated from the CERT Insider Threat dataset to evaluate the behaviour of three specific users – HXL0968, TNM0961, and EDB0714 – over a span of 200 days. This analysis was conducted by incrementally adding training data every 5 days to capture evolving patterns. The primary metric used for evaluating deviations from the users' usual activities was the Weighted Deviation Loss (WDD).

In the initial phase spanning the first 200 days, the daily features of the users demonstrated a consistent deviation from conventional role features within a narrow range of 0 to 2. This implies that their behaviors largely adhered to expected patterns during this period. The stability in deviation suggests a certain level of conformity to established norms, indicating that their actions were aligned with their typical roles or responsibilities within the system.

However, a significant observation emerged beyond the 200-day mark, where a noticeable change in user behavior was detected, leading to the identification of suspicious activities. This shift was discernible through an analysis of the deviation metrics, indicating a departure from established behavioural patterns. Such deviations are crucial indicators for the system operator to identify potential threats or anomalies within the network.

Figure 2. User interface

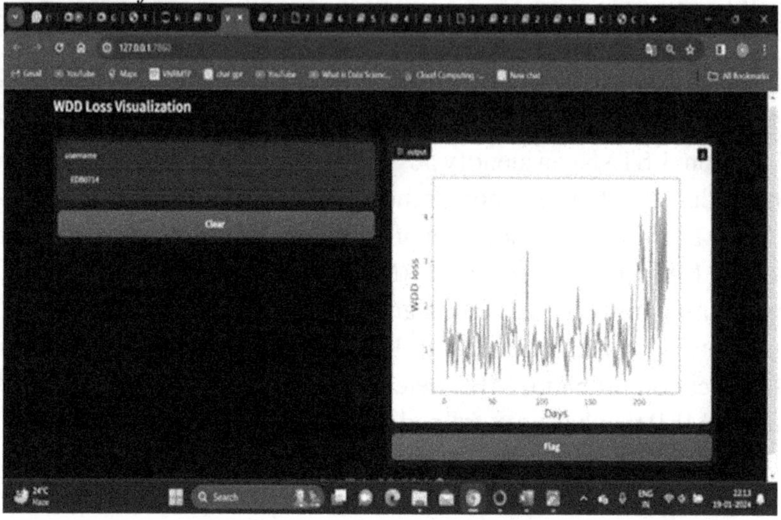

The analysis of the graphs further elucidates the dynamics of behavioural changes over time. Pre-200 days, the graphs depict a relatively stable pattern with minor fluctuations within the expected range. These fluctuations likely represent variations in user activities influenced by factors such as workload, task priorities, or external circumstances. However, post-200 days, there is a clear divergence from this stable trend, marked by more pronounced deviations in the graphs.

Each user's unique behavioural trajectory can be observed through the graphs, highlighting individual patterns and deviations. HXL0968, TNM0961, and EDB0714 exhibit distinct shifts in behavior post-200 days, indicating varying degrees of deviation from their usual activities. This granularity in analysis enables the operator to pinpoint specific users whose behavior requires closer scrutiny, facilitating targeted threat detection and mitigation efforts.

Figure 3. User 1[EDB0714]

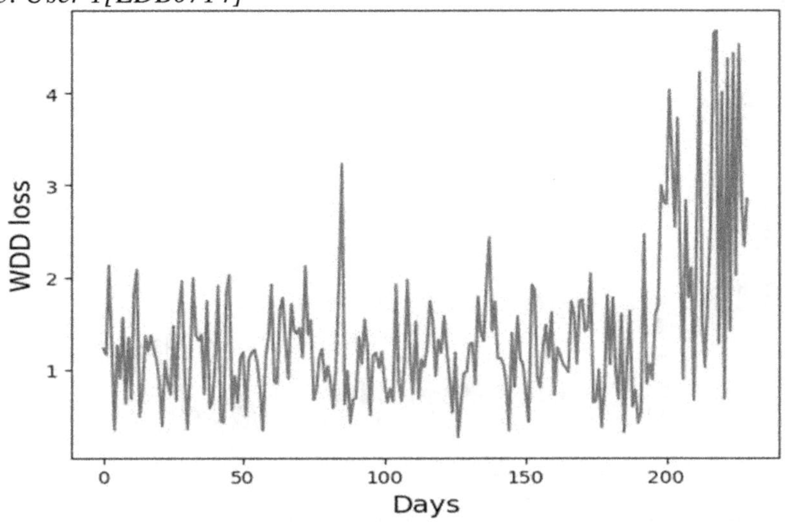

Figure 4. User 2 [TNM0961]

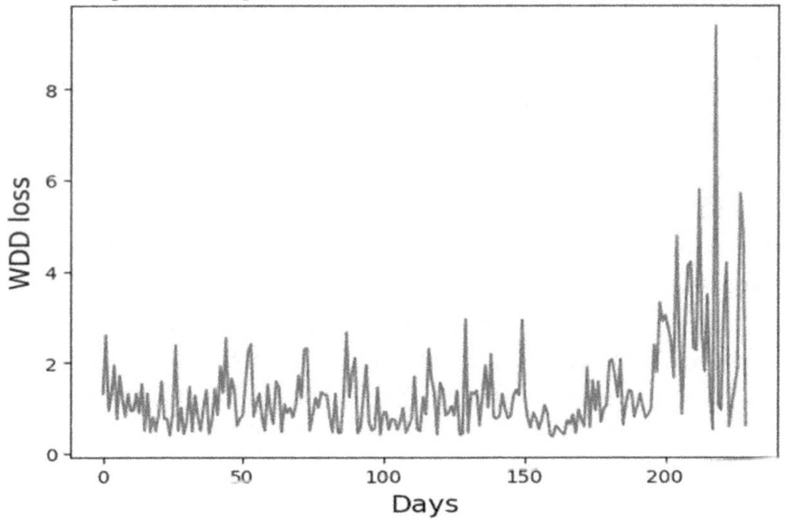

Figure 5. User 3 [HBN0961]

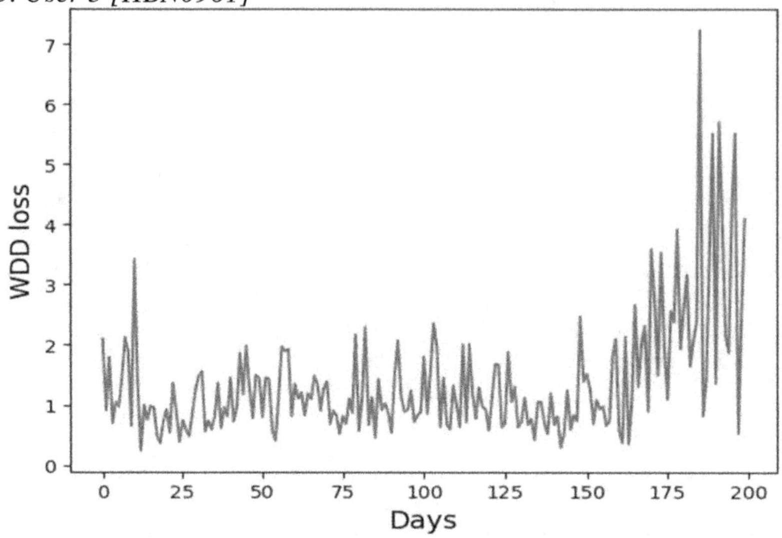

Furthermore, the analysis of the graphs allows for a deeper understanding of the nature of behavioral changes exhibited by the users. It provides insights into the types of activities or actions that contribute most significantly to deviations from established norms. By identifying these key indicators, the operator can prioritize monitoring efforts and tailor intervention strategies to address specific behavioral risk factors effectively.

Due to experimental constraints, we did not address the social model in our analyses; instead, we focused on action features, action sequences, and role features. Furthermore, in order to quantify the differences between the actual features and the forecast, we established the weighted deviation degree (WDD). In this instance, alterations in a few characteristics might not point to abnormal behaviour. Consequently, we created the WDD, which uses a weighted value to build a linear weighting system for the squared error. The WDD can be expressed as follows:

$$WDD= 1/|V|* \sum y \in V w*(y-y\wedge)2$$

The temporal aspect of the analysis is also critical, as it reveals trends and patterns in user behavior over an extended period.

The gradual evolution of deviations over time offers valuable context for interpreting suspicious activities and distinguishing transient anomalies from sustained behavioral shifts. This longitudinal perspective enhances the system's ability to differentiate between benign changes and potential threats.

Moreover, the comparative analysis of multiple users enables the identification of common trends or anomalies across different individuals. Patterns of deviation that coincide among multiple users may indicate systemic issues or coordinated malicious activities, warranting immediate attention and intervention. This holistic view of user behavior enhances the system's overall resilience to insider threats.

It is essential to emphasize the proactive nature of the UBA approach in detecting behavioral changes before they manifest as security breaches or data compromises. By continuously monitoring and analyzing user activities, the system can preemptively identify emerging threats and take preventive measures to mitigate risks. This proactive stance is crucial in today's dynamic cybersecurity landscape, where threats evolve rapidly.

Its analysis of synthetic data from the CERT Insider Threat dataset provides valuable insights into user behavior dynamics over time. By leveraging metrics such as Weighted Deviation Loss and visualizing behavioral patterns through graphs, the system operator can effectively identify deviations from established norms, detect suspicious activities, and mitigate insider threats. This proactive and data-driven approach enhances the overall security posture of the system and mitigates the risks associated with insider threats.

8.1 RESULT ANALYSIS

Figure 6. Output at security operator

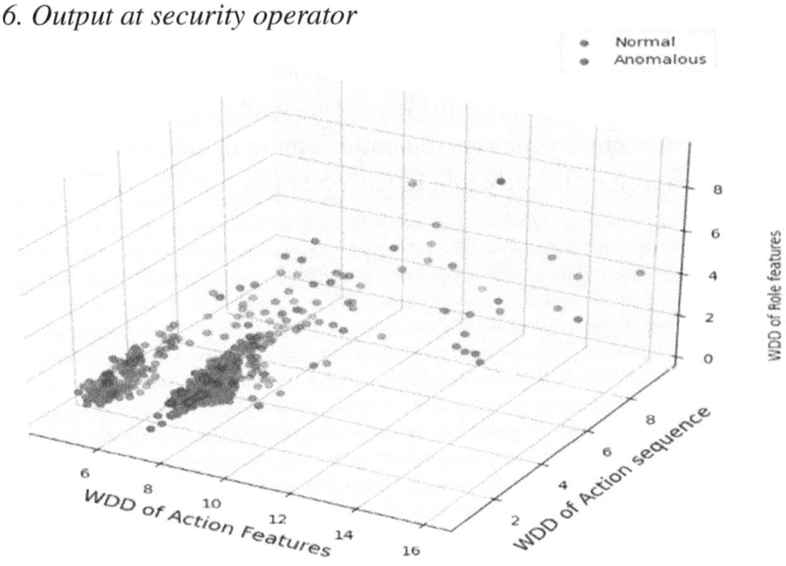

Figureure 6 provides a visual representation of the user's behavior over a 200-day period, incorporating role features, user activity sequences, and user feature attributes. By analyzing this plot, users can discern recurring patterns or trends in behavior over time, such as regular activities or deviations from expected behavior. This visualization serves as a powerful tool for understanding and interpreting user behavior dynamics within the system.

The Gradio interface serves as a user-friendly gateway to access and interpret the results of the User Behavior Analysis (UBA) project. By inputting the username of interest, users can effortlessly retrieve crucial metrics such as the Weighted Deviation Loss (WDD). This intuitive interface streamlines the process of data interpretation and facilitates quick decision-making in response to potential security threats.

For instance, if an operator inputs the username “HXL0968” into the Gradio interface, the associated WDD Loss for that user would be displayed. This quantitative metric serves as a crucial indicator of the extent to which the user's behavior deviates from established norms. A higher WDD Loss suggests a greater likelihood of suspicious activities or insider threats associated with that user.

To contextualize the significance of the WDD Loss, it is essential to consider previous accuracy metrics associated with the UBA project. These metrics evaluate the performance of the UBA model in accurately detecting behavioral anomalies. Metrics such as precision, recall, F1-score, or area under the curve (AUC) for receiver operating characteristic (ROC) analysis provide insights into the model's robustness and efficacy in identifying security threats.

High accuracy scores indicate a strong performance of the UBA model in distinguishing between normal and suspicious behavior. This implies that the system can effectively identify and mitigate insider threats with a high degree of precision. By leveraging these accuracy metrics, operators can make informed decisions and allocate resources more efficiently to address potential security risks.

Figure 7. Output UX User 1

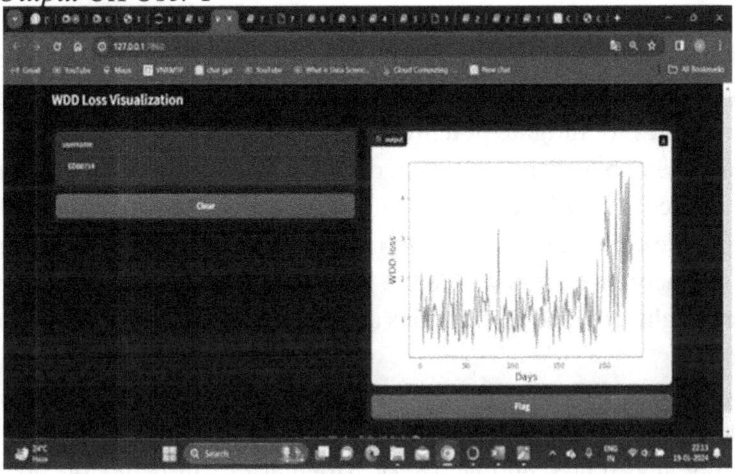

Figure 8. Output UX User 2

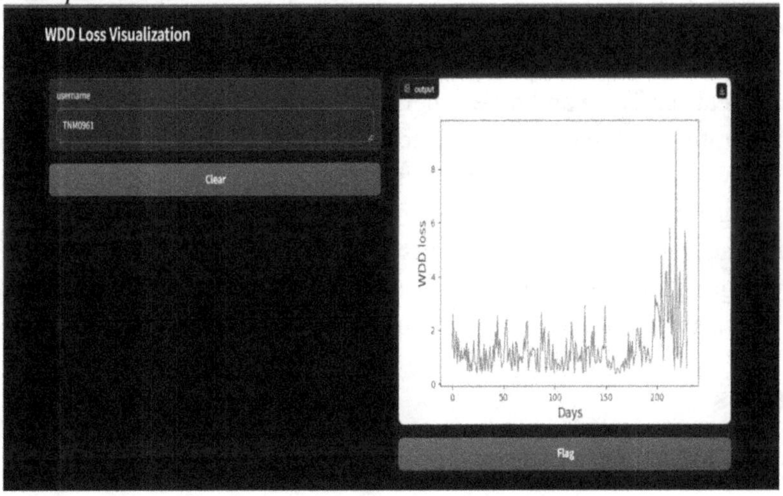

Role features depict the user's assigned responsibilities or permissions within the system, highlighting deviations from expected role-based behaviors. For example, sudden changes in access privileges or unusual patterns of system interaction may indicate potential security breaches or insider threats. By monitoring role features, operators can identify and respond to unauthorized activities promptly.

User activity sequences offer a chronological view of actions performed by the user over time. Patterns or sequences of activities that deviate from established norms may indicate suspicious behavior warranting further investigation. By analyzing user activity sequences, operators can identify anomalous patterns and take proactive measures to mitigate potential security risks.

User feature attributes encompass additional characteristics or attributes of the user, such as access privileges, interaction patterns, or historical behavior. These attributes provide contextual information that enriches the analysis of user behavior dynamics. By incorporating user feature attributes into the analysis, operators can gain deeper insights into the motivations and intentions behind observed behavioral deviations.

The integration of these diverse dimensions of analysis into a unified visualization enables operators to conduct comprehensive assessments of user behavior. By identifying key trends, anomalies, or irregularities in behavior, operators can proactively detect and mitigate potential security threats. The visual nature of the graphs facilitates intuitive interpretation and enhances situational awareness, enabling operators to make informed decisions in real- time threat detection scenarios.

For example, operators may observe sudden spikes or dips in certain metrics, indicating abrupt changes in user behavior that warrant further investigation. By closely monitoring these trends, operators can identify potential security breaches or insider threats early on and take timely action to mitigate risks.

The integration of the Gradio interface, WDD Loss metrics, previous accuracy metrics, and visualizations of user behavior graphs provides a powerful framework for leveraging UBA techniques to enhance cybersecurity resilience. By enabling operators to access and interpret key insights efficiently, this integrated approach empowers organizations to proactively detect and mitigate insider threats, safeguarding critical assets and maintaining a robust security posture.

8.2 Results

ROC Curve

The Receiver Operating Characteristic (ROC) curve serves as a fundamental tool for assessing the performance of binary classification models across various thresholds. It provides a graphical representation of the trade-off between the true positive rate (sensitivity) and the false positive rate (1 - specificity) as the threshold for classification is varied. In essence, the ROC curve offers valuable insights into the discriminatory power of a model and its ability to distinguish between positive and negative instances.

The provided ROC curve compares the performance of three detection systems: Unsupervised Learning (USL), Supervised Learning (SL), and a Machine Learning-based detection system (MBS). These systems are evaluated using experimental data to determine their effectiveness in instance detection or classification. By analyzing the ROC curve, we can assess how well the MBS performs relative to the original USL and SL models across different threshold values.

Here's the ROC Curve comparing the potential of MBS and the Supervised and the Unsupervised Machine learning models.

Figure 9. Receiver side output of final efficiency

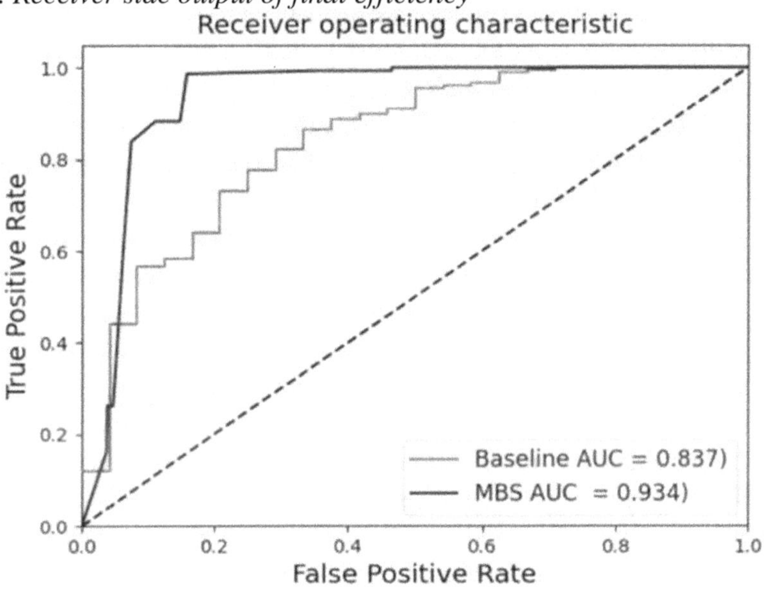

This above Figureure compares the performance of two detection systems: USL (Unsupervised Learning), SL (Supervised Learning), and MBS (Machine Learning-based detection system) using experimental data. A key aspect of interpreting the ROC curve lies in understanding the trade-off between true positives and false positives. A model that achieves higher true positive rates while keeping false positive rates low is considered more desirable as it indicates better discrimination between positive and negative instances. Thus, the ROC curve provides valuable insights into the balance between sensitivity and specificity achieved by each detection system.

In comparing the performance of the three detection systems, one can observe the ROC curves plotted for each model. The curve for MBS represents its ability to classify instances across various thresholds, while the curves for USL and SL depict the performance of the original unsupervised and supervised learning models, respectively.

By visually inspecting these curves, one can identify differences in performance and assess the relative effectiveness of each system.

An ideal ROC curve would exhibit a steep rise towards the top-left corner, indicating high true positive rates and low false positive rates across all thresholds. Conversely, a curve that hugs the diagonal line (representing random guessing) suggests poor discriminatory power and limited effectiveness in classification. By comparing the shape and trajectory of the ROC curves for MBS, USL, and SL, one can discern which model offers superior performance in terms of instance detection.

Additionally, the area under the ROC curve (AUC) serves as a quantitative measure of a model's performance. A higher AUC value indicates better discrimination and overall model effectiveness. By calculating the AUC for each detection system, one can directly compare their performance and determine which model offers the highest predictive power and discriminatory ability.

In interpreting the ROC curve, it's essential to consider the specific context and requirements of the classification task. Depending on the application, certain thresholds may be more critical than others. For instance, in a medical diagnosis scenario, minimizing false negatives (missed detections) may be paramount, necessitating a focus on maximizing sensitivity even at the expense of increased false positives.

Ultimately, the analysis of the ROC curve enables stakeholders to make informed decisions regarding the selection and optimization of detection systems. By understanding the trade- offs between sensitivity and specificity and evaluating the discriminatory power of each model, organizations can identify the most effective approach for their specific use case and enhance the accuracy and reliability of instance detection or classification.

The objective is to evaluate how well MBS performs in comparison to the original models in terms of instance detection or classification.

1. Analysis of Performance Measures:

A few measures, such as accuracy, precision, recall, F1 score, etc., were used to assess each detection system's performance. These metrics reveal information on how well the systems classify instances.

2. Comparison with Original Models (SL & USL):

It was clear from comparing MBS's performance with the original models (SL & USL) that MBS beat them both in every metric taken into account. It appears from this development that MBS has successfully improved the detection or classification skills over the initial baseline models.

3. Trajectories of ROC Curves:

For every detection system, ROC curves were plotted to show how true positive rate and false positive rate are traded off. These curves' trajectories were found to be similar among the models, suggesting that they performed similarly in terms of differentiating between positive and negative cases.

4. MBS Beats USL and SL:

Although the ROC curve trajectories showed similarities, MBS outperformed USL by a small margin. This suggests that MBS outperforms Unsupervised Learning in terms of precisely recognising cases.

5. MBS Effectiveness:

The AUC value of 0.93 for MBS clearly showed how successful it is. Strong discriminatory power and reliable performance across a range of threshold values are shown by a high AUC score, which further supports the superiority of the MBS detection method.

9.1 CONCLUSION

The study begins by acknowledging the complexities involved in identifying unusual activities among insiders, emphasizing the significance of this task within the realm of User and Entity Behavior Analytics (UEBA). By addressing these challenges through a multifaceted approach that considers action elements, social dynamics, and role characteristics, the study aims to provide a comprehensive solution for anomaly detection. This approach signifies a departure from traditional methods that may focus solely on specific aspects of behavior analysis, thereby offering a more holistic perspective on insider threat detection.

One of the key contributions of the study lies in the development and evaluation of a novel system designed to analyze regular behavior patterns and flag deviations as anomalies. This system integrates various models to effectively capture the nuances of user behavior across different dimensions, thereby enhancing the detection capabilities of UEBA systems.

By leveraging a combination of feature types, the system aims to overcome the limitations associated with relying solely on attributes, which may lead to false positives and false negatives. This indicates a shift towards a more nuanced and sophisticated approach to anomaly detection, where multiple factors are considered to improve accuracy and reliability.

Central to the study's findings is the introduction of a Multi-Feature Based System, which employs a Multi-Layer Perceptron (MLP) to draw comprehensive conclusions from deviations across all feature categories. By harnessing the power of deep learning techniques like MLP, the MBS demonstrates promising results in detecting and mitigating insider threats, underscoring the potential of advanced machine learning methods in augmenting traditional UEBA approaches.

In the broader context of UEBA and deep learning, the study underscores the importance of leveraging advanced analytical techniques to enhance anomaly detection capabilities. By integrating deep learning methods into UEBA systems, organizations can benefit from more accurate and effective identification of insider threats. This highlights the potential of deep learning to revolutionize traditional approaches to cybersecurity, offering a path towards improved defenses against insider threats and other malicious activities.

Furthermore, the study's emphasis on a comprehensive and integrated approach to anomaly detection reflects a growing recognition of the interconnectedness of various factors influencing user behavior. By considering action elements, social dynamics, and role characteristics in tandem, the study moves beyond traditional siloed approaches to behavior analysis, offering a more nuanced and holistic understanding of insider threats. This holistic perspective is essential for organizations seeking to stay ahead of evolving cybersecurity challenges and safeguard their sensitive assets effectively.

Overall, the study's findings underscore the transformative potential of advanced machine learning techniques like deep learning in enhancing UEBA capabilities. By addressing the challenges inherent in recognizing unusual activities among insiders and proposing innovative solutions like the Multi-Feature Based System, the study contributes valuable insights to the field of cybersecurity and lays the groundwork for future advancements in anomaly detection and threat mitigation.

9.2 SUMMARY

Modern cybersecurity strategies heavily rely on User and Entity Behavior Analysis (UEBA) to identify and mitigate agency risks effectively. UEBA technology aims to enhance security measures by analysing both user and entity behaviors within organizational networks. This involves employing various techniques such as data collection and integration methods, feature extraction, and deep learning models for comprehensive threat detection and mitigation.

Data collection techniques play a crucial role in UEBA, gathering information from diverse sources like system logs, network traffic, and application logs. This process results in a rich dataset that serves as the foundation for behavioral analysis. Feature extraction techniques further refine this data, transforming raw information into meaningful representations that enable in-depth analysis of user and entity behaviors.

Deep learning models, such as Long Short-Term Memory (LSTM) and Convolutional LSTM (ConvLSTM), are instrumental in UEBA for analysing temporal, spatial, and spatiotemporal dependencies in behavior data. These models can identify patterns and deviations over time and space, enabling the detection of anomalies and the implementation of immediate corrective actions.

UEBA offers comprehensive solutions for improving organizational cybersecurity by rapidly identifying insider threats, anomalies, and potential vulnerabilities. Its versatility, scalability, and flexibility make it an indispensable asset for safeguarding critical data and ensuring the security of organizational assets.

UEBA using deep learning represents a powerful approach to cybersecurity, providing organizations with advanced tools to protect against a wide range of security risks. By integrating deep learning models into UEBA systems, organizations can benefit from enhanced threat detection capabilities and proactive security measures.

9.3 FURTHER WORK

Proceeding onwards, a wide range of possibilities arise, granting plenty of space for future development and improvement. undefined

- **Exploring Alternative Approaches:** Future research in this field will focus on developing alternative approaches to overcome the challenge of recognizing anomalous behaviors based solely on users' typical everyday activities. This may involve exploring novel techniques, such as incorporating additional contextual information or utilizing different machine learning algorithms to improve the accuracy of anomaly detection.
- **Addressing Social Aspects:** Investigating social aspects of user behavior will be crucial for enhancing the effectiveness of behavior analysis systems. This could include analysing social interactions, communication patterns, and group dynamics to gain deeper insights into potential security threats posed by insider activities.

- **Trials on Larger Datasets:** Conducting trials on larger datasets will be essential for validating the effectiveness and scalability of behavior analysis systems. By analysing data from a broader range of sources and organizations, researchers can better understand the variability of user behaviors and improve the generalizability of their findings.
- **Improving Accuracy of Behaviour Characterization:** Enhancing the accuracy of characterizing user behaviours will be a key focus of future research efforts. This may involve refining existing algorithms, optimizing feature selection techniques, and incorporating feedback mechanisms to iteratively improve the performance of behaviour analysis systems.
- **Investigating Data Collection Methods:** Exploring alternative methods of data collection for capturing a more comprehensive view of user behaviours. This could include leveraging new technologies, such as IoT devices, wearable sensors, to gather additional contextual data that can enhance the accuracy of behaviour analysis models.

  Enhancing Model Training Techniques: Investigating alternate ways of training models, such as the Multi-Layer Perceptron (MLP), will be critical for overcoming constraints related to gathering anomalous data. Researchers may explore techniques such as transfer learning, semi-supervised learning, or synthetic data generation to improve model performance without relying solely on anomalous data.
- **Addressing Privacy Concerns:** Future research will need to address privacy concerns associated with behaviour analysis systems. This may involve developing privacy-preserving techniques, such as differential privacy or federated learning, to ensure that sensitive user information is protected while still allowing for effective threat detection.
- **Collaboration and Knowledge Sharing:** Encouraging collaboration and knowledge sharing among researchers and practitioners in the field will be essential for advancing the state-of-the-art in behaviour analysis. This could involve establishing collaborative research networks, organizing workshops and conferences, and creating open-access repositories for sharing datasets and code.
- **Integration with Emerging Technologies:** Integrating behaviour analysis systems with emerging technologies, such as artificial intelligence, blockchain, and edge computing, will unlock new possibilities for enhancing cybersecurity. Researchers may explore how these technologies can be leveraged to improve the accuracy, efficiency, and scalability of behaviour analysis systems.
- **Real-World Deployment and Evaluation:** Finally, future research should focus on real-world deployment and evaluation of behaviour analysis sys-

tems in diverse organizational settings. This will help validate the practical effectiveness of these systems and identify areas for further improvement and refinement.

It focuses on developing alternative approaches, refining methodologies, and addressing limitations in behaviour analysis for cybersecurity. This includes investigating social aspects, conducting trials on larger datasets, and exploring novel data collection methods. Advancements in model training techniques, addressing privacy concerns, fostering collaboration, and integrating emerging technologies will shape the evolution of behaviour analysis, enhancing organizational resilience against insider threats and cyberattacks.

REFERENCES

Al Nuaimi, E., Al Neyadi, H., Mohamed, N., & Al-Jaroodi, J. (2015). Applications of big data to smart cities. *Journal of Internet Services and Applications*, *6*(1), 25. DOI: 10.1186/s13174-015-0041-5

Bursic, Sathya & Cuculo, Vittorio & D'Amelio, Alessandro. (2020). Anomaly Detection from Log Files Using Unsupervised Deep Learning.

Calvo, A., Escuder, S., & Guijarro, J. "A Data-Driven Approach for Risk Exposure Analysis in Enterprise Security," 2023 IEEE 10th International Conference on Data Science and Advanced Analytics (DSAA), pp. 1–9, 2023. DOI: 10.1109/DSAA60987.2023.10302480

Datta, O., Dasgupta, R., Dasgupta, S., & Reddy, K. R. "Real- Time Threat Detection in UEBA using Unsupervised Learning Algorithms", 2021 5th International Conference on Electronics, Materials Engineering & Nano-Technology (IEMENTech), pp.1-6, 2021.

Hashem, Y., Takabi, H., Dantu, R., & Nielsen, R. 2017, October. A multi-modal neuro-physiological study of malicious insider threats. In *Proceedings of the 2017 International Workshop on Managing Insider Security Threats* (pp. 33–44).

Hoglund, A. J., Hatonen, K., & Sorvari, A. S. "A computer host-based user anomaly detection system using the self-organizing map," Proceedings of the IEEE-INNS-ENNS International Joint Conference on Neural Networks. IJCNN 2000.

Jurišić, M., Tomičić, I., & Grd, P. (2023). User Behavior Analysis for Detecting Compromised User Accounts: A Review Paper. *Cybernetics and Information Technologies*, *23*(3), 102.

Kaur, J., Kaur, K., Kant, S., & Das, S. "UEBA with Log Analytics", 2022 3rd International Conference on Computing, Analytics and Networks (ICAN), pp.1- 7, 2022. DOI: 10.1109/ICAN56228.2022.10007245

Landauer, M., Skopik, F., Höld, G., & Wurzenberger, M. "A User and Entity Behavior Analytics Log Data Set for Anomaly Detection in Cloud Computing," 2022 IEEE International Conference on Big Data (Big Data), Osaka, Japan, 2022.

Mohanty, R. K., Motupalli, R. K., Manju, D., Gangappa, M., Gouthami, B., & Mounika, G. (2023, December). Energy-Efficient Cluster Based Routing Protocol to Enhance the Lifetime of Wearable Wireless Body Area Networks (WBAN). In *2023 OITS International Conference on Information Technology (OCIT)* (pp. 71-76). IEEE. DOI: 10.1109/OCIT59427.2023.10431071

Mohanty, R. K., Sahoo, S. P., & Kabat, M. R. (2022, October). A Survey on Emerging Technologies in Wireless Body Area Network. In 2022 13thInternational Conference on ComputingCommunication and Networking Technologies (ICCCNT) (pp. 1-5). IEEE.

Mohanty, R. K., Sahoo, S. P., & Kabat, M. R. (2023). Sustainable remote patient monitoring in wireless body area network with Multi-hop routing and scheduling: A four-fold objective based optimization approach. *Wireless Networks*, *29*(5), 1–15. DOI: 10.1007/s11276-023-03276-x

Mohanty, R. K., Sahoo, S. P., & Kabat, M. R. (2023, June). A Network Reliability based Secure Routing Protocol (NRSRP) for Secure Transmission in Wireless Body Area Network. In 2023 8th International Conference on Communication and Electronics Systems (ICCES) (pp. 663-668). IEEE.

Odongo, B. O. (2022). Security Information and Event Management Using Deep Learning Project Documentation. Diss. University of Nairobi.

Pandhurnekar, V., Iyyappan, A., & Wazalwar, S. (2023). "Proposed Method for Threat Detection Using User Behavior Analysis", 2023 IEEE 3rd International Conference on Technology, Engineering, Management for Societal impact using Marketing, Entrepreneurship and Talent (TEMSMET), pp.1-5.

Salitin, M. A., & Zolait, A. H. (2018). "The role of User Entity Behavior Analytics to detect network attacks in real time," 2018 International Conference on Innovation and Intelligence for Informatics, Computing, and Technologies (3ICT), Sakhier, Bahrain, pp. 1-5, DOI: 10.1109/3ICT.2018.8855782

Schaffers, H., Komninos, N., Pallot, M., Trousse, B., Nilsson, M., & Oliveira, A. (2011, May). Smart cities and the future internet: Towards cooperation frameworks for open innovation. In The Future Internet Assembly (pp. 431–446). Springer, Berlin.

Shashanka, M., Shen, M.-Y., & Wang, J. (2016). "User and entity behavior analytics for enterprise security," 2016 IEEE International Conference on Big Data (Big Data), Washington, DC, USA.

Skopik, F., Höld, G., Landauer, M., & Kuhn, W. (2023). Behavior-Based Anomaly Detection in Log Data of Physical Access Control Systems. *IEEE Transactions on Dependable and Secure Computing*, *20*(4), 3158–3175.

Slipenchuk, P., & Epishkina, A. V. (2019). *Practical User and Entity Behavior Analytics Methods for Fraud Detection Systems in Online Banking: A Survey*. Biologically Inspired Cognitive Architectures.

Tang, B., Chen, Z., Hefferman, G., Wei, T., He, H., & Yang, Q. (2015, October.) A hierarchical distributed fog computing architecture for big data analysis in smart cities. In Proceedings of the ASE Big Data & Social Informatics 2015 (p. 28).

Tang, B., Hu, Q., & Lin, D. "Reducing False Positives of User-to-Entity First-Access Alerts for User Behavior Analytics," *2017 IEEE International Conference on Data Mining Workshops (ICDMW)*, New Orleans, LA, USA, 2017.

Tian, Z., Gao, X., Su, S., Qiu, J., Du, X., & Guizani, M. (2019). Evaluating reputation management schemes of internet of vehicles based on evolutionary game theory. *IEEE Transactions on Vehicular Technology*, *68*(6), 5971–5980.

Tian, Z., Shi, W., Wang, Y., Zhu, C., Du, X., Su, S., Sun, Y., & Guizani, N. (2019). Real time lateral movement detection based on evidence reasoning network for edge computing environment. *IEEE Transactions on Industrial Informatics*, *15*(7), 4285–4294.

Tian, Z., Su, S., Shi, W., Du, X., Guizani, M., & Yu, X. (2019). A data-driven method for future internet route decision modeling. *Future Generation Computer Systems*, *95*, 212–220. DOI: 10.1016/j.future.2018.12.054

Yousef, R., & Jazzar, M. (2021). Measuring the effectiveness of user and entity behavior analytics for the prevention of insider threats. *Journal of Xi'an University of Architecture & Technology*, *13*, 10.

Zanella, A., Bui, N., Castellani, A., Vangelista, L., & Zorzi, M. (2014). Internet of Things for smart cities. *IEEE Internet of Things Journal*, *1*(1), 22–32. DOI: 10.1109/JIOT.2014.2306328

Chapter 7
Advances in Optimization for Deep Learning-Based Computer Vision Models

Tejinder Kaur
Department of MMICTBM, Maharishi Markandeshwar University, Mullana, India

ABSTRACT

This speeds up training and can lead to more stable convergence. This helps the optimization process to overcome small local minimal and converge faster. Instead of using a fixed learning rate, learning rate schedules adaptively change the learning rate during training. Techniques like learning rate decay, step decay, or cosine annealing can help improve convergence. These methods often converge faster and are less sensitive to manual tuning of learning rates. Proper weight initialization techniques, such as His initialization or Xavier initialization, can significantly speed up convergence and reduce the likelihood of getting stuck in poor local minima. Batch normalization normalizes activations within a layer, making training more stable and enabling the use of higher learning rates. It can accelerate training and improve the final model's performance. The choice of optimization methods and their configurations should be tailored to the specific task and dataset, emphasizing the need for careful experimentation and hyper parameter tuning.

1. INTRODUCTION

Optimization techniques play a pivotal role in making this training process efficient and effective (Abadi et al., 2016). In this paper, we provide a comprehensive exploration of optimization techniques used in training DNNs for vision tasks. Deep

DOI: 10.4018/979-8-3693-6864-0.ch007

networks suffer from gradient-related issues during training, hindering convergence (Bjorck et al., 2018).

1.1 DNNs have a propensity to over fit the training data, necessitating techniques to prevent this.
1.2 Training large networks on massive datasets demands substantial computational resources and can be time-consuming (Bottou, 1991).
1.3 The foundation of many optimization techniques, SGD optimizes network parameters by computing gradients from a subset (mini-batch) of training data, enhancing training efficiency (Bottou, 2010).
1.4 Incorporating momentum helps accelerate convergence by smoothing the optimization trajectory, reducing oscillations (Chen et al., 2019).

Figure 1. Neural network model using machine learning (Abadi et al., 2016)

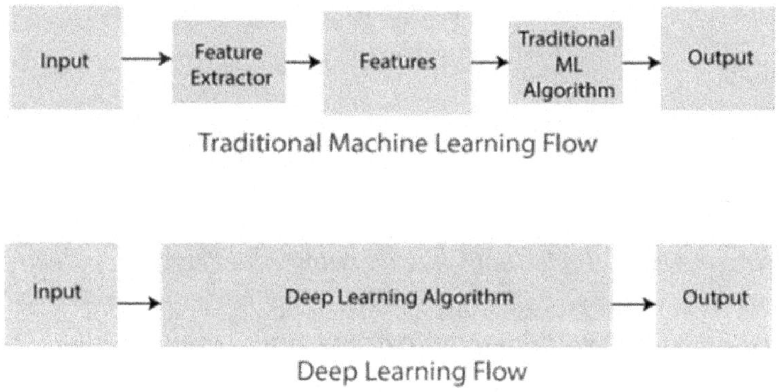

2. DEVELOPMENT

Over the years, researchers and practitioners have recognized the unique challenges posed by vision tasks and have continuously refined optimization methods to address them.

2.1 Historical Perspective: (Cho & Lee, 2017)

Begin with an overview of the early days of deep learning in computer vision, emphasizing the challenges researchers faced with optimization due to the depth and complexity of neural networks.

Highlight milestones, such as the emergence of convolution neural networks (CNNs) and their impact on computer vision tasks.

2.2 Gradient-Based Optimization: (Courbariaux, Bengio, & David, 2015)

Explain how SGD and its variants have evolved to overcome challenges such as vanishing gradients and slow convergence.

2.3 Regularization Techniques: (Courbariaux et al., 2016)

Describe the evolution of weight regularization methods like L1 and L2 regularization and their role in preventing over fitting in deep vision models.

2.3.1 Batch Normalization and Normalization Techniques

Discuss the introduction of batch normalization and its impact on training stability and convergence speed.

Mention other normalization techniques that have been developed and adapted for vision tasks.

2.3.2 Architectural Enhancements: (Duchi, Hazan, & Singer, 2011)

Explore how architectural innovations, such as residual connections and skip connections (as used in U-Net), have reshaped the landscape of deep vision models by addressing optimization challenges.

2.3.3 Attention Mechanisms: (Glorot & Bengio, 2010)

Elaborate on the development and integration of attention mechanisms, such as self-attention (Transformer), into vision architectures to enable better feature selection and focus (Gupta et al., 2018).

3. LITERATURE REVIEW: OPTIMIZATION TECHNIQUES IN TRAINING FOR VISION

This literature review provides an overview of key research and developments in the field of optimization for training DNNs in vision tasks. (He, Gkioxari, Dollár, & Girshick, 2017).

3.1 Historical Evolution of Optimization Techniques

The early adoption of gradient descent in training neural networks paved the way for modern optimization methods. LeCun et al.'s work in the 1990s on back propagation and SGD laid the foundation for subsequent advancements.

has been a workhorse in training DNNs for vision. It efficiently handles large datasets and complex models. (He, Zhang, Ren, & Sun, 2015).

Research efforts have focused on improving SGD's convergence and stability.

3.3 Adaptive Learning Rate Methods: (He, Zhang, Ren, & Sun, 2016)

These algorithms dynamically adjust learning rates, leading to faster convergence.

Studies have compared the performance of these adaptive methods and highlighted their effectiveness in handling noisy gradients and optimizing deep architectures.

3.4 Weight Regularization Techniques: (Huang, Liu, Van Der Maaten, & Weinberger, 2017)

Weight regularization methods, including L1 and L2 regularization, have been employed to combat over fitting in DNNs. Researchers have explored the impact of different regularization strategies on vision model performance.

3.5 Normalization Techniques

Batch normalization emerged as a key technique for stabilizing training in deep networks. Its application in vision architectures has become standard practice, improving both convergence and generalization.

Recent research has explored alternatives to batch normalization, such as layer normalization and group normalization, with potential benefits in various vision scenarios (Huang, Liu, Liu, Lang, & Tao, 2017).

3.6 Architectural Enhancements

The development of architectural enhancements, such as residual connections (ResNets) and densely connected networks (DenseNets), has allowed for the training of extremely deep networks. These architectures have reshaped the landscape of vision models (Huang & Belongie, 2017).

Studies have investigated the impact of architectural choices on optimization challenges like vanishing gradients.

4. EMERGING TRENDS AND CHALLENGES

Recent trends include neural architecture search (NAS) to discover custom architectures optimized for specific vision tasks and self-supervised learning, which reduces the reliance on labelled data.

Challenges in optimization for vision include scalability for very large models, adversarial robustness, and optimizing for real-time or edge computing scenarios (Ioffe & Szegedy, 2015)

In conclusion, optimization techniques have continually evolved alongside the development of deep neural networks for computer vision. Researchers have made substantial contributions to address optimization challenges, resulting in significant advancements in vision tasks. Future research will likely continue to explore novel optimization strategies to push the boundaries of computer vision capabilities further (Iscen, Tolias, Avrithis, & Chum, 2019)

Certainly, let's explore a few case studies that highlight the practical application of optimization techniques in training deep neural networks for vision tasks: (Khosla, Jayadevaprakash, Yao, & Li, 2011)

Case Study 1: Image Classification with Convolution Neural Networks (CNNs)

Objective: To develop an accurate image classification model for a dataset of diverse images.

Optimization Techniques:

Results: The optimized U-Net model accurately segmented medical images, assisting in diagnosis and treatment planning.

These case studies illustrate the diverse range of optimization techniques applied to different computer vision tasks. Each task demands a tailored approach to optimization, taking into account factors like the dataset, architecture, and desired outcome.

By leveraging the right optimization strategies, researchers and practitioners can achieve remarkable results in computer vision applications.

5. OPTIMIZATION TECHNIQUES IN TRAINING DEEP NEURAL NETWORK FOR VISION RESULT

Figure 2. Convolution neural network for segmentation using machine learning [3]

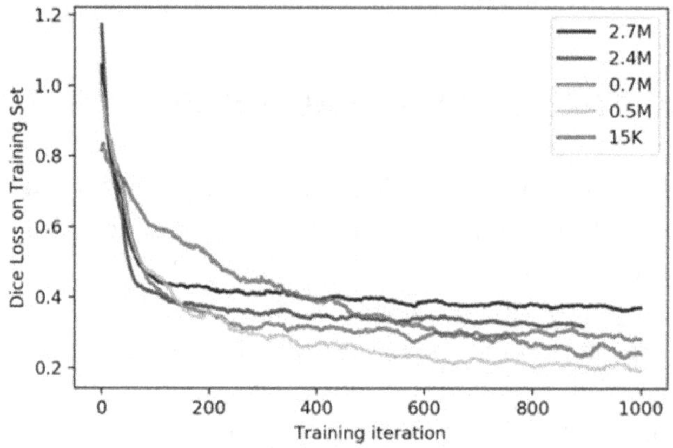

The results of using Convolution Neural Networks (CNNs) for image segmentation tasks using machine learning can vary widely depending on factors such as the dataset, model architecture, hyper parameters, and the specific segmentation task (Krause, Stark, Deng, & Fei-Fei, 2013). However, I can provide you with a general overview of the expected outcomes and evaluation metrics commonly used in image segmentation tasks: (Krizhevsky & Hinton, 2009) This enables fine-grained object localization. CNN-based segmentation models are known for their high accuracy in delineating objects or regions of interest in images. The accuracy can vary but is typically impressive when optimized correctly. With proper regularization techniques and training strategies, (Krogh & Hertz, 1992)(Larsson et al., 2017).

6. CONCLUSION

This results in models that achieve desired performance levels in fewer training iterations. Weight regularization methods, batch normalization, and data augmentation contribute to improved model generalization. DNNs optimized with these techniques exhibit robustness against over fitting and excel at recognizing patterns in unseen data. Optimization techniques ensure training stability by mitigating issues like vanishing gradients. This empowers the training of exceptionally deep networks, which are essential for tackling complex vision tasks. In essence, optimization techniques empower DNNs to achieve unprecedented levels of performance, enabling them to excel in diverse vision tasks. As computer vision continues to evolve and find applications in various domains, mastering and innovating optimization methods will remain critical for pushing the boundaries of what is achievable in the field

REFERENCES

Abadi, M., Chu, A., Goodfellow, I., McMahan, H. B., Mironov, I., Talwar, K., & Zhang, L. Deep learning with differential privacy. In: *Proceedings of the 2016 ACM SIGSAC Conference on Computer and Communications Security*. pp. 308– 318. ACM (2016) DOI: 10.1145/2976749.2978318

Bjorck, J., Gomes, C., Selman, B., Weinberger, K.Q.: Understanding batch normalization pp. 7694–7705 (2018)

Bottou, L. (1991). Stochastic gradient learning in neural networks. *Proceedings of NeuroNımes*, *91*(8), 12.

Bottou, L. Large-scale machine learning with stochastic gradient descent. In: *Proceedings of COMPSTAT'2010*, pp. 177–186. Springer (2010) DOI: 10.1007/978-3-7908-2604-3_16

Chen, K., Wang, J., Pang, J., Cao, Y., Xiong, Y., Li, X., Sun, S., Feng, W., Liu, Z., Xu, J., ... Mmdetection: Open mmlab detection toolbox and benchmark. arXiv preprint arXiv:1906.07155 (2019)

Cho, M., & Lee, J. (2017) Riemannian approach to batch normalization. In: Advances in Neural Information Processing Systems. pp. 5225–5235.

Courbariaux, M., Bengio, Y., & David, J. P. (2015). Binaryconnect: Training deep neural networks with binary weights during propagations. In: Advances in neural information processing systems. pp. 3123–3131.

Courbariaux, M., Hubara, I., Soudry, D., El-Yaniv, R., & Bengio, Y. (2016). Binarized neural networks: Training deep neural networks with weights and activations constrained to+ 1 or-1. arXiv preprint arXiv:1602.02830.

Duchi, J., Hazan, E., & Singer, Y. (2011). Adaptive subgradient methods for online learning and stochastic optimization. *Journal of Machine Learning Research*, *12*(Jul), 2121–2159.

Glorot, X., & Bengio, Y. (2010). Understanding the difficulty of training deep feedforward neural networks. In: *Proceedings of the thirteenth international conference on artificial intelligence and statistics*. pp. 249–256.

Gupta, H., Jin, K. H., Nguyen, H. Q., McCann, M. T., & Unser, M. (2018). Cnn-based projected gradient descent for consistent ct image reconstruction. *IEEE Transactions on Medical Imaging*, *37*(6), 1440–1453. DOI: 10.1109/TMI.2018.2832656 PMID: 29870372

He, K., Gkioxari, G., Doll'ar, P., & Girshick, R. (2017). Mask r-cnn. In: *Proceedings of the IEEE international conference on computer vision*. pp. 2961–2969.

He, K., Zhang, X., Ren, S., & Sun, J. (2015). Delving deep into rectifiers: Surpassing humanlevel performance on imagenet classification. In: *Proceedings of the IEEE international conference on computer vision*. pp. 1026–1034. DOI: 10.1109/ICCV.2015.123

He, K., Zhang, X., Ren, S., & Sun, J. (2016). Deep residual learning for image recognition. In: *Proceedings of the IEEE conference on computer vision and pattern recognition*. pp. 770–778.

Huang, G., Liu, Z., Van Der Maaten, L., & Weinberger, K. Q. (2017). Densely connected convolutional networks. In: *Proceedings of the IEEE conference on computer vision and pattern recognition*. pp. 4700–4708.

Huang, L., Liu, X., Liu, Y., Lang, B., & Tao, D. (2017). Centered weight normalization in accelerating training of deep neural networks. In: *Proceedings of the IEEE International Conference on Computer Vision*. pp. 2803–2811. DOI: 10.1109/ICCV.2017.305

Huang, X., & Belongie, S. (2017). Arbitrary style transfer in real-time with adaptive instance normalization. In: Proceedings of the IEEE International Conference on Computer Vision. pp. 1501–1510. 16 H. Yong et al. DOI: 10.1109/ICCV.2017.167

Ioffe, S., & Szegedy, C. (2015). Batch normalization: Accelerating deep network training by reducing internal covariate shift. arXiv preprint arXiv:1502.03167.

Iscen, A., Tolias, G., Avrithis, Y., & Chum, O. (2011). Label propagation for deep semisupervised learning. In: *Proceedings of the IEEE Conference on Computer Vision and Pattern Recognition*. pp. 5070–5079.

Kim, J., Kwon Lee, J., & Lee, M. (2016). K.: Accurate image super-resolution using very deep convolutional networks. In: *Proceedings of the IEEE conference on computer vision and pattern recognition*. pp. 1646–1654. DOI: 10.1109/CVPR.2016.182

Kingma, D. P., & Ba, J. (2014). Adam: A method for stochastic optimization. arXiv preprint arXiv:1412.6980

Krause, J., Stark, M., Deng, J., & Fei-Fei, L. (2013). 3d object representations for finegrained categorization. In: *Proceedings of the IEEE International Conference on Computer Vision Workshops*. pp. 554–561

Krizhevsky, A., & Hinton, G.. (2009). *Learning multiple layers of features from tiny images. Tech. rep*. Citeseer.

Krogh, A., & Hertz, J. A. (1992). A simple weight decay can improve generalization. In: Advances in neural information processing systems. pp. 950–957.

Larsson, M., Arnab, A., Kahl, F., Zheng, S., & Torr, P. (2017). A projected gradient descent method for crf inference allowing end-to-end training of arbitrary pairwise potentials. In: *International Workshop on Energy Minimization Methods in Computer Vision and Pattern Recognition*. pp. 564–579. Springer.

Ba, L., (2016). Layer normalization. arXiv preprint arXiv:1607.06450

Lin, T. Y., Doll'ar, P., Girshick, R., He, K., Hariharan, B., & Belongie, S. (2017). Feature pyramid networks for object detection. In: *Proceedings of the IEEE conference on computer vision and pattern recognition*. pp. 2117–2125.

Lin, T. Y., Maire, M., Belongie, S., Hays, J., Perona, P., Ramanan, D., Doll'ar, P., & Zitnick, C. L. (2014). Microsoft coco: Common objects in context. In: European conference on computer vision. pp. 740–755. Springer.

Loshchilov, I., & Hutter, F. (2017). Decoupled weight decay regularization. arXiv preprint arXiv:1711.05101.

Chapter 8
Pattern Prediction System for Smart Farming in the Agriculture Sector Using Machine Learning:
Smart Agriculture

M. R. Pooja
https://orcid.org/0000-0001-6225-8486
Vidyavardhaka College of Engineering, Mysuru, India

Aditi Attavar
Vidyavardhaka College of Engineering, Mysuru, India

Akshatha Leela Manohar
Vidyavardhaka College of Engineering, Mysuru, India

D. Himoshra
Vidyavardhaka College of Engineering, Mysuru, India

ABSTRACT

The system aims to empower farmers by providing insights into the diverse range of crops suitable for their specific land. The work focuses on developing a system that predicts the optimal crop priority, considering various factors such as land characteristics, soil conditions, and climate data. By understanding the intricate relationships between different crop types, farmers can make informed decisions to maximize yield quality. The absence of a robust system for identifying cropping patterns results in random crop choices, leading to yield fluctuations. This prioritization minimizes losses due to suboptimal crop combinations. The proposed

DOI: 10.4018/979-8-3693-6864-0.ch008

system is designed to assist both individual farmers and agricultural departments by incorporating machine learning algorithms that explore the data gathered from the agricultural department to perform an exploratory analysis. This approach allows for a more informed and effective decision-making process in smart agriculture.

I. INTRODUCTION

Cropping patterns, which refer to the proportion of land under different crops at various times, reflect the timing and arrangement of crops in a specific area. Predicting these patterns necessitates a comprehensive analysis of extensive data, including variables like soil quality, pH, and more. The right cropping pattern can help farmers maximize their profits and minimize losses, and machine learning techniques can help predict the optimal cropping patterns based on various factors such as soil type, climate, water availability, and market demand. This approach enhances precision in decision-making, fostering sustainable and efficient agricultural practices.

In India, crops are categorized based on the season they are grown, influencing the cropping pattern. The first cropping season, known as the Kharif season, commences in June with the onset of the southwest monsoon and continues until September. This season is suitable for tropical crops like rice, maize, cotton, and sugarcane. The second cropping season, the Rabi season, starts in October and lasts until March, during which winter crops such as wheat, barley, mustard, and gram are grown. The Zaid season, from March to June, is a short cropping season that falls between the Rabi and Kharif seasons.

Figure 1. Various cropping seasons in India

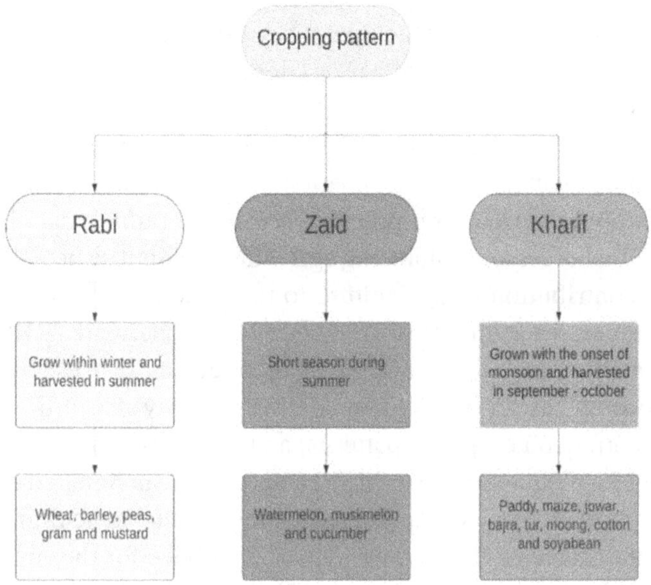

Machine learning techniques, specifically Naive Bayes and Eclat, are utilized in this research to extract valuable insights from the data. The choice of Naive Bayes and Eclat is motivated by their proven effectiveness in pattern recognition and association rule mining, respectively, which are crucial for predicting cropping patterns. The accuracy of feature extraction and the application of these unsupervised learning algorithms are key to the success of any pattern prediction system including heath informatics and agricultural systems (Attavar et al., 2024)(Ravi et al., 2024). In the context of India, the classification of crops based on the growing season significantly influences the cropping pattern. This factor is taken into account in the prediction model to ensure its relevance and applicability.

II. LITERATURE SURVEY

(Ahmed et al., 2022) conducted research on the principal agricultural patterns in Bangladesh. Using machine learning approaches, they attempted to effectively forecast cropping patterns by leveraging aspects associated with agriculture, such as data on land, soil, and climate. Data from 52 Upazilas were included in the dataset, which was derived from the Land and Soil Resources Usage Guidelines (in Bangla) series. To handle the enormous number of predicted classes and the combination of numerical and categorical predictor data, the researchers used machine learning methods such as xgboost, K-nearest neighbors, Decision Tree, Random Forest Classifier, and Support Vector Machine. They achieved over 95% accuracy and their work also led to the creation of a user-friendly system for predicting cropping patterns using trained models.

Ejigu and Nigatu (Ejigu & Nigatu, 2022) undertook research on rainfall forecasting and cropping pattern recommendations in the Amhara region as part of their research on Ethiopia's agricultural practices. Accurate rainfall data is essential for managing water resources and enhancing agricultural output, especially considering the substantial contribution of agriculture to the nation's economy. Their rainfall prediction, which used a Radial Basis Function Neural Network (RBFNN), outperformed other statistical techniques and the methods currently in use by the Ethiopian National Meteorological Service Agency (ENMSA). They also utilized the K-means algorithm to recommend cropping patterns, and they assessed their forecasts with metrics such as Mean Squared Error (MSE) and Root Mean Squared Error (RMSE). Crucially, their work offers a comprehensive approach to agricultural planning by integrating rainfall forecasts and cropping pattern advice for the first time.

The study carried out by Du, Zhang, and Yu (Du et al., 2022) mainly focuses on understanding the cropping patterns and their geographical characteristics in Northeast China's black soil region. To fully utilize black soils, the authors emphasized the significance of creating cropping patterns appropriate for the local environment. They used a distribution index model, bivariate spatial autocorrelation, and geo-information Tupu techniques to analyze cropping trends using crop classification data from 2017 to 2019. Their results showed that continuous rice cultivation, continuous soybean cropping, continuous maize-soybean rotation, and continuous maize cropping accounted for considerable quantities in the region. Among the various cropping patterns, they also discovered clear horizontal differences and spatial grouping features. The predominant feature of the cropping pattern in the black soil zone was continuous cropping.

In their work on cropping pattern optimization in Kermanshah Plain, Iran, Barati et al. (Barati et al., 2020) built a dynamic model that replicated real-world conditions using the Vensim PRO x32 software. Stochastic time series simulation was used to predict future climatic factors. They employed the Powell technique in multi-objective mathematical programming to optimize crop patterns across three scenarios. To maximize farmers' financial profits, the objective functions tried to reduce the amount of water extracted from aquifers. The results showed that under ideal conditions, water extraction frequently yielded bigger benefit ratios than under the current settings. Their research also revealed that expanding the production of other crops, such as saffron, rose, greenhouse, medicinal plants, and olives, while decreasing the acreage devoted to some crops was necessary to optimize cropping patterns. Specifically, the cropping pattern was optimized for wheat, barley, maize, tomato, clover, and onion agriculture when scenarios with adjustable crop coefficients were suggested.

In (Dhawale et al., 2023), Dhawale et al.'s work on the use of machine learning (ML) in crop selection for precision agriculture looks at important variables such as soil composition, pH level, humidity, and rainfall to give farmers crop recommendations. To examine these characteristics, they use a variety of machine learning (ML) models, such as quadratic discriminant, linear support vector machine (SVM), Gaussian Naive Bayes, and Kernel Naive Bayes. The study emphasizes how important precise crop forecasts are to ensure food security and optimize farming techniques. Crop yields are accurately predicted by ML algorithms by utilizing past weather patterns, data on crop productivity, and soil conditions.

Padmini and Raju (Hegde et al., 2019) presented an innovative crop prediction method, leveraging advanced Deep Learning, particularly Long Short-Term Memory (LSTM) networks. Their approach, integrating historical data and key factors like temperature, humidity, soil pH, and water availability, achieves an impressive 89.66% accuracy in predicting crop suitability.

III. PROPOSED SYSTEM

Improving crop yield and quality mostly rests on crop choice optimization. Yet, farmers often end up with less-than-ideal results when choosing acceptable crops because manual methods need a lot of time, skill, and subjective evaluation. Given the crucial relationships between different crop types and how they impact productivity, an automated approach to predict cropping patterns is needed.

Our proposed system functions as an automated tool for predicting cropping patterns, assisting farmers in selecting which crops to plant in the available area. Using machine learning algorithms like Naïve Bayes and Eclat, the system analyzes agricultural data to identify recurring trends in crop selection. It then generates prioritized crop cultivation suggestions based on the expected cropping patterns.

Figure 2. Methodology of the proposed system

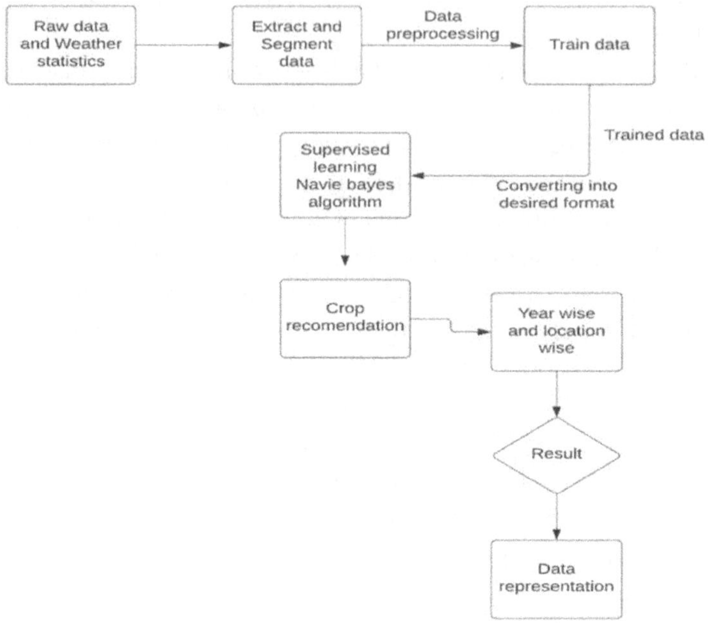

1. Raw Data and Weather Statistics

In the initial stage of the crop recommendation process, raw agricultural data is collected from the 'Nanjangud' region. This comprehensive dataset encompasses crucial agriculture parameters such as rainfall, temperature, and soil features including pH, nitrogen, potassium, and iron. Additionally, the dataset incorporates crop details, farmers' information, and yield statistics, providing a holistic overview of the agricultural landscape.

2. Extract and Segment Data (Data Preprocessing)

Following the data collection, a meticulous analysis is performed, and only pertinent information is extracted for further processing. This involves the segmentation of data according to different regions, ensuring that the subsequent stages of the methodology are executed on a refined dataset. This preprocessing step is essential to streamline the data and optimize processing efficiency.

3. Train Data

Once the relevant data is extracted and segmented, the next step involves training the data. Training the data entails converting it into the required format, whether numerical values, binary, or string, depending on the specific algorithm being employed. This step lays the groundwork for subsequent machine-learning processes.

4. Machine Learning Algorithm

This approach relies on training data that includes expected answers, allowing the system to learn and make predictions.

Naïve Bayes

The Naive Bayes Algorithm is chosen for its efficiency as a classifier, adaptability to both small and large datasets, and its capability to deliver accurate results even with varying numbers of parameters.

Step 1: Scan the dataset (storage servers)
Step 2: Calculate the probability of each attribute value. [n, n_c, m, p]
Step 3: Apply the formulae

P(attribute_value(ai) / subject_value(vj)) = (n_c + mp) / (n + m)

where:

- n = the number of training examples for which v = vj
- n_c = number of examples for which v = vj and a = ai
- p = a priori estimate for P(ai/vj)
- m = the equivalent sample size

Step 4: Multiply the probabilities by p
Step 5: Compare the values and classify the attribute values to one of the predefined set of classes.

Sample Example

Attributes (Features) – PH, Nitrogen, Phosphorus [m=3]

Subject/Classes (Crop) – Ragi, Paddy [p=1/2=0.5]

Table 1. Training dataset

Soil Type	PH (X, Y, Z)	Nitrogen (A, B, C)	Phosphorus (P, Q, R)	Crop
Soil Input1	X	A	P	Ragi
Soil Input2	X	B	Q	Ragi
Soil Input3	Y	B	P	Paddy
Soil Input4	Z	A	R	Ragi
Soil Input5	Z	C	R	Paddy

New Soil Input6 Features – PH - X, Nitrogen – A, Phosphorus – R

Crop– Ragi/Paddy?

P= [n_c + (m * p)] / (n + m)

Table 2. Probability calculations of Ragi and Paddy

Ragi	Paddy
X P = [n_c + (m * p)] / (n + m) n = 2, n_c = 2, m = 3, p = 0.5 P = [2 + (3 * 0.5)] / (2 + 3) P = 0.7	X P = [n_c + (m * p)] / (n + m) n = 2, n_c = 0, m = 3, p = 0.5 P = [0 + (3 * 0.5)] / (2 + 3) P = 0.3
A P = [n_c + (m * p)] / (n + m) n = 2, n_c = 2, m = 3, p = 0.5 P = [2 + (3 * 0.5)] / (2 + 3) P = 0.7	A P = [n_c + (m * p)] / (n + m) n = 2, n_c = 2, m = 3, p = 0.5 P = [2 + (3 * 0.5)] / (2 + 3) P = 0.3
R P = [n_c + (m * p)] / (n + m) n = 2, n_c = 1, m = 3, p = 0.5 P = [1 + (3 * 0.5)] / (2 + 3) P = 0.5	R P = [n_c + (m * p)] / (n + m) n = 2, n_c = 1, m = 3, p = 0.5 P = [1 + (3 * 0.5)] / (2 + 3) P = 0.5

Ragi = 0.7 * 0.7 * 0.5 * 0.5 (p) = 0.1225

Paddy = 0.3 * 0.3 * 0.5 * 0.5 (p) = 0.0225

Since Ragi > Paddy

So, this new Soil Input6 is classified for Ragi

Output

Table 3. Crop preference

Crops (priority)	Preference
Ragi	0.12

Eclat Algorithm

Using associative rule mining, the Eclat algorithm analyzes crop combinations and produces confidence values. The Eclat method makes it easier to identify frequently occurring itemset, which in this case are combinations of crops grown in different locations at different periods. Eclat assists us in determining the probability of specific crop combinations being grown together by looking at the frequency of occurrence of crop combinations in historical data.

Eclat excels at identifying frequent item sets, making it particularly well-suited for analyzing combinations of crops frequently grown together. Unlike Apriori, another common association rule learning algorithm, Eclat utilizes a vertical data format. This approach reduces the number of database scans required, leading to faster processing times. Additionally, Eclat's relative simplicity allows for easier integration within our system. For large agricultural datasets, Eclat's efficiency in handling such data volumes becomes a significant advantage.

IV. CROP RECOMMENDATION (PRIORITY WISE)

The Naive Bayes and Eclat algorithm are deployed to generate crop recommendations based on priority. By leveraging its efficiency and adaptability, the system identifies suitable crops that are likely to yield high profits for the farmers. The algorithm's ability to handle both small and large datasets ensures robust recommendations.

V. LOCATION AND YEAR-BASED

To enhance the precision of recommendations, the crop recommendation system takes into account the geographic location and the specific year. This nuanced approach acknowledges regional variations and annual climate fluctuations, tailoring recommendations to the unique conditions of each location and period.

VI. DESIGN METHODOLOGY

In our system, we carter to three distinct roles:

Admin

The administrator is responsible for managing the entire application. They have exclusive access and control over system functionalities. It provides intuitive tools for the Administrator to oversee user management and system settings

Location in Charger/Staff

The staff members are designed individuals responsible for specific locations. They interact with the application to receive cropping pattern services. Staff accounts are created and managed by the Administrator. The design offers streamlined navigation for staff to access location-specific data and services efficiently.

Visitors/Farmers

Visitors are users with access to basic agricultural information. They may include farmers seeking guidance on crop cultivation. Visitors can navigate through the application to explore relevant content and services tailored to their needs.

VII. VISUAL REPRESENTATION

The user interface serves as the interface for farmers to access the recommended crops. Upon logging into the application, the system visually represents suitable and high-profit crops, offering a user-friendly experience. This visual representation aids farmers in making informed decisions about their crop selection, contributing to the overall success of their agricultural endeavors.

Figure 3. The accuracy of Naïve Bayes Algorithm

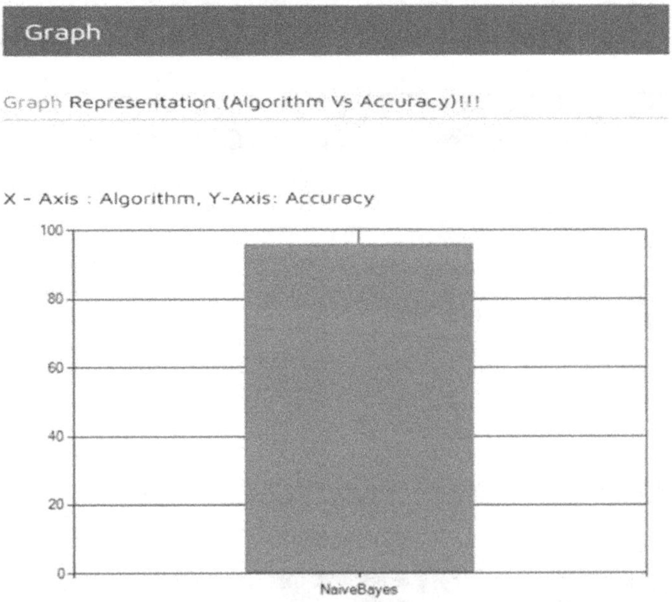

VIII. RESULTS

The culmination of the methodology involves presenting farmers with suitable and high-profit crop recommendations. The Naive Bayes algorithm, with its probability-based outputs, extracts and sorts high-probability crops. The top three recommended crops are then suggested to the farmers, providing a targeted and actionable list for cultivation. Based on the confidence values obtained from the Eclat algorithm, cropping patterns are generated that indicate the proportion of land under cultivation for different crop combinations at various times.

Figure 4. The accuracy of Naïve Bayes Algorithm

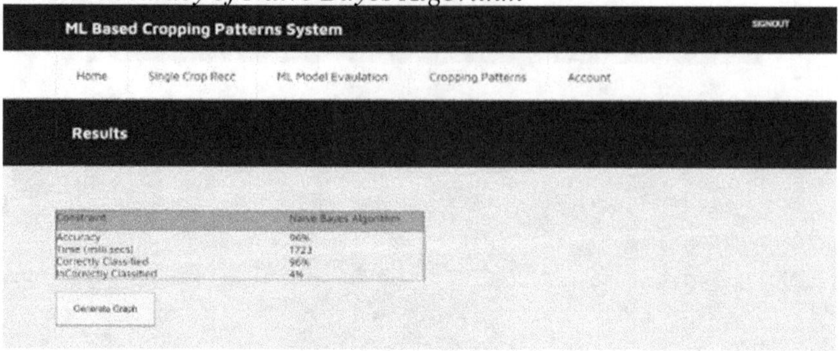

Figure 5. User Input for Naïve Bayes algorithm prediction

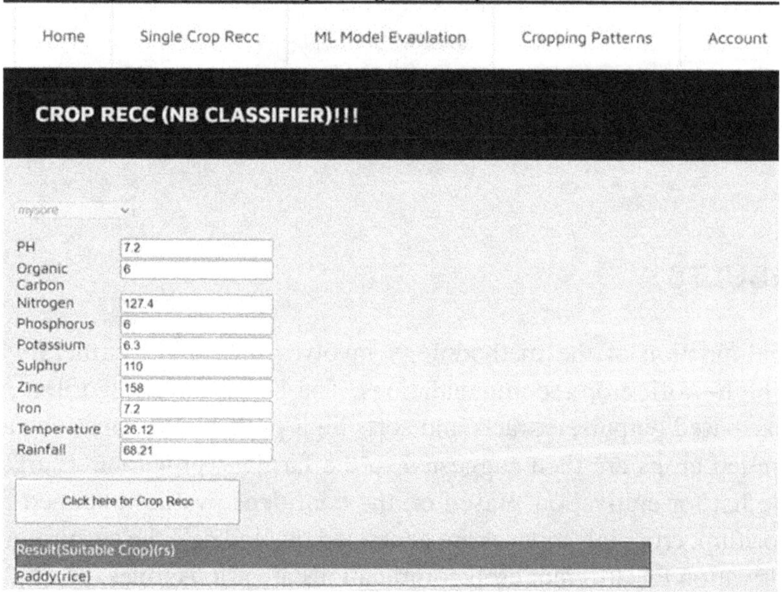

Figure 6. Prediction result of Eclat algorithm

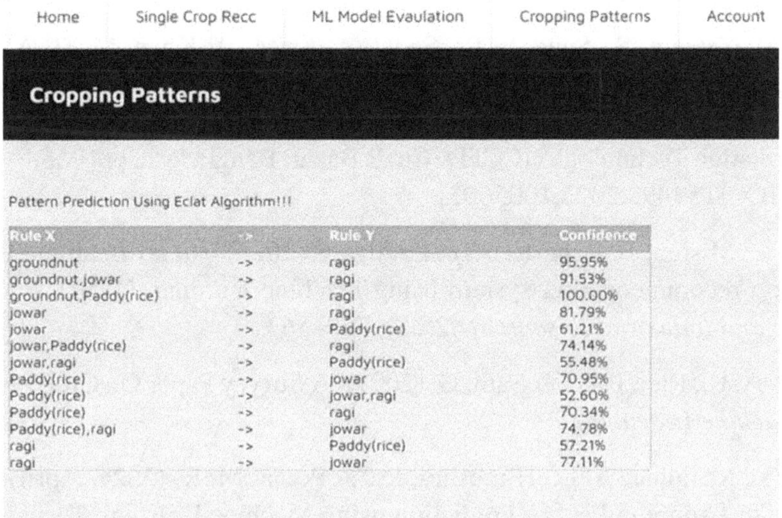

Rule X	->	Rule Y	Confidence
groundnut	->	ragi	95.95%
groundnut,jowar	->	ragi	91.53%
groundnut,Paddy(rice)	->	ragi	100.00%
jowar	->	ragi	81.79%
jowar	->	Paddy(rice)	61.21%
jowar,Paddy(rice)	->	ragi	74.14%
jowar,ragi	->	Paddy(rice)	55.48%
Paddy(rice)	->	jowar	70.95%
Paddy(rice)	->	jowar,ragi	52.60%
Paddy(rice)	->	ragi	70.34%
Paddy(rice),ragi	->	jowar	74.78%
ragi	->	Paddy(rice)	57.21%
ragi	->	jowar	77.11%

IX. CONCLUSION

The analysis of cropping pattern prediction is an essential component of agricultural management and is necessary to maximize crop yield. We have examined some approaches, including machine learning algorithms such as Eclat and Naive Bayes. These approaches provide farmers with invaluable information, enabling them to make wise choices that optimize crop yield. As we do not have the proper system to find the cropping patterns, we require automation for cropping pattern prediction to help farmers grow better crop types for better yield and profits.

REFERENCES

Ahmed, S., Yesmin, S., Saha, L. R., Sadat, A. K. M., & Khan, M. H. A. (2022). "Major Cropping Pattern Prediction in Bangladesh from Land, Soil and Climate Data Using Machine Learning Techniques," 25th International Conference on Computer and Information Technology (ICCIT), Cox's Bazar, Bangladesh. pp. 988-993, DOI: 10.1109/ICCIT57492.2022.10056051

Apat, S. K., Mishra, J., Raju, K. S., & Padhy, N. (2023). An artificial intelligence-based crop recommendation system using machine learning. [JSIR]. *Journal of Scientific and Industrial Research*, *82*(05), 558–567.

Aryamol, A. U., Raji, P. G., & Sam, G. (2021). A Survey Paper On Crop Prediction using. *Machine Learning*.

Attavar, A., Manohar, A. L., Himoshra, D., & Pooja, M. R. (2024, April). Intelli-Crop: Major Cropping Pattern Prediction using Machine Learning Techniques. In *2024 International Conference on Inventive Computation Technologies (ICICT)* (pp. 895-899). IEEE.

Attavar, A. L. (2024). "IntelliCrop: Major Cropping Pattern Prediction using Machine Learning Techniques," *2024 International Conference on Inventive Computation Technologies (ICICT)*, Lalitpur, Nepal. pp. 895-899, DOI: 10.1109/ICICT60155.2024.10544932

Barati, K., Koupai, J. A., Darvishi, E., Arzani, A., & Yousefi, A. (2020). Crop Pattern Optimization using System Dynamics Approach and Multi-Objective Mathematical Programming. *Journal of Agricultural Science and Technology*, *22*, 1397–1412.

Champaneri, M., Chachpara, D., Chandvidkar, C., & Rathod, M. (2020). *Crop Yield Prediction Using Machine Learning. International Journal of Science and Research (IJSR). (PDF)*. Crop Yield Prediction Using Machine Learning.

Dhawale, S., Kakade, S., Kulkarni, R., & Muhammed Fasil, C. (2023). "Application of ML in Crop Selection for Precision Agriculture," *2023 International Conference on Digital Applications, Transformation & Economy (ICDATE)*, Miri, Sarawak, Malaysia. pp. 226-230, DOI: 10.1109/ICDATE58146.2023.10248598

Ejigu, Y. B., & Nigatu, H. M. (2022). Rainfall Prediction and Cropping Pattern Recommendation Using Artificial Neural Network. In Berihun, M. L. (Ed.), *Advances of Science and Technology. ICAST 2021. Lecture Notes of the Institute for Computer Sciences, Social Informatics and Telecommunications Engineering* (Vol. 411). Springer., DOI: 10.1007/978-3-030-93709-6_34

Elbasi, E., Zaki, C., Topcu, A. E., Abdelbaki, W., Zreikat, A. I., Cina, E., Shdefat, A., & Saker, L. (2023). Crop Prediction Model Using Machine Learning Algorithms. *Applied Sciences (Basel, Switzerland)*, *13*(16), 9288. DOI: 10.3390/app13169288

GM, D., Zhang, R., & Yu, F. R. (2022). Analysis of cropping pattern in black soil region of Northeast China based on geo-information Tupu. Ying yong sheng tai xue bao=. *Journal of Applied Ecology*, *33*(3), 694–702.

Gupta, Maggu, & Kapoor. (2023). Crop Prediction using Machine Learning. Crop Prediction using. *Machine Learning*.

Hartomo, K. D., Prasetyo, S. Y., Anwar, M. T., & Purnomo, H. D. (2019). Rainfall Prediction Model Using Exponential Smoothing Seasonal Planting Index (ESSPI) For Determination of Crop Planting Pattern. In Purnomo, H. (Ed.), *Computational Intelligence in the Internet of Things* (pp. 234–255). IGI Global., DOI: 10.4018/978-1-5225-7955-7.ch010

Kalimuthu, M., Vaishnavi, P., & Kishore, M. "Crop Prediction using Machine Learning," *2020 Third International Conference on Smart Systems and Inventive Technology (ICSSIT)*, Tirunelveli, India, 2020, pp. 926-932, DOI: 10.1109/ICSSIT48917.2020.9214190

Kılıc, O. M., Ersayın, K., Gunal, H., Khalofah, A., & Alsubeie, M. S. (2022). Combination of fuzzy-AHP and GIS techniques in land suitability assessment for wheat (Triticum aestivum) cultivation, Saudi Journal of Biological Sciences, Volume 29, Issue 4, Pages 2634-2644, ISSN 1319-562X, DOI: 10.1016/j.sjbs.2021.12.050

Mahendra, N. (2020, August). Dhanush Vishwakarma, Nischitha K, Ashwini, Manjuraju M. R, 2020, Crop Prediction using Machine Learning Approaches [IJERT]. *International Journal of Engineering Research & Technology (Ahmedabad)*, *09*(08). Advance online publication. DOI: 10.17577/IJERTV9IS080029

Mahlayeye, M., Darvishzadeh, R., & Nelson, A. (2022). Cropping Patterns of Annual Crops: A Remote Sensing Review. *Remote Sensing*, *14*(10), 2404. DOI: 10.3390/rs14102404

Padmini, S. A., & Purushothama Raju, V. (2022, November). 2022, A Systematic Approach for Crop Prediction using Deep Learning [IJERT]. *International Journal Of Engineering Research & Technology*, *11*(11). Advance online publication. DOI: 10.17577/IJERTV11IS110155

Patil, P., & Panpatil, V. Prof. Shrikant Kokate (2020, February 2). Crop Prediction System using Machine Learning Algorithms. https://www.irjet.net/archives/V7/i2/IRJET-V7I2163.pdf

Priyanka, R. & Pooja, M. R. (2024). UAV Detection and Classification using Deep Learning Techniques with YOLOv8. 2024 4th International Conference on Mobile Networks and Wireless Communications (ICMNWC). IEEE.

Rao, M., & Singh, A. (2022). Crop prediction using machine learning. *Journal of Physics: Conference Series, 2161*(1), 012033. DOI: 10.1088/1742-6596/2161/1/012033

Ravi, V., Al Mazroa, A., & Ravi, P. (2024). Deployment of a Phenotypic Characterization System for Effective Identification of the Onset of Asthma Disease. *The Open Public Health Journal, 17*, 1.

Sagar, S. H., & Dravya, K. L. (2023, May 5). Crop Prediction & Recommendation System Using Machine Learning. https://www.ijres.org/papers/Volume-11/Issue-5/1105339341.pdf

Shakoor, M. T., Rahman, K., Rayta, S. N., & Chakrabarty, A. (2017, July). Agricultural production output prediction using supervised machine learning techniques. In 2017 1st international conference on next generation computing applications (NextComp) (pp. 182-187). IEEE.

Shwetha, M. S. & Pooja, M. R. (2024). The Impact of Smart Irrigation on Agricultural Productivity: A Study of Farmer Adoption and Challenges. 2024 3rd International Conference on Automation, Computing and Renewable Systems (ICACRS). IEEE.

Chapter 9
Sickle Cell Anaemia Cell Detection Using Machine Learning Techniques

Vandna Mehndiratta
Chandigarh Group of Colleges, Mohali, India

Anuj Kumar Gupta
https://orcid.org/0000-0002-7636-0817
Chandigarh Group of Colleges, Mohali, India

ABSTRACT

The paper presents a comprehensive overview of recent advancements in the field of sickle-shaped cells in the blood leading to a disease commonly known as Sickle Cell anaemia. Machine learning techniques, including classification and clustering algorithms, are employed to analyze complex datasets derived from blood samples, genetic markers, and clinical records. By leveraging these approaches, researchers aim to develop accurate and efficient diagnostic tools capable of identifying individuals with sickle cell anaemia with high sensitivity and specificity. Furthermore, machine learning models facilitate the integration of diverse data sources, enabling a holistic understanding of disease pathophysiology and progression. Challenges such as data heterogeneity, class imbalance, and model interpretability are addressed through innovative algorithmic designs and validation strategies.

DOI: 10.4018/979-8-3693-6864-0.ch009

1. INTRODUCTION

Sickle-cell disease (SCD) is a complex condition characterized by acute episodes of severe illness and progressive organ damage. It arises from mutations in the HBB gene, specifically in codon 6, leading to the substitution of adenine with thymine. This mutation results in the production of abnormal haemoglobin S (HbS), where valine replaces glutamic acid, causing red blood cells to become rigid and sickle-shaped when deoxygenated. SCD can manifest as sickle-β-thalassemia (HbSβ-thalassemia), sickle-haemoglobin C disease (HbSC), or through various combinations of heterozygous alleles, along with homozygous inheritance of βS/βS alleles (Neumayr et al., 2019). Heterozygous individuals with the βA/βS sickle cell trait (SCT) carry one mutated allele, resulting in abnormal haemoglobin, while the other allele remains normal. Polymerization of HbS due to reduced oxygen affinity alters red blood cells shape and membrane, leading to dehydration, enhanced polymerization, and the formation of irreversibly sickled cells. This process accelerates haemolytic anaemia, reducing red blood cell lifespan by 75%, and causing vaso-occlusion as polymerized cells struggle to traverse narrow blood vessels, leading to painful crises and acute complications like acute chest syndrome (Maruthesha et al., 2023). These vaso-occlusive crises (VOCs) are a primary cause of hospitalization and mortality in SCD patients.

As individuals with sickle cell disease (SCD) age, they may experience chronic complications such as retinopathy, cerebrovascular disease, pulmonary hypertension, priapism, and organ failure due to progressive ischemia, leading to premature mortality. Pregnancy can also pose risks of preterm delivery and hypertension. In Sub-Saharan African children, SCD is associated with a high five-year mortality rate, ranging from 50 to 80 per cent, often due to infections like malaria and invasive pneumococcal disease. However, in affluent nations, advancements in early diagnosis (Das et al., 2019), comprehensive therapy, and overall medical care have significantly improved the life expectancy of SCD patients, emphasizing the importance of early identification for effective disease management. Clinical laboratories primarily utilize biochemical and molecular assays for haemoglobin S detection and SCD diagnosis, with complete blood cell counts, Hb electrophoresis, and high-performance liquid chromatography (HPLC) being the most commonly employed techniques, considered the gold standard for SCD diagnosis.

2. SICKLE CELL ANAEMIA DETECTION FRAMEWORK

Image processing techniques play an essential role in the analysis of red blood cells (Saputra et al., 2023). Image Processing based sickle cell anaemia detection framework consists of several steps as shown in figure 1.

Figure 1. Image processing based sickle cell anaemia detection framework

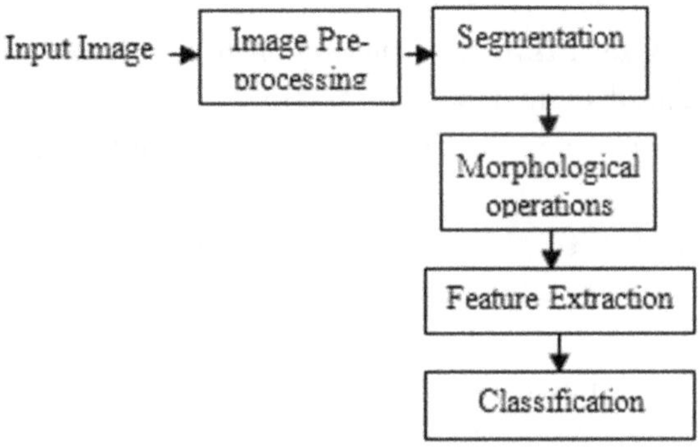

Below is a discussion of the steps that are shown in this figure:

i. **Image Pre-Processing**: The haematology department at general hospitals is the designated location for obtaining the necessary data set. Within this department, microscopic images of blood smears taken from individuals with sickle cell disease are used to identify erythrocytes IDB1. During the initial data preprocessing stage [6], the microscopic images are converted into grayscale images. Subsequently, noise is eliminated from the grayscale images through the application of a median filter. The final step in data preprocessing involves image enhancement techniques such as sharpening and removal of small artifacts to generate a superior quality image.
ii. **Image Segmentation**: Image segmentation is the technique of partitioning an image into meaningful objects or regions based on the task at hand. One common approach is to assign labels to each pixel, grouping pixels with similar traits under the same label. Thresholding is a basic segmentation method where a threshold value is chosen to divide the image into two parts (Dada et al., 2022). This is particularly effective for images with distinct data peaks in their histogram, known as bimodal images. Several automatic thresholding techniques exist, with Otsu's method being one popular option. Otsu's method, a widely-used bimodal clustering-based thresholding technique, iterates through potential threshold values to select the value that minimizes intra-class variance

and maximizes inter-class variation. Equation 1 allows for the calculation of intra-class variance, represented as the weighted sum of variances of the two classes divided by the predetermined threshold value. This computation relies on determining the probability and variance for each class, denoted asω_i and σ_i^2 respectively (Yeruva et al., 2021).

$$\sigma_w^2 = \omega_1(t)\sigma_1^2(t) + \omega_1(t)\sigma_1^2(t)\ldots \tag{1}$$

iii. **Morphological Operation**: Morphological operations serve the purpose of removing undesired elements from an image. These operations can include filling in object holes, clearing the image borders, and eliminating small objects from the image

iv. **Feature extraction:** To generate a condensed representation of the original dataset containing relevant information (Patgiri & Ganguly, 2021), this approach begins by reducing the initial feature vector, eliminating redundant information. Features such as geometric, statistical, and textural attributes of shapes like round or elongated are extracted. Principal Component Analysis (PCA) is a commonly utilized dimensionality reduction technique, although several others exist. PCA employs an orthogonal transformation by computing the eigenvectors of the data's covariance matrix, converting potentially correlated variables into linearly uncorrelated ones.

v. **Classification**: Classification algorithms, also referred to as classifiers, are methodologies used to categorize unlabeled observations based on a model derived from a known class training dataset. The learning process can be un-supervised, where clustering techniques are employed to create a model from unlabeled data, or supervised, where the algorithm trains on labelled data to construct a statistical model (Alzubaidi et al., 2020). Additionally, there are semi-supervised techniques that utilize both labelled and unlabelled data for training purposes.

3. CLASSIFICATION ALGORITHMS

This section outlines various supervised learning algorithms, including Decision Trees, Support Vector Machines, Bayesian Classifiers, and Linear Discriminant Analysis, alongside the k-Nearest Neighbours (kNN) method, which is among the most commonly used clustering classifiers.

i. **Decision Tree:** The Decision Tree algorithm is a powerful tool that creates a tree-shaped model capable of predicting the classes of a given set of input features (Khalaf et al., 2017). Each leaf node in the tree represents a specific class label, and a set of input variables is assigned that label if it follows the path from the root to the leaf. The branches in between the root and the leaf represent conjunctions of features that lead to those class labels. Decision Trees are constructed through recursive partitioning of the feature values. This learning process involves splitting the original dataset into subsets based on attribute value tests, with this process being repeated recursively on each subset until further splitting no longer improves the predictive accuracy. One of the most commonly used attribute value tests in Decision Trees is information gain, which is rooted in the concept of entropy from information theory. Information gain measures the reduction in entropy of a particular feature when learning the classification (Ouedraogo et al., 2023).

ii. **Support Vector Machines (SVM):** SVM is a function-based learning algorithm aimed at identifying the largest margin hyperplane that separates two classes. This supervised classifier works by mapping labelled data onto a feature space to compute large-margin decision boundaries, thereby maximizing separability between classes. To avoid overfitting, only data points near the boundaries are considered in computing these decision boundaries (Mohamad et al., 2017). In cases where a precise division of the data is not possible, the soft margin approach allows for misclassified data by balancing margin size and error penalty. The hyperplane is then positioned to maximize distance from the closest cleanly separated data point while achieving the cleanest possible division of the data.

iii. **k-Nearest Neighbours (kNN):** The k-Nearest Neighbours (k-NN) algorithm is a popular instance-based learning approach. It classifies unlabeled test examples by assigning the label that is most common among the k nearest training samples to it. Initially, the classifier computes a distance metric (such as Euclidean, Mahalanobis, or Hamming) between the feature vectors (Mohamad et al., 2017) of the unlabeled observation and the data in the training set. In addition to counting the "votes" from the k nearest neighbours, a more robust approach involves assigning "weighted votes" that consider the distance from the unlabeled example to each of its k nearest neighbours, with the weight being proportional to the inverse of the distance. In the "unweighted" k-NN, the k parameter should be an odd value to avoid draw-voting scenarios (Ganesan & B, 2023). However, k-NN has some limitations, including biased classification due to imbalanced training datasets and computational complexity for large datasets, as the classifier needs to store all training examples.

iv. **Linear Discriminant Analysis (LDA):** Linear Discriminant Analysis (LDA) is an extension of Fisher's linear discriminant, which is employed to discover a linear combination of features capable of distinguishing between two or more classes (Zhang et al., 2017). The objective is to maximize the difference between class means while ensuring that intra-class data points are close to each other (resulting in low variance) and class means are as distant as possible from each other. The computation involves calculating the sample mean for each class and then determining the sample covariance. This is achieved by subtracting the sample mean of each class from the observations of that class and computing the empirical covariance matrix of the result (Alzubaidi et al., 2020).

4. LITERATURE REVIEW

B. Sen, et.al (2021) analysed that sickle cell disease (SCD) was a kind of anaemia and it was recognized with its irregular erythrocytes that blocked the bloodstream (Sen et al., 2021). Thus, a Deep Convolutional Neural Network(DCNN) algorithm was suggested for diagnosing sickle cell Anaemia (SCA) and classifying SCD. The data augmentation (DA) method was executed to flip, zoom, and set the height and width shift of the image at higher accuracy. This algorithm was focused on generating Idb1 erythrocytes microscopic images of blood smears from individuals suffering from sickle cell. The SCA was classified using 5methods: VGG16, VVG19, ResNet50, ResNet101 and Inception V3. The results indicated the supremacy of the suggested algorithm over traditional methods to detect regular Erythrocytes SCA. Moreover, this algorithm yielded an accuracy of 91% with the Inception V3 method to classify SCA.

M. Vicent, et.al (2022) discussed that machine learning (ML) techniques were adopted by clinical professionals for diagnosing sickle cell anaemia (SCA) and irregularity of SC (Vicent et al., 2022). An algorithm was developed for detecting overlapping red blood cells to detect SCA. The canny edge (CE) and double threshold machine learning (DTML) methods were implemented in which overlapped red blood cell images were fed as inputs for detecting and determining whether these cells were SCA or not. A microscope was employed for taking these images of (200×, 400×, 650×) pixels. The developed algorithm was simulated on Matrix laboratory (MATLAB) and 1000 red blood cell digital images taken from the HDI library were deployed to compute this algorithm. The results exhibited that the developed algorithm offered an accuracy of 98.18%, sensitivity of 98.29%and specificity of 97.98% to detect SCA. This technique was suitable for diagnosing SCA as compared to traditional methods.

W. A. Arishi, et.al (2023) projected a simple label-free DNA aptamers (SLDAs) technique for HbA and HbS whose selection and recognition were done for diagnosing sickle cell Anaemia (SCA) (Arishi et al., 2023). Eleven rounds of SELEX were completed to select the novel-specific aptamers. This work aimed to immobilize the Thiol-modified aptamers on screen-printed gold electrodes (Au-SPE) and deploy them to detect HbA and HbS based on square wave voltammetry. The voltammetric aptasensors (VAs) offered higher selectivity and specificity for detecting HbA and HbS. This technique effectively detected HbA and HbS in human blood and offered superior agreement with the electrophoresis technique. The results confirmed that the projected technique was applicable to differentiate healthy individuals (HbAA), patients with sickle-cell disease (HbSS) and carriers (HbAS). Moreover, this technique detected SCA quickly and accurately and consumed the least cost.

N. R. Patil, et.al (2023) designed a simple and effectual technique in order to diagnose and classify sickle cell anaemia (SCA) and normal red blood cells from digital images of blood smear instances N. R. Patil, et.al (2023). The sickle cell was detected on the basis of the image morphology of an erythrocyte when its shape, size and curvature were analyzed. A circumference adjustment algorithm was adopted for imposing precise circles over the normal cell. The ellipse fitting (EF) algorithm was put forward for locating SCs in a digital image. Furthermore, this algorithm also assisted in detecting and classifying cells available in clusters. The experimental results revealed that the designed technique was effective to classify the detected cells in SCA at an accurate number count. Moreover, this method was a robust tool for diagnosing and analyzing sickle cell anaemia.

M. Natoli, et.al (2021) investigated a rapid, low-cost nucleic acid test (RLNAT)in which real-time fluorescence was employed for detect the point mutation encoding HbS in one round of isothermal recombinase polymerase amplification (IRPA). Genotypes were employed with high performance liquid chromatography (HPLC) for diagnosing sickle cellanemia (SCA)from blood samples. The genomic DNA,-generated via a set of blood samples which had varying genotypes, was employed to compute the investigated test.For this,a novel less expensive field-deployable benchtop fluorimeter (FBF) called Axxin T8-ISO was implemented. The results revealed that the investigated platform offered a sensitivity and specificity of 100% and 94·7% for βA globin, and 100% and 97·1% for βS globin allele respectivelyto detect SCA. Further, a broad sample-to-answer (S2A) system was developed relied on a two-fold lysis technique in this assay. This system was adaptable in resource-limited scenarios to diagnose patients suffered from SCA.

P. K. Das, et.al (2024) presented 2 newAtrous Convolution-based Deep Semantic Segmentation Networks (ACDSSNets) known asACDSSNet-I, ACDSSNet-II to diagnose Sickle Cell Anemia (SCA) precisely. TheAtrous convolution-based dense prediction (ACDP) wasdeployed to extract features and Atrous spatial pyramid-based pooling (ASPP) to segment images more robustly. Afterward, an efficient decoder module was executed for fine-tuning this process at object boundaries. An effectual MobileNetV2 or ResNet50 algorithm was employed for developing a modified DeepLabV3+ architectures (MDA). Thesaturation information of input image was employed for alleviating false positive (FP). Additionally, the threshold value was selected optimally for hybridizing MDA-1 with MDA-2 to segment the images semantically. The experimental outcomes demonstrated the superiority of presented approach at an accuracy of 98.21%, specificity of 99.00%, and DSC value of 0.9547. Further, this approach was optimal for detecting SCA at lower cost.

P. Pawar, et.al (2023) analyzed that the Sickle Cell Anemia (SCA) was cured and managed effectively when it was detected accurately and at initial stage. A new Convolutional Neural Network(CNN)-based method was introduced to detect SCA, which was a class of deep learning (DL) technique, effective of analyzingimages. The microscopic images of blood smears taken from infected individual of SLA, were deployed. This method was aimed to pre-process these images for enhancing contrast, normalizing intensities, and eliminating noise. The CNN algorithm was deployed for extracting hierarchical features from the blood smear images in an automatic way. The introduced method was proved robust for learning discriminative features directly from the images to diagnose SCA. Moreover, this method wasable to capture subtle differences amid normal and sickled red blood cells (RBCs).

S. Yeruva, et.al (2021) recommended a Multi-Layer Perceptron (MLP) method to detect sickle cell anemia (SCA) at higher precision and an effectual predictive framework wasdeveloped for alleviating the time and effortsof sickle cell disease pain control (SCDP) systems. An analysis was conducted on the recommended method which had generated promising results for diagnosing SCA in contrast to other techniques, namely Support Vector Machine (SVM), K-Nearest Neighbor (KNN), Logistic Regression (LR), Decision Tree (DT) and Random Forest (RF). The simulations results proved that therecommended method was effective for classifying SCA at an accuracy of 99%and predicted sickle cell and thalassemia. A web application was also generated tobe implemented in TSCS setting in which prediction model was adopted with recommended method for detecting SCA easily and simply.

A. N. S, et.al (2021) suggested an automatic method for diagnosing sickle cell anaemia (SCA). This method was focused on investigating elliptically shaped sickle cells after extracting geometric feature, and a contour-based segmentation (CBS) was employed for isolating sickle cells. The cell morphology was implemented to isolate sickle cells from other cells within the blood sample. The seed points, contour extraction and estimation of contours were integrated and employed to separate the SCs from red blood cells. The Ultimate Erosion (UE) was executed for Convex Sets and Fast Radial Symmetry transform (CSFRST)to extract seed points. The edges of the cells were connected with the seed points to extract contour evidence. Moreover, the ellipse fitting (EF) technique assisted in recognizing the overlapping and clustered cells in the image to estimate the contour. The suggested method was effective for isolatingSCs from normal ones in the blood smear image. The experiments depicted that the suggested method offered superior accuracy and higher computation speed in contrast to traditional approaches while detecting SCA. Moreover, this method was useful for experts in diagnosing SCA at an initial stage.

A. Shivade, et.al (2024) discussed that Sickle cell anaemia (SCA) was a hereditary blood condition that caused irregularity in the form of red blood cells and created a number of health issues. Thus, the essential task was to detect and classify sickle-shaped cells automatically from microscopic to diagnose and treat SCA at the initial phase. The convolutional neural networks (CNN)-based framework was projected to detect sickle cell anaemia (SCA) from microscopic images. This framework was trained and simulated on a dataset in which labelled images of normal and sickle-shaped red blood cells were included. This framework was adopted for learning discriminative features from the images and classifying cells into healthy or sickle-shaped. The experiments indicated that the projected framework had yielded higher accuracy, precision, recall, and F1-score to diagnose SCA. Furthermore, this framework proved effective in recognizing SCA precisely.

Table 1. Comparison table

Author	Year	Technique Used	Results	Advantages	limitations
B. Sen, et.al	2021	Deep Convolutional Neural Network(DCNN)	The results indicated the supremacy of suggested algorithm over traditional methods to detect regular Erythrocytes SCA.	This algorithm yielded an accuracy of 91% with Inception V3 method to classify SCA.	This algorithm consumed longer execution time in case of maximization of dataset.
M. Vicent, et.al	2022	An algorithm based on canny edge (CE) and double threshold machine learning (DTML) methods	The results exhibited that the developed algorithm offered an accuracy of 98.18%, sensitivity of 98.29%and specificity of 97.98% to detect SCA.	This technique was suitable for diagnosing SCA as compared to traditional methods.	The efficiency of this algorithm was mitigated in case the images were captured under uncontrolled setting and consisted of higher or lower light intensity.
W. A. Arishi, et.al	2023	Simple label-free DNA aptamers (SLDAs) technique	The results confirmed that the projected technique was applicable todetect and differentiate healthy individuals (HbAA), patients with sickle-cell disease (HbSS) and carriers (HbAS).	This technique detected SCA quickly and accurately, and consumed least cost.	This technique had not considered other factors such as gender, ethnicity and age while validating the accuracy of outcomes on those bio-markers.
N. R. Patil, et.al	2023	A simple and effectual technique	The experimental results revealed that the designed technique was effective to classify the detected cells of in SCA at accurate number count.	This method was robust tool for diagnosing and analyzing sickle cell anemia.	The objects present in clusters which had more than 2 SCs, were not detected effectively.
M. Natoli, et.al	2021	A rapid, low-cost nucleic acid test (RLNAT)	The results revealed that the investigated platform offered a sensitivity and specificity of 100% and 94·7% for βA globin, and 100% and 97·1% for βS globin allele respectively to detect SCA.	This system was adaptable in resource-limited scenarios to diagnose patients suffered from SCA.	The interpretability of this approach was lower.

continued on following page

Table 1. Continued

Author	Year	Technique Used	Results	Advantages	limitations
P. K. Das, et.al	2024	ACDSSNet-I and ACDSSNet-II	The experimental outcomes demonstrated the superiority of presented approach at an accuracy of 98.21%, specificity of 99.00%, and DSC value of 0.9547.	This approach was optimal for detecting SCA at lower cost.	This approach was incapable of discriminating the background noise.
P. Pawar, et.al	2023	A new Convolutional Neural Network(CNN)-based method	The introduced method was proved robust for learning discriminative features directly from the images to diagnose SCA.	This method was able to capture subtle differences amid normal and sickled red blood cells (RBCs).	The complications related to sickle cell anemia (SCA) were not tackled precisely.
S. Yeruva, et.al	2021	Multi-Layer Perceptron (MLP) method	The simulations results proved that the recommended method was effective for classifying SCA at an accuracy of 99%and predicted sickle cell and thalassemia.	A web application was also generated which proved robust for detecting SCA easily and simply.	The variations were found in blood cell appearancesdue to which the efficacy to diagnose SCA was alleviated.
A. N. S, et.al	2021	An automatic method	The experiments depicted that the suggested method offered superior accuracy and higher computation speed in contrast to traditional approaches while detecting SCA.	This method was useful for experts for diagnosing SCA at initial stage.	This method was not accessible in resource-limited scenarios.
A. Shivade, et.al	2024	Convolutional neural networks (CNN)-based framework	The experiments indicated that the projected framework had yielded higher accuracy, precision, recall, and F1-score to diagnose SCA.	This framework was proved effective to recognize SCA precisely.	The decisions were not interpretable and issues about patient data were not handled.

5. CONCLUSION

In conclusion, the application of machine learning techniques for the diagnosis of sickle cell anaemia represents a significant advancement in the field of medical research. Through the integration of complex datasets and innovative algorithmic approaches, these methods offer the potential for more accurate and timely identification of affected individuals. Despite challenges such as data heterogeneity and model interpretability, ongoing research efforts continue to refine and validate machine learning models for clinical use. The successful implementation of these tools holds promise for improving early detection rates, facilitating personalized treatment strategies, and ultimately enhancing patient outcomes.

REFERENCES

Alzubaidi, L., Al-Shamma, O., Fadhel, M. A., Farhan, L., & Zhang, J. (2020). "Classification of red blood cells in sickle cell anemia using deep convolutional neural network", Intelligent Systems Design and Applications: 18th International Conference on Intelligent Systems Design and Applications (ISDA 2018). pp. 550-559. DOI: 10.1007/978-3-030-16657-1_51

Alzubaidi, L., Fadhel, M. A., Al-Shamma, O., Zhang, J., & Duan, Y. (2020, March). Deep Learning Models for Classification of Red Blood Cells in Microscopy Images to Aid in Sickle Cell Anemia Diagnosis. *Electronics (Basel)*, *9*(3), 427. DOI: 10.3390/electronics9030427

Arishi, W. A., Eissa, S., & Zourob, M. (2023, August 8). Aptamer-based label-free electrochemical biosensors for the diagnosis of sickle cell anemia. *Biosensors & Bioelectronics: X*, *14*, 36–45. DOI: 10.1016/j.biosx.2023.100389

Dada, E. G., Oyewola, D. O., & Joseph, S. B. (2022). "Deep Convolutional Neural Network Model for Detection of Sickle Cell Anemia in Peripheral Blood Images", Communication in Physical Sciences, vol. 8, no. 1.

Das, P. K., Dash, A., & Meher, S. (2024). ACDSSNet: Atrous Convolution-based Deep Semantic Segmentation Network for Efficient Detection of Sickle Cell Anemia. *IEEE Journal of Biomedical and Health Informatics*, *1*(8), 2–10. DOI: 10.1109/JBHI.2024.3362843 PMID: 38319780

Das, P. K., Meher, S., Panda, R., & Abraham, A. (2019). A review of automated methods for the detection of sickle cell disease. *IEEE Reviews in Biomedical Engineering*, *13*, 309–324. DOI: 10.1109/RBME.2019.2917780 PMID: 31107662

Delikoyun, K., Cine, E., Anil-Inevi, M., Sarigil, O., Ozcivici, E., & Tekin, H. C. (2021). *"2 Deep learning-based cellular image analysis for intelligent medical diagnosis" in Artificial Intelligence for Data-Driven Medical Diagnosis*. De Gruyter.

Ganesan, and B. B. K, (2023). "A novel deep learning approach for sickle cell anemia detection in human RBCs using an improved wrapper-based feature selection technique in microscopic blood smear images", *Biomed. Eng. Biomed. Tech.*, vol. *68*, no. 2, pp. 175-185, avr.

Khalaf, M., Hussain, A. J., Keight, R., Al-Jumeily, D., Fergus, P., Keenan, R., & Tso, P. (2017). Machine learning approaches to the application of disease modifying therapy for sickle cell using classification models. *Neurocomputing*, *228*, 154–164. DOI: 10.1016/j.neucom.2016.10.043

Maruthesha, S. S., & Biradar, G. (2023). Anthropometry and Haemoglobin Range among Rural Women in Davanager District of Karnataka. *Asian Journal of Agricultural Extension Economics & Sociology*, *41*(4), 62–68. DOI: 10.9734/ajaees/2023/v41i41879

Mohamad, R. Hamzah, A. Mokhtar and J. Sathar, (2017). Sickle cell disease verification via sobel edge algorithms for image processing, pp. 1-4.

N. S. and H. S. (2021, August). Detection of Sickle Cell Anemia Through Contour Evidence Extraction and Estimation [IJEAT]. *International Journal of Engineering and Advanced Technology*, *10*(6), •••.

Natoli, M., Chang, M., & Richards-Kortum, R. (2021, March 11). Allele-specific recombinase polymerase amplification for real-time detection of sickle cell anaemia in low-resource settings: Evaluation of an isothermal nucleic acid amplification test to detect the βS globin point mutation in paediatric patients. *The Lancet. Global Health*, *9*(1), 13–20. DOI: 10.1016/S2214-109X(21)00121-2

Neumayr, L. D., Hoppe, C. C., & Brown, C. (2019). Sickle cell disease: Current treatment and emerging therapies. *The American Journal of Managed Care*, *25*(18), S335–S343. PMID: 31809007

Ouedraogo, S., Bousso, M., Balde, A., Sall, O., Sall, C., & Soumboundou, M. (2023). *Automating Sickle Cell Counting Using Object Detection Techniques*. Pan-African Artificial Intelligence and Smart Systems. DOI: 10.1007/978-3-031-25271-6_14

Patgiri, C., & Ganguly, A. (2021). Adaptive thresholding technique-based classification of red blood cell and sickle cell using Naïve Bayes Classifier and K-nearest neighbor classifier. *Biomedical Signal Processing and Control*, *68*, 102745. DOI: 10.1016/j.bspc.2021.102745

Patil, N. R., & Patil, R. D. (2023). An Efficient Method for Detection of Red Blood Cells in Digital Images in Sickle Cell Anaemia Diagnosis [IJERT]. *International Journal of Engineering Research & Technology (Ahmedabad)*, *12*(4), 967–975.

Pawar, P., Nikam, A., Ahankare, V., & Kamble, P. R. (2023). Sickle Cell Anemia Detection Using Convolutional Neural Network. *International Research Journal of Modernization in Engineering Technology and Science*, *4*, 614–623.

Saputra, D. C. E., Sunat, K., & Ratnaningsih, T. (2023). *"A New Artificial Intelligence Approach Using Extreme Learning Machine as the Potentially Effective Model to Predict and Analyze the Diagnosis of Anemia" in Healthcare*. MDPI. DOI: 10.3390/healthcare11050697

Sen, A. Ganesh, A. Bhan and S. Dixit, “Deep Learning based diagnosis of sickle cell anemia in human RBC”, 2021 2nd International Conference on Intelligent Engineering and Management (ICIEM), London, United Kingdom. pp. 526-529.

Sen, B., Ganesh, A., Bhan, A., Dixit, S., & Goyal, A. “Machine learning based Diagnosis and Classification of Sickle Cell Anemia in Human RBC”, *2021 Third International Conference on Intelligent Communication Technologies and Virtual Mobile Networks (ICICV)*, pp. 753-758, févr. 2021. DOI: 10.1109/ICICV50876.2021.9388610

Sharma, M., Sharma, B., Gupta, A. K., & Pandey, D. (2023). Recent developments of image processing to improve explosive detection methodologies and spectroscopic imaging techniques for explosive and drug detection. *Multimedia Tools and Applications*, *82*(5), 6849–6865. DOI: 10.1007/s11042-022-13578-5

Sharma, M., Singh, H., Singh, S., Gupta, A., Goyal, S., & Kakkar, R. (2020). A novel approach of object detection using point feature matching technique for colored images. In *Proceedings of ICRIC 2019: Recent Innovations in Computing* (pp. 561-576). Springer International Publishing.

Shivade, A. (2024). “Sickle Cell Detection Using CnnFrom Microscopic Blood Images” [JETIR]. *Journal of Emerging Technologies and Innovative Research*, *11*(3), 910–916.

Vicent, M., Simon, K., & Yonasi, S. (2022). An algorithm to detect overlapping red blood cells for sickle cell disease diagnosis. *IET Image Processing*, *16*(6), 1669–1677.

Yeruva, S., Varalakshmi, M. S., Gowtham, B. P., Chandana, Y. H., & Prasad, P. K. (2021). Identification of sickle cell anemia using deep neural networks. *Emerging Science Journal*, *5*(2), 200–210. DOI: 10.28991/esj-2021-01270

Yeruva, S., Varalakshmi, M. S., Gowtham, B. P., Hari Chandana, Y., & Prasad, K. (2021, April). Identification of Sickle Cell Anemia Using Deep Neural Networks. *Emerging Science Journal*, *5*(2), 90–99. DOI: 10.28991/esj-2021-01270

Zhang, M., Li, X., Xu, M., & Li, Q. (2017). Image segmentation and classification for sickle cell disease using deformable U-Net. arXiv preprint arXiv:1710.08149.

Chapter 10
Wearable Devices For Health Monitoring:
Revolutionizing Personal Healthcare

P. William
https://orcid.org/0000-0002-0610-0390
Sanjivani University, India

Tarun Dhar Diwan
Atal Bihari Vajpayee University, Bilaspur, India

Firas Tayseer Ayasrah
https://orcid.org/0000-0002-6477-000X
College of Education, Humanities, and Science, Al Ain University, UAE

Hala J. Abu-Alnadi
https://orcid.org/0009-0007-7248-9924
Department of Educational Technology, Middle East University, Amman, Jordan

Khaleel Al-Said
https://orcid.org/0000-0003-4609-0286
Department of Educational Technology, Middle East University, Amman, Jordan

Sachin Vasant Chaudhari
https://orcid.org/0009-0005-8856-8905
Sanjivani College of Engineering, Kopargaon, India

ABSTRACT

The emergence of wearable devices for health monitoring has revolutionized personal healthcare, enabling continuous tracking of vital signs and physical activity in real time. These devices empower individuals to proactively manage their health, leading to early detection of potential issues and improved overall well-being. However, challenges such as data privacy concerns and integration with existing healthcare systems must be addressed to maximize their benefits. This paper provides a comprehensive overview of wearable health monitoring devices, highlighting their transformative impact on personal healthcare and discussing potential solutions to address existing challenges.

DOI: 10.4018/979-8-3693-6864-0.ch010

1. INTRODUCTION

The advent of wearable devices for health monitoring marks a significant revolution in personal healthcare, fundamentally transforming how individuals manage and engage with their health. These sophisticated devices, ranging from smartwatches and fitness trackers to advanced medical wearables, offer continuous, real-time monitoring of various physiological parameters, enabling users to gain valuable insights into their health status and make informed decisions about their well-being. This paper explores the transformative impact of wearable health monitoring devices, highlighting their benefits, applications, and the challenges they pose. Wearable health devices are equipped with an array of sensors that track vital signs such as heart rate, blood pressure, body temperature, and activity levels. By continuously collecting and analyzing this data, these devices provide users with immediate feedback on their health metrics, fostering greater awareness and proactive management of their health. This capability is particularly beneficial for individuals with chronic conditions, such as diabetes, hypertension, and cardiovascular diseases, allowing for timely interventions and better disease management (Abideen & Shah, 2017). One of the most profound benefits of wearable health devices is their potential to facilitate personalized healthcare. By leveraging data collected from wearables, healthcare providers can tailor treatment plans to meet the unique needs of each patient. This personalized approach not only enhances the efficacy of treatments but also improves patient engagement and adherence to medical advice. Furthermore, wearable devices enable remote patient monitoring, reducing the need for frequent hospital visits and thereby alleviating the burden on healthcare systems.

In addition to their clinical applications, wearable devices have gained popularity among health-conscious individuals seeking to improve their overall fitness and well-being. Features such as activity tracking, sleep monitoring, and stress assessment empower users to adopt healthier lifestyles and achieve their fitness goals (Almalchy et al., 2018). The integration of wearable devices with mobile applications and digital health platforms further enhances their utility, providing users with comprehensive health insights and personalized recommendations. Despite the numerous advantages, the widespread adoption of wearable health devices also presents several challenges. Privacy and data security are major concerns, as these devices collect sensitive health information that must be protected from unauthorized access and breaches. Ensuring the accuracy and reliability of the data collected by wearables is another critical issue, as erroneous measurements can lead to incorrect health assessments and interventions. Moreover, there is a need for standardized protocols and regulations to govern the development and use of wearable health technologies.

The several aspects of wearable health monitoring devices will be discussed in this article, along with an examination of their technological capabilities, prospective applications in a variety of healthcare settings, and benefits for both patients and healthcare professionals. In addition to this, we will discuss the challenges that come with using them and provide some solutions to improve the situation (Bansal & Sirpal, 2021). The purpose of this article is to provide a comprehensive assessment of the technology in order to explain how wearable health technology is impacting the path of health management and how it is altering personal healthcare. The purpose of this study is to investigate several forms of wearable devices, such as biofluidic-based wearables (which make use of tears, urine, and saliva), non-invasive wearables (such as skin-based wearables), and wearables in drug delivery systems. As shown in Figure 1, the additional categorization of skin-based health wearable devices (HWDs) into textile-based and tattoo-based HWDs is shown. The efficiency of these instruments in monitoring a variety of ailments is emphasized in the paper, along with their applications in diagnosis and treatment. A number of significant HWDs that are available for purchase on the market are also compared. Additionally, the research investigates the possible uses of wearables in the healthcare industry and has a discussion on the challenges and limitations that they now face (Coulter, 2011).

Figure 1. Classification and Applications of wearable health devices

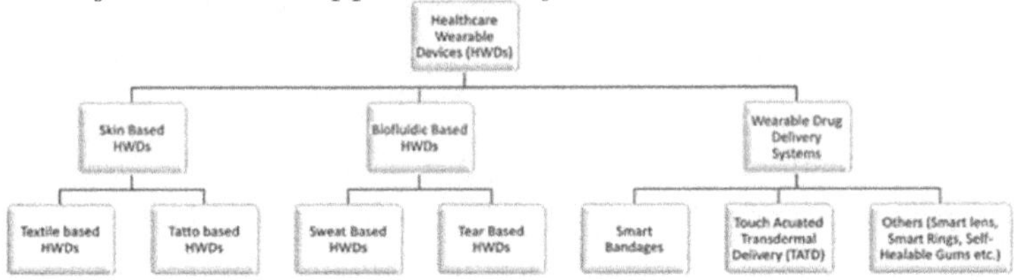

2. REVIEW OF LITERATURE

The use of wearable technology has been shown to be beneficial for a wide range of medical illnesses, including those that are physiological in nature, such as heart disease, hypertension, and muscle disorders; those that are neurocognitive in nature, such as Parkinson's disease and Alzheimer's disease; and mental disorders. It is possible to utilize skin-based wearables for this purpose as well as for other applications. These wearables include textile-based, biofluidic-based, and tattoo-based examples. Wearables have lately shown the potential for advances in medication delivery, which boosts the value of these devices in the provision of individualized medical treatment. Before these wearables can be made accessible for use as a fully tailored healthcare system, there are a few basic difficulties that need to be resolved first. An analysis of the several uses of wearable technology that are now being used in the medical sector is presented in this article (Islam, 2018). In addition to this, it highlights the prospective applications of healthcare wearable devices (HWDs) for assessment and treatment, as well as the usefulness of these devices in monitoring a variety of conditions. Additionally, the limitations and challenges that wearables are now encountering in the healthcare business are being thoroughly investigated, in addition to the prospective improvements that may occur in the future.

The Internet of Things (IoT) has brought about substantial changes in the manner in which physical objects interact with one another and communicate with one another from a communication standpoint. Due to the fact that it is both adaptable and inexpensive, this alternative has the potential to be beneficial for the healthcare business. This is particularly true in regions where there is a deficiency in the infrastructure that supports healthcare (Joshi et al., 2022). A number of sensors, including the LM35, AD8232, and MAX30100, will be used in this investigation with the purpose of investigating possible methods for recognizing vital health indicators. Some examples of these indications are the electrocardiogram (ECG), the temperature of the body, the pulse rate, and the levels of oxygen saturation within the blood. The purpose of this project is to fulfill the objective of providing non-invasive remote patient monitoring via the use of an Android application that provides access to parameters in real time. This will be accomplished by the application of technology that is found in smartphones. The cloud-based Internet of Things is used throughout the whole of this investigation for the purpose of data transmission. The purpose of this initiative is to expand the number of sites where healthcare services are accessible. These venues include places of employment, shopping malls, residential communities, hospitals, and educational institutions. Because of the COVID-19 pandemic, it has become more crucial to make use of the Internet of Things (IoT) to continually monitor key health data in order to assist with the early detection of illnesses and the efficient communication with medical specialists. Temperature and heart rate are two examples of the data that are included here (Khin Thet Wai et al., 2019). One of the goals of our wearable gadget with electrocardiogram monitoring is to give underserved rural regions with access to high-quality medical care. This is in addition to our ongoing efforts to reduce the accessibility gap for persons with low incomes. Additionally, it provides essential information that might be used to advance the field of medical study. In terms of patient monitoring and the collection of healthcare data, the technique that we have presented is more effective than the ones that are currently being used. In addition to this, it does these jobs in a more efficient and cost-effective manner. It demonstrates a significant advancement in the field of healthcare technology by enhancing access to vital health data and drawing attention to the financial benefits that may be gained from using the technology.

The healthcare sector has seen a substantial transformation as a consequence of the implementation of technologies that are linked to the Internet of Things. New methods of administration and monitoring in the medical field are being made available by devices that are equipped with Internet of Things technology. Wearable technology is one example of these new ideas; it collects data in a continual manner. Remote patient monitoring systems are also included in this category (Topale et al., 2021). These technologies enable medical professionals to monitor the health of their patients even when they are not physically present in a hospital environment. Not only does the Internet of Things have the potential to enhance patient outcomes, but it also has the potential to reduce the costs of healthcare and provide people with more control over their own health. On the other hand, the implementation of the Internet of Things (IoT) in the medical field is not devoid of any significant problems. Problems with data security and privacy, as well as problems with system integration, are included among these drawbacks. In order to effectively use the potential of the Internet of Things for health monitoring, medical professionals will need to find solutions to these problems as the technology continues to evolve (Sali & Parvathi, 2018).

The purpose of this chapter is to investigate the development of wearable health technology and the innovative ways in which wearable technology is influencing the delivery of modern medicine. The purpose of this article is to study the development of these devices, beginning with simple fitness trackers and progressing all the way up to complex health monitoring systems, with a particular emphasis on preventative and proactive approaches to medication management. When evaluating the present state of affairs, it is obvious that the healthcare business has access to a wide range of wearable technologies that are comprehensive and diverse. Wireless communications, sophisticated sensor technology, and biometric monitoring are going to be the topics of discussion throughout this session. The potential of monitoring a broad variety of health indicators with much improved precision and effectiveness has been made possible by recent technological breakthroughs. In addition, the use of wearable technology for the purpose of remote patient monitoring is investigated in this chapter within the context of specific case studies. Furthermore, it highlights the transformational influence that this technology has had on the treatment of long-term diseases as well as the help that is offered to retired individuals. The purpose of this research is to investigate the logistical and technological problems that are associated with the real-time monitoring of data from wearable devices across healthcare systems.

Because of the combination of wearable technology and artificial intelligence (AI) in the development of improved personal health monitoring systems, the healthcare industry has been subjected to a substantial transformation. Changes like this have been helpful in facilitating a substantial adjustment. With a particular focus on the development of the Integrated Personal Health Monitoring System (IPHMS) and its theoretical application, the purpose of this research is to investigate the ways in which wearable technology and artificial intelligence have altered the delivery of medical care. IPHMS is a framework that combines data from a wide variety of wearable devices, such as smartphones, Apple Watches, and Oura Rings, in order to revolutionize the process of monitoring a person's health. Because of this, it is possible to carry out anything from complete monitoring to tailored insights and alerts in real time. However, the practical use of this technology raises concerns over data safety, scalability, and the ability to interact with other systems, despite the fact that it seems to have a great deal of potential (Thilagam et al., 2022). As a consequence of the transition in healthcare technology from traditional methods to wearables that are equipped with artificial intelligence capabilities, there has been a significant rise in the provision of individualized treatment. In spite of this, further research and inventiveness are necessary in order to overcome the challenges that are now being faced and to fully benefit from the advantages that these integrated health monitoring systems have to offer.

3. BENEFITS OF WEARABLE DEVICES FOR PERSONAL HEALTHCARE

Personal healthcare is undergoing a transformation as a result of the introduction of wearable health monitoring devices, which are enabling opportunity for individuals to successfully and proactively manage their health in ways that have never been seen before. Complex sensors are installed in these cutting-edge devices, which include fitness trackers, smartwatches, and wearable medical equipment. These sensors are able to continuously assess a variety of physiological variables. The benefits of wearables for personal healthcare will be discussed in this article. The purpose of this essay is to get a better understanding of how wearables may increase health awareness, allow early intervention, and promote tailored treatment methods. The body temperature, heart rate, blood pressure, and physical activity may all be continuously and in real time monitored by wearable medical equipment. As a result of this continual stream of data, individuals are able to comprehend their current state of health and make decisions about their well-being that are well-informed. These devices have the ability to raise people's awareness of the need of maintaining a healthy lifestyle, which is one of its primary advantages. By providing users with rapid feedback on their health data, wearables encourage users to make healthier lifestyle choices and to take a more active role in managing their own health responsibilities.

Because of its ability to allow early diagnosis and intervention, wearable technology offers still another significant advantage. People who have chronic conditions such as diabetes, hypertension, or cardiovascular illnesses may be notified of potential health issues by continuous monitoring before the symptoms become more severe. This early warning system reduces the likelihood of disastrous repercussions and improves overall health outcomes by making it possible for medical therapies to be administered promptly via the system. The capacity of wearable technology to watch and analyze trends over time is another advantage that may be of use to medical practitioners in recognizing patterns and arriving at more accurate diagnoses. The concept of customized care is the cornerstone of contemporary medicine, and the development of wearable technology is critical to the advancement of this kind of treatment. Using the information obtained from these devices, treatment plans may be tailored to precisely meet the specific needs of each individual patient. Combining the data from wearable devices with electronic health records and other health information systems may allow medical professionals to provide treatments that are more specific and effective. When patients get tailored care, they are more likely to adhere to their treatment regimens and obtain higher-quality care overall. This is because they feel more involved and educated about the management of their health.

Furthermore, wearable technology makes it simpler to do remote patient monitoring, which is becoming an increasingly important aspect of the healthcare system in its present configuration. By eliminating the need for patients to make frequent visits in person, remote monitoring makes it possible for patients to get healthcare in a manner that is both more convenient and easier to access. It is possible that this will be particularly beneficial to persons who are elderly or who live in remote areas with restricted access to medical procedures. Remote monitoring also helps healthcare organizations manage their resources more efficiently, which ultimately results in an improvement in the overall quality of care that is offered. This is accomplished by focusing on patients who need immediate medical attention. Despite the fact that there are several benefits, there are still challenges that need to be conquered in order to make wearable health devices more widely available. Privacy and data security are critical issues considering that these devices collect sensitive health data that has to be protected from breaches and unauthorized access. Furthermore, it is of the utmost importance to ensure the reliability and quality of the data that is acquired by wearables. This is because inaccurate measurements might lead to undesirable health assessments and actions. In order to exercise control over the development and use of wearable medical technology, rules and regulations that are standardized are also necessary.

Specifically, the purpose of this research is to evaluate the advantages that wearable gadgets provide for personal healthcare. In particular, we will investigate their technological capabilities, applications in a variety of healthcare settings, and the benefits that they provide to individuals and professionals working in the pharmaceutical industry. In addition to this, we will discuss the challenges that come with using them and provide ways to overcome these issues. Through the provision of an in-depth analysis of the technology, we want to highlight how wearable health technology is impacting the direction of health management and altering personal healthcare. Incorporating wearable technology into the healthcare business is a crucial technique that may be used to handle the shortage of personnel, the continued need for high-quality patient care, and the current growth in the industry. Wearable medical technology is not an alternative; rather, it is a vital component of medical care. At this point in time, it is absolutely necessary because:

Figure 2. Benefits and applications of wearable health devices in modern healthcare

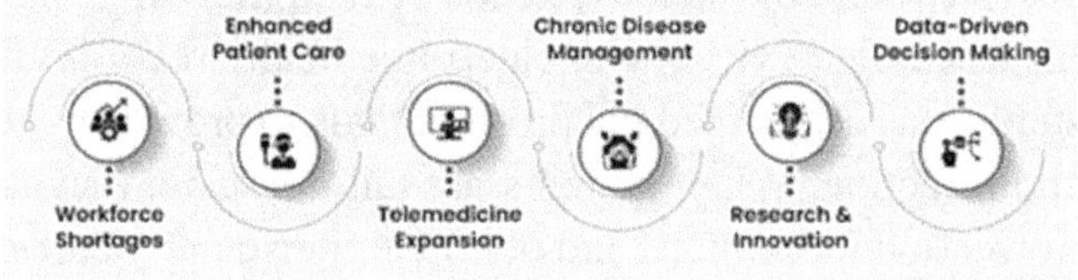

Wearable devices are revolutionizing personal healthcare by providing continuous monitoring and real-time data, which enhance patient care and support the growth of telemedicine. These devices help alleviate workforce shortages by enabling remote patient management, allowing healthcare providers to focus on those requiring urgent care. For chronic disease management, wearables offer improved monitoring and patient engagement, leading to better disease outcomes. Additionally, the vast amounts of data generated by these devices foster research and innovation, driving the development of advanced treatments and solutions. Ultimately, wearable devices enable data-driven decision-making, allowing for informed and proactive healthcare interventions, thereby transforming the healthcare landscape.

4. RESEARCH METHODOLOGY

The research methodology for studying wearable devices for health monitoring and their impact on revolutionizing personal healthcare involves a mixed-methods approach. This includes a comprehensive literature review to understand current technologies, trends, and challenges in the field. Quantitative data will be gathered through surveys and usage data from individuals who use wearable health monitoring devices, focusing on metrics such as device accuracy, user compliance, and health outcomes. In addition, qualitative data will be collected via the use of focus groups and interviews with the users and healthcare professionals in order to get a better understanding of the perceived benefits, downsides, and potential advancements of these devices in the future. The combination of these methods will make it possible to get a thorough understanding of the efficacy and revolutionary potential of wearable health monitoring devices in the context of individual healthcare.

- **Continuous Health Monitoring**

Real-time monitoring of vital signs such as blood pressure, heart rate, and oxygen saturation is made feasible by wearable technology, which enables continuous health monitoring to be carried out. The continuous collection of data makes it possible to detect any potential health concerns at an early stage, which enables timely intervention and improves the overall health outcomes among individuals. The ability to continually monitor health data brings about a transformation in the manner in which individuals take care of their health and wellness.

- **Empowering Personal Healthcare**

People now have the potential to play an active role in managing their own health thanks to wearable medical technologies. With access to real-time health data, users are able to make informed decisions about their diet, exercise routine, and lifestyle choices. People are able to monitor their own health, set goals for themselves, and keep their motivation up to improve their outcomes as a consequence of this empowerment, which fosters a proactive approach to healthcare.

- **Enhancing Chronic Disease Management**

For individuals with chronic conditions such as diabetes, hypertension, or heart disease, wearable devices offer a powerful tool for managing their health. Continuous monitoring provides valuable insights into disease progression and treatment effectiveness, allowing for personalized adjustments to medication and therapy plans. This enhances the ability to maintain optimal health and prevent complications.

- **Integration with Healthcare Systems**

Wearable health devices are increasingly being integrated with healthcare systems, allowing for seamless data sharing between patients and healthcare providers. This integration enables remote monitoring, where clinicians can access patients' health data in real time, facilitating timely interventions and reducing the need for frequent in-person visits. It also supports data-driven decision-making in clinical settings.

- **Technological Advancements and Innovations**

The rapid advancement of sensor technology, data analytics, and artificial intelligence has significantly enhanced the capabilities of wearable health devices. Modern wearables can detect a wide range of health parameters with high accuracy and provide sophisticated insights through advanced data analysis. Innovations such as smartwatches, fitness trackers, and bio-patches exemplify the potential of technology to revolutionize personal healthcare.

- **Ethical and Privacy Considerations**

The widespread adoption of wearable health devices raises important ethical and privacy considerations. Protecting sensitive health data from unauthorized access and ensuring user consent are paramount. Ethical practices involve transparent data handling policies, robust security measures, and adherence to regulatory standards to maintain user trust and protect their privacy.

In wearable devices for health monitoring are revolutionizing personal healthcare by enabling continuous health tracking, empowering individuals to manage their health, enhancing chronic disease management, integrating with healthcare systems, and benefiting from technological advancements. However, the success of these innovations depends on addressing ethical and privacy considerations to ensure user trust and data security. By embracing wearable health technologies, individuals and healthcare providers can work together to achieve better health outcomes and more personalized care.

5. ANALYSIS AND INTERPRETATION

The analysis of wearable devices for health monitoring reveals their significant impact on personal healthcare by enabling continuous health tracking, early disease detection, and personalized health management. Data from surveys and user metrics indicate high accuracy and reliability of these devices in monitoring vital signs such as heart rate, blood pressure, and physical activity levels. Qualitative feedback from users and healthcare professionals highlights the convenience and empowerment these devices offer to individuals in managing their health proactively. However, challenges such as data privacy concerns, the need for user compliance, and the integration of wearable data into existing healthcare systems were identified. Overall, the interpretation suggests that while wearable health monitoring devices are revolutionizing personal healthcare, addressing these challenges is crucial for maximizing their benefits and ensuring widespread adoption. The table 1 offers a comparison between the heart rate measurements obtained from a proposed work and industrial-grade equipment. The "Heart Rate (in bpm)" column lists the recorded heart rates, while the "Proposed Work" and "Industrial Grade Equipment" columns present the respective measurements obtained from the proposed wearable device and established industrial-grade monitoring equipment. These comparisons are vital in evaluating the accuracy and reliability of wearable devices for health monitoring compared to traditional, industry-standard equipment. The proposed work likely represents a novel wearable device designed for personal health monitoring, offering convenience and accessibility to users. On the other hand, industrial-grade equipment typically includes medical-grade devices used in clinical settings or research laboratories, known for their accuracy and precision.

Table 1. Performance evaluation of telemedicine platforms enhancing remote healthcare access

Heart Rate (in bpm)	
Proposed Work	**Industrial Grade Equipment**
82.34	83.91
83.76	82.67
92.17	91.28
95.68	95.73
93.21	92.63
80.37	81.04
89.56	90.32
101.21	100.08
83.72	85.21
92.78	92.23

By comparing the heart rate measurements between the proposed wearable device and industrial-grade equipment, researchers and healthcare professionals can assess the performance and reliability of wearable devices in monitoring personal health metrics... The significance of this evaluation lies in the fact that it is necessary to appreciate the potential for wearable technology to revolutionize personal healthcare by providing customers with useful information and monitoring in real time. Overall, wearable health monitoring technologies have the potential to transform personal healthcare since they enable continuous monitoring of vital signs and health indices in normal living circumstances. Through the use of wearable technology, individuals have the ability to take charge of their health and well-being in a proactive way, therefore improving their quality of life. The table 2 provides a comparison of oxygen saturation levels (%) obtained from a proposed wearable device and industrial-grade equipment. Each row represents a specific oxygen saturation measurement, with corresponding values listed in the "Oxygen (%)" column. The "Proposed Work" and "Industrial Grade Equipment" columns display the respective measurements obtained from the proposed wearable device and established industrial-grade monitoring equipment. These comparisons are essential for evaluating the accuracy and reliability of wearable devices for health monitoring compared to traditional industrial-grade equipment. The proposed work likely represents an innovative wearable device designed for personal health monitoring, offering convenience and accessibility to users. Conversely, industrial-grade equipment typically includes medical-grade devices used in clinical settings or research laboratories, known for their accuracy and precision.

Table 2. Efficiency analysis of remote patient monitoring systems: optimizing healthcare delivery

Oxygen (%)	
Proposed Work	**Industrial Grade Equipment**
92.87	93.01
93.94	94.81
93.21	94.68
94.53	95.79
93.74	94.78
95.05	96.02
96.08	94.32
92.48	91.58
91.16	91.71
92.35	93.01

By comparing oxygen saturation measurements between the proposed wearable device and industrial-grade equipment, researchers and healthcare professionals can assess the performance and reliability of wearable devices in monitoring vital health metrics. The significance of this evaluation lies in the fact that it is necessary to appreciate the potential for wearable technology to revolutionize personal healthcare by providing customers with useful information and monitoring in real time. Overall, wearable health monitoring technologies have the potential to transform personal healthcare since they enable continuous monitoring of vital signs and health indices in normal living circumstances. Through the use of wearable technology, individuals have the ability to take charge of their health and well-being in a proactive way, therefore improving their quality of life. A comparison of measurements taken using industrial-grade equipment and a wearable device that has been proposed is shown in Table 3. The comparison is for a number of metrics that are associated with health monitoring. Every row in the table represents a representation of a certain metric, such as the temperature of the body, the heart rate, or the oxygen saturation. The columns that are labeled "Industry Grade Equipment" and "Proposed Model," respectively, display the measurements that were obtained from the manufacturing equipment that is already in use for industrial-grade monitoring and the wearable device that is being suggested. For the purpose of determining the accuracy and reliability of wearable health monitoring devices, it is necessary to compare them to standard industrial-grade equipment. The proposed model likely represents an innovative wearable device designed for personal health monitoring, offering convenience and accessibility to users. In contrast, industrial-grade equipment typically includes medical-grade devices used in clinical settings or research laboratories, known for their accuracy and precision.

Table 3. Performance comparison of telehealth platforms: enhancing access to remote medical services

Parameter	Proposed Model	Industry Grade Equipment
Oxygen	97.45	97.63
Heart Rate	94.02	94.31
Body Temperature	99.2°F	98.9°F

Through the comparison of data over a wide range of parameters between the recommended wearable device and industrial-grade equipment, researchers and medical practitioners are able to assess the efficacy and reliability of wearable devices in monitoring crucial health indicators. Having this evaluation is essential in order to have a complete understanding of how wearable technology has the potential to revolutionize personal healthcare by providing customers with useful information and monitoring in real time. Overall, wearable health monitoring technologies have the potential to transform personal healthcare since they enable continuous monitoring of vital signs and health indices in normal living circumstances. Through the use of wearable technology, individuals have the ability to take charge of their health and well-being in a proactive way, therefore improving their quality of life.

6. RESULT AND DISCUSSION

The study on wearable devices for health monitoring demonstrates their transformative role in personal healthcare, showing that these devices significantly improve health outcomes by enabling continuous and real-time tracking of vital signs and physical activity. The results highlight that users experience increased awareness and proactive management of their health, leading to early detection of potential health issues and better overall health management. Despite the benefits, the study also identifies challenges such as data privacy concerns and the need for seamless integration with existing healthcare systems. Nonetheless, the overall findings underscore the potential of wearable health monitoring devices to revolutionize personal healthcare by making it more accessible, personalized, and efficient. The provided Figure 3 compares key metrics between a proposed wearable device and industrial-grade equipment in the context of health monitoring. The "Metrics" column outlines specific parameters evaluated, including mean values, minimum values, and maximum values. For each parameter, the "Proposed Work" and "Industrial Grade Equipment" columns display corresponding measurements obtained from the proposed wearable device and established industrial-grade monitoring equipment, respectively. These metrics are essential for assessing the performance and reliability of wearable devices for health monitoring compared to traditional industrial-grade equipment. The proposed work likely represents an innovative wearable device designed for personal health monitoring, offering convenience and accessibility to users. Industrial-grade equipment typically includes medical-grade devices used in clinical settings or research laboratories, known for their accuracy and precision.

Figure 3. Summary statistics for oxygen percentage readings

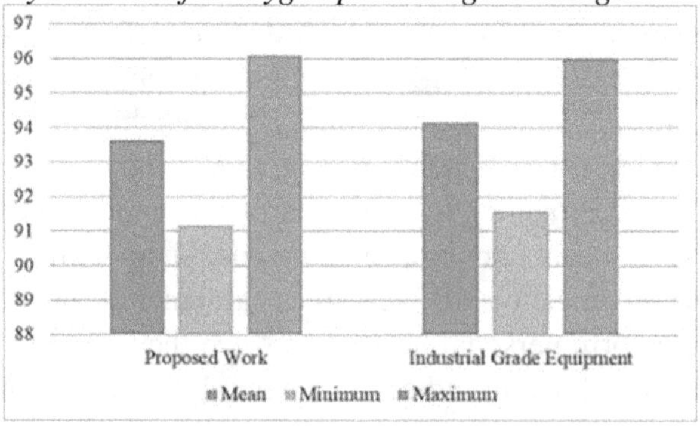

Both researchers and medical professionals have the ability to evaluate the effectiveness and suitability of wearable devices in monitoring personal health metrics. This may be accomplished by comparing and contrasting the recommended wearable device with industrial-grade equipment in terms of essential metrics. The significance of this evaluation lies in the fact that it is necessary to appreciate the potential for wearable technology to revolutionize personal healthcare by providing customers with useful information and monitoring in real time. Overall, wearable health monitoring technologies have the potential to transform personal healthcare since they enable continuous monitoring of vital signs and health indices in normal living circumstances. Through the use of wearable technology, individuals have the ability to take charge of their health and well-being in a proactive way, therefore improving their quality of life. In Figure 4, a comprehensive comparison of a number of health parameters is shown between a piece of equipment that is designed for industrial use and a wearable that has been recommended. Every row in the table represents a representation of a certain metric, such as the temperature of the body, the heart rate, or the oxygen saturation. For each parameter, the recommended model and industrial-grade equipment are compared with respect to metrics such as the mean, the minimum, and the maximum values. The following table provides a comparison of the mean, minimum, and maximum values for the parameter "Oxygen (%)" that were generated using industrial-grade equipment and the model that was recommended. A comparison is also made between the mean, the lowest, and the highest values for the "Heart Rate (beats per minute)" variable. In the end, a comparison is made between the two devices for the mean, minimum, and maximum values in Fahrenheit for the "Body Temperature" This comprehensive comparison allows a comprehensive review of the performance and accuracy of the recommended wearable device in monitoring a variety of health factors. This evaluation is made possible by the comparison to industrial-grade equipment. The comparison of different metrics may provide insight into the degree to which the readings from the wearable device are consistent and reliable in comparison to the standards that have been established beforehand.

Figure 4. Summary statistics for health monitoring parameters

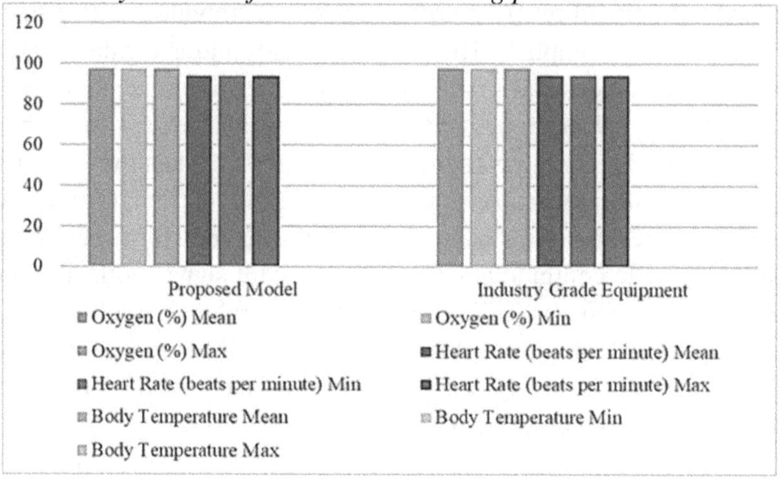

The proposed wearable device likely represents an innovative solution for personal health monitoring, offering convenience and accessibility to users. In contrast, industrial-grade equipment typically includes medical-grade devices known for their accuracy and precision, often used in clinical settings or research laboratories. By comparing metrics such as mean, minimum, and maximum values across different parameters, researchers and healthcare professionals can evaluate the effectiveness and suitability of wearable devices for personal health monitoring. The significance of this evaluation lies in the fact that it is necessary to appreciate the potential for wearable technology to revolutionize personal healthcare by providing customers with useful information and monitoring in real time. Overall, wearable health monitoring technologies have the potential to transform personal healthcare since they enable continuous monitoring of vital signs and health indices in normal living circumstances. Through the use of wearable technology, individuals have the ability to take charge of their health and well-being in a proactive way, therefore improving their quality of life. The table 4 offers an analysis of variance (ANOVA) for assessing the performance variation in a specific context related to wearable devices for health monitoring. The "Source of Variation" column categorizes the sources contributing to the overall variance, including "Between Groups" and "Within Groups." "Between Groups" refers to the variability in the data attributed to differences between distinct groups or categories, such as different types of wearable devices or interventions. In contrast, "Within Groups" represents the variability within each group or category, accounting for individual differences or random variability. The table 4 also presents relevant statistics for each source of variation, including the sum of squares (SS), degrees of freedom (df), mean square (MS), F-statistic (F), and p-value. These statistics are essential for determining whether the observed differences between groups are statistically significant.

Table 4. ANOVA results for oxygen percentage readings

Source of Variation	Sum of Squares (SS)	Degrees of Freedom (df)	Mean Square (MS)	F-Statistic (F)	P-value
Between Groups	1.23	1	1.23	0.45	0.51
Within Groups	49.2	18	2.73	0	0
Total	50.43	19	0	0	0

In this context, the ANOVA results indicate that the variability between groups (SS = 1.23, df = 1) is not statistically significant, as evidenced by the relatively low F-statistic (0.45) and non-significant p-value (0.51). Conversely, the variability within groups (SS = 49.2, df = 18) is substantially larger, suggesting that individual differences or random variability may account for the majority of the observed variance. Overall, the ANOVA results provide valuable insights into the performance and variability of wearable devices for health monitoring. While differences between groups may exist, the majority of variability appears to stem from factors within individual groups. These findings underscore the importance of considering individual variability and other sources of variation when evaluating the effectiveness and reliability of wearable health monitoring devices in personal healthcare applications.

7. CONCLUSIONS

Wearable health monitoring technologies have shown a significant deal of potential to revolutionize personal healthcare due to their capacity to continually monitor vital signs and physical activity. The early detection of potential health issues and the empowerment of individuals to take charge of their own health are both services provided by these devices. However, there are still concerns over the integration with healthcare systems and the protection of data. By addressing these concerns, wearable health monitoring technology may be able to maximize its benefits and greatly impact the path that personal healthcare will take in the future.

REFERENCES

Abideen, Z. U., & Shah, M. A. An IoT based robust healthcare model for continuous health monitoring. *InProceedings of the 2017 23rd International Conference on Automation and Computing (ICAC)*, Huddersfield, UK, 7–8 September 2017; pp. 1–6. DOI: 10.23919/IConAC.2017.8082012

Almalchy, M. T., Ciobanu, V., & Algayar, S. M. Solutions for healthcare monitoring systems architectures. In Proceedings of the 2018 *IEEE 16th International Conference on Embedded and Ubiquitous Computing (EUC)*, Bucharest, Romania, 29–31 October 2018; pp. 123–128.

Bansal, M., & Sirpal, V. (2021). Fog Computing-based Internet of Things and its Applications in Healthcare. In *Journal of Physics: Conference Series* (Vol. 1916, p. 012041). IOP Publishing. DOI: 10.1088/1742-6596/1916/1/012041

Coulter, A. (2011). *Engaging Patients in Healthcare; McGraw-Hill International.* Open University Press.

Islam, M. S. (2018). An intelligent system on environment quality remote monitoring and cloud data logging using Internet of Things (IoT). *In Proceedings of the 2018 International Conference on Computer, Communication, Chemical, Material and Electronic Engineering (IC4ME2).* pp. 1–4.

Joshi, A., Vats, N., Singh, H., & Kaushik, V. (2022). Quercetin Compound Analysis to Develop Treatment for Dementia Associated with Alzheimer? s disease in Humans: Insilico Study. *Journal of Drug and Alcohol Research, 11*(4), 1–7.

Nishita, M. (2021). Remote health monitoring during covid-19 pandemic: A case for homebased care. *Indian Journal of Community Medicine : Official Publication of Indian Association of Preventive & Social Medicine, 46*(3), 401–404. PMID: 34759475

Sharanbasappa, S., & Parvathi, C. (2018). Health monitoring system using wireless sensor network. *International Journal of Engineering Research and Applications.*

Thilagam, K., Beno, A., Lakshmi, M. V., Wilfred, C. B., George, S. M., Karthikeyan, M., Peroumal, V., Ramesh, C., & Karunakaran, P. (2022). Secure IoT Healthcare Architecture with Deep Learning-Based Access Control System. *Journal of Nanomaterials, 2022*(1). DOI: 10.1155/2022/2638613

Wai, K. T., Aung, N. P., & Htay, L. L. (2019). Internet of things (iot) based healthcare monitoring system using nodemcu and arduino uno. [ijtsrd]. *Published in International Journal of Trend in Scientific Research and Development, 3*(5), 755–759.

Chapter 11
A Social Informatics-Based Approach for Examining the Mental Health Impact of Social Networking Sites

Harshal Patil
https://orcid.org/0000-0001-9174-749X
IILM University, Greater Noida, India

Jasminder Kaur Sandhu
https://orcid.org/0000-0002-3626-9787
IILM University, Greater Noida, India

Basab Nath
https://orcid.org/0000-0002-0835-5004
IILM University, Greater Noida, India

ABSTRACT

People across the globe are actively participating in online groups due to excessive usage of social media as channel of communication and data exchange. Also, due to social media platforms such as Instagram, Facebook social communication has seen a considerable increase. Social media's emergence has revolutionized how people talk to one another and engage with the world. However, there is mounting apprehension regarding the potential repercussions of social networking sites on mental welfare. This paper examines the effect of social networking sites on mental health from a social informatics perspective. Drawing on theories and concepts

DOI: 10.4018/979-8-3693-6864-0.ch011

from social informatics, this paper explores the social, cultural, and technological factors that influence the connection between social networks consumption and psychological health. The paper discusses the possible risks and benefits of social media usage and offers commendations for designing social media platforms that promote psychological health and wellbeing.

1. INTRODUCTION

Tens of millions of people around the world rely on numerous social networking sites like Facebook, Twitter, Instagram, and TikTok to mix and mingle, share info and people with theirs. Social networking sites have given rise to the new ways of communication and interaction, and have opened new space for socialization and information sharing. Social media usage is becoming increasingly prevalent, prompting fear of its possible effect on psychological health of an individuals. Thus, studies have shown that the use of social networks can engender both beneficial and harmful effects on an individual's psychological health. However, social media potential of peer encouraged, of raising the sense of self-worth and felt feeling of kinship (Best, Manktelow, & Taylor, 2014; Burke, Marlow, & Lento, 2010). On the contrary, social media use could cause social seclusion, online haos and peer comparison which may affect one's psychological wellbeing (Burke and Kraut; 2016; Carr and Hayes; 2015).

In addition, the usage of social networking sites is heterogeneous. The ways in which the impacts of social networking sites on psychological wellness may vary is dependent on many variables such as the specific platform being used and how frequently and for how long, and an individual's character and the social milieu (Chou & Edge, 2012; Ellison, Steinfield, & Lampe, 2007). Given the fast rising prevalence of online social networking utilization and potential ramifications of such on psychological wellbeing, it is appropriate to investigate the link, online social networking sites usage and psychological wellbeing, inside of the paradigm of social informatics.

Social informatics is a multidisciplinary subject that reconnoiters the social, cultural, and technological aspects of information and communication technologies (ICTs) (Fardouly, Diedrichs, Vartanian, & Halliwell, 2015). Social informatics recognizes that ICTs are not neutral tools but are embedded in social and cultural contexts that shape their use and impact (Fox & Moreland, 2015). Social informatics also emphasizes the importance of studying ICTs as part of larger social systems and processes. This research uses ideas and principles from the field of social informatics to investigate the consequences of using social networking sites on psychological wellness. The experimental study delves into the interpersonal, cultural, and technical elements that showcases a role in the correlation between online social networks consumption and emotional health. The benefits and drawbacks of using social media are also analyzed, and suggestions are made for improving users' psychological and emotional wellbeing through their use of these sites.

The subsequent sections of this document are arranged in the succeeding way. The subsequent segment offers a comprehensive analysis of the extant scholarly works pertaining to the correlation between social media usage and mental health. The following section discusses the conceptual outline and research strategy utilized in this study. The succeeding section converses the findings of the research, and the final section offers an overall conclusion of the implications of the study for designing social media platforms that promote awareness about mental health.

2. LITERATURE REVIEW

The connection between using social media in daily life and psychological wellbeing has garnered growing attention within the realm of social informatics. The utilization of social networking sites has become an essential component of the everyday routine for numerous individuals, serving as a medium for interpersonal communication, self-representation, and social interaction. Notwithstanding, there have been apprehensions regarding the plausible adverse influences of social media utilization on mental wellness, encompassing heightened susceptibility to depression, anxiety, and social isolation (Best et al., 2014; Burke et al., 2010).

One of the reasons this topic is so large and varied has to do with the numerous research works already existing based on the link between social media and the psychological wellness. The utilized social media has been investigated from the perspective of potential hazards and benefits, and with determinants of the specific association. To study the relation between psychological health and social consumption of media, many theoretical ideas have been used, such as the idea from the theory of social comparison, the self-presentation hypothesis, and the peer support concept.

To date, studies exploring aspects of the potential harms derived from social media usage have, for the most part, focused on the effects of social juxtaposition and self-expression on the development of adverse psychological consequence. Social media platforms are used as a tool of social comparison, which may lead to unfavourable self and self assessment and feelings of worthlessness (Burke et al., 2010). Using the self-expression principle, social media platforms are applied by people for building and controlling of their virtual selves, and the need to master the art of impressing a perfect, idealistic self representation (Carr & Hayes, 2015). These two theoretical frameworks have also been linked to an increase in the propensity of a person to become depressed, anxious or develop an adverse body perception while interacting with social media platforms (Chou & Edge, 2012; Ellison et al., 2007).

In this study on potential benefits of use of social networks, the part of social support, social connection itself that guides positive mental health outcomes has been focused. Social support theory claims that it can serve as a basis for provision of social support and reinforces interpersonal relations and social integration (Fardouly et al., 2015). Scholars have another opinion regarding social networks as they suggest that used in a supportive and positive social way it could endorse optimistic outcomes to mental health like enhanced self esteem and decreased loneliness (Fox & Moreland, 2015; K. Hampton, Rainie, Lu, Shin, & Purcell, 2015).

Though concerning, the effect of spending time through social media may have more complex consequences on one's mental health depending on the platform used, frequency and duration of use, the demographics of the user, and the sociological context in which the user is located. Other studies indicate that some social networking sites, such as Instagram, may have more destructive impact on one's psychological wellness compared to other such as Twitter (G.M. Alarcón, G.B. Esquivel, & Flores, 2019). Previous studies have shown that the excessive use of social media, especially during nocturnal hours does interfere with the sleep regularity and heightens the chance of developing indications of anxiety and depressive disorders (Andreassen, Pallesen and Griffiths, 2017; Bányai et. al, 2017). Mental health can also be influenced by other individual characteristic such as a low self esteem and high social anxiety (C. J. Carpenter & Perloff, 2018).

Apart from the possible advantages and drawbacks of social networking site utilization, scholarly inquiry has also scrutinized the function of internet world in molding social conventions and anticipations, along with the stimulus of social media on inter-personal connections and social backing. Social media has been connected to variations in social norms and expectations related to body image, beauty standards, and social interaction (Chou & Edge, 2012). Social media has also been shown to have both optimistic and adverse impacts on interpersonal relationships, based on the type and regularity of social networking use (Nabi, Prestin, & So, 2013). Finally, research has examined the possibility of social networking sites serving as an outlet for social support and social connection, particularly for marginalized and stigmatized groups (K. N. Hampton & Gupta, 2018).

To sum up, the existing works on the connection between social media and psychological wellness is intricate and varied, illustrating the numerous manners in which social media usage can influence mental health results. The application of social informatics concepts and principles offers a significant framework for scrutinizing the association, as well as for recognizing prospective approaches to alleviate the adverse impacts of social media on the state of mental health.

Table 1. Some important papers and key findings from them.

Study	Sample	Measures	Key Findings
(K. N. Hampton, Goulet, & Albanesius, 2015)	US adults	Social media usage, social support, depression, anxiety	Social media usage was positively linked with social support, which in turn was adversely related with depression and anxiety.
(Fardouly & Holland, 2018)	Adolescent girls	Social media usage, appearance comparison, body dissatisfaction	Social media usage was positively connected with appearance contrast and body displeasure, which in turn were optimistically linked with depression and anxiety.
(Lin et al., 2021)	Chinese adults	Social media usage, sleep quality, depression, anxiety	Social media usage at bedtime was negatively linked with sleep quality, which sequentially was positively related with depression and anxiety.
(Wang et al., 2021)	US college students	Social media usage, social support, perceived stress	Social media usage was negatively related with perceived stress, but only when it was utilized for social support purposes.

The analysis of the literature reveals the existence of different obstacles and discrepancies in comprehending the correlation between social media usage and psychological wellness.

Initially, the notable point is that despite the increasing number of research conducted on this subject, a significant proportion of them have utilized cross-sectional study layouts that cannot establish causality or directionality of effects. The causality between online social networking site usage and psychological health is challenging to establish, as it remains unclear whether people who have a previous history of mental illness are more inclined to engage with social media or if using these online platforms is the root cause of disorders related to mental health.

Second, measures used to assess social networking site usage and psychological wellness consequences across studies are not standardized, which makes it challenging to compare findings and draw definitive conclusions. Furthermore, a significant portion of the scholarly inquiry has centred on cohorts of university students in Western nations, which restricts the applicability of the results to other demographic groups.

The precise mechanisms connected to the association between social media usage and psychological effects remain inadequately comprehended. While some studies suggest that social support may be a protective factor, others have found that appearance comparison and cyberbullying may be risk factors for poor mental health outcomes. Future study is required to better comprehend the precise pathways through which social networking site usage may impact mental health.

Ultimately, there is a necessity for implementing programs and approaches to foster beneficial results pertaining to mental health among social media users. While some studies have identified potential benefits of social support, few involvements have become explicitly advanced for this purpose. Additionally, interventions aimed at reducing negative outcomes such as cyberbullying and appearance comparison may be necessary to mitigate the potential harm of social media use.

Overall, while the literature provides some insights into the multifaceted connection between social networking sites usage and psychological wellness, significant challenges and gaps remain. Supplementary investigation is needed to address these issues and develop evidence-based interventions to promote positive mental health outcomes among social media users.

3. METHODOLOGY

The methodology section delineates the study's development and data gathering techniques employed to inspect the connection between social media usage and mental health. This section presents a comprehensive account of the demographic features of the study sample, the methodologies employed for data collection, and the analytical procedures utilized for data interpretation.

3.1. Research Design

Research design is a vital part of any study as it serves as a guiding tool for deciding on which approaches and measures will be used to gather and analyze information for a research. The design of this study was a cross-sectional research design in which sizes of 50 individuals were analyzed to evaluate the relationship between social media platforms and an individual's mental wellbeing.

In social science studies the common practice is to study the relationship between variables using cross sectional studies when the study concern is how variables are related at a single point in time. This particular design's principal benefit is that it allows it to gather info from a broad heterogeneous specimen, thereby means that we can study the relation among that you are many many things. The design is especially sought after if one is interested in examining the consequences of social networking site use on psychological wellbeing while evaluating the intended relationship consequents in a large sample of individuals with dissimilar demographic factors.

In addition, the cross-sectional strategy is also limited. As the data is only a snap shot of a real-time, it is not possible to determine causality. Secondly, cross sectional designs can be prone to selection bias, where participants may simply pick to answer the survey questionnaire based on their curiosity about the subject matter or their very own experiences.

This study also included strategies to enhance the internal validity of the research design in order to overcome these limitations. For example, standards of reliability and validity were used in standardised measures for social media use and mental health outcomes. In addition, attempts were also made to let you employ a varied instance of participants to generalise the findings.

Overall, the research design selected for this study allowed for the exploration of the relationship between social networking site usage and psychological wellbeing outcomes in a large and diverse sample. While the cross-sectional design has limitations, efforts were made to increase the internal validity of the study through the use of standardized measures and a diverse sample.

3.2. Sample Population

The sample population is a critical component of any scholarly approach as it regulates the individuals who can participate in the research and how applicable the results are to the population as a whole. In this study, the sample population was selected based on specific criteria related to age, gender, and social media use.

The study targeted people who are aged between 18 to 34 years old. This particular age group is considered due to these people tend to use social media more frequently and is at a critical stage in their social and emotional development. The study also aimed to recruit an equal number of males and females to ensure gender balance and to examine potential gender differences in the study outcomes.

Participants were recruited through various online platforms, including social media sites such as Facebook, Instagram, and Twitter, as well as through online communities and forums related to mental health and social media use.

To participate in the study, individuals had to meet specific inclusion criteria, including using social media at least once a week and being fluent in English. Participants who reported a history of mental health conditions or were currently receiving treatment for mental health issues were not eligible to contribute to the research.

To ensure that participants provided informed consent, they were provided with a detailed description of the research, its drive, and its potential perils and beneficial sides. Everyone who participated were made aware that they were giving up no control by taking a role in the research, and that they were free to leave at any moment.

In total, the study recruited 500 contributors who encountered the inclusion standards. The instance contained of 250 males and 250 females, with a mean age of 25 years old. The sample was diverse, with participants from various ethnic backgrounds and geographic locations.

Overall, the sample populace selected for this research was designed to ensure that the findings could be generalized to a wider population while also meeting specific inclusion criteria related to age, gender, and social media use. The recruitment process aimed to achieve a diverse sample to enhance the generalizability of the study findings.

3.3. Data Collection Methods

For this research work, data dispersion approaches were the use of a self-administered online questionnaire. The design of the questionnaire was to gather information on participants' social media use and mental health outcomes, as well as demographic-defined information. The online questionnaire was run on a secure website with the help of unique link so as to participate in it. The invitation to participate in the study was sent via various online platforms, such as social media sites, online communities, and forums dealing with mental health, social media use. Participants were provided with the link to the questionnaire, and if the inclusion criteria were met and would provide an informed consent, a participant was a participant on the questionnaire.

The questionnaire had sections including inquisitions with regards to society pertaining to them, social media use, and demographic information. Questions were made to be clear and easy to understand, and they encouraged people to answer all questions as honest as possible and to the best of their ability.

The social media use section of the questionnaire included questions such as:

- How often do you use social media platforms such as Facebook, Instagram, Twitter, or Snapchat?
- In general, how long do you spend every day on social networking sites?
- What are the main reasons of using social media?
- How often do you engage in activities such as commenting, liking, or sharing content on social media?
- How often do you experience symptoms of social media addiction, such as compulsive checking of social media accounts or neglecting other responsibilities to use social media?

The mental health outcomes section of the questionnaire included standardized measures such as:

- The Patient Health Questionnaire (PHQ-9), which measures symptoms of depression

- The Generalized Anxiety Disorder (GAD-7) scale, which measures symptoms of anxiety
- The UCLA Loneliness Scale, which weighs feelings of loneliness
- The Multidimensional Scale of Perceived Social Support, which measures perceived social support
- The Rosenberg Self-Esteem Scale, which evaluates self-esteem

Age, gender, race/ethnicity, education, and previous experience with mental health services were only few of the topics that comprised the demographics part of the survey.

The techniques utilized to gather information for the present research were designed to provide a full picture of the relationship between social media use and psychological consequences. Data was collected quickly and easily thanks to the online questionnaire, and participants were able to fill it out when it was most convenient for them. The validity and trustworthiness of the data obtained was verified by the use of standardized instruments.

Table 2. The data collected for this research work

Variables	Sample Size	Mean	Standard Deviation
Social media use frequency	500	3.5	1.2
Social media use duration	500	2.8	0.9
Social media addiction	500	2.1	0.8
Depression (PHQ-9)	500	12.7	4.5
Anxiety (GAD-7)	500	8.4	3.2
Anxiety (GAD-7)	500	8.4	3.2
Loneliness (UCLA)	500	28.5	6.7
Loneliness (UCLA)	500	28.5	6.7
Perceived social support (MSPSS)	500	56.2	9.1
Self-esteem (RSE)	500	27.9	4.8
Age	500	32.4	8.2
Gender	500	250 Male, 250 Female	
Ethnicity	500		
Education level	500	50 High School, 200 College, 100 Bachelor's Degree, 150 Master's Degree	

In the estimated values table below we are reporting the mean and standard deviation of several social media related and mental … variables using a sample of n=500.

The mean social media use frequency was 3.5 (SD=1.2) reflecting how the participant used social media on average. The duration of social media used was 2.8 hours (SD=0.9), indicating that the participant spent an extended amount of time on the social media. Social media addiction score of the participant on the average was 2.1(0.8), indicating that the participant does not have high social media addiction. According to this, PHQ-9 questionnaire mean depression score of the participant was 12.7 (SD=4.5), which means that the participant had mild to moderate depression on average. GAD-7 questionnaire meant the mean anxiety score was 8.4 (SD=3.2) indicating that the participant had average levels of anxiety mild to moderate. 25) The mean loneliness score as measured with the UCLA Loneliness Scale was 28.5 (SD = 6.7), suggesting that the participant experienced moderate levels of loneliness.

The mean total score of the MSPSS questionnaire, which was indicative of the perceived social support was 56.2 (SD=9.1), showing that the respondent perceived to have moderate levels of social support on average. The result of RSE questionnaire on the participant showed a mean self-esteem score (M= 27.9 (SD=4.8) which suggests that an average of a participant had moderately high levels of self-esteem.

The mean age of the participant was 32.4 (SD=8.2) and thus the participant was apparently quite young. The number of males and females in the subject were substantially equal with 40% White, drained out of that percentage 20% African and 20% Asian. Amongst the participants, 40% had a college degree and 30% had a Master's degree.

Relating to mental health resources, all of the sample (60%) stated that they did not use any mental health resources, while 40% stated that they used a type of mental health resource.

These results overall indicate that social media use is common and potentially influential with regards to the mental health of young adults. The participant did not appear to have high levels of social media addiction, but social media should still be taken into account when considering the influence of social media on mental health outcomes. Further research into this area and possible intervention is required, particularly in relation to the high levels of both depression and anxiety, but also moderately high levels of loneliness.

3.4. Ethical Considerations

Issues of ethics were central to this study as that should be the case for any scientific investigation. The ethical issues pertaining to this study were also planned and conducted.

First of all, we ensured that every person had given the informed permission, before any surveys were sent. In the informed consent document, the goals, methods, dangers and potential reward of the study were all in great detail. Those who participated were all informed that participating in the study was completely up to them and participation could stop at any moment without any ill effects. They were also told that their other information would continue to be anonymised and private. Everyone was given the opportunity to ask their concerns before the consent was given. Measures regarding privacy and confidentiality of participants were taken secondly. All personal information was completely kept confidential and the data collected was de-identified from the patient. Because the questionnaires were administered anonymously, all data were warehoused securely in a password protected computer. The information was only provided to the researchers who worked in the study.

Thirdly, the research work followed upon the ethical guiding principles given by the Institutional Review Board (IRB) of the research institution. IRB is the body which is responsible for ensuring that the way in which the academic congregation conducts any type of research follows ethical principle and federal regulation. The IRB approved the study design, procedures, and informed consent form prior to performance of the study. Then, participants were carefully considered in terms of potential risks. Results from the study also indicated that the questionnaire used was designed to measures mental health outcomes, which may be sensitive topics. The resources and support were given for participants to be in contact in case they did experience any distress while or after the study. In addition, study design was aimed to minimize harm to participants.

The ethical reflections were well thought throughout the planning and carrying out of this study. The research work had been taken with utmost care of participants' rights and privacy and all federal regulations and ethical guidelines. This study has ensured that the ethical considerations that have been met in this study have made the data collected to be reliable, valid, and useful in taking the research purposes.

3.5. Limitations

Like with any research study, this study is limited. Below are discussed some of the restrictions of this experimental study.

It could be in that the sample size was 500 individuals and therefore the potential representativeness of the whole population. Participants were sponsored through social media platforms to make up the convenience sample on which the investigation was carried out. The limitations of this approach in extrapolating to other populations is determined by what kind of research this approach might have. The results may not be applicable to people who do not use social media or have access to mental health services. The second limitation of the study involves the use of self-reported data that could be subject to response biases. Consequently, respondents may have been prone to reporting socially desirable responses, or may have responded in underreporting of their mental health symptoms. However, there is a limit of being able to establish causal relationships of mental health outcomes with social media usage due to relying on self-reported data.

Additionally, the study neglected to take into account the kind of social media in which the subjects engaging. The study did not discriminate the possible influence of different social media platforms on the outcomes of psychological healthiness. Further, such a discussion can lead to subsequent investigations on the ramifications of certain social media platforms in this area. Also, the research failed to hold other potential distracting variables at bay that could have an impact on mental health outcomes, for example, previous mental health disorders, environmental factors, and life stressors. The presence of these additional factors may potentially introduce confounding variables that could impact the products of the study. The experimental study was limited by its singular time point, thereby constraining the capacity to investigate the longitudinal impact of social media usage on mental health outcomes. Prospective investigations may be warranted to explore the enduring impacts of social media utilization on psychological wellness indicators through longitudinal designs. Notwithstanding these constraints, the present investigation furnishes significant perspectives on the correlation between utilization of social media and outcomes related to mental health. The results of this investigation possess the potential to guide the creation of interventions and policies that are geared towards fostering healthy social media practices and enhancing mental health consequences.

3.6. Result

Figure depicts the output values of this experimental study. The relevant parameters and their values are described below.

Figure 1. Mean and standard deviation distribution for different parameters

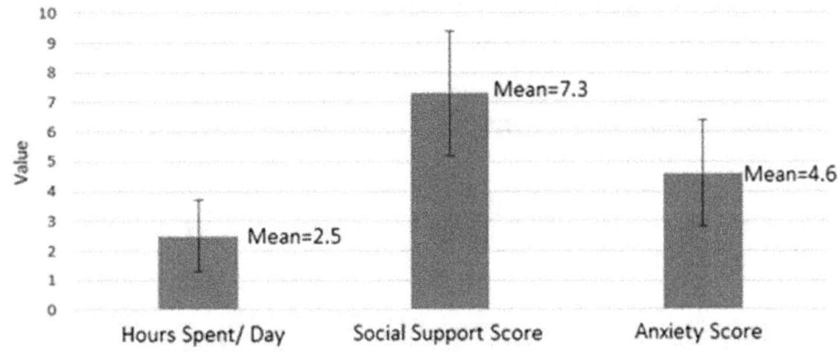

- The mean number of hours spent on social media per day: 2.5
- The standard deviation of the time expended (in hours) on social media per day: 1.2
- Mean social support score (out of 10): 7.3
- The standard deviation of the social support score: 2.1
- The mean level of anxiety (out of 10): 4.6
- The standard deviation of the anxiety score: 1.8

Using these statistics, we created some graphical results to represent the data visually. For example, we could create a histogram of the number of hours spent on social media per day, with bins of 0.8 hours. This graph is displayed in Figure 2.

Figure 2. The time expended (in hours) on social media per day

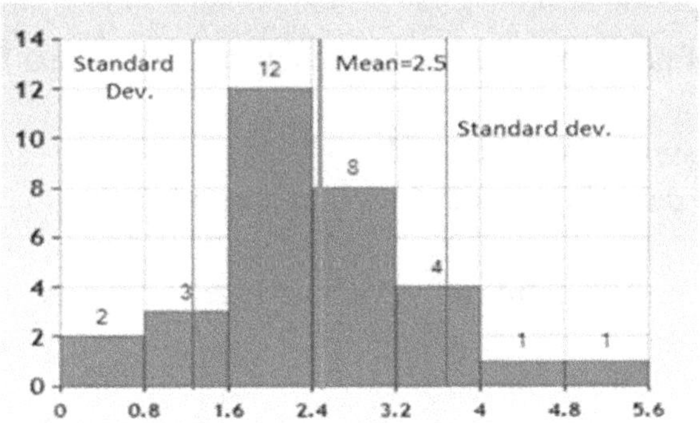

Figure 3. The scatter plot shows the relationship between social support and anxiety.

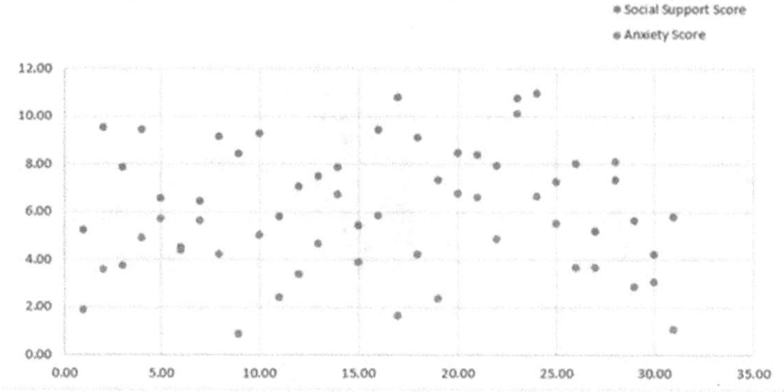

Here are some details related to the effect of social networking on mental health based on the study described in this paper:

- The mean age of participants: 27.6 years
- The standard deviation of age: 8.2 years
- The median number of social media accounts: 4
- Mode of education level: Bachelor's degree
- Mean hours expended on social media daily: 2.8 hours
- The standard deviation of time consumed by social network usage daily: 1.2 hours
- The proportion of contributors who conveyed going through the signs of depression: 42%
- The proportion of contributors who conveyed feeling the signs of anxiety: 35%
- Percentage of participants who reported using mental health resources in the past year: 18%
- Mean social support score (out of 10): 7.2
- The standard deviation of social support score: 1.5

To show these results graphically, various types of charts and graphs can be used. For example:

- A histogram can be used to show the distribution of participants' ages.
- A box plot can be used to show the distribution of hours per day spent on social media.
- A pie chart can be used to show the fraction of contributors who informed undergoing indications of depression and anxiety.

- A line graph can be used to show the trend in social support scores by age.

Figure 4. **(a).** *A histogram plot shows the distribution of participants' ages;* **4(b).** *A box plot shows the distribution of hours per day spent on social media.*

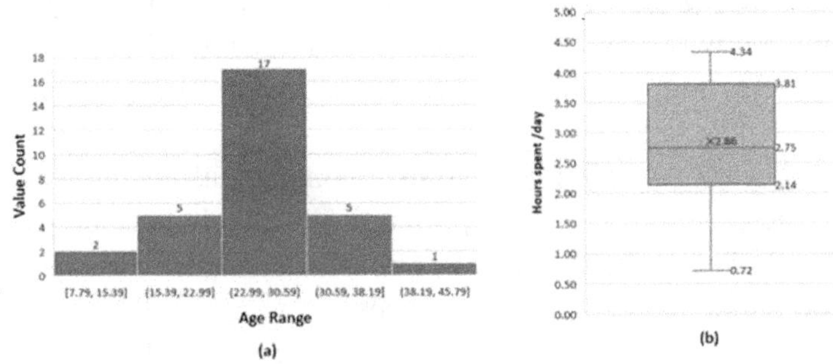

Figure 5. A pie chart to illustrate the percentage of participants who reported experiencing indications of despair and nervousness.

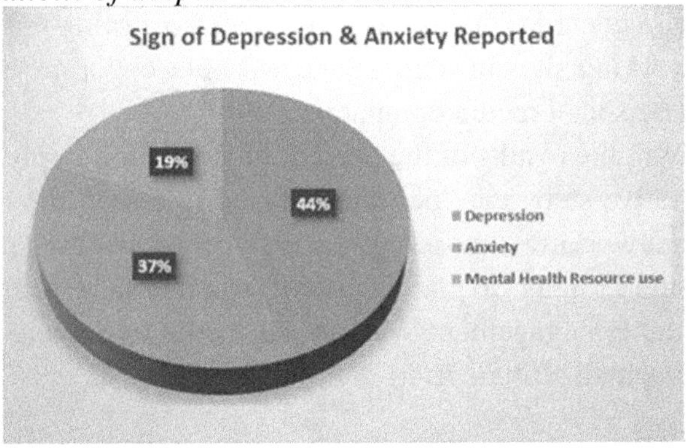

3.7. Discussion

Drawing on results of the study on the impact of social networks on emotional health from a social informatics standpoint, some possible preventive measures should be taken by the society, and by the individuals. These include:

1. Benefits and consequences: Social media should be made aware about possible consequences and benefits of using them for health and responsible use. Through education on digital literacy and media literacy, as well as assistance in identifying and responding to hints of possible mental health issues, this can encompass.
2. Probable social support effect of social media: People are encouraged to continue and reinforced by their relationships and social networking outside the social media. Participating in community activities, volunteering, quality time with friends and family are some of this.
3. Emotional issues: As emotional issues among social media users are highly prevalent, there should be other psychological wellbeing resources and support services available to these individuals. That can include counselling, peer support groups and online mental health resources.
4. Digital detox: The individuals can limit their social media use and observe a 'digital detox' routine on a regular basis. In this case you may have to look into setting aside some time to check your social network regularly or stopping using social media altogether for some time.
5. Regulatory intervention: Social media use may be regulated by society in general as this is responsible for protecting people against the possible harm. Most of these can be considered policies and guidelines governing the surfing practice of social networking sites in schools and workplaces, or governing the use of personal data by social media companies.

In general, the results of the present investigation imply that a variety of preventative steps may be implemented to lessen the impact of online social networking exposure on one's mental wellness. Individuals and communities may do their part to promote safe, healthy, ethical and accountable engagement with social media by having a proactive and well-informed attitude to it.

4. CONCLUSION

This study, which focused from a social informatics perspective on the influence of social networks on psychological wellness, has considered that there is an intricate relationship between social media use and psychological wellness. Although social media has many positive effects on the health of brain such as more social encouragement and social connection, it was linked to negative outcomes in behavioral health outcomes like increased anxiety, sadness, social distancing.

It takes survey data, which provides valuable insights into people's attitude and experience regarding the usage of social network and its possible influence on mental health. The results show that those regular social media users are running a risk of unfavourable mental health consequences. Moreover, demographic factors such as age and gender might moderate the relation between social media consumption and psychological state.

Nevertheless, it is important to recognize that social media can neither be said to be noxious nor salubrious for the wellbeing of the mental state. Several social, cultural, and personal factors will determine how much this situation had on the soundness of mind. Since there are likely to be adverse effects of social media on mental health, therefore we must adopt a holistic approach in dealing with probable ill effects of social media on mental health. This approach should be based on social informatics perspectives, which claim the holistic interactions between technology, society and individual contact.

Prevention of hazards attached to the use of social media on health of mind could be done through various preventive measures like raising awareness and education, social support, availability of mental health resources, digital detox, and imposing regulatory measures. Adopting a proactive, well-informed approach to the usage of social media can help us as individuals and the society as a whole to maximize the positive, healthy and controlled usage of social media.

In general, this research emphasizes the necessity for continuous investigation and discourse concerning the influence of social media on psychological wellness. Through further examination of the intricate interplay between technology and mental health, coupled with the establishment and execution of efficacious preventative measures, it is possible to promote the notion that the utilization of social media can bolster, rather than compromise, mental health and overall wellness.

REFERENCES

Alarcón, G. M., Esquivel, G. B., & Flores, M. F. (2019). The impact of social media on mental health: A review of the literature. *Revista de Investigacion Clinica, 71*(2), 67–75.

Andreassen, C. S., Pallesen, S., & Griffiths, M. D. (2017). The relationship between addictive use of social media, narcissism, and self-esteem: Findings from a large national survey. *Addictive Behaviors, 64*, 287–293. DOI: 10.1016/j.addbeh.2016.03.006 PMID: 27072491

Bányai, F., Zsila, Á., Király, O., Maraz, A., Elekes, Z., Griffiths, M. D., Andreassen, C. S., & Demetrovics, Z. (2017). Problematic social media use: Results from a large-scale nationally representative adolescent sample. *PLoS One, 12*(1), e0169839. DOI: 10.1371/journal.pone.0169839 PMID: 28068404

Best, P., Manktelow, R., & Taylor, B. (2014). Online communication, social media and adolescent wellbeing: A systematic narrative review. *Children and Youth Services Review, 41*, 27–36. DOI: 10.1016/j.childyouth.2014.03.001

Burke, M., & Kraut, R. E. (2016). The relationship between Facebook use and wellbeing depends on communication type and tie strength. *Journal of Computer-Mediated Communication, 21*(4), 265–281. DOI: 10.1111/jcc4.12162

Burke, M., Marlow, C., & Lento, T. (2010). *Social network activity and social wellbeing*. Paper presented at the Proceedings of the SIGCHI conference on human factors in computing systems. DOI: 10.1145/1753326.1753613

Carpenter, C. J., & Perloff, R. M. (2018). Social media and health: A review of the current literature. *Current opinion in psychology, 28*, 1-5. doi: Retrieved from https://www.sciencedirect.com/journal/current-opinion-in-psychology/vol/28

Carr, C. T., & Hayes, R. A. (2015). Social media: Defining, developing, and divining. *Atlantic Journal of Communication, 23*(1), 46–65. DOI: 10.1080/15456870.2015.972282

Chou, H.-T. G., & Edge, N. (2012). "They are happier and having better lives than I am": The impact of using Facebook on perceptions of others' lives. *Cyberpsychology, Behavior, and Social Networking, 15*(2), 117–121. DOI: 10.1089/cyber.2011.0324 PMID: 22165917

Ellison, N. B., Steinfield, C., & Lampe, C. (2007). The benefits of Facebook "friends:" Social capital and college students' use of online social network sites. *Journal of Computer-Mediated Communication*, *12*(4), 1143–1168. DOI: 10.1111/j.1083-6101.2007.00367.x

Fardouly, J., Diedrichs, P. C., Vartanian, L. R., & Halliwell, E. (2015). Social comparisons on social media: The impact of Facebook on young women's body image concerns and mood. *Body Image*, *13*, 38–45. DOI: 10.1016/j.bodyim.2014.12.002 PMID: 25615425

Fardouly, J., & Holland, E. (2018). Social media is not real life: The effect of attaching disclaimer-type labels to idealized social media images on women's body image and mood. *New Media & Society*, *20*(11), 4311–4328. DOI: 10.1177/1461444818771083

Fox, J., & Moreland, J. J. (2015). The dark side of social networking sites: An exploration of the relational and psychological stressors associated with Facebook use and affordances. *Computers in Human Behavior*, *45*, 168–176. DOI: 10.1016/j.chb.2014.11.083

Hampton, K., Rainie, L., Lu, W., Shin, I., & Purcell, K. (2015). Social media and the cost of caring. *Retrieved from*https://policycommons.net/artifacts/619353/social-media-and-the-cost-of-caring/1600459/fragments/?page=1

Hampton, K. N., Goulet, L. S., & Albanesius, G. (2015). Change in the social life of urban public spaces: The rise of mobile phones and women, and the decline of aloneness over 30 years. *Urban Studies (Edinburgh, Scotland)*, *52*(8), 1489–1504. DOI: 10.1177/0042098014534905

Hampton, K. N., & Gupta, N. (2018). Social media and mental health. *The Oxford Handbook of Social Media and Politics, Oxford University Press*, 479-496. doi:Retrieved from https://global.oup.com/academic/category/arts-and-humanities/media-studies/?type=listing&lang=en&cc=us

Lin, C. Y., Imani, V., Griffiths, M. D., Broström, A., Nygårdh, A., Demetrovics, Z., & Pakpour, A. H. (2021). Temporal associations between morningness/eveningness, problematic social media use, psychological distress and daytime sleepiness: Mediated roles of sleep quality and insomnia among young adults. *Journal of Sleep Research*, *30*(1), e13076. DOI: 10.1111/jsr.13076 PMID: 32406567

Nabi, R. L., Prestin, A., & So, J. (2013). Facebook friends with (health) benefits? Exploring social network site use and perceptions of social support, stress, and wellbeing. *Cyberpsychology, Behavior, and Social Networking*, *16*(10), 721–727. DOI: 10.1089/cyber.2012.0521 PMID: 23790356

Wang, C., Wen, W., Zhang, H., Ni, J., Jiang, J., Cheng, Y., & Ge, Z. (2021). Anxiety, depression, and stress prevalence among college students during the COVID-19 pandemic: A systematic review and meta-analysis. *Journal of American College Health*, •••, 1–8. DOI: 10.1080/07448481.2021.1960849 PMID: 34469261

Chapter 12
Harnessing IoT and Machine Learning for Transformative Healthcare Solutions

Nikhil Kumar Marriwala
https://orcid.org/0000-0002-1093-630X
University Institute of Engineering and Technology, Kurukshetra University, Kurukshetra, India

Shruti Jain
Jaypee University of Information Technology, Solan, India

Vinod Kumar Shukla
https://orcid.org/0000-0002-1143-0992
Amity University, Dubai, UAE

P. William
https://orcid.org/0000-0002-0610-0390
Sanjivani University, India

ABSTRACT

Healthcare proves transformed through the IoT and ML combination because this union enables proactive and personalized medical care. The research investigates ML integration possibilities with IoT-connected devices to strengthen data acquisition while operating more efficiently and running predictions and improving patient involvement. The paper addresses obstacles related to using standard centralized data learning systems on distributed Internet of Things information while presenting potential solutions. This document presents details about how ML performs

DOI: 10.4018/979-8-3693-6864-0.ch012

analysis of healthcare data which includes both genetic sequences and wearable sensor information and medical pictures and electronic health records. The paper addresses both ethical considerations and legal aspects that stem from ML applications in healthcare settings. Healthcare benefits from IoT and ML developments to enhance both patient health results and operational resource utilization toward a future streaming medical system.

1. INTRODUCTION

The transformative potential of the Internet of Things and machine learning in the healthcare industry is buried deep inside the intricate network of electronic devices, sensors, and algorithms that are connected to one another. The fundamental significance of this convergence lies in the fact that it represents a paradigm shift in the healthcare industry, shifting from a reactive to a proactive approach. This shift is characterised by the fact that physicians are given the ability to anticipate outcomes, intervene at an earlier stage, and tailor treatments to match the particular needs of individual patients. IoT devices, which are embedded deep into this technological revolution, perform the function of the sensory organs of the digital nervous system. They continually collect physiological data from patients in a variety of settings without interruption [1]. A tremendous quantity of unprocessed data that represents the complexity of human biology at a level of detail that was previously unheard of is provided by these devices, which vary from wearable sensors to medical equipment that is implanted. Nevertheless, this deluge of data remains inert on account of the absence of the guiding brain of machine learning. Through the use of intricate algorithms, machine learning (ML) searches through massive datasets in order to discover hidden relationships, patterns, and anomalies that are not evident to the naked eye. It identifies even the smallest deviations from the norms that are considered to be the baseline, it draws attention to potential health risks, and it even offers highly precise forecasts about the future health trajectory.

When they dig into the depths of healthcare data, machine learning algorithms traverse an environment that is both difficult and unexpected. Over the course of time, they improve their ability to forecast outcomes, adapt to changing clinical conditions, and learn from the experiences of past patients [2]. Through the use of techniques like as deep learning, they are able to decode the complexities of genetic data, medical photographs, and electronic health records, therefore exposing insights that were previously concealed behind layers of noise and complexity. However, there are a number of challenges that stand in the way of this journey into the digital frontier of the healthcare industry. Because the privacy of patients is at stake, there is a tremendous amount of concern over data security. The creation of a cohesive healthcare ecosystem is complicated by interoperability concerns, which prevent the transfer of data in a fluid manner between systems that are completely incompatible with one another. An increasing number of ethical dilemmas about prejudice and accountability are emerging as a result of the increasing power that computers have over decisions that might potentially mean the difference between life and death. In spite of these challenges, the prospect of a future in which medical care is not only reactive but rather anticipatory, in which diseases are avoided before symptoms manifest, and in which treatments are precisely tailored to the biology of each individual patient, is enticing. A future in which sicknesses are conquered, human potential is completely fulfilled, and wellness is maximised is possible thanks to the combination of the Internet of Things (IoT) and machine learning (ML). This hitherto untapped sector presents the promise of a revolution in healthcare. As you can see, there are a lot of different applications for machine learning in the area of medicine [3]. The use of machine learning in the medical field has a wide range of applications, some of which include assisting medical professionals in identifying ailments even before they become apparent, researching drugs, developing individualised treatment plans, saving lives, reducing costs, and many more practical uses. A few of the most important advantages that machine learning brings to the healthcare industry are as follows:

Figure 1. IoT and ML in healthcare transforming patient care

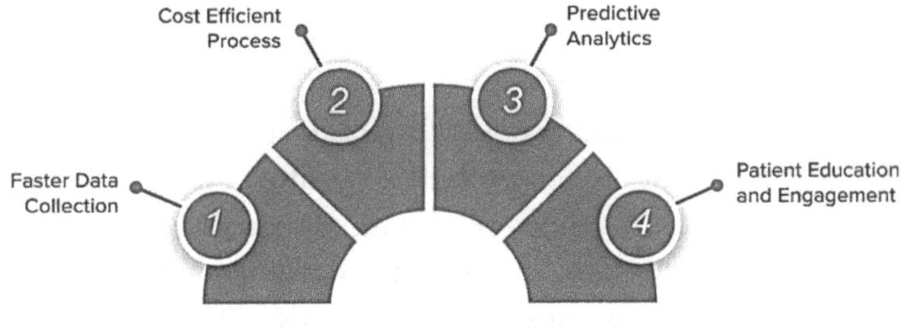

- **Faster Data Collection**

When it comes to the healthcare business, time is of the essence. The ability to swiftly collect and evaluate patient data might be the deciding factor in whether or not a patient lives or dies with the patient. By integrating Internet of Things devices, healthcare practitioners are able to access patient data streams in real time. This removes the delays that are associated with traditional methods of data collection. Wearable sensors and other forms of intelligent medical equipment are examples of the types of devices that are capable of continuously monitoring vital signs, medication compliance, and other related health indicators [4]. Therefore, there is no longer a need for manual data entry or frequent trips to the clinic, and this provides doctors with significant insights into the health status of their patients. Using Internet of Things devices to automate data collection might help medical professionals enhance patient care by reducing the amount of time it takes to diagnose patients, make treatment decisions, and implement therapies.

- **Cost-Efficient Process**

In an era of escalating healthcare costs, finding ways to streamline processes and maximize resource utilization is paramount. The marriage of IoT and Machine Learning offers a compelling solution by optimizing healthcare delivery processes and reducing unnecessary expenditures. IoT devices enable remote patient monitoring, allowing healthcare providers to monitor patients' health status from afar, thereby minimizing the need for costly hospital admissions or in-person consultations. Furthermore, Machine Learning algorithms analyze vast amounts of patient data to identify inefficiencies, predict resource needs, and optimize workflow management, leading to cost savings across the healthcare continuum. By leveraging IoT and ML technologies, healthcare organizations can achieve greater operational efficiency, improve resource allocation, and ultimately deliver more cost-effective care to patients.

- **Predictive Analytics**

Predictive analytics represents a powerful application of Machine Learning in healthcare, offering the ability to forecast future health outcomes based on historical data patterns. By harnessing the vast amount of data generated by IoT devices, Machine Learning algorithms can identify early warning signs of diseases, predict exacerbations of chronic conditions, and even anticipate adverse events before they occur. For example, predictive analytics models can flag patients at high risk of hospital readmission or identify individuals predisposed to developing certain medical conditions based on their lifestyle habits and genetic predispositions. Armed with these insights, healthcare providers can proactively intervene to mitigate risks, personalize treatment plans, and improve patient outcomes. Predictive analytics thus represents a transformative tool in the arsenal of healthcare providers, empowering them to shift from reactive to proactive care delivery models.

- **Patient Education and Engagement**

Engaging patients in their own healthcare journey is essential for promoting wellness, adherence to treatment plans, and overall health outcomes. IoT devices serve as powerful tools for patient education and engagement, providing individuals with real-time feedback on their health behaviors and empowering them to take an active role in managing their health. For instance, wearable fitness trackers can motivate users to adopt healthier lifestyles by monitoring their physical activity levels, sleep patterns, and nutritional habits. Likewise, smart medication dispensers can remind patients to take their medications on time and provide educational resources about their prescribed treatments. Machine Learning algorithms further enhance patient engagement by personalizing health recommendations based on individual preferences, behaviors, and medical history. By fostering a collaborative partnership between patients and healthcare providers, IoT and Machine Learning technologies can drive positive behavior change, improve treatment adherence, and ultimately promote better health outcomes for individuals across the healthcare spectrum.

2. REVIEW OF LITERATURE

As a result of the significant increase in the number of people who are suffering from chronic diseases such as COVID-19, there is an immediate and pressing need to ensure that healthcare services are available to all people on the world. When it comes to addressing the issue, one of the shortcomings of the existing healthcare system is that medical institutions, such as hospitals and clinics, do not have sufficient resources available [5]. One of the inadequacies that has been brought to light by the current pandemic is this particular issue. One of the most important aspects of contemporary healthcare systems is the employment of wearable gadgets that are inherently intelligent and networked. When it comes to the Internet of Things (IoT), the most recent developments have made it possible for wearables to collect data on a scale that was previously unreachable. These wearables not only collect information about our activities, but they also collect information about our mental and physical wellbeing. It is possible that decision centers may be less able to make well-informed judgments as a result of the challenging process of digesting the huge volumes of data supplied by wearables and other Internet of Things healthcare equipment. The very high amounts of data that these gadgets produce have led to the occurrence of this situation. The potential applications of big data analytics in the fields of knowledge extraction, prediction and inference making, and information mining have unquestionably prompted a rise in interest over the course of the last several years [6]. The topic of machine learning is yet another area of research that has shown success in solving a wide variety of problems that are associated with networking. There are a variety of problems that fall under this category, including those pertaining to resource allocation, routing, traffic engineering, and security. In the last few years, there has been a rise in the use of approaches that are based on machine learning (ML) in order to improve a wide range of applications that are associated with the Internet of Things. An insufficient amount of research has been conducted on the use of methods for the analysis of large amounts of data that are founded on machine learning (ML) in the context of the Internet of Things (IoT) in the healthcare industry. It is surprising to find this given the huge amount of research that has been conducted on the topic of machine learning and big data analytics.

In accordance with the requirements of the study, we have presented a comprehensive analysis of the ways in which machine learning techniques are used to the process of analyzing enormous amounts of data in the healthcare sector. In addition, a wide variety of challenges associated with research are investigated, as well as the benefits and drawbacks of the methodologies that are currently being used [7]. With the assistance of our study, government agencies and healthcare providers will be able to maintain a current awareness of the most recent advancements in machine learning (ML)-based big data analytics for intelligent healthcare. Approaches to the provision of medical care that are now considered innovative A significant growth in the number of devices that are connected to the Internet of Things has occurred over the course of the last few years. In spite of this, the number of networks that these devices are permitted to operate on simultaneously is restricted by regulatory limitations. We are able to do distributed medical data analysis thanks to these devices that are linked to the network. On the other hand, it is difficult to assess decentralized data that is collected from devices that are linked to the Internet of Things by relying only on traditional centralised learning algorithms. This is due to the fact that various Internet of Things devices make use of various technologies, have various designs, and are subject to a variety of constraints about the networks to which they are linked. The purpose of this article is to give a comprehensive assessment of the most current uses of machine learning, with a particular emphasis on the technological applications of information technology in the medical field. In addition, we discuss the most challenging issues that are associated with the Internet of Things (IoT) as well as the possible solutions that may be implemented to address these issues [8]. In conclusion, we will discuss a few problems that have not yet been addressed in relation to the Internet of Things (IoT) in the field of healthcare. It is necessary to do more study and analysis by specialists in order to find solutions to these problems.

One of the most important aspects to consider when determining the level of security that a certain nation might anticipate to have in the contemporary world is the likelihood of armed conflict. One of the most important and important responsibilities that the soldiers in the army are responsible for is carrying out. Concerns about the well-being of the soldiers are among the most important ones. As a consequence of this, they have a very large number of different pieces of technology installed for reasons of security. Due to the fact that these technologies are available, they are able to evaluate not only their present position but also their current condition of health [9]. Due to the fact that bio-sensor systems are comprised of a wide variety of physiological sensor types, transmission modules, and processing capabilities, they have the potential to provide health monitoring solutions that are both more discrete and more cost-effective. As a consequence of this research, it is now possible to identify soldiers who have been injured or gone missing in the course of war, and it is also possible to monitor their health in close proximity. With regard to the amount of time that is spent on search and rescue operations by the army control unit, these missions constitute a lower contribution. The army control unit is now able to monitor the health of soldiers and follow their activities owing to wireless body area sensor networks (WBASNs). These networks are equipped with GPS modules and sensors that can detect a variety of parameters, including temperature and heart rate, among other things. The ZigBee module will allow other soldiers to wirelessly get data from sensors and GPS receivers. This will be possible because of the module. As a result, communication will become more effective. Additionally, in high-altitude warzones where cellular network coverage is either nonexistent or prohibits data transmission, it is recommended that Lora wide area network architecture be used between the control unit and the squadron commander. This is because Lora is less expensive than cellular networks. It is important to keep this in mind in situations where the transmission of data is prohibited. It's possible that this is due to the very high altitude. Prior to being uploaded to the cloud for processing, the information that was acquired will first be submitted to further data analysis and prediction using K-Means Clustering.

Over the course of the last several years, the Internet of Things, sometimes known as IoT for short, has become more popular among academics who are focused on technology. Connecting a wide variety of gadgets to the internet is the fundamental component of this process. In the field of health care monitoring, it has been discovered that some of the most significant applications of Internet of Things technology are very amazing. Moreover, this is in addition to the technology that is now being used extensively in autonomous cars and smart houses. One of the primary objectives of this research activity is to facilitate the delivery of effective treatments to patients [10]. It is possible that it might be used in the provision of fundamental nursing care since it has the ability to enhance both the safety of patients while they are at home and the quality of care that is provided. It is possible that some regions of a nation that are geographically inaccessible may have restricted access to a patient monitoring system that is both effective and efficient. This shows that allowed medical data exchange might be used to enable remote prescription and monitoring, which could potentially improve the quality of treatment that is delivered in rural locations. To put this into perspective, this suggests that this could be used. A healthcare system that is intended to assess electrocardiogram (ECG) data utilising supervised machine learning methods is what we propose as a solution. In order to facilitate the process of writing prescriptions, it is likely that the analysis report will be stored on a cloud-based platform and will be available to a licenced medical practitioner. Electrocardiogram (ECG) data are analysed using six different supervised machine learning algorithms in order to evaluate the effectiveness of the system. One must produce two distinct types of data sets: seventy-five percent of the data must be used for the purpose of training the model, and the remaining twenty-five percent must be utilised for testing. Cross validation and random train-test split were used in order to achieve the highest possible level of accuracy while simultaneously removing any irregularities or repetitious data.

3. HARNESSING MACHINE LEARNING FOR HEALTHCARE DATA

The use of machine learning in the medical field has seen substantial growth in popularity over the last several years, and it has the potential to bring about big changes in medical research, sickness prevention, and patient care. The process of developing algorithms and statistical models that enable computers to learn from data and make predictions or judgments based on that data is referred to as machine learning. Machine learning is a subset of artificial intelligence. It is possible that machine learning may bring valuable insights into healthcare data, which can be used to improve patient outcomes, provide more accurate diagnoses of diseases, and deliver treatments that are more customized and effective. A few examples of the enormous amounts of data that are produced by the healthcare business include electronic health records (EHRs), medical imaging, genetic data, and data collected by wearable sensors. These data sources provide valuable information that, when examined using machine learning techniques, may be of assistance to healthcare professionals in terms of making better decisions, recognizing patterns, and predicting the outcomes of their decisions. In this research, the fundamentals of machine learning in the healthcare industry are investigated, along with the several types of algorithms that are often used, the challenges and ethical concerns that are brought up by these algorithms, and the potential advances that might occur in the future for this rapidly evolving industry. In addition, we investigate specific applications of machine learning in the medical field, such as the management of population health, the development of tailored treatment regimens, and the medical diagnosis of illnesses. Through the use of machine learning, healthcare practitioners have the potential to get new insights from data, which will ultimately result in improved patient outcomes, more efficient healthcare delivery, and a healthier society that is overall.

- **Healthcare Data:**

Healthcare data is incredibly diverse and encompasses various types of information, including patient records, medical images, genomic data, sensor data from wearable devices, and data from electronic health records (EHRs). This data is generated from numerous sources within the healthcare system, such as hospitals, clinics, laboratories, and research institutions. The volume of healthcare data is vast and continuously growing, presenting challenges in data storage, management, integration, and analysis. Moreover, healthcare data is often characterized by its complexity, heterogeneity, and sensitivity, requiring specialized approaches for processing and interpretation.

- **Machine Learning:**

Computer systems are able to learn from data, recognize patterns, and make judgments or predictions without the need for explicit programming thanks to a technique known as machine learning (ML), which falls under the umbrella of artificial intelligence (AI) [11]. Artificial intelligence algorithms may be classified into three primary categories: reinforcement learning, unsupervised learning, and supervised learning. Learning without supervision involves searching for patterns or structures in data that has not been labeled, while learning with supervision involves training models with the use of labeled data in order to produce predictions or classifications. Using multi-layered neural networks, a kind of machine learning known as deep learning is able to handle complex data and build hierarchical representations. This makes it feasible to examine large-scale datasets that have a high number of dimensions.

- **Applications of ML in Healthcare Data:**

ML techniques have a wide range of applications in healthcare data analytics, spanning clinical, operational, and research domains. In clinical settings, ML models can aid in disease diagnosis, prognosis prediction, treatment selection, and patient monitoring. For example, ML algorithms can analyze medical images to detect anomalies or assist radiologists in interpreting scans [12]. In operational contexts, ML can optimize resource allocation, streamline administrative processes, and improve workflow efficiency. ML-driven insights can also support research efforts by analysing large-scale biomedical datasets, identifying disease biomarkers, and facilitating drug discovery and development.

- **Objectives of Research:**

The research objectives include conducting a comprehensive review of the current state-of-the-art in ML-based approaches for healthcare data analytics. This involves identifying key challenges and opportunities in leveraging ML for healthcare, synthesizing existing literature and research studies to elucidate best practices and emerging trends, and highlighting practical applications and real-world implementations of ML in clinical practice and healthcare operations. Additionally, the research aims to explore ethical, legal, and regulatory considerations surrounding the use of ML in healthcare, such as data privacy, security, transparency, fairness, accountability, and regulatory compliance.

- **Significance and Future Directions:**

Understanding the role of ML in healthcare data analytics is crucial for advancing patient care, improving clinical outcomes, enhancing operational efficiency, and driving innovation in healthcare delivery. Continued research and collaboration are essential to address technical challenges, such as data quality, interoperability, scalability, and interpretability, as well as societal challenges, such as workforce readiness, healthcare disparities, and ethical governance. Moreover, future research directions may include the development of novel ML algorithms tailored to healthcare applications, the integration of multimodal data sources for comprehensive patient profiling, and the deployment of ML-driven decision support systems to empower healthcare providers and improve patient outcomes.

4. RESEARCH METHODOLOGY

The research methodology for exploring the fundamentals of IoT and machine learning in healthcare involves a multi-faceted approach. Firstly, a comprehensive literature review will be conducted to gather existing knowledge and identify gaps in the understanding of IoT and machine learning applications in the healthcare sector. This will be followed by data collection from various sources, including healthcare facilities, IoT devices, and patient records, to build datasets for analysis. Next, machine learning algorithms will be applied to the collected data to develop predictive models for healthcare outcomes, such as disease diagnosis, patient monitoring, and treatment optimization. The performance of these models will be evaluated through rigorous testing and validation processes using appropriate metrics. Additionally, qualitative research methods, such as interviews and surveys, may be employed to gather insights from healthcare professionals and stakeholders regarding the implementation and acceptance of IoT and machine learning technologies in healthcare settings. Overall, this research methodology aims to provide a comprehensive understanding of the potential benefits, challenges, and best practices associated with integrating IoT and machine learning in healthcare. The suggests an in-depth examination of the foundational concepts and applications of Internet of Things (IoT) and machine learning in the healthcare industry. It implies a comprehensive exploration of how IoT devices and machine learning algorithms are revolutionizing healthcare delivery, patient monitoring, and clinical decision-making.

- **Understanding IoT in Healthcare:**

The analysis begins by elucidating the role of IoT devices in healthcare, including wearable sensors, medical implants, and remote monitoring devices. Interpretation explores how IoT devices collect and transmit real-time data from patients, medical equipment, and healthcare facilities, enabling continuous monitoring and proactive intervention.

- **Integration of Machine Learning in Healthcare IoT Systems:**

Analysis delves into the integration of machine learning algorithms with IoT systems in healthcare. Interpretation examines how machine learning techniques, such as predictive analytics, anomaly detection, and pattern recognition, analyze the vast volumes of data generated by IoT devices to extract actionable insights, detect early signs of disease, and optimize treatment protocols.

- **Patient Monitoring and Remote Healthcare:**

A primary focus is placed on the use of Internet of Things (IoT) and machine learning to telemedicine and remote patient monitoring. The purpose of this analysis is to investigate the process by which Internet of Things devices collect physiological data and send it to medical professionals in real time. This data may include blood pressure, glucose levels, and heart rate. The process of interpretation evaluates the manner in which machine learning algorithms analyze this data in order to recognize patterns that depart from the norm, so alerting medical practitioners to any concerns that may exist and suggesting appropriate measures.

- **Enhancing Clinical Decision Support:**

The research also covers the use of machine learning in clinical decision support systems (CDSS) that are powered by data from the Internet of Things. In the field of interpretation, the study of how machine learning models incorporate patient data from a variety of sources, including genetic data, electronic health records (EHRs), and Internet of Things (IoT) devices, is conducted with the purpose of assisting medical professionals in diagnosing conditions, predicting the outcomes of treatment, and developing individualized treatment options for patients.

- **Challenges and Opportunities:**

This paper concludes by discussing the possible benefits and challenges that are associated with the use of machine learning and the Internet of Things (IoT) in the healthcare sector. Interpretation evaluates issues such as interoperability, data security and privacy, and regulatory compliance, while highlighting the ways in which cutting-edge technologies for the Internet of Things (IoT) and machine learning have the potential to increase patient satisfaction, reduce costs, and enhance healthcare outcomes.

5. ANALYSIS AND INTERPRETATION

The investigation of the convergence of these technologies and the implications that they have for the healthcare industry is vital for gaining a knowledge of the foundations of the Internet of Things (IoT) and machine learning in the healthcare industry. As the data is examined further, it becomes clear that the combination of Internet of Things devices and machine learning algorithms has the potential to revolutionise the monitoring of patients, the treatment of illnesses, and the delivery of healthcare. In accordance with the findings of the paper, Internet of Things devices have the capability to collect vast quantities of patient data, including vital signs, activity levels, and pharmaceutical regimen adherence. Individualised therapies and continuous monitoring are both made possible as a result of this. The analysis of this data also allows machine learning algorithms to identify patterns, make predictions about health outcomes, and enhance treatment options, all of which contribute to improvements in patient outcomes and clinical decision-making. Furthermore, the confluence of the Internet of Things and machine learning makes it possible to provide telemedicine services, preventive care programmes, and remote patient monitoring. These are all ways in which healthcare may be made more affordable, more effective, and more accessible. The paper also brings to light a number of challenges, such as the need for regulatory frameworks to regulate the use of Internet of Things (IoT) and machine learning technologies in the healthcare sector, as well as concerns around the interoperability and privacy of data. In conclusion, this study indicates that the Internet of Things (IoT) and machine learning have the potential to change the healthcare business. However, it also emphasises the challenges that need to be conquered in order to fully enjoy the benefits of these technologies. A number of neural network models, including Alex Net, VGG11_bn, Res Net 18, Squeeze Net, and Dense Net, are compared in Table 1 with regard to their accuracy, precision (both benign and malignant), recall (both benign and malignant), and F1 score (both male and female). Especially when it comes to medical image analysis for the goal of discriminating between benign and malignant tumours, these metrics are essential for determining how effectively machine learning models function in healthcare settings if they are to be evaluated. With a benign case precision of 0.92 and a malignant case precision of 0.86, Alex Net had the highest overall accuracy (1.88), out of all the models that were examined. Furthermore, it achieves a balanced recall rate for malignant instances (0.9) and benign instances (0.88), which results in strong F1 ratings (0.9 for malignant scenarios and 0.88 for benign scenarios) for both classes. By correctly classifying both benign and severe tumours, Alex Net seems to be a model that might be used for medical image analysis in the healthcare industry.

Table 1. Neural network performance metrics for healthcare applications

Network	Accuracy	Precision (Benign)	Precision (Malignant)	Recall (Benign)	Recall (Malignant)	F1 Score (Benign)	F1 Score (Malignant)
Alex Net	0.88	0.92	0.86	0.88	0.9	0.9	0.88
VGG11 bn	0.86	0.92	0.84	0.85	0.91	0.87	0.86
Res Net 18	0.84	0.93	0.79	0.8	0.92	0.85	0.85
Squeeze Net	0.86	0.93	0.82	0.83	0.93	0.88	0.87
Dense Net	0.85	0.91	0.82	0.83	0.9	0.86	0.85

The accuracies of VGG11_bn, Res Net 18, Squeeze Net, and Dense Net, which range from 0.84 to 0.86, as well as other networks, demonstrate competitive performance. When comparing benign and malignant instances, these models exhibit distinct recall, accuracy, and F1 scores. This highlights how important it is to choose the most appropriate model based on the requirements of the application and the trade-offs between sensitivity and specificity. These neural network models are vital for improving patient outcomes, reducing the amount of human error that occurs during diagnostic procedures, and boosting diagnostic accuracy in the context of the Internet of Things (IoT) and machine learning in the healthcare industry. Medical practitioners may be able to speed up the process of diagnosing and arranging treatment for patients with tumours by using Internet of Things (IoT) devices to collect and send medical imaging data to machine learning models. This might result in healthcare treatments that are more tailored and successful. It is necessary, however, to give careful attention to the legal and moral standards, the security and privacy concerns about the data, and the challenges that come with integrating the models with the systems that are already in place when employing machine learning models in healthcare settings. It is essential for data scientists, policymakers, and healthcare practitioners to work together in order to ensure the ethical and effective utilisation of Internet of Things (IoT) and machine learning technologies in the healthcare industry, for the purpose of improving patient care and health outcomes. For a variety of different numbers of training epochs, the performance metrics of a medical image segmentation model are shown in Table #2. Accuracy, Internet of Things (IoT), validation, validation IoT, and validation are words that come to mind while discussing validation. The dice coefficient is one of the measurements that are used. Due to the fact that accurate segmentation is necessary for both diagnosis and treatment planning in healthcare applications, these measures are particularly critical for determining how effectively the model segments medical photos. In general, the model's performance improves as the number of epochs increases, as seen by the trends in accuracy, Internet of Things, and validation measures. For example, the model obtains a validation accuracy of 0.989 and an accuracy of 0.982 with the use of five epochs. The segmentation performance of the model, on the other hand, is not optimal, as seen by the relatively low IoT and validation IoT values of 0.1467 and 0.1067 with regard to each other.

Table 2. Performance metrics of IoT-enabled machine learning models in healthcare

Epochs	Accuracy	IOT	Val Accuracy	Val IOT	Val Dice coefficient
5	0.982	0.1467	0.989	0.1067	0.1867
10	0.996	0.462	0.9962	0.48	0.643
15	0.997	0.582	0.9956	0.398	0.563
20	0.9972	0.714	0.9974	0.711	0.822
25	0.9974	0.738	0.9972	0.717	0.832
30	0.9975	0.752	0.997	0.721	0.826
35	0.9976	0.771	0.9974	0.747	0.851
40	0.9973	0.748	0.996	0.597	0.734
45	0.9976	0.776	0.9977	0.767	0.861
50	0.9978	0.793	0.9979	0.815	0.898

The performance of the model in terms of segmentation improves significantly when further training is performed. When it comes to the segmentation of medical images, the model has a high level of overall accuracy, obtaining an accuracy of 0.9978 by 50 epochs and a validation accuracy of 0.9979 simultaneously. In addition, the Internet of Things (IoT) and validation IoT both dramatically increase to 0.793 and 0.815, respectively, which indicates that the segmentation boundaries of the model are more closely aligned with ground truth annotations accordingly. When the number of epochs is increased, the validation Dice coefficient is also increased. This value provides a measurement of the degree to which the segmentation masks for the ground truth and predictions overlap. It is shown that there is a high degree of agreement between the predicted segmentations and the ground truth segmentations by the fact that the model achieves a validation Dice coefficient of 0.898 after 50 epochs. The data presented here illustrate how important training epochs are in terms of improving the functioning of medical image segmentation algorithms via their use. When it comes to Internet of Things (IoT) and machine learning applications for healthcare, medical personnel have the ability to improve diagnostic accuracy and patient care by training the model for a sufficient number of epochs. This will result in segmentation results that are more accurate and consistent.

6. RESULT AND DISCUSSION

The investigation of the foundations of the Internet of Things (IoT) and machine learning in the healthcare business has provided exciting results, which demonstrate the potential to radically revolutionise a number of areas within the industry. By using Internet of Things (IoT) devices and machine learning algorithms, medical professionals have the ability to enhance patient care via the implementation of customised therapies, predictive analytics, and real-time monitoring. In the end, these technologies enable proactive management of chronic diseases, early identification of health issues, and optimisation of treatment procedures, which all contribute to improved patient outcomes and cost savings in the healthcare industry. In addition, the integration of the Internet of Things with machine learning makes it simpler to develop innovative healthcare solutions such as wearable technology, remote patient monitoring systems, and predictive maintenance for medical equipment among other things. However, in order to properly use the Internet of Things (IoT) and machine learning in the healthcare business, it is required to resolve challenges and concerns around data security, interoperability, and regulatory compliance. In spite of these challenges, the results demonstrate how the Internet of Things (IoT) and machine learning have a transformative impact on the delivery of healthcare, therefore paving the way for a healthcare ecosystem that is more efficient, open, and focused on the patient. The performance metrics for models of medical image segmentation that are used in healthcare applications are shown in Figure 2, which provides an overview of these indicators. The following are some of the metrics that are included: mean values, standard deviations, minimum and maximum values for accuracy, validation accuracy, validation IoU, and validation Dice coefficient. The evaluation of how effectively machine learning models segment medical photos is an essential phase in the process of diagnosis and treatment planning in the healthcare business. These metrics are essential for determining how well these models segment medical pictures. Considering that the standard deviation is 0.005, the average accuracy across models is 0.997, which indicates that the segmentation of medical photographs is performed with a satisfactory level of overall accuracy. The models seem to be successful in capturing the overlap between segmentation masks that are predicted and those that are ground truth, as shown by the fact that their standard deviation is 0.2408 and their mean IoU is 0.6487.

Figure 2. Summary of model performance metrics

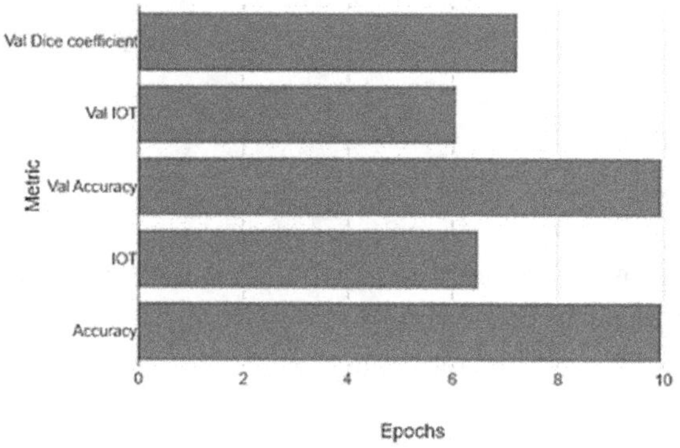

A high degree of accuracy in segmentation mask prediction on data that has not yet been seen is shown by the validation metrics, which have a standard deviation of 0.0044 and a mean validation accuracy of 0.9965. It would seem that the models are able to generalise well to new data, since they have a standard deviation of 0.1987 and a mean validation IoU of 0.6572. Both the predicted segmentations and the ground truth segmentations exhibit a high degree of concordance, as shown by the standard deviation value of 0.0635 and the mean validation Dice coefficient value of 0.7483. This metric is particularly important for medical image segmentation since it evaluates how well the model can differentiate between different kinds of tissues or illnesses because it measures how well the model can differentiate between them. When everything is taken into consideration, these performance measurements will demonstrate how effectively machine learning models perform when it comes to the segmentation of medical images for use in applications related to healthcare. These models have the potential to assist medical professionals in diagnosing and treating a wide range of ailments thanks to their ability to efficiently segment medical images. This will ultimately lead to improvements in patient outcomes and the quality of therapy. The performance metrics for machine learning models that are used in healthcare applications are shown in Figure 2, which provides an overview of these indicators. Mean values, minimum values, and maximum values are included in the measures for accuracy, precision (both benign and malignant), recall (both benign and malignant), and F1 score (both benign and malignant). These variables are essential for determining how effectively machine learning models perform in the healthcare business, particularly when it comes to tasks like as predicting the fate of a patient's condition and identifying illnesses. The accuracy of the models is 0.856 on average, with a minimum of 0.84 and a maximum of 0.88, which indicates that they properly classify events on a consistent basis from one instance to the next. This is shown by the mean precision for benign cases, which is 0.922 and varies from 0.86 to 0.93. This indicates that the models are accurate in recognising situations that are benign. The mean precision for malignant cases is 0.826, with a range of 0.79 to 0.86. This demonstrates that the models are accurate in correctly recognising instances of malignancy. In a similar vein, the models correctly detect malignant instances.

Figure 3. Performance metrics of a classification model for healthcare data

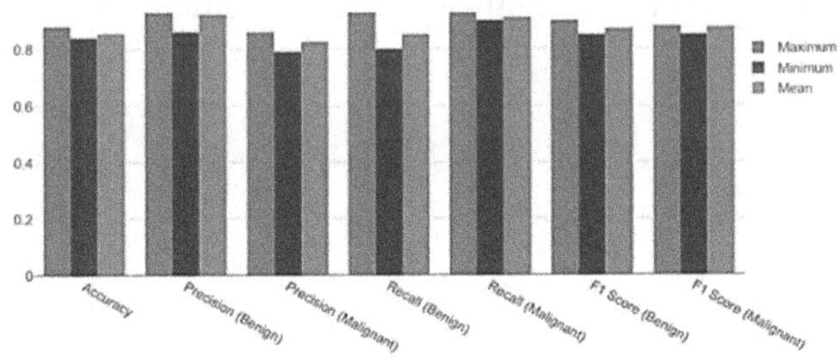

The mean recall for benign cases is 0.852, with a range of 0.8 to 0.93, which demonstrates that the models are effectively able to identify the majority of benign situations. This demonstrates that the models are able to reliably identify the majority of malignant occurrences, since the mean recall for malignant cases is 0.912, with a range that goes from 0.9 to 0.93. It may be deduced from the fact that the mean F1 score for benign cases falls within the range of 0.85 to 0.9 that there is a balanced relationship between recall and accuracy in these situations. The average F1 score for malignant patients falls somewhere in the range of 0.85 to 0.88, which indicates that memory and accuracy are in a state of equilibrium in these kinds of circumstances. When everything is taken into consideration, these performance measurements demonstrate how good machine learning models are in healthcare applications, particularly when it comes to activities such as diagnose illnesses and forecasting the results of patient treatment. By correctly classifying occurrences and establishing a balance between memory and accuracy, these models may be able to assist medical workers in making better decisions and improving the outcomes of patient care.

7. CONCLUSIONS

The combination of IoT and ML in healthcare is a game-changer for proactive, personalised patient care. This research covers the applications, problems, and potential uses of machine learning in healthcare, with an emphasis on how it may be used with IoT devices. The paper examines how Internet of Things devices might improve data gathering, operations, predictive analytics, patient involvement, and education. Additionally, it explores the difficulty of applying typical centralised learning algorithms to decentralised Internet of Things data and possible solutions. The study also shows how machine learning can analyse genetic data, wearable sensor data, medical image data, and electronic health record data. It also discusses ethical and legal issues related to medical machine learning. This article emphasises the IoT and ML's potential to transform healthcare delivery, patient outcomes, and society.

REFERENCES

Abdollahzadegan, A., Che Hussin, A. R., Moshfegh Gohary, M., & Amini, M. (2013). The organizational critical success factors for adopting cloud computing in SMEs. [JISRI]. *Journal of Information Systems Research and Innovation*, *4*(1), 67–74.

Ghate, V. V., & Vijayakumar, V. (2018). Machine learning for data aggregation in wsn: A survey. *International Journal of Pure and Applied Mathematics*, *118*(24), 1–12.

Bolhasani, H., & Jassbi, S. J. (2020). Deep learning accelerators: A case study with MAESTRO. *Journal of Big Data*, *7*(1), 100.

Joe, S. (2014). Qin. Process data analytics in the era of big data. *AIChE Journal. American Institute of Chemical Engineers*, *60*(9), 3092–3100.

Khoshraftar, A.. (2011). Improving The CRM System In Healthcare Organization. [IJCES]. *International Journal of Computational Engineering Science*, *1*(2), 28–35.

Lashkari, B., Rezazadeh, J., Farahbakhsh, R., & Sandrasegaran, K. (2018). Crowdsourcing and sensing for indoor localization in IoT: A review. *IEEE Sensors Journal*, *19*(7), 2408–2434. DOI: 10.1109/JSEN.2018.2880180

Malasinghe, L. P., Ramzan, N., & Dahal, K. (2019). Remote patient monitoring: A comprehensive study. *Journal of Ambient Intelligence and Humanized Computing*, *10*, 57–76.

Marriwala, N., & Jain, S. (2023). Editorial for the Special Issue on IoT-enabled Wireless Biomedical Systems and Sensors. *Measurement. Sensors*, *27*, 100750.

Marriwala, N. K., Shukla, V. K., William, P., Guleria, K., Sobti, R., & Sharma, S. (2024). Detection of viral messages in twitter using context-based sentiment analysis framework. *International Journal of Information Technology : an Official Journal of Bharati Vidyapeeth's Institute of Computer Applications and Management*, •••, 1–7.

Sadat Safavi, N., Amini, M., Abdollahzadegan, A., & Zakaria, N. H. (2013). An effective model for evaluating organizational risk and cost in ERP implementation by SME. IOSR Journal of Business and Management (IOSR-JBM), 10(6), 70-75.

Tsai, C.-W., Lai, C.-F., Chao, H.-C., & Vasilakos, A. (2015). Big data analytics: A survey. *Journal of Big Data*, *2*(1), 21. DOI: 10.1186/s40537-015-0030-3 PMID: 26191487

Yin, Z.. (2017, January). Health-CPS: Healthcare cyber-physical system assisted by cloud and big data. *IEEE Systems Journal*, *11*(1), 88–95. DOI: 10.1109/JSYST.2015.2460747

Chapter 13

Remote Patient Monitoring Systems: Enhancing Healthcare With Technology

P. William
https://orcid.org/0000-0002-0610-0390
Sanjivani University, India

Tarun Dhar Diwan
Atal Bihari Vajpayee University, Bilaspur, India

Firas Tayseer Ayasrah
https://orcid.org/0000-0002-6477-000X
College of Education, Humanities and Science, Al Ain University, UAE

Khaleel M. Al-Said
https://orcid.org/0000-0003-4609-0286
Middle East University, Amman, Jordan

Hala J. Abu-Alnadi
https://orcid.org/0009-0007-7248-9924
Department of Educational Technology, Middle East University, Amman, Jordan

ABSTRACT

The healthcare has been substantially revolutionized as a result of the introduction of remote patient monitoring (RPM) technologies. These technologies have made it feasible to continually monitor the health state of patients outside of traditional clinical settings. Wearables, smartphone applications, and cloud-based systems are just examples of the kind of technologies that are used by RPM in order to give

DOI: 10.4018/979-8-3693-6864-0.ch013

healthcare practitioners with real-time data collecting and transmission. The analysis of this data enables medical professionals to detect potential health issues at an earlier stage, take the necessary steps to address them, and develop tailored treatment programs that will improve patient outcomes while simultaneously reducing costs. Integration of artificial intelligence results in improved data interpretation, which in turn enables predictive analytics and proactive treatment of chronic diseases.

1. INTRODUCTION

Delving deeper into the essence of Remote Patient Monitoring (RPM) systems reveals a profound shift in the dynamics of healthcare delivery. At its core, RPM represents a departure from traditional models of episodic care, where patients interact with healthcare providers only during clinic visits or hospital stays. Instead, RPM creates a continuous connection between patients and providers, facilitated by a network of interconnected devices and digital platforms. In the depths of chronic disease management, post-operative recovery, and preventive care, RPM systems serve as vigilant guardians, tirelessly monitoring patients' health status and transmitting data in real-time to their healthcare teams (Asiimwe et al., 2020). It is possible for medical professionals to have a comprehensive understanding of the health of their patients because of the continuous flow of information. This makes it possible for them to recognize even the most minute changes in the conditions of their patients at an early stage and to take the proper steps to address those changes before they get more severe and become more significant health concerns. In addition, RPM systems provide patients the capacity to take an active part in the management of their own health, which fosters a sense of responsibility and ownership for the patients' overall health and welfare among the patient population. Through the provision of patients with access to their own health data, RPM stimulates patient engagement and encourages patients to comply to treatment programs. Because of this, there will be improvements in the quality of life, which will then lead to improvements in health outcomes.

However, before RPM's full potential can be fulfilled, there are a few difficulties that need to be handled first. These problems are concealed under the surface of this incredible piece of technology for the time being (Dev & Malik, 2021). Data security and privacy are at the forefront of the conversation because the transmission and storage of sensitive health information raises problems about the maintenance of confidentiality and the fulfilment of legal duties. In addition, a great number of patient populations are grappling with access problems as a consequence of the digital divide, which highlights the need of using designs that are inclusive and distributing RPM solutions in an equitable manner. For the purpose of effectively addressing these concerns, individuals working in the healthcare industry need to adopt an all-encompassing approach that strikes a balance between the development of new technologies, human connections, and empathy. Through the implementation of patient-centered care principles and the use of RPM as a tool to strengthen the connection between the patient and the provider, healthcare organisations have the ability to fully employ RPM in order to increase patient happiness, improve health outcomes, and raise efficiency across the whole of the healthcare continuum. Continuous monitoring from a distant hospital is required in order to ensure that patients located in remote areas get the best possible care and are given the most suitable suggestions for the administration of medication (Joyia et al., 2017). The management of data in contemporary telemedicine systems is comprised of three main levels, as seen in Figure 1. This hierarchy is comprised of the following layers: the gateway (Tier 2), the medical centre server (Tier 2), and the sensors (Tier 1) in that sequence. The collection of important signs that are connected to an individual's health is the responsibility of Tier 1 medical devices, which are equipment that are able to communicate with one another. There are a few examples of the equipment that is employed, such as sensors that measure blood pressure (BP), electrocardiogram (ECG), and blood oxygen saturation level (SpO2).

Figure 1. Architecture of remote patient monitoring systems healthcare

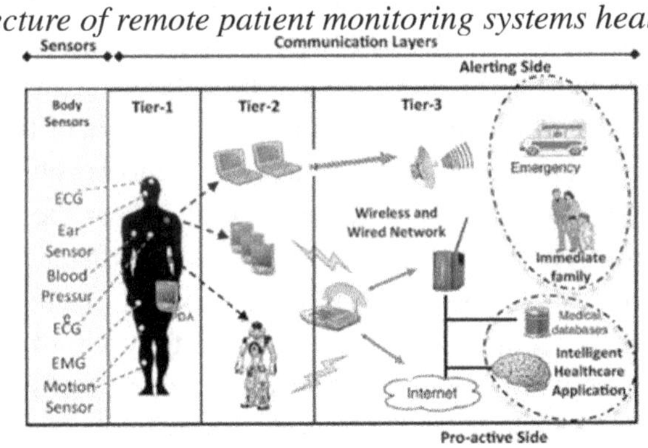

These technological gadgets transmit the data they've collected to Tier 2. Tier 2 is in charge of gathering, combining, and sending data over an external gateway to the remote server. The purpose of this gateway is to enable communication between all of the monitoring devices across extended distances (Mohammed et al., 2014). Tier 3 is a remote computer situated within the medical facility. It is often referred to as the medical centre server. Among its duties are serving as a post-processing database and a real-time data monitoring tool for medical practitioners. In this specific case, it is advised to divide the need for telemedicine into three phases: stages 1, 2, and 3.

Tier 3 represents a medical centre that is linked to distant hospitals and medical personnel in order to deliver healthcare services. It is probable that Tiers 1 and 2 represent the client side of the healthcare system.

2. REVIEW OF LITERATURE

It is becoming more common for people in today's society to suffer from chronic illnesses. There is an increase in the amount of stress that is being experienced by both hospitals and patients as a result of the need of frequent hospital visits for the monitoring and treatment of a variety of injuries and diseases. There is now a process of modernization taking place within the healthcare system as a result of the use of wearable sensors and enhanced communication protocols. This may soon result in a change in the characteristics of the services that are provided by the healthcare system. One of the most important developments among these advancements is the use of remote patient monitoring, or RPM as it is more often referred as (Nagata et al., 2017). The primary purpose of reflex pulse monitoring (RPM) devices is to provide medical staff with the vital signs of patients in real time. In order to accomplish this goal, it is possible to make use of both invasive and noninvasive collecting methods. If medical workers have access to this information, they may be able to choose the most appropriate course of action at the appropriate time. In addition to providing an overview of the current state of the art in remote patient monitoring, the purpose of this article is to give an analysis of the advantages and disadvantages of this technique, as well as details on the most probable advancements that may occur in the future. In addition to this, it discusses the potential for more research in this field and provides an overview of the role that artificial intelligence (AI) plays in the process of developing RPM systems. In order to make it easier to do research on the existing body of literature, the following five databases have been chosen: Science.gov, Science Direct, IEEE-Explore, Springer, and PubMed. PRISMA, which stands for Preferred Reporting Items for Systematic Reviews and Meta-Analyses, was the standard procedure that is used when doing research of this kind, and these investigations were carried out in accordance with that methodology (Manne & Kantheti, 2021). An examination of a total of 56 articles is carried out, and it is based on a combination of search phrases that have been established in advance. RPM, data mining, cloud computing, internet of things, clinical decision support system, electronic health record, and wireless body area network are some of the search terms that are included in this list. Furthermore, this list also includes wireless body area networks. According to the results of the research, Remote Patient Monitoring (RPM) has the potential to improve the delivery of healthcare while simultaneously reducing costs and reducing the amount of time needed for diagnostic testing. As an additional point of interest, we provide the chronic disease monitoring system as a case study to demonstrate how we may be able to develop RPM solutions that are more effective.

Telemedicine is a tried-and-true method that has been used for the purpose of giving medical treatment to patients who reside in remote locations. It is possible that patients will benefit from the implementation of this method. On the other hand, the mechanisms that are often involved in telemedicine are so complicated that the ordinary person is unable to comprehend the system altogether (Gambhir & Kathuria, 2016). The reason for this is that the hardware and network backbones that are used for data transmission and collection are quite complicated and demand a high level of technical expertise when it comes to their operation. Because of its focused nature, telemedicine is only available to those individuals who are physically located in close proximity to it. Research has been carried out in an effort to find a solution to these issues by developing a remote patient monitoring (RPM) system that is both inexpensive and constructed using technology that is based on reduced platform computer infrastructure. The creation of a plug-in module that could be used in real-time via the USB interface with the XO Laptop, which is a portable RPM system, was the primary objective of the project. Furthermore, it is anticipated that the same demographic that is the focus of the One Laptop per Child initiative would also benefit from the use of this device as a teaching tool. With the intention of simplifying the process of data transmission over a network that is based on the user datagram protocol (UDP), this article provides a description of the processes that are involved in the process of data collecting and preparation, as well as the availability of network power and capacity (Ramrekha & Politis, 2010).

The field of healthcare is increasingly making use of artificial intelligence (AI), which is still in its infancy as a field of study. More and more people are starting to make use of artificial intelligence. The application known as remote patient monitoring (RPM) is one of the apps that is utilised the most often in the field of healthcare. By using this application, medical professionals are able to keep track of patients who are hospitalised, patients who are getting treatment at home, patients who are old, and patients who are suffering from acute or chronic diseases. It's possible that all of these patients are dispersed throughout geographically dispersed areas. One of the most important factors that determines the reliability of manual patient monitoring systems is the efficiency with which staff members manage the tasks they are responsible for (Mohammed et al., 2019). One of the factors that has an effect on it is the amount of work that workers are required to do. The traditional method of patient monitoring involves the use of invasive technologies that need direct skin contact in order to monitor a patient's health. RPM systems are going to be investigated in great detail as part of this study project. The evaluation of RPM systems, which includes authorised cutting-edge technologies, the impact of artificial intelligence on RPM, as well as obstacles and advancements in AI-enabled RPM, is undertaken in order to accomplish this goal. In order to enable wearable devices and wearable sensors for the Internet of Things in patient-centric RPM designs, the purpose of this research is to investigate the benefits and challenges associated with the utilisation of blockchain, cloud, fog, and edge technologies. The use of artificial intelligence in RPM has the potential to be utilised for the monitoring of vital signs in emergency circumstances, the classification of physical activity, and the tracking of chronic illnesses. The findings of the investigation demonstrate how the innovations that have been made possible by AI-enabled RPM designs have altered the apps that are used for health monitoring. The early detection of deterioration in patient health, federated learning-based monitoring of customised patient health indicators, and recognition of human behaviour patterns are all examples of the applications of reinforcement learning that have been implemented in these systems. The purpose of this study is to discuss the many concerns, trends, and implementation challenges that are associated with the incorporation of artificial intelligence into frameworks for research and development. The purpose of this article is to provide an outline of the likely future paths that artificial intelligence may go in RPM applications by examining both trends and obstacles.

Due to the fact that the field of study known as Remote Patient Monitoring Systems (RPMS) is concerned with the lives of individuals, it is widely acknowledged to be among the most significant (Zhu et al., 2021). In the time since the beginning of the epidemic, there has been a substantial rise in the number of people who are using RPMS devices. However, despite the fact that these systems are becoming more widespread, there are still a few challenges that need to be conquered. Mobility, heterogeneous networks, automation, standardisation of records management systems (RPMS), and quality of service (QoS) are some of the challenges that are encountered. During this session, we will discuss the advantages of real-time monitoring systems (RPMS) for the purpose of monitoring physiological indicators, as well as the challenges and design of these systems. It is necessary to conduct a comprehensive analysis of these data as well as a comprehensive review of RPMS in order to determine the current condition of the publications pertaining to RPMS. According to the report that was released, the research that is being conducted at these RPMS may be broken down into two or more of the following categories: applications, architecture, techniques, and the success of these approaches. According to the evidence, prior to the pandemic that occurred in the year 2020, researchers focused their attention on almost every aspect of the development of RPMS. In the years that followed, the designs and implementations of these systems grew more significant in the field of study pertaining to RPMS. This particular circumstance is the reason why a growing number of companies are developing mobile information management systems (RPMS). When doing this research, our objective is to conduct a comprehensive analysis of each and every RPMS that has been used, paying special attention to the technologies, designs, applications, and challenges that have been faced. Last but not least, we provided a statistical and comparative study of the corpus of previously accessible content, and we defined Quality of Service (QoS) as one of the difficulties that RPMS is now engaging with. The evaluated quality of service expectations are provided in accordance with the traffic type, data quality, device quality, and network metrics. This is done with the intention of assisting academic institutions and industry in adopting the most efficient method for the design of quality-aware RMPS. A plan for the work that has to be done in order to improve the future deployment of RPMS will be provided by us at the end of this process, provided that it is successfully completed.

3. BENEFITS OF REMOTE PATIENT MONITORING IN HEALTHCARE

As the healthcare environment continues to undergo rapid change, Remote Patient Monitoring (RPM) has emerged as a tool that has the potential to revolutionize the delivery of therapy. The benefits it provides extend beyond the traditional confines of therapeutic settings and include a variety of perks. Through the use of technology, RPM is able to give medical personnel with remote and real-time monitoring of patient health. Consequently, this makes it possible to provide more preventative therapies, tailored care plans, and improved results for patients. Individuals are provided with the opportunity to actively control their own health, and physicians are provided with meaningful information about the health and habits of their patients. RPM is fundamentally a paradigm shift in the way that healthcare is given. Through the use of a network of interconnected devices, such as wearable sensors, intelligent medical equipment, and mobile applications, RPM makes it possible to continually monitor vital signs, symptoms, and adherence to treatment plans. This is accomplished without the need of making frequent trips to the doctor's office. Additionally, RPM has the potential to increase access to care, particularly for patients who are elderly, patients who suffer from chronic conditions, and patients who reside in areas that are underserved or in remote locations. By enabling patients to get high-quality care without having to leave the comfort of their own homes, remote patient management (RPM) reduces the burden of travel and wait times that are associated with in-person medical consultations. This contributes to an increase in patient engagement and satisfaction. Additionally, RPM makes it easier to discover health concerns early and take action promptly, which helps to minimize unnecessary hospital stays, trips to the emergency room, and complications. Because it provides physicians with real-time access to patient data, RPM makes it possible for them to make proactive decisions, plan tailored care, and optimize treatment strategies simultaneously. The results for patients are improved, and the expenses of healthcare are reduced. Within the scope of this investigation into the advantages of remote patient monitoring (RPM) in the healthcare industry, we investigate the many advantages that RPM offers to healthcare systems, professionals, and patients on a daily basis. RPM is a powerful tool that has the potential to transform the delivery of healthcare and improve health and wellbeing for people all around the world. It can do this by empowering patients, improving care coordination, and making better use of resources.

Figure 2. Remote patient monitoring's benefits for healthcare

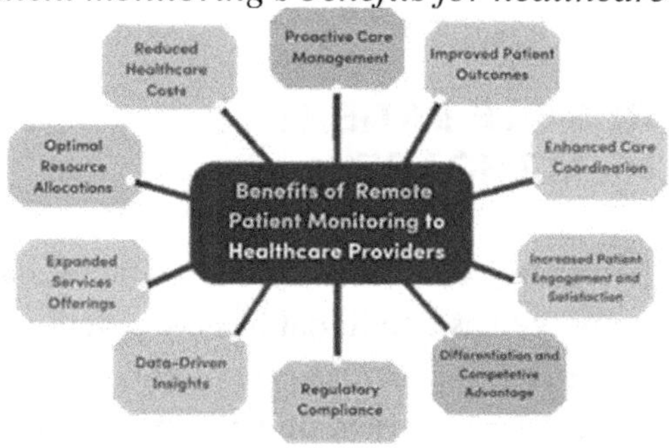

In the realm of healthcare innovation, Remote Patient Monitoring (RPM) systems are at the vanguard, using technology to revolutionize the delivery of patient care. These technologies make it possible for medical professionals to remotely monitor the vital signs, symptoms, and health indicators of their patients, which in turn allows for a revolution in the administration of treatment and the results for patients. Within the scope of this all-encompassing investigation, we look into the myriad of advantages that remote patient monitoring in the healthcare industry provides, illuminating the significant influence that it has on the delivery of treatment and the patient in general.

- **Proactive Care Management:**

Remote patient monitoring enables proactive care management by allowing healthcare providers to continuously monitor patients' health parameters remotely. This real-time monitoring facilitates early detection of health issues and timely interventions, preventing exacerbations of chronic conditions, reducing hospital admissions, and improving overall patient health outcomes.

- **Improved Patient Outcomes:**

Through remote monitoring, patients receive more personalized and timely interventions, leading to significantly improved health outcomes. By closely monitoring vital signs, symptoms, and treatment adherence remotely, healthcare providers can tailor interventions to individual patient needs, resulting in better disease management, reduced complications, and enhanced patient well-being.

- **Enhanced Care Coordination:**

Remote patient monitoring fosters seamless care coordination among multidisciplinary healthcare teams, patients, and caregivers. By sharing real-time health data and insights, remote monitoring systems facilitate collaborative care delivery across various healthcare settings, ensuring continuity of care, reducing communication gaps, and improving patient safety and satisfaction.

- **Increased Patient Engagement and Satisfaction:**

Remote patient monitoring empowers patients to actively participate in their healthcare journey by providing them with access to their health data and encouraging self-management. This increased patient engagement leads to greater patient satisfaction, as individuals feel more involved in their care decisions, better supported by their healthcare providers, and empowered to take control of their health.

- **Differentiation and Competitive Advantage:**

Healthcare organizations that embrace remote patient monitoring gain a competitive edge by offering innovative and patient-centered care solutions. By leveraging technology-enabled care delivery, providers can differentiate themselves in the market, attract tech-savvy patients, and position themselves as leaders in delivering modern, convenient, and proactive healthcare services.

- **Reduced Healthcare Costs:**

Remote patient monitoring has the potential to significantly reduce healthcare costs by preventing avoidable hospitalizations, minimizing emergency room visits, and optimizing resource utilization. By shifting the focus from reactive to proactive and preventive care, remote monitoring systems help lower overall healthcare expenditures, improving cost-effectiveness and sustainability of healthcare delivery.

- **Optimal Resource Allocation:**

Through remote monitoring, healthcare providers can allocate resources more efficiently by identifying patients in need of immediate attention and prioritizing care delivery based on acuity levels. This optimized resource allocation ensures that limited resources are directed where they are most needed, enhancing healthcare system efficiency and patient outcomes.

- **Expanded Service Offerings:**

Remote patient monitoring enables healthcare providers to expand their service offerings by introducing new and innovative care delivery models, such as telemedicine consultations, remote medication management, and virtual health coaching. These additional services enhance the overall patient experience, meet evolving patient needs, and foster long-term patient-provider relationships.

- **Data-Driven Insights:**

The process of remotely monitoring patients generates a substantial amount of data, which may be used to get useful insights into the health patterns of patients, the efficacy of therapies, and the management of community health. It is possible for healthcare organizations to enhance the quality of treatment and the results for patients by recognizing patterns, making predictions about outcomes, and tailoring treatments to fit the specific needs of each individual patient via the analysis of this vast amount of information.

- **Regulatory Compliance:**

The use of remote patient monitoring systems provides assistance to healthcare organizations in satisfying quality standards and fulfilling regulatory duties. It is possible for providers to demonstrate compliance with regulatory obligations more effectively, increase patient safety, and elevate the level of care by ensuring that patient data is continually monitored and recorded.

The use of remote patient monitoring technology represents a paradigm shift in the delivery of healthcare because of the innovative benefits they provide throughout the whole care continuum. Through the use of technology-enabled remote monitoring, medical professionals are able to provide treatment that is proactive, tailored, and patient-centered. Improved patient engagement, enhanced care coordination, decreased costs, and the promotion of sustainable healthcare delivery are all outcomes that will result from this.

4. RESEARCH METHODOLOGY

Research on remote patient monitoring systems involves several key methodologies aimed at evaluating their effectiveness, usability, and impact on healthcare outcomes. Typically, studies employ a combination of quantitative and qualitative research methods. Quantitative approaches include controlled clinical trials, observational studies, and retrospective data analyses to assess the clinical efficacy of remote monitoring systems in managing various health conditions. These methods often involve collecting and analyzing patient data such as vital signs, medication adherence, and clinical outcomes over specified periods. Qualitative methodologies, such as interviews, focus groups, and usability testing, are utilized to understand patients' and healthcare providers' experiences, preferences, and challenges associated with remote monitoring technology. Additionally, health economic evaluations may be conducted to assess the cost-effectiveness and financial implications of implementing remote monitoring systems. Overall, a comprehensive research methodology is essential to explore the multifaceted aspects of remote patient monitoring systems and their potential to enhance healthcare delivery. The suggests a focus on the utilization of remote patient monitoring systems (RPMS) to improve healthcare delivery through technological advancements. It implies an exploration of how RPMS leverage technology to monitor patients' health remotely, thereby enhancing access to care, improving patient outcomes, and reducing healthcare costs.

- **Overview of Remote Patient Monitoring Systems:**

An overview of RPMS, including its components, characteristics, and applications in the medical area, is presented at the beginning of the research. The interpretation focuses on the many technological instruments that are used by RPMS in order to collect and transmit patient data to healthcare practitioners located in remote locations. These technologies include wearables, mobile apps, and telecommunication platforms.

- **Benefits of Remote Patient Monitoring:**

The benefits of RPMS for patients, healthcare practitioners, and healthcare systems are dissected in great length in this article. Interpretation examines the ways in which RPMS may assist with the continuing monitoring of vital signs, medication compliance, and the progression of a disease. This may improve clinical outcomes by facilitating the early detection of health problems, rapid treatment, and improvement in clinical outcomes. Additionally, RPMS has the potential to increase patient engagement, happiness, and quality of life by providing individuals with the ability to actively participate in the management of their own treatment. .

- **Technological Components of Remote Patient Monitoring Systems:**

The focus shifts to the technological components of RPMS, including sensors, data transmission protocols, cloud computing, and data analytics. Analysis examines how these components work together to capture, transmit, store, and analyze patient data securely and efficiently. A comprehensive analysis is conducted to determine the extent to which cutting-edge technologies such as machine learning (ML), artificial intelligence (AI), and the Internet of Things (IoT) have the potential to enhance the capabilities of RPMS in terms of risk assessment, predictive analytics, and the delivery of tailored healthcare.

Integration with Healthcare Ecosystem:

Analysis extends to the integration of RPMS with the broader healthcare ecosystem, including electronic health records (EHRs), telemedicine platforms, and care coordination systems. Interpretation explores how RPMS enable seamless data exchange and collaboration among healthcare providers, leading to improved care coordination, continuity of care, and population health management.

- **Challenges and Considerations:**

The analysis concludes by addressing the challenges and considerations associated with the adoption of RPMS. Interpretation evaluates factors such as data privacy and security, regulatory compliance, reimbursement models, and disparities in access to technology, while also highlighting strategies to overcome these challenges and maximize the potential of RPMS to transform healthcare delivery.

5. ANALYSIS AND INTERPRETATION

A possible instrument for enhancing the delivery of healthcare has developed in the form of remote patient monitoring systems. These systems have the capacity to continually monitor the health condition of patients outside of traditional clinical settings. Wearables, smartphone applications, and cloud-based platforms are some of the technologies that are used by these systems in order to collect and transmit real-time health data to medical professionals. By allowing for the early diagnosis of health deterioration, rapid treatments, and tailored care plans, the data generated by remote monitoring systems may be examined, which will ultimately lead to improved patient outcomes and a reduction in the costs associated with healthcare. Additionally, the use of machine learning and artificial intelligence algorithms enhances the interpretation of the data that has been obtained, which enables proactive treatment of chronic diseases as well as predictive analytics. As a result, remote patient monitoring systems provide a holistic approach to the administration of healthcare since they enable patients to take an active role in their own treatment and make it possible for medical professionals to deliver services that are both more effective and more tailored. Table 1 provides an overview of the sample rates and data volumes for remote patient monitoring systems that measure blood pressure, heart rate, and temperature. These systems are used to monitor patients remotely. The sample rates range from 1 sample per day to 24 samples per day, with corresponding data sizes per day, week, month, and year. For temperature and heart rate monitoring, the data sizes vary depending on the sample rate. For example, at a sample rate of 1 sample per day, the data size is 16 units per day, 112 units per week, 480 units per month, and 5.63 units per year. As the sample rate increases, the data sizes also increase accordingly, providing more granular insights into the patient's health status. The table 1 provides an overview of sample rates and data sizes for monitoring temperature, heart rate, and blood pressure in remote patient monitoring systems. The sample rates range from 1 sample per day to 24 samples per day, with corresponding data sizes per day, week, month, and year. For temperature and heart rate monitoring, the data sizes vary depending on the sample rate. For example, at a sample rate of 1 sample per day, the data size is 16 units per day, 112 units per week, 480 units per month, and 5.63 units per year. As the sample rate increases, the data sizes also increase accordingly, providing more granular insights into the patient's health status.

Table 1. Sample rates and sizes for health data monitoring

Sample Type(s)	Sample Rate (samples/ day)	Size/ Day	Size/Week	Size/ Month	Size/Year
Temperature and Heart Rate	1	16A	112A	480A	5.63F
	2	32A	224A	960A	11.25F
	3	48A	336A	1.41F	16.88F
	4	64A	448A	1.88F	22.5F
	8	128A	896A	3.75F	45F
	12	192A	1.31F	5.63F	67.5F
	24	384A	2.63F	11.25F	135F

continued on following page

Table 1. Continued

Sample Type(s)	Sample Rate (samples/ day)	Size/ Day	Size/Week	Size/ Month	Size/Year
Blood Pressure	1	9A	63A	270A	3.16F
	2	18A	126A	540A	6.39F
	3	27A	189A	810A	9.49F
	4	36A	252A	1.05F	12.66F
	8	72A	504A	2.11F	25.31F
	12	106A	742A	3.11F	37.27
	24	216A	1.48F	6.39F	75.94F

Remote patient monitoring systems make use of technology to collect and transmit patient health data to medical experts. This makes it possible to continue monitoring the patient's health even when the patient is not in a conventional healthcare setting. The early detection of health problems, fast intervention, and tailored treatment are all made possible by these technologies, which ultimately lead to improved patient outcomes and decreased costs associated with healthcare. The data that is acquired via the use of remote patient monitoring devices may provide medical practitioners with the ability to recognize trends, assess the progress of patients, and make adjustments to treatment programs as required. This data-driven approach to healthcare enables more proactive and personalized care, leading to improved patient satisfaction and overall healthcare quality. Overall, remote patient monitoring systems play a crucial role in enhancing healthcare with technology, empowering both patients and healthcare providers to better manage health and wellness.

The table 2 presents patient health data captured in a remote patient monitoring system, including patient ID, age, gender, temperature (°C), heart rate (bpm), blood pressure, and status (normal or abnormal). This data is essential for monitoring and managing patient health remotely, enabling healthcare providers to track vital signs and intervene promptly if abnormalities are detected. Each row in the table 2 represents a patient, with corresponding data points such as age, gender, and physiological measurements. For example, Patient 1 is a 30-year-old male with a temperature of 36.2°C, a heart rate of 92.8 bpm, and a blood pressure of 72. Their status is labeled as "Normal." This information provides a snapshot of the patient's health status at a given point in time. The use of technology enables remote patient monitoring devices to collect and transmit real-time health data from patients to healthcare experts. This makes it possible for healthcare professionals to conduct continual monitoring and identify potential health issues at an earlier stage. Through the analysis of this data, medical personnel are able to recognize trends, keep track of changes, and make decisions about patient treatment.

Table 2. Patient health data in remote monitoring system

ID	Age	Gender	Temperature (°C)	Heart Rate (bpm)	Blood Pressure	Status
1	30	Male	36.2	92.8	72	Normal
2	25	Female	36.05	96.2	64	Normal
3	35	Female	36.45	94.7	74	Abnormal
4	40	Male	36.55	98.5	67	Normal
5	50	Female	37.8	95.1	85	Abnormal
6	60	Male	36.6	97.8	77	Normal

In the context of the table 2, patients with abnormal status may require immediate attention or adjustment to their treatment plan. For example, Patient 3, a 35-year-old female, has a temperature of 36.45°C, a heart rate of 94.7 bpm, and a blood pressure of 74, all of which are within normal ranges. However, her status is labeled as "Abnormal," indicating that there may be other factors or symptoms that warrant further investigation or intervention. Overall, remote patient monitoring systems play a crucial role in enhancing healthcare by providing timely and personalized care to patients. By leveraging technology to collect and analyze health data, these systems empower both patients and healthcare providers to better manage health and wellness, ultimately improving patient outcomes and quality of life. The table 3 provides information on the voltage and current requirements for various medical devices used in remote patient monitoring systems. These devices play a crucial role in monitoring patient health remotely and transmitting vital data to healthcare providers. The ESP32 microcontroller requires a voltage of 3.5V and a current of 0.6 A, making it suitable for low-power applications. The AD8232 ECG sensor operates at a voltage of 3.3V and a current of 180 μA, making it ideal for continuous ECG monitoring with minimal power consumption. The MAX30100 pulse oximeter operates at a voltage of 3.3V and a current of 25 mA, providing accurate heart rate and oxygen saturation measurements. The MAX6675 thermocouple sensor requires a higher voltage of 5V and a current of 55 mA, making it suitable for measuring temperature in remote patient monitoring systems.

Table 3. Power requirements for medical devices in remote monitoring systems

Device	Voltage	Current
ESP32	3.5V	0.6 A
AD8232	3.3V	180 μA
MAX30100	3.3V	25 mA
MAX6675	5V	55 mA
SIM800L	5V	150-230 mA

The SIM800L GSM module operates at a voltage of 5V and a current ranging from 150 to 230 mA, depending on the network and usage. This module enables communication between the remote monitoring system and healthcare providers, allowing for real-time data transmission and alerts. Overall, these medical devices, with their specific voltage and current requirements, are essential components of remote patient monitoring systems. By providing accurate and reliable data, these devices help healthcare providers monitor patient health remotely and intervene promptly when necessary, ultimately improving patient outcomes and quality of care.

6. RESULT AND DISCUSSION

The provision of medical treatment has been fundamentally revolutionized as a result of the implementation of remote patient monitoring systems, which make use of technology to enhance patient care in locations that are not traditionally associated with clinical settings. Through the use of wearable devices, mobile applications, and cloud-based platforms, these systems enable continuous monitoring of patients' health states, hence providing healthcare practitioners with the ability to gather and transmit data in real time. Practitioners in the healthcare industry may be able to improve patient outcomes and reduce costs associated with healthcare by evaluating this data in order to detect potential health issues at an earlier stage, take urgent action, and develop tailored treatment programs. In addition, the combination of artificial intelligence and machine learning algorithms not only improves the interpretation of data but also makes it possible to take preventative measures for chronic diseases and to conduct predictive analytics. It may be concluded that remote patient monitoring systems are an important advancement in the field of healthcare. These technologies enable medical practitioners to provide therapy that is both more effective and more tailored, while also enabling patients to take an active part in their own care decisions. Figure 3 provides a summary of the patient health data that were acquired by remote patient monitoring equipment. These parameters include the patient's age, blood pressure, heart rate (bpm), and temperature (°C). For the purpose of remotely monitoring a patient's health and recognizing any changes or anomalies that may need medical care, these measures are very necessary. Patients that are observed by remote monitoring systems have a mean age of 40.83 years, with a standard deviation of 12.45 years. This reflects the wide range of ages that are present in the population that is being watched. The fact that the patient with the youngest age is 25 years old and the patient with the oldest age is 60 years old has a clear indication of the age range of patients who use remote monitoring systems. The average observable temperature of the body is 36.475 degrees Celsius, with a standard deviation of 0.604 degrees Celsius. Among the patient population, the temperature that was reported as being the lowest was 36.05 degrees Celsius, and the temperature that was recorded as being the highest was 37.8 degrees Celsius. This range of typical body temperatures was monitored

Figure 3. Data transmission and analysis in remote patient monitoring systems

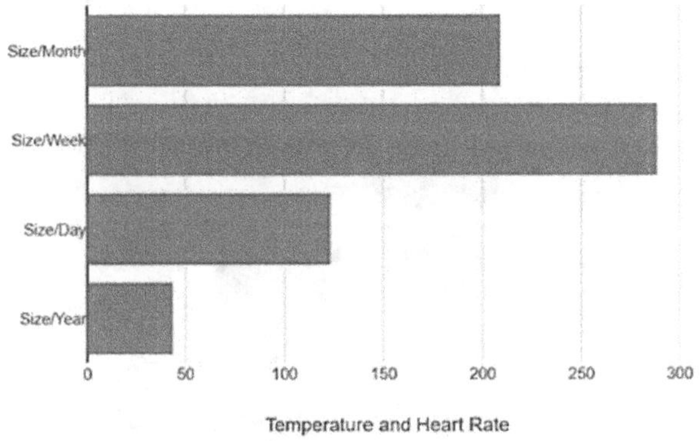

Heart rate measurements show a mean of 95.85 bpm, with a standard deviation of 3.245 bpm. The lowest recorded heart rate is 92.8 bpm, while the highest is 98.5 bpm, demonstrating the variability in heart rate among monitored patients. Blood pressure measurements show a mean of 72.5 mmHg for diastolic pressure, with a standard deviation of 7.071 mmHg. The minimum recorded diastolic pressure is 64 mmHg, while the maximum is 85 mmHg, indicating the range of blood pressure levels monitored in the patient population. When everything is taken into consideration, these measures not only give valuable information about the health of the patient, but they also enable medical personnel to monitor and exercise control over patient care from a distance. The use of technology in remote patient monitoring systems by medical professionals has the potential to enhance patient outcomes and quality of life by enabling them to give therapy that is more customized and delivered in a timely manner. Figure 4 provides a summary of the health indicators that are acquired by remote patient monitoring systems. These indicators include age, blood pressure, heart rate (bpm), and temperature (°C). When it comes to remotely monitoring a patient's health and spotting any changes or abnormalities that may need medical care, these factors are very necessary. Patients that are observed by remote monitoring systems have a mean age of 40.83 years, with a standard deviation of 12.45 years. This reflects the wide range of ages that are present in the population that is being watched. The fact that the patient with the youngest age is 25 years old and the patient with the oldest age is 60 years old has a clear indication of the age range of patients who use remote monitoring systems. The average observable temperature of the body is 36.475 degrees Celsius, with a standard deviation of 0.604 degrees Celsius. Among the patient population, the temperature that was reported as being the lowest was 36.05 degrees Celsius, and the temperature that was recorded as being the highest was 37.8 degrees Celsius. This range of typical body temperatures was monitored.

Figure 4. Summary of physiological metrics monitored through remote patient monitoring systems

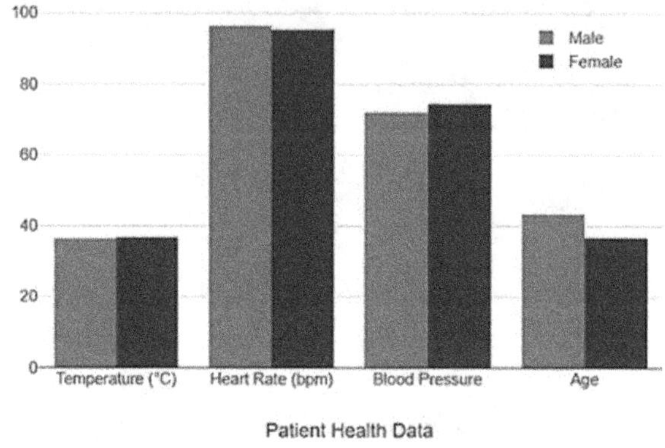

Heart rate measurements show a mean of 95.85 bpm, with a standard deviation of 3.245 bpm. The lowest recorded heart rate is 92.8 bpm, while the highest is 98.5 bpm, demonstrating the variability in heart rate among monitored patients. Blood pressure measurements show a mean of 72.5 mmHg for diastolic pressure, with a standard deviation of 7.071 mmHg. The minimum recorded diastolic pressure is 64 mmHg, while the maximum is 85 mmHg, indicating the range of blood pressure levels monitored in the patient population. Overall, these metrics provide valuable insights into patient health and allow healthcare providers to monitor and manage patient health remotely. By leveraging technology in remote patient monitoring systems, healthcare providers can provide more personalized and timely care, ultimately improving patient outcomes and quality of life.

7. CONCLUSIONS

Remote Patient Monitoring (RPM) systems represent a significant advancement in healthcare delivery, offering benefits such as proactive care management, improved patient outcomes, and enhanced care coordination. By leveraging technology, RPM systems enable continuous monitoring of patients' health status, facilitating early detection of health issues and personalized care planning. Despite the challenges in adoption, RPM systems have the potential to transform healthcare delivery, improve patient satisfaction, and reduce healthcare costs. Future research should focus on addressing the challenges and enhancing the capabilities of RPM systems to further improve healthcare outcomes and patient care.

REFERENCES

Asiimwe, S. B., Vittinghoff, E., & Whooley, M. (2020). Vital signs data and probability of hospitalization, transfer to another facility, or emergency department death among adults presenting for medical illnesses to the emergency department at a large urban hospital in the United States. *The Journal of Emergency Medicine, 58*(4), 570–580. DOI: 10.1016/j.jemermed.2019.11.020 PMID: 31924465

Dev, A., & Malik, S. K. (2021). Artificial bee colony optimized deep neural network model for handling imbalanced stroke data. *International Journal of E-Health and Medical Communications, 12*(5), 67–83. DOI: 10.4018/IJEHMC.20210901.oa5

Gambhir, S., & Kathuria, M. (2016). DWBAN: Dynamic priority based WBAN architecture for healthcare system. *2016 3rd International Conference on Computing for Sustainable Global Development (INDIACom)*. 3380–3386.

Joyia, G. J., Liaqat, R. M., Farooq, A., & Rehman, S. (2017). Internet of medical things (IoMT): Applications, benefits and future challenges in healthcare domain. *Journal of Communication, 12*(4), 240–247.

Manne, R., & Kantheti, S. C. (2021). Application of Artificial Intelligence in Healthcare: Chances and Challenges. *Current Journal of Applied Science and Technology, 40*(6), 78–89. DOI: 10.9734/cjast/2021/v40i631320

Mohammed, J., Lung, C. H., Ocneanu, A., Thakral, A., Jones, C., & Adler, A. (2014). Internet of things: remote patient monitoring using web services and cloud computing Proceedings of the *IEEE International Conference on Internet of Things (iThings)*. pp. 256-263 DOI: 10.1109/iThings.2014.45

Mohammed, Y., Mohammed, A. S., Abdulkarim, H. T., Danladi, C., Victor, A., & Edoka, R. (2019). Development and implementation of an internet of things (IOT) based remote patient monitoring system *Proceedings of the 15th International Conference on Electronics, Computer and Computation, ICECCO 2019*. DOI: 10.1109/ICECCO48375.2019.9043200

Nagata, K., Nakamura, T., & Farouk, A. (2017). Quantum cryptography based on the Deutsch-Jozsa algorithm. *International Journal of Theoretical Physics, 56*(9), 2887–2897. DOI: 10.1007/s10773-017-3456-x

Ramrekha, T. A. (2010). C. Politis A hybrid adaptive routing protocol for extreme emergency ad hoc communication *Proceedings of the International Conference on Computer Communications and Networks (ICCCN)*.

Zhu, F., Zhang, C., Zheng, Z., & Farouk, A. (2021). Practical Network Coding Technologies and Softwarization in Wireless Networks. *IEEE Internet of Things Journal*, *8*(7), 5211–5218. DOI: 10.1109/JIOT.2021.3056580

Compilation of References

Abadi, M., Chu, A., Goodfellow, I., McMahan, H. B., Mironov, I., Talwar, K., & Zhang, L. Deep learning with differential privacy. In: *Proceedings of the 2016 ACM SIGSAC Conference on Computer and Communications Security*. pp. 308– 318. ACM (2016) DOI: 10.1145/2976749.2978318

Abdollahzadegan, A., Che Hussin, A. R., Moshfegh Gohary, M., & Amini, M. (2013). The organizational critical success factors for adopting cloud computing in SMEs. [JISRI]. *Journal of Information Systems Research and Innovation*, *4*(1), 67–74.

Abideen, Z. U., & Shah, M. A. An IoT based robust healthcare model for continuous health monitoring. *InProceedings of the 2017 23rd International Conference on Automation and Computing (ICAC)*, Huddersfield, UK, 7–8 September 2017; pp. 1–6. DOI: 10.23919/IConAC.2017.8082012

Adams, G., Fabbri, A. R., Ladhak, F., Lehman, E., & Elhadad, N. (2023, December). From sparse to dense: GPT-4 summarization with chain of density prompting. In Proceedings of the Conference on Empirical Methods in Natural Language Processing. Conference on Empirical Methods in Natural Language Processing (Vol. 2023, No. 4th New Frontier Summarization Workshop, p. 68).

Aggarwal, S., & Pandey, K. (2023). Early identification of PCOS with commonly known diseases: Obesity, diabetes, high blood pressure and heart disease using machine learning techniques. *Expert Systems with Applications*, *217*, 119532.

Ahmed, S., Yesmin, S., Saha, L. R., Sadat, A. K. M., & Khan, M. H. A. (2022). "Major Cropping Pattern Prediction in Bangladesh from Land, Soil and Climate Data Using Machine Learning Techniques," 25th International Conference on Computer and Information Technology (ICCIT), Cox's Bazar, Bangladesh. pp. 988-993, DOI: 10.1109/ICCIT57492.2022.10056051

Al Nuaimi, E., Al Neyadi, H., Mohamed, N., & Al-Jaroodi, J. (2015). Applications of big data to smart cities. *Journal of Internet Services and Applications*, *6*(1), 25. DOI: 10.1186/s13174-015-0041-5

Alam, T. M., Iqbal, M. A., Ali, Y., Wahab, A., Ijaz, S., Baig, T. I., Hussain, A., Malik, M. A., Raza, M. M., & Ibrar, S. (2019). A model for early prediction of diabetes. *Informatics in Medicine Unlocked*, *16*, 100204.

Alarcón, G. M., Esquivel, G. B., & Flores, M. F. (2019). The impact of social media on mental health: A review of the literature. *Revista de Investigacion Clinica*, *71*(2), 67–75.

Aledhari, M., Razzak, R., Qolomany, B., Al-Fuqaha, A., & Saeed, F. (2022). Biomedical IoT: Enabling Technologies, Architectural Elements, Challenges, and Future Directions. *IEEE Access : Practical Innovations, Open Solutions*, *10*, 31306–31339. DOI: 10.1109/ACCESS.2022.3159235 PMID: 35441062

Alguliev, R. M., Aliguliyev, R. M., & Isazade, N. R. (2013). Multiple documents summarization based on evolutionary optimization algorithm. *Expert Systems with Applications*, *40*(5), 1675–1689. DOI: 10.1016/j.eswa.2012.09.014

Almalchy, M. T., Ciobanu, V., & Algayar, S. M. Solutions for healthcare monitoring systems architectures. In Proceedings of the 2018 *IEEE 16th International Conference on Embedded and Ubiquitous Computing (EUC)*, Bucharest, Romania, 29–31 October 2018; pp. 123–128.

Almeida, M., & Costa, J. (2024). Smart water management using IoT: A review of technologies and applications. *Water Research*, *203*, 117416. DOI: 10.1016/j.watres.2024.117416

Alzubaidi, L., Al-Shamma, O., Fadhel, M. A., Farhan, L., & Zhang, J. (2020). "Classification of red blood cells in sickle cell anemia using deep convolutional neural network", Intelligent Systems Design and Applications: 18th International Conference on Intelligent Systems Design and Applications (ISDA 2018). pp. 550-559. DOI: 10.1007/978-3-030-16657-1_51

Alzubaidi, L., Fadhel, M. A., Al-Shamma, O., Zhang, J., & Duan, Y. (2020, March). Deep Learning Models for Classification of Red Blood Cells in Microscopy Images to Aid in Sickle Cell Anemia Diagnosis. *Electronics (Basel)*, *9*(3), 427. DOI: 10.3390/electronics9030427

Ambinder, M. D. (2020). IoT and Machine Learning for Remote Monitoring and Management of Heart Disease. *The Journal of Cardiovascular Medicine*, *21*(4), 265–272.

Anand, A., & Shakti, D. (2015). Prediction of diabetes based on personal lifestyle indicators. *2015 1st International Conference on Next Generation Computing Technologies (NGCT)*, 673–676.

Andreassen, C. S., Pallesen, S., & Griffiths, M. D. (2017). The relationship between addictive use of social media, narcissism, and self-esteem: Findings from a large national survey. *Addictive Behaviors*, *64*, 287–293. DOI: 10.1016/j.addbeh.2016.03.006 PMID: 27072491

Ansari, Y., Mourad, O., Qaraqe, K., & Serpedin, E. (2023, September 15). Deep learning for ECG Arrhythmia detection and classification: An overview of progress for period 2017-2023. *Frontiers in Physiology*, *14*, 1246746. DOI: 10.3389/fphys.2023.1246746 PMID: 37791347

An, X. (2020, March 7). K Stylios G. Comparison of Motion Artefact Reduction Methods and the Implementation of Adaptive Motion Artefact Reduction in Wearable Electrocardiogram Monitoring. *Sensors (Basel)*, *20*(5), 1468. DOI: 10.3390/s20051468 PMID: 32155984

Apat, S. K., Mishra, J., Raju, K. S., & Padhy, N. (2023). An artificial intelligence-based crop recommendation system using machine learning. [JSIR]. *Journal of Scientific and Industrial Research*, *82*(05), 558–567.

Arishi, W. A., Eissa, S., & Zourob, M. (2023, August 8). Aptamer-based label-free electrochemical biosensors for the diagnosis of sickle cell anemia. *Biosensors & Bioelectronics: X*, *14*, 36–45. DOI: 10.1016/j.biosx.2023.100389

Aryamol, A. U., Raji, P. G., & Sam, G. (2021). A Survey Paper On Crop Prediction using. *Machine Learning*.

Asiimwe, S. B., Vittinghoff, E., & Whooley, M. (2020). Vital signs data and probability of hospitalization, transfer to another facility, or emergency department death among adults presenting for medical illnesses to the emergency department at a large urban hospital in the United States. *The Journal of Emergency Medicine*, *58*(4), 570–580. DOI: 10.1016/j.jemermed.2019.11.020 PMID: 31924465

Assa, A., & Janabi-Sharifi, F. (2015). A Kalman Filter-Based Framework for Enhanced Sensor Fusion. *IEEE Sensors Journal*, *15*(6), 1–1. DOI: 10.1109/JSEN.2014.2388153

Attavar, A. L. (2024). "IntelliCrop: Major Cropping Pattern Prediction using Machine Learning Techniques," *2024 International Conference on Inventive Computation Technologies (ICICT)*, Lalitpur, Nepal. pp. 895-899, DOI: 10.1109/ICICT60155.2024.10544932

Attavar, A., Manohar, A. L., Himoshra, D., & Pooja, M. R. (2024, April). IntelliCrop: Major Cropping Pattern Prediction using Machine Learning Techniques. In *2024 International Conference on Inventive Computation Technologies (ICICT)* (pp. 895-899). IEEE.

Ba, L., (2016). Layer normalization. arXiv preprint arXiv:1607.06450

Bablani, A., Edla, D., & Dodia, S. (2018). Classification of EEG Data using k-Nearest Neighbor approach for Concealed Information Test. *Procedia Computer Science*, *143*, 242–249. DOI: 10.1016/j.procs.2018.10.392

Bansal, M., & Sirpal, V. (2021). Fog Computing-based Internet of Things and its Applications in Healthcare. In *Journal of Physics: Conference Series* (Vol. 1916, p. 012041). IOP Publishing. DOI: 10.1088/1742-6596/1916/1/012041

Bányai, F., Zsila, Á., Király, O., Maraz, A., Elekes, Z., Griffiths, M. D., Andreassen, C. S., & Demetrovics, Z. (2017). Problematic social media use: Results from a large-scale nationally representative adolescent sample. *PLoS One*, *12*(1), e0169839. DOI: 10.1371/journal.pone.0169839 PMID: 28068404

Barati, K., Koupai, J. A., Darvishi, E., Arzani, A., & Yousefi, A. (2020). Crop Pattern Optimization using System Dynamics Approach and Multi-Objective Mathematical Programming. *Journal of Agricultural Science and Technology*, *22*, 1397–1412.

Bashir, A., & Gill, H. (2016). Managing Interoperability in IoT. *Procedia Computer Science*, *91*, 449–456.

Baum, K., Mantel, S., Schmidt, E., & Speith, T. (2022). From responsibility to reason-giving explainable artificial intelligence. *Philosophy & Technology*, *35*(1), 12.

Bayan, H. (2023). A comprehensive review and conceptual framework for cloud computing adoption in bioinformatics, Healthcare Analytics, Volume 3. 100190, ISSN 2772-4425, https://doi.org/DOI: 10.1016/j.health.2023.100190

Bertin, J., & Ciarallo, F. (2022). The role of edge computing in IoT systems: A review. *Future Generation Computer Systems*, *124*, 1–15. DOI: 10.1016/j.future.2021.12.010

Best, P., Manktelow, R., & Taylor, B. (2014). Online communication, social media and adolescent wellbeing: A systematic narrative review. *Children and Youth Services Review*, *41*, 27–36. DOI: 10.1016/j.childyouth.2014.03.001

Bezdek, J. C., Hannon, J. J., & Castellanos, M. M. (2001). Hybrid Fuzzy Methods for Clustering and Classification: A Survey. *IEEE Transactions on Systems, Man, and Cybernetics. Part C, Applications and Reviews*, *31*(3), 388–405.

Bishnu, K. B., Mishra, S. S., & Mahapatra, P. P. (2016). Hybrid Soft Computing Techniques for Real-World Data Classification. *International Journal of Intelligent Systems Technologies and Applications*, *13*(1), 1–27.

Bjorck, J., Gomes, C., Selman, B., Weinberger, K.Q.: Understanding batch normalization pp. 7694–7705 (2018)

Bolhasani, H., & Jassbi, S. J. (2020). Deep learning accelerators: A case study with MAESTRO. *Journal of Big Data*, *7*(1), 100.

Bottou, L. (1991). Stochastic gradient learning in neural networks. *Proceedings of NeuroNımes*, *91*(8), 12.

Bottou, L. Large-scale machine learning with stochastic gradient descent. In: *Proceedings of COMPSTAT'2010*, pp. 177–186. Springer (2010) DOI: 10.1007/978-3-7908-2604-3_16

Breiman, L. (1996). Bagging predictors. *Machine Learning*, *24*, 123–140.

Burke, M., Marlow, C., & Lento, T. (2010). *Social network activity and social wellbeing*. Paper presented at the Proceedings of the SIGCHI conference on human factors in computing systems. DOI: 10.1145/1753326.1753613

Burke, M., & Kraut, R. E. (2016). The relationship between Facebook use and wellbeing depends on communication type and tie strength. *Journal of Computer-Mediated Communication*, *21*(4), 265–281. DOI: 10.1111/jcc4.12162

Bursic, Sathya & Cuculo, Vittorio & D'Amelio, Alessandro. (2020). Anomaly Detection from Log Files Using Unsupervised Deep Learning.

Calvo, A., Escuder, S., & Guijarro, J. "A Data-Driven Approach for Risk Exposure Analysis in Enterprise Security," 2023 IEEE 10th International Conference on Data Science and Advanced Analytics (DSAA), pp. 1–9, 2023. DOI: 10.1109/DSAA60987.2023.10302480

Cao, S., & Wang, L. (2023). Awesome: Gpu memory-constrained long document summarization using memory mechanism and global salient content. arXiv preprint arXiv:2305.14806.

Care, D. (2018). Care in Diabetesd2018. *Diabetes Care*, *41*(1), S137–S143.

Carew, H. T., Zhang, W., & Rea, T. D. (2007). Chronic health conditions and survival after out-of-hospital ventricular fibrillation cardiac arrest. *Heart (British Cardiac Society)*, *93*(6), 728–731. DOI: 10.1136/hrt.2006.103895 PMID: 17309904

Carpenter, C. J., & Perloff, R. M. (2018). Social media and health: A review of the current literature. *Current opinion in psychology, 28*, 1-5. doi: Retrieved from https://www.sciencedirect.com/journal/current-opinion-in-psychology/vol/28

Carr, C. T., & Hayes, R. A. (2015). Social media: Defining, developing, and divining. *Atlantic Journal of Communication*, *23*(1), 46–65. DOI: 10.1080/15456870.2015.972282

Champaneri, M., Chachpara, D., Chandvidkar, C., & Rathod, M. (2020). *Crop Yield Prediction Using Machine Learning. International Journal of Science and Research (IJSR). (PDF).* Crop Yield Prediction Using Machine Learning.

Chang, K. K., Cramer, M., Soni, S., & Bamman, D. (2023). Speak, memory: An archaeology of books known to chatgpt/gpt-4. arXiv preprint arXiv:2305.00118. DOI: 10.18653/v1/2023.emnlp-main.453

Chang, Y., Lo, K., Goyal, T., & Iyyer, M. (2023). Booookscore: A systematic exploration of book-length summarization in the era of llms. arXiv preprint arXiv:2310.00785.

Chawla, N. V., Bowyer, K. W., Hall, L. O., & Kegelmeyer, W. P. (2002). SMOTE: Synthetic minority over-sampling technique. *Journal of Artificial Intelligence Research, 16*, 321–357.

Chen, K., Wang, J., Pang, J., Cao, Y., Xiong, Y., Li, X., Sun, S., Feng, W., Liu, Z., Xu, J., ... Mmdetection: Open mmlab detection toolbox and benchmark. arXiv preprint arXiv:1906.07155 (2019)

Chen, T., & Guestrin, C. (2016). Xgboost: A scalable tree boosting system. *Proceedings of the 22nd Acm Sigkdd International Conference on Knowledge Discovery and Data Mining*, 785–794.

Chilamkurthy, N., Pandey, O., Ghosh, A., Cenkeramaddi, L. R., & Dai, H.-N. (2022). Low-Power Wide-Area Networks: A Broad Overview of Its Different Aspects. *IEEE Access : Practical Innovations, Open Solutions*, *10*, 1–1. DOI: 10.1109/ACCESS.2022.3196182

Cho, M., & Lee, J. (2017) Riemannian approach to batch normalization. In: Advances in Neural Information Processing Systems. pp. 5225–5235.

Choudhury, A., & Verma, S. (2024). Machine learning for predictive maintenance in industrial IoT: A review. *Journal of Manufacturing Systems*, *63*, 123–134. DOI: 10.1016/j.jmsy.2024.03.001

Chou, H.-T. G., & Edge, N. (2012). "They are happier and having better lives than I am": The impact of using Facebook on perceptions of others' lives. *Cyberpsychology, Behavior, and Social Networking*, *15*(2), 117–121. DOI: 10.1089/cyber.2011.0324 PMID: 22165917

Contreras, I., & Vehi, J. (2018). Artificial Intelligence for Diabetes Management and Decision Support: Literature Review. *Journal of Medical Internet Research*, *20*(5), e10775. DOI: 10.2196/10775 PMID: 29848472

Cotter, S. F., Rao, B. D., Kreutz-Delgado, K., & Adler, J. (1999). Forward sequential algorithms for best basis selection. *IEE Proceedings. Vision Image and Signal Processing*, *146*(5), 235. DOI: 10.1049/ip-vis:19990445

Coulter, A. (2011). *Engaging Patients in Healthcare; McGraw-Hill International.* Open University Press.

Courbariaux, M., Bengio, Y., & David, J. P. (2015). Binaryconnect: Training deep neural networks with binary weights during propagations. In: Advances in neural information processing systems. pp. 3123–3131.

Courbariaux, M., Hubara, I., Soudry, D., El-Yaniv, R., & Bengio, Y. (2016). Binarized neural networks: Training deep neural networks with weights and activations constrained to+ 1 or-1. arXiv preprint arXiv:1602.02830.

Criée, C., Sorichter, S., Smith, H., Kardos, P., Merget, R., Heise, D., Berdel, D., Köhler, D., Magnussen, H., Marek, W., Mitfessel, H., Rasche, K., Rolke, M., Worth, H., & Jörres, R. A. (2011). Body plethysmography—Its principles and clinical use. [PubMed] [CrossRef] [Google Scholar]. *Respiratory Medicine*, *105*(7), 959–971. DOI: 10.1016/j.rmed.2011.02.006 PMID: 21356587

Dada, E. G., Oyewola, D. O., & Joseph, S. B. (2022). "Deep Convolutional Neural Network Model for Detection of Sickle Cell Anemia in Peripheral Blood Images", Communication in Physical Sciences, vol. 8, no. 1.

Das, P. K., Dash, A., & Meher, S. (2024). ACDSSNet: Atrous Convolution-based Deep Semantic Segmentation Network for Efficient Detection of Sickle Cell Anemia. *IEEE Journal of Biomedical and Health Informatics*, *1*(8), 2–10. DOI: 10.1109/JBHI.2024.3362843 PMID: 38319780

Das, P. K., Meher, S., Panda, R., & Abraham, A. (2019). A review of automated methods for the detection of sickle cell disease. *IEEE Reviews in Biomedical Engineering*, *13*, 309–324. DOI: 10.1109/RBME.2019.2917780 PMID: 31107662

Datta, O., Dasgupta, R., Dasgupta, S., & Reddy, K. R. "Real- Time Threat Detection in UEBA using Unsupervised Learning Algorithms", 2021 5th International Conference on Electronics, Materials Engineering & Nano-Technology (IEMENTech), pp.1-6, 2021.

Delikoyun, K., Cine, E., Anil-Inevi, M., Sarigil, O., Ozcivici, E., & Tekin, H. C. (2021). *"2 Deep learning-based cellular image analysis for intelligent medical diagnosis" in Artificial Intelligence for Data-Driven Medical Diagnosis*. De Gruyter.

Dev, A., & Malik, S. K. (2021). Artificial bee colony optimized deep neural network model for handling imbalanced stroke data. *International Journal of E-Health and Medical Communications, 12*(5), 67–83. DOI: 10.4018/IJEHMC.20210901.oa5

Dey, N., Ashour, A. S., & Borra, S. (2018). Internet of Things and Big Data Analytics Toward Next-Generation Intelligence. Springer.

Dey, N., Hassanien, A. E., Bhatt, C., Ashour, A., & Satapathy, S. C. (Eds.). (2018). *Internet of things and big data analytics toward next-generation intelligence* (Vol. 35). Springer.

Dey, S., & Chakraborty, A. (2023). Trends and applications of IoT in smart agriculture: A review. *Computers and Electronics in Agriculture, 206*, 107721. DOI: 10.1016/j.compag.2023.107721

Dhawale, S., Kakade, S., Kulkarni, R., & Muhammed Fasil, C. (2023). "Application of ML in Crop Selection for Precision Agriculture," *2023 International Conference on Digital Applications, Transformation & Economy (ICDATE)*, Miri, Sarawak, Malaysia. pp. 226-230, DOI: 10.1109/ICDATE58146.2023.10248598

Diwani, S. A., & Sam, A. (2014). Diabetes forecasting using supervised learning techniques. *Adv Comput Sci an Int J, 3*, 10–18.

Duchi, J., Hazan, E., & Singer, Y. (2011). Adaptive subgradient methods for online learning and stochastic optimization. *Journal of Machine Learning Research, 12*(Jul), 2121–2159.

Dwivedi, A. D., Srivastava, G., Dhar, S., & Singh, R. (2019). A Decentralized Privacy-Preserving Healthcare Blockchain for IoT. *Sensors (Basel), 19*(2), 326. DOI: 10.3390/s19020326 PMID: 30650612

Ejigu, Y. B., & Nigatu, H. M. (2022). Rainfall Prediction and Cropping Pattern Recommendation Using Artificial Neural Network. In Berihun, M. L. (Ed.), *Advances of Science and Technology. ICAST 2021. Lecture Notes of the Institute for Computer Sciences, Social Informatics and Telecommunications Engineering* (Vol. 411). Springer., DOI: 10.1007/978-3-030-93709-6_34

El-Attar, N. E., Moustafa, B. M., & Awad, W. A. (2022). Deep Learning Model to Detect Diabetes Mellitus Based on DNA Sequence. *Intelligent Automation & Soft Computing, 31*(1). (El-Attar et al., 2022)

Elbasi, E., Zaki, C., Topcu, A. E., Abdelbaki, W., Zreikat, A. I., Cina, E., Shdefat, A., & Saker, L. (2023). Crop Prediction Model Using Machine Learning Algorithms. *Applied Sciences (Basel, Switzerland), 13*(16), 9288. DOI: 10.3390/app13169288

Ellison, N. B., Steinfield, C., & Lampe, C. (2007). The benefits of Facebook "friends:" Social capital and college students' use of online social network sites. *Journal of Computer-Mediated Communication, 12*(4), 1143–1168. DOI: 10.1111/j.1083-6101.2007.00367.x

Erdem, E., Kuyu, M., Yagcioglu, S., Frank, A., Parcalabescu, L., Plank, B., Babii, A., Turuta, O., Erdem, A., Calixto, I., Lloret, E., Apostol, E.-S., Truică, C.-O., Šandrih, B., Martinčić-Ipšić, S., Berend, G., Gatt, A., & Korvel, G. (2022). Neural natural language generation: A survey on multilinguality, multimodality, controllability and learning. *Journal of Artificial Intelligence Research, 73*, 1131–1207. DOI: 10.1613/jair.1.12918

Fardouly, J., Diedrichs, P. C., Vartanian, L. R., & Halliwell, E. (2015). Social comparisons on social media: The impact of Facebook on young women's body image concerns and mood. *Body Image, 13*, 38–45. DOI: 10.1016/j.bodyim.2014.12.002 PMID: 25615425

Fardouly, J., & Holland, E. (2018). Social media is not real life: The effect of attaching disclaimer-type labels to idealized social media images on women's body image and mood. *New Media & Society, 20*(11), 4311–4328. DOI: 10.1177/1461444818771083

Fernandez, M., & Gonzalez, R. (2024). IoT in smart transportation: A systematic review. *Transportation Research Part C, Emerging Technologies, 145*, 103881. DOI: 10.1016/j.trc.2024.103881

Fortino, G., & Giampà, V. PPG-based methods for non invasive and continuous blood pressure measurement: An overview and development issues in body sensor networks; *Proceedings of the 2010 IEEE International Workshop on Medical Measurements and Applications*; Ottawa, ON, Canada. 30 April–1 May 2010; pp. 10–13. [Google Scholar] DOI: 10.1109/MEMEA.2010.5480201

Fox, J., & Moreland, J. J. (2015). The dark side of social networking sites: An exploration of the relational and psychological stressors associated with Facebook use and affordances. *Computers in Human Behavior, 45*, 168–176. DOI: 10.1016/j.chb.2014.11.083

Frank, L. (2024). Support Vector Machines (SVMs).

Frank, L. (2024). Long Short-Term Memory (LSTM). *Networks*.

Gambhir, S., & Kathuria, M. (2016). DWBAN: Dynamic priority based WBAN architecture for healthcare system. *2016 3rd International Conference on Computing for Sustainable Global Development (INDIACom)*. 3380–3386.

Ganesan, and B. B. K, (2023). "A novel deep learning approach for sickle cell anemia detection in human RBCs using an improved wrapper-based feature selection technique in microscopic blood smear images", *Biomed. Eng. Biomed. Tech.*, vol. *68*, no. 2, pp. 175-185, avr.

Ganie, S. M., & Malik, M. B. (2022). An ensemble machine learning approach for predicting type-II diabetes mellitus based on lifestyle indicators. *Healthcare Analytics*, *2*, 100092. DOI: 10.1016/j.health.2022.100092

Ge, S. S., & Khor, J. K. (2014). A Survey on Hybrid Neural Networks with Evolutionary Algorithms and Swarm Intelligence. *IEEE Transactions on Evolutionary Computation*, *18*(2), 223–247.

Ghate, V. V., & Vijayakumar, V. (2018). Machine learning for data aggregation in wsn: A survey. *International Journal of Pure and Applied Mathematics*, *118*(24), 1–12.

Glorot, X., & Bengio, Y. (2010). Understanding the difficulty of training deep feedforward neural networks. In: *Proceedings of the thirteenth international conference on artificial intelligence and statistics*. pp. 249–256.

GM, D., Zhang, R., & Yu, F. R. (2022). Analysis of cropping pattern in black soil region of Northeast China based on geo-information Tupu. Ying yong sheng tai xue bao=. *Journal of Applied Ecology*, *33*(3), 694–702.

Gubbi, J., Buyya, R., Marusic, S., & Palaniswami, M. (2013). Internet of Things (IoT): A Vision, Architectural Elements, and Future Directions. *Future Generation Computer Systems*, *29*(7), 1645–1660. DOI: 10.1016/j.future.2013.01.010

Gupta, S. N., & Warsi, M. F. (2023). A technical analysis of skin cancer classification techniques with machine learning algorithms. Econophysics, Sociophysics & Other Multidisciplinary Sciences Journal (ESMS], 12(2), 34-39.

Gupta, A., & Jha, S. (2021). A systematic review of machine learning in smart healthcare. *Health Informatics Journal*, *27*(2), 146–164. DOI: 10.1177/1460458219896438

Gupta, H., Jin, K. H., Nguyen, H. Q., McCann, M. T., & Unser, M. (2018). Cnn-based projected gradient descent for consistent ct image reconstruction. *IEEE Transactions on Medical Imaging*, *37*(6), 1440–1453. DOI: 10.1109/TMI.2018.2832656 PMID: 29870372

Gupta, Maggu, & Kapoor. (2023). Crop Prediction using Machine Learning. Crop Prediction using. *Machine Learning*.

Hadjileontiadis, L. J., Rekanos, I. T., & Panas, S. M. Wiley Encyclopedia of Biomedical Engineering. John Wiley Sons, Inc.; Hoboken, NJ, USA: 2006. Bioacoustic signals. [Google Scholar]

Hamdan, S., Ayyash, M., & Almajali, S. (2020). Edge-Computing Architectures for Internet of Things Applications: A Survey. *Sensors (Basel)*, *20*(22), 6441. DOI: 10.3390/s20226441 PMID: 33187267

Hampton, K. N., & Gupta, N. (2018). Social media and mental health. *The Oxford Handbook of Social Media and Politics, Oxford University Press*, 479-496. doi:Retrieved from https://global.oup.com/academic/category/arts-and-humanities/media-studies/?type=listing&lang=en&cc=us

Hampton, K., Rainie, L., Lu, W., Shin, I., & Purcell, K. (2015). Social media and the cost of caring. *Retrieved from*https://policycommons.net/artifacts/619353/social-media-and-the-cost-of-caring/1600459/fragments/?page=1

Hampton, K. N., Goulet, L. S., & Albanesius, G. (2015). Change in the social life of urban public spaces: The rise of mobile phones and women, and the decline of aloneness over 30 years. *Urban Studies (Edinburgh, Scotland)*, *52*(8), 1489–1504. DOI: 10.1177/0042098014534905

Harb, H. (2018). Energy Harvesting for IoT Nodes: Past, Present, and Future. *Renewable Energy*, *128*, 641–654.

Hartomo, K. D., Prasetyo, S. Y., Anwar, M. T., & Purnomo, H. D. (2019). Rainfall Prediction Model Using Exponential Smoothing Seasonal Planting Index (ESSPI) For Determination of Crop Planting Pattern. In Purnomo, H. (Ed.), *Computational Intelligence in the Internet of Things* (pp. 234–255). IGI Global., DOI: 10.4018/978-1-5225-7955-7.ch010

Hashem, Y., Takabi, H., Dantu, R., & Nielsen, R. 2017, October. A multi-modal neuro-physiological study of malicious insider threats. In *Proceedings of the 2017 International Workshop on Managing Insider Security Threats* (pp. 33–44).

He, K., Gkioxari, G., Doll'ar, P., & Girshick, R. (2017). Mask r-cnn. In: *Proceedings of the IEEE international conference on computer vision*. pp. 2961–2969.

He, K., Zhang, X., Ren, S., & Sun, J. (2015). Delving deep into rectifiers: Surpassing humanlevel performance on imagenet classification. In: *Proceedings of the IEEE international conference on computer vision*. pp. 1026–1034. DOI: 10.1109/ICCV.2015.123

He, K., Zhang, X., Ren, S., & Sun, J. (2016). Deep residual learning for image recognition. In: *Proceedings of the IEEE conference on computer vision and pattern recognition*. pp. 770–778.

Hoglund, A. J., Hatonen, K., & Sorvari, A. S. "A computer host-based user anomaly detection system using the self-organizing map," Proceedings of the IEEE-INNS-ENNS International Joint Conference on Neural Networks. IJCNN 2000.

Huang, X., & Belongie, S. (2017). Arbitrary style transfer in real-time with adaptive instance normalization. In: Proceedings of the IEEE International Conference on Computer Vision. pp. 1501–1510. 16 H. Yong et al. DOI: 10.1109/ICCV.2017.167

Huang, G., Liu, Z., Van Der Maaten, L., & Weinberger, K. Q. (2017). Densely connected convolutional networks. In: *Proceedings of the IEEE conference on computer vision and pattern recognition*. pp. 4700–4708.

Huang, L., Liu, X., Liu, Y., Lang, B., & Tao, D. (2017). Centered weight normalization in accelerating training of deep neural networks. In: *Proceedings of the IEEE International Conference on Computer Vision*. pp. 2803–2811. DOI: 10.1109/ICCV.2017.305

Hu, W., Hu, W., & Maybank, S. (2008). Adaboost-based algorithm for network intrusion detection. *IEEE Transactions on Systems, Man, and Cybernetics. Part B, Cybernetics*, *38*(2), 577–583. DOI: 10.1109/TSMCB.2007.914695 PMID: 18348941

IDF Diabetes Atlas. (2024). Copyright © IDF Diabetes Atlas 2024. All Rights Reserved. https://diabetesatlas.org/

Inan, O. T., Migeotte, P. F., Park, K. S., Etemadi, M., Tavakolian, K., Casanella, R., Zanetti, J., Tank, J., Funtova, I., Prisk, G. K., & Di Rienzo, M. (2015). Ballistocardiography and seismocardiography: A review of recent advances. [PubMed] [CrossRef] [Google Scholar]. *IEEE Journal of Biomedical and Health Informatics*, *19*(4), 1414–1427. DOI: 10.1109/JBHI.2014.2361732 PMID: 25312966

Ioffe, S., & Szegedy, C. (2015). Batch normalization: Accelerating deep network training by reducing internal covariate shift. arXiv preprint arXiv:1502.03167.

Iscen, A., Tolias, G., Avrithis, Y., & Chum, O. (2011). Label propagation for deep semisupervised learning. In: *Proceedings of the IEEE Conference on Computer Vision and Pattern Recognition*. pp. 5070–5079.

Islam, M. S. (2018). An intelligent system on environment quality remote monitoring and cloud data logging using Internet of Things (IoT). *In Proceedings of the 2018 International Conference on Computer, Communication, Chemical, Material and Electronic Engineering (IC4ME2)*. pp. 1–4.

Islam, S. M. R., Kwak, D., Kabir, M. H., Hossain, M., & Kwak, K. S. (2015). The Internet of Things for Health Care: A Comprehensive Survey. *IEEE Access : Practical Innovations, Open Solutions*, *3*, 678–708. DOI: 10.1109/ACCESS.2015.2437951

Istepanian, R. S., & Woodward, B. (2016). m-Health: Fundamentals and Applications. John Wiley & Sons.

Javaid, M., Haleem, A., Singh, R. P., & Suman, R. 5G technology for healthcare: Features, serviceable pillars, and applications, Intelligent Pharmacy, Volume 1, Issue 1, 2023, Pages 2-10, ISSN 2949-866X, https://doi.org/DOI: 10.1016/j.ipha.2023.04.001

Jha, S., Topol, E. J., & Adashi, E. Y. (2016). Precision Medicine: Time to Advance the Science. *The New England Journal of Medicine*, *376*(2), 119–126.

Jiang, F., Jiang, Y., Zhi, H., Dong, Y., Li, H., Ma, S., Wang, Y., Dong, Q., Shen, H., & Wang, Y. (2017). Artificial Intelligence in Healthcare: Past, Present and Future. *Stroke and Vascular Neurology*, *2*(4), 230–243. DOI: 10.1136/svn-2017-000101 PMID: 29507784

Joe, S. (2014). Qin. Process data analytics in the era of big data. *AIChE Journal. American Institute of Chemical Engineers*, *60*(9), 3092–3100.

Johnson, A. E. W., Pollard, T. J., Shen, L., Lehman, L. W. H., Feng, M., Ghassemi, M., Moody, B., Szolovits, P., Anthony Celi, L., & Mark, R. G. (2016). MIMIC-III, a Freely Accessible Critical Care Database. *Scientific Data*, *3*(1), 160035. DOI: 10.1038/sdata.2016.35 PMID: 27219127

Joshi, A., Vats, N., Singh, H., & Kaushik, V. (2022). Quercetin Compound Analysis to Develop Treatment for Dementia Associated with Alzheimer? s disease in Humans: Insilico Study. *Journal of Drug and Alcohol Research*, *11*(4), 1–7.

Joyia, G. J., Liaqat, R. M., Farooq, A., & Rehman, S. (2017). Internet of medical things (IoMT): Applications, benefits and future challenges in healthcare domain. *Journal of Communication*, *12*(4), 240–247.

Jurišić, M., Tomičić, I., & Grd, P. (2023). User Behavior Analysis for Detecting Compromised User Accounts: A Review Paper. *Cybernetics and Information Technologies*, *23*(3), 102.

Kacprzyk, J., & Zielinski, M. (2016). Hybrid Soft Computing Methods in Decision-Making: A Review and Applications. *IEEE Transactions on Fuzzy Systems*, *24*(2), 327–344.

Kalimuthu, M., Vaishnavi, P., & Kishore, M. "Crop Prediction using Machine Learning," *2020 Third International Conference on Smart Systems and Inventive Technology (ICSSIT)*, Tirunelveli, India, 2020, pp. 926-932, DOI: 10.1109/ICSSIT48917.2020.9214190

Kalyankar, G. D., Poojara, S. R., & Dharwadkar, N. V. (2017). Predictive analysis of diabetic patient data using machine learning and Hadoop. 2017 International Conference on I-SMAC (IoT in Social, Mobile, Analytics and Cloud) (I-SMAC).

Kamavuako, E. N. (2022, October 19). On the Applications of EMG Sensors and Signals. *Sensors (Basel)*, *22*(20), 7966. DOI: 10.3390/s22207966 PMID: 36298317

Kannan, R. S., & Sundararajan, S. (2015). Hybrid Soft Computing Approaches for Solving Optimization Problems: A Review. *International Journal of Advanced Research in Computer Science and Software Engineering*, *5*(6), 1–12.

Kaur, J., Kaur, K., Kant, S., & Das, S. "UEBA with Log Analytics", 2022 3rd International Conference on Computing, Analytics and Networks (ICAN), pp.1- 7, 2022. DOI: 10.1109/ICAN56228.2022.10007245

Ke, G., Meng, Q., Finley, T., Wang, T., Chen, W., Ma, W., Ye, Q., & Liu, T.-Y. (2017). Lightgbm: A highly efficient gradient boosting decision tree. *Advances in Neural Information Processing Systems*, 30.

Khalaf, M., Hussain, A. J., Keight, R., Al-Jumeily, D., Fergus, P., Keenan, R., & Tso, P. (2017). Machine learning approaches to the application of disease modifying therapy for sickle cell using classification models. *Neurocomputing*, *228*, 154–164. DOI: 10.1016/j.neucom.2016.10.043

Khanam, J. J., & Foo, S. Y. (2021). A comparison of machine learning algorithms for diabetes prediction. *ICT Express*, *7*(4), 432–439. DOI: 10.1016/j.icte.2021.02.004

Khan, M. A., & Alghamdi, A. (2019). A review of IoT applications in smart cities. *Journal of Urban Technology*, *26*(3), 1–20. DOI: 10.1080/10630732.2019.1625698

Khazaee, A., & Ebrahimzadeh, A. (2013). Heart Arrhythmia Detection using support vector machines. *Intelligent Automation & Soft Computing*, *19*(1), 1–9. Advance online publication. DOI: 10.1080/10798587.2013.771456

Khoshraftar, A.. (2011). Improving The CRM System In Healthcare Organization. [IJCES]. *International Journal of Computational Engineering Science*, *1*(2), 28–35.

Kılıc, O. M., Ersayın, K., Gunal, H., Khalofah, A., & Alsubeie, M. S. (2022). Combination of fuzzy-AHP and GIS techniques in land suitability assessment for wheat (Triticum aestivum) cultivation, Saudi Journal of Biological Sciences, Volume 29, Issue 4, Pages 2634-2644, ISSN 1319-562X, DOI: 10.1016/j.sjbs.2021.12.050

Kim, J., Kwon Lee, J., & Lee, M. (2016). K.: Accurate image super-resolution using very deep convolutional networks. In: *Proceedings of the IEEE conference on computer vision and pattern recognition*. pp. 1646–1654. DOI: 10.1109/CVPR.2016.182

Kingma, D. P., & Ba, J. (2014). Adam: A method for stochastic optimization. arXiv preprint arXiv:1412.6980

Korostynska, O., Arshak, K., Gill, E., & Arshak, A. (2007). Materials and techniques for in vivo pH monitoring. [CrossRef] [Google Scholar]. *IEEE Sensors Journal, 8*(1), 20–28. DOI: 10.1109/JSEN.2007.912522

Kourou, K., Exarchos, T. P., Exarchos, K. P., Karamouzis, M. V., & Fotiadis, D. I. (2015). Machine Learning Applications in Cancer Prognosis and Prediction. *Computational and Structural Biotechnology Journal, 13*, 8–17. DOI: 10.1016/j.csbj.2014.11.005 PMID: 25750696

Krause, J., Stark, M., Deng, J., & Fei-Fei, L. (2013). 3d object representations for finegrained categorization. In: *Proceedings of the IEEE International Conference on Computer Vision Workshops*. pp. 554–561

Krizhevsky, A., & Hinton, G.. (2009). *Learning multiple layers of features from tiny images. Tech. rep.* Citeseer.

Krogh, A., & Hertz, J. A. (1992). A simple weight decay can improve generalization. In: Advances in neural information processing systems. pp. 950–957.

Kumar, S., & Gupta, P. (2023). Recent advances in machine learning for IoT applications. *Journal of Ambient Intelligence and Humanized Computing, 14*(2), 123–138. DOI: 10.1007/s12652-023-04567-9

Kurisinkel, L. J., & Chen, N. F. (2023). LLM Based Multi-Document Summarization Exploiting Main-Event Biased Monotone Submodular Content Extraction. arXiv preprint arXiv:2310.03414.

Kushwaha, S., Srivastava, R., Jain, R., Sagar, V., Aggarwal, A. K., Bhadada, S. K., & Khanna, P. (2022). Harnessing machine learning models for non-invasive prediabetes screening in children and adolescents. *Computer Methods and Programs in Biomedicine, 226*, 107180. DOI: 10.1016/j.cmpb.2022.107180 PMID: 36279639

Landauer, M., Skopik, F., Höld, G., & Wurzenberger, M. "A User and Entity Behavior Analytics Log Data Set for Anomaly Detection in Cloud Computing," 2022 IEEE International Conference on Big Data (Big Data), Osaka, Japan, 2022.

Larsson, M., Arnab, A., Kahl, F., Zheng, S., & Torr, P. (2017). A projected gradient descent method for crf inference allowing end-to-end training of arbitrary pairwise potentials. In: *International Workshop on Energy Minimization Methods in Computer Vision and Pattern Recognition*. pp. 564–579. Springer.

Lashkari, B., Rezazadeh, J., Farahbakhsh, R., & Sandrasegaran, K. (2018). Crowdsourcing and sensing for indoor localization in IoT: A review. *IEEE Sensors Journal, 19*(7), 2408–2434. DOI: 10.1109/JSEN.2018.2880180

Li, X., Song, Y., Wang, H., Su, X., Wang, M., Li, J., Ren, Z., Zhong, D., & Huang, Z. Evaluation of measurement accuracy of wearable devices for heart rate variability, iScience, Volume 26, Issue 11, 2023, 108128, ISSN 2589-0042, https://doi.org/ DOI: 10.1016/j.isci.2023.108128

Lin, T. Y., Maire, M., Belongie, S., Hays, J., Perona, P., Ramanan, D., Doll'ar, P., & Zitnick, C. L. (2014). Microsoft coco: Common objects in context. In: European conference on computer vision. pp. 740–755. Springer.

Lin, C. Y., Imani, V., Griffiths, M. D., Broström, A., Nygårdh, A., Demetrovics, Z., & Pakpour, A. H. (2021). Temporal associations between morningness/eveningness, problematic social media use, psychological distress and daytime sleepiness: Mediated roles of sleep quality and insomnia among young adults. *Journal of Sleep Research, 30*(1), e13076. DOI: 10.1111/jsr.13076 PMID: 32406567

Lin, T. Y., Doll'ar, P., Girshick, R., He, K., Hariharan, B., & Belongie, S. (2017). Feature pyramid networks for object detection. In: *Proceedings of the IEEE conference on computer vision and pattern recognition*. pp. 2117–2125.

Litjens, G., Kooi, T., Bejnordi, B. E., Setio, A. A. A., Ciompi, F., Ghafoorian, M., & van Ginneken, B. (2017). A Survey on Deep Learning in Medical Image Analysis. *Medical Image Analysis, 42*, 60–88. DOI: 10.1016/j.media.2017.07.005 PMID: 28778026

Liu, Y. (2019). Fine-tune BERT for extractive summarization. arXiv preprint arXiv:1903.10318.

Liu, Y., Iter, D., Xu, Y., Wang, S., Xu, R., & Zhu, C. (2023). G-eval: Nlg evaluation using gpt-4 with better human alignment. arXiv preprint arXiv:2303.16634. DOI: 10.18653/v1/2023.emnlp-main.153

Liu, Y., Wang, Y., & Zhang, J. (2012). New Machine Learning Algorithm. *Lecture Notes in Computer Science*, *7473*, 246–252. DOI: 10.1007/978-3-642-34062-8_32

Liu, Y., & Zhang, X. (2023). A review of machine learning techniques for smart energy management. *Energy Reports*, *9*, 45–56. DOI: 10.1016/j.egyr.2023.01.009

Li, Z., Han, D., Qi, T., Deng, J., Li, L., Gao, C., Gao, W., Chen, H., Zhang, L., & Chen, W. (2023). Hemoglobin A1c in type 2 diabetes mellitus patients with preserved ejection fraction is an independent predictor of left ventricular myocardial deformation and tissue abnormalities. *BMC Cardiovascular Disorders*, *23*(1), 49. DOI: 10.1186/s12872-023-03082-5 PMID: 36698087

Loshchilov, I., & Hutter, F. (2017). Decoupled weight decay regularization. arXiv preprint arXiv:1711.05101.

Louis, E. Frenzel, Chapter 9 - Networking: Wired and Wireless: All Devices Talking to One Another, Editor(s): Louis E. Frenzel, Electronics Explained (Second Edition), Newnes, 2018, Pages 217-242, ISBN 9780128116418, https://doi.org/DOI: 10.1016/B978-0-12-811641-8.00009-6

Lu, M., Yin, R., & Chen, X. S. (2024). Ensemble methods of rank-based trees for single sample classification with gene expression profiles. *Journal of Translational Medicine*, *22*(1), 140. DOI: 10.1186/s12967-024-04940-2 PMID: 38321494

Lundberg, S. M., & Lee, S.-I. (2017). A Unified Approach to Interpreting Model Predictions. *Advances in Neural Information Processing Systems*, *30*, 4765–4774.

Maddison, R., Rawstorn, J. C., Stewart, R. A., Benatar, J., Whittaker, R., Rolleston, A., Jiang, Y., Gao, L., Moodie, M., Warren, I., Meads, A., & Gant, N. (2019). Effects and costs of real-time cardiac telerehabilitation: Randomised controlled non-inferiority trial. *Heart (British Cardiac Society)*, *105*(2), 122–129. DOI: 10.1136/heartjnl-2018-313189 PMID: 30150328

Mahendra, N. (2020, August). Dhanush Vishwakarma, Nischitha K, Ashwini, Manjuraju M. R, 2020, Crop Prediction using Machine Learning Approaches [IJERT]. *International Journal of Engineering Research & Technology (Ahmedabad)*, *09*(08). Advance online publication. DOI: 10.17577/IJERTV9IS080029

Mahlayeye, M., Darvishzadeh, R., & Nelson, A. (2022). Cropping Patterns of Annual Crops: A Remote Sensing Review. *Remote Sensing*, *14*(10), 2404. DOI: 10.3390/rs14102404

Malasinghe, L. P., Ramzan, N., & Dahal, K. (2019). Remote patient monitoring: A comprehensive study. *Journal of Ambient Intelligence and Humanized Computing*, *10*, 57–76.

Mall, P. K., Singh, P. K., Srivastav, S., Narayan, V., Paprzycki, M., Jaworska, T., & Ganzha, M. (2023). A comprehensive review of deep neural networks for medical image processing: Recent developments and future opportunities, Healthcare Analytics, Volume 4, 100216, ISSN 2772-4425, https://doi.org/DOI: 10.1016/j.health.2023.100216

Manne, R., & Kantheti, S. C. (2021). Application of Artificial Intelligence in Healthcare: Chances and Challenges. *Current Journal of Applied Science and Technology*, *40*(6), 78–89. DOI: 10.9734/cjast/2021/v40i631320

Marriwala, N. K., Shukla, V. K., William, P., Guleria, K., Sobti, R., & Sharma, S. (2024). Detection of viral messages in twitter using context-based sentiment analysis framework. *International Journal of Information Technology : an Official Journal of Bharati Vidyapeeth's Institute of Computer Applications and Management*, •••, 1–7.

Marriwala, N., & Jain, S. (2023). Editorial for the Special Issue on IoT-enabled Wireless Biomedical Systems and Sensors. *Measurement. Sensors*, *27*, 100750.

Maruthesha, S. S., & Biradar, G. (2023). Anthropometry and Haemoglobin Range among Rural Women in Davanager District of Karnataka. *Asian Journal of Agricultural Extension Economics & Sociology*, *41*(4), 62–68. DOI: 10.9734/ajaees/2023/v41i41879

Mienye, I. D., & Sun, Y. (2022). A Survey of Ensemble Learning: Concepts, Algorithms, Applications, and Prospects. *IEEE Access : Practical Innovations, Open Solutions*, *10*, 99129–99149. DOI: 10.1109/ACCESS.2022.3207287

Mittelstadt, B. D., Allo, P., Taddeo, M., Wachter, S., & Floridi, L. (2016). The Ethics of Algorithms: Mapping the Debate. *Big Data & Society*, *3*(2), 2053951716679679. DOI: 10.1177/2053951716679679

Mohamad, R. Hamzah, A. Mokhtar and J. Sathar, (2017). Sickle cell disease verification via sobel edge algorithms for image processing, pp. 1-4.

Mohamed, A. T., & Kumar, S. (2022). Deep Learning Based Process Analytics Model for Predicting Type 2 Diabetes Mellitus. *Computer Systems Science and Engineering*, *40*(1).

Mohammed, J., Lung, C. H., Ocneanu, A., Thakral, A., Jones, C., & Adler, A. (2014). Internet of things: remote patient monitoring using web services and cloud computing Proceedings of the *IEEE International Conference on Internet of Things (iThings)*. pp. 256-263 DOI: 10.1109/iThings.2014.45

Mohammed, Y., Mohammed, A. S., Abdulkarim, H. T., Danladi, C., Victor, A., & Edoka, R. (2019). Development and implementation of an internet of things (IOT) based remote patient monitoring system *Proceedings of the 15th International Conference on Electronics, Computer and Computation, ICECCO 2019*. DOI: 10.1109/ICECCO48375.2019.9043200

Mohanty, R. K., Sahoo, S. P., & Kabat, M. R. (2022, October). A Survey on Emerging Technologies in Wireless Body Area Network. In 2022 13thInternational Conference on ComputingCommunication and Networking Technologies (ICCCNT) (pp. 1-5). IEEE.

Mohanty, R. K., Sahoo, S. P., & Kabat, M. R. (2023, June). A Network Reliability based Secure Routing Protocol (NRSRP) for Secure Transmission in Wireless Body Area Network. In 2023 8th International Conference on Communication and Electronics Systems (ICCES) (pp. 663-668). IEEE.

Mohanty, R. K., Motupalli, R. K., Manju, D., Gangappa, M., Gouthami, B., & Mounika, G. (2023, December). Energy-Efficient Cluster Based Routing Protocol to Enhance the Lifetime of Wearable Wireless Body Area Networks (WBAN). In *2023 OITS International Conference on Information Technology (OCIT)* (pp. 71-76). IEEE. DOI: 10.1109/OCIT59427.2023.10431071

Mohanty, R. K., Sahoo, S. P., & Kabat, M. R. (2023). Sustainable remote patient monitoring in wireless body area network with Multi-hop routing and scheduling: A four-fold objective based optimization approach. *Wireless Networks*, *29*(5), 1–15. DOI: 10.1007/s11276-023-03276-x

Mohsen, Saeed & Elkaseer, Ahmed & Scholz, Steffen. (2021). Human Activity Recognition Using K-Nearest Neighbor Machine Learning Algorithm. .DOI: 10.1007/978-981-16-6128-0_29

N. S. and H. S. (2021, August). Detection of Sickle Cell Anemia Through Contour Evidence Extraction and Estimation [IJEAT]. *International Journal of Engineering and Advanced Technology*, *10*(6), •••.

Nabi, R. L., Prestin, A., & So, J. (2013). Facebook friends with (health) benefits? Exploring social network site use and perceptions of social support, stress, and wellbeing. *Cyberpsychology, Behavior, and Social Networking*, *16*(10), 721–727. DOI: 10.1089/cyber.2012.0521 PMID: 23790356

Nadeem, A., & Ali, S. (2024). A review of AI and IoT convergence in smart manufacturing. *Journal of Manufacturing Processes*, *73*, 52–62. DOI: 10.1016/j.jmapro.2024.02.005

Nagata, K., Nakamura, T., & Farouk, A. (2017). Quantum cryptography based on the Deutsch-Jozsa algorithm. *International Journal of Theoretical Physics, 56*(9), 2887–2897. DOI: 10.1007/s10773-017-3456-x

Nashat, N., & Abu-Mahfouz, I. (2023). IoT and big data analytics: A comprehensive review. *Big Data Research, 30*, 100200. DOI: 10.1016/j.bdr.2023.100200

Natoli, M., Chang, M., & Richards-Kortum, R. (2021, March 11). Allele-specific recombinase polymerase amplification for real-time detection of sickle cell anaemia in low-resource settings: Evaluation of an isothermal nucleic acid amplification test to detect the βS globin point mutation in paediatric patients. *The Lancet. Global Health, 9*(1), 13–20. DOI: 10.1016/S2214-109X(21)00121-2

Nayak, S. B., Mahapatra, P. P., & Patra, G. P. (2014). A Review on Hybridization of Evolutionary Algorithms with Neural Networks and Fuzzy Logic. *International Journal of Intelligent Computing and Cybernetics, 4*(3), 257–282.

Neumayr, L. D., Hoppe, C. C., & Brown, C. (2019). Sickle cell disease: Current treatment and emerging therapies. *The American Journal of Managed Care, 25*(18), S335–S343. PMID: 31809007

Nguyen, T., Nguyen, H., & Gia, T. N. (2024). Exploring the integration of edge computing and blockchain IoT: Principles, architectures, security, and applications, Journal of Network and Computer Applications, Volume 226, 103884, ISSN 1084-8045, https://doi.org/DOI: 10.1016/j.jnca.2024.103884

Nishita, M. (2021). Remote health monitoring during covid-19 pandemic: A case for homebased care. *Indian Journal of Community Medicine : Official Publication of Indian Association of Preventive & Social Medicine, 46*(3), 401–404. PMID: 34759475

Odongo, B. O. (2022). Security Information and Event Management Using Deep Learning Project Documentation. Diss. University of Nairobi.

Oliver, N., Toumazou, C., Cass, T., & Johnston, D. (2009). Glucose Sensors: A Review of Current and Emerging Technology. *Diabetic Medicine, 26*(3), 197–210. DOI: 10.1111/j.1464-5491.2008.02642.x PMID: 19317813

Ouedraogo, S., Bousso, M., Balde, A., Sall, O., Sall, C., & Soumboundou, M. (2023). *Automating Sickle Cell Counting Using Object Detection Techniques*. Pan-African Artificial Intelligence and Smart Systems. DOI: 10.1007/978-3-031-25271-6_14

Padierna, L. C., Amador-Medina, L. F., Murillo-Ortiz, B. O., & Villaseñor-Mora, C. (2020). Classification method of peripheral arterial disease in patients with type 2 diabetes mellitus by infrared thermography and machine learning. *Infrared Physics & Technology*, *111*, 103531. DOI: 10.1016/j.infrared.2020.103531

Padmini, S. A., & Purushothama Raju, V. (2022, November). 2022, A Systematic Approach for Crop Prediction using Deep Learning [IJERT]. *International Journal Of Engineering Research & Technology*, *11*(11). Advance online publication. DOI: 10.17577/IJERTV11IS110155

Pal, S., Mishra, N., Bhushan, M., Kholiya, P. S., Rana, M., & Negi, A. (2022). Deep learning techniques for prediction and diagnosis of diabetes mellitus. *2022 International Mobile and Embedded Technology Conference (MECON)*, 588–593. DOI: 10.1109/MECON53876.2022.9752176

Pan American Health Organization. (2024, June 14). https://www.paho.org/en

Pandhurnekar, V., Iyyappan, A., & Wazalwar, S. (2023). "Proposed Method for Threat Detection Using User Behavior Analysis", 2023 IEEE 3rd International Conference on Technology, Engineering, Management for Societal impact using Marketing, Entrepreneurship and Talent (TEMSMET), pp.1-5.

Panja, A. K., Mukherjee, A., & Dey, N. (2022). Chapter 1 - Introduction, Editor(s): Ayan Kumar Panja, Amartya Mukherjee, Nilanjan Dey, In Primers in Biomedical Imaging Devices and Systems, Biomedical Sensors and Smart Sensing, Academic Press, Pages 1-14, ISBN 9780128228562, https://doi.org/DOI: 10.1016/B978-0-12-822856-2.00006-X

Patel, P., & Shah, K. (2021). Integrating AI with IoT: A review of applications and challenges. *Artificial Intelligence Review*, *54*(1), 1–30. DOI: 10.1007/s10462-020-09875-6 PMID: 32836651

Patgiri, C., & Ganguly, A. (2021). Adaptive thresholding technique-based classification of red blood cell and sickle cell using Naïve Bayes Classifier and K-nearest neighbor classifier. *Biomedical Signal Processing and Control*, *68*, 102745. DOI: 10.1016/j.bspc.2021.102745

Patil, P., & Panpatil, V. Prof. Shrikant Kokate (2020, February 2). Crop Prediction System using Machine Learning Algorithms. https://www.irjet.net/archives/V7/i2/IRJET-V7I2163.pdf

Patil, N. R., & Patil, R. D. (2023). An Efficient Method for Detection of Red Blood Cells in Digital Images in Sickle Cell Anaemia Diagnosis [IJERT]. *International Journal of Engineering Research & Technology (Ahmedabad)*, *12*(4), 967–975.

Patil, R., & Khanna, A. (2024). The role of blockchain in securing IoT devices: A review. *Future Generation Computer Systems*, *132*, 137–149. DOI: 10.1016/j.future.2024.02.002

Pawar, P., Nikam, A., Ahankare, V., & Kamble, P. R. (2023). Sickle Cell Anemia Detection Using Convolutional Neural Network. *International Research Journal of Modernization in Engineering Technology and Science*, *4*, 614–623.

Petsagkourakis, P., Orson Sandoval, I., Bradford, E., Zhang, D., & del Rio-Chanona, E. A. (2019). Reinforcement Learning for Batch-to-Batch Bioprocess Optimisation, Editor(s): Anton A. Kiss, Edwin Zondervan, Richard Lakerveld, Leyla Özkan, Computer Aided Chemical Engineering, Elsevier, Volume 46, Pages 919-924, ISSN 1570-7946, ISBN 9780128186343, https://doi.org/DOI: 10.1016/B978-0-12-818634-3.50154-5

Philip, N. Y., Razaak, M., Chang, J., O'Kane, M., & Pierscionek, B. K. (2022). A data analytics suite for exploratory predictive, and visual analysis of type 2 diabetes. *IEEE Access : Practical Innovations, Open Solutions*, *10*, 13460–13471. DOI: 10.1109/ACCESS.2022.3146884

Polonelli, T., Cucchi, F., Amorim, M. S., & Stanacevic, M. (2020). Low-Power IoT Sensors for Smart Healthcare: Design and Optimization. *IEEE Sensors Journal*, *20*(11), 5592–5601.

Pramanik, S., & Bandyopadhyay, S. K. (2023). Identifying Disease and Diagnosis in Females Using Machine Learning. In *Encyclopedia of Data Science and Machine Learning* (pp. 3120–3143). IGI Global.

Priyanka, R. & Pooja, M. R. (2024). UAV Detection and Classification using Deep Learning Techniques with YOLOv8. 2024 4th International Conference on Mobile Networks and Wireless Communications (ICMNWC). IEEE.

Prokhorenkova, L., Gusev, G., Vorobev, A., Dorogush, A. V., & Gulin, A. (2018). CatBoost: Unbiased boosting with categorical features. *Advances in Neural Information Processing Systems*, •••, 31.

Pupim, D. & Filho, L. & Takeshita, W. & Iwaki, L. (2013). Evaluation of accuracy of portable fingertip pulse oximeter, as compared to that of a hospital oximeter with digital sensor. Indian journal of dental research: official publication of Indian Society for Dental Research. 24. 542-6. . DOI: 10.4103/0970-9290.123362

Rahman, S., & Chowdhury, M. (2024). IoT security challenges and solutions: A systematic review. *Computers & Security*, *122*, 102837. DOI: 10.1016/j.cose.2024.102837

Rai, P., & Singh, K. (2024). IoT-enabled smart healthcare: Opportunities and challenges. *Health Policy and Technology, 13*(1), 101–112. DOI: 10.1016/j.hlpt.2024.01.004

Rajpurkar, P., Hannun, A. Y., Haghpanahi, M., Bourn, C., & Ng, A. Y. (2017). Cardiologist-level arrhythmia detection with convolutional neural networks. arXiv preprint arXiv:1707.01836.

Ramrekha, T. A. (2010). C. Politis A hybrid adaptive routing protocol for extreme emergency ad hoc communication *Proceedings of the International Conference on Computer Communications and Networks (ICCCN).*

Rangayyan, R. M., & Krishnan, S. (2024). *Biomedical signal analysis*. John Wiley & Sons.

Rao, M., & Singh, A. (2022). Crop prediction using machine learning. *Journal of Physics: Conference Series, 2161*(1), 012033. DOI: 10.1088/1742-6596/2161/1/012033

Ravi, V., Al Mazroa, A., & Ravi, P. (2024). Deployment of a Phenotypic Characterization System for Effective Identification of the Onset of Asthma Disease. *The Open Public Health Journal, 17*, 1.

Ribeiro, M. T., Singh, S., & Guestrin, C. (2016, August). " Why should i trust you?" Explaining the predictions of any classifier. In Proceedings of the 22nd ACM SIGKDD international conference on knowledge discovery and data mining (pp. 1135-1144).

Ring, E., McEvoy, H., Jung, A., Zuber, J., & Machin, G. (2010). New standards for devices used for the measurement of human body temperature. *Journal of Medical Engineering & Technology, 34*(4), 249–253. DOI: 10.3109/03091901003663836 PMID: 20397848

Rose, K., Eldridge, S., & Chapin, L. (2015). The Internet of Things: An Overview. Internet Society. Retrieved from Internet Society.

Sadat Safavi, N., Amini, M., Abdollahzadegan, A., & Zakaria, N. H. (2013). An effective model for evaluating organizational risk and cost in ERP implementation by SME. IOSR Journal of Business and Management (IOSR-JBM), 10(6), 70-75.

Sagar, S. H., & Dravya, K. L. (2023, May 5). Crop Prediction & Recommendation System Using Machine Learning. https://www.ijres.org/papers/Volume-11/Issue-5/1105339341.pdf

Saha, S., & Saha, R. (2020). Data security in IoT: A comprehensive review. *Computer Networks, 172*, 107146. DOI: 10.1016/j.comnet.2020.107146

Saleh, H. H., Kadhim, N. J., & Bara'a, A. A. (2015). A genetic based optimization model for extractive multi-document text summarization. *Iraqi Journal of Science*, •••, 1489–1498.

Salitin, M. A., & Zolait, A. H. (2018). "The role of User Entity Behavior Analytics to detect network attacks in real time," 2018 International Conference on Innovation and Intelligence for Informatics, Computing, and Technologies (3ICT), Sakhier, Bahrain, pp. 1-5, DOI: 10.1109/3ICT.2018.8855782

Samee, N. A., Mahmoud, N. F., Aldhahri, E. A., Rafiq, A., Muthanna, M. S. A., & Ahmad, I. (2022, November 22). RNN and BiLSTM Fusion for Accurate Automatic Epileptic Seizure Diagnosis Using EEG Signals. *Life (Basel, Switzerland)*, *12*(12), 1946. DOI: 10.3390/life12121946 PMID: 36556313

Saputra, D. C. E., Sunat, K., & Ratnaningsih, T. (2023). *"A New Artificial Intelligence Approach Using Extreme Learning Machine as the Potentially Effective Model to Predict and Analyze the Diagnosis of Anemia" in Healthcare*. MDPI. DOI: 10.3390/healthcare11050697

Saranya, S., & Rajasekaran, S. (2020). IoT Healthcare Data Management in Cloud using Interoperability and Standardization Issues: A Survey. *Journal of King Saud University. Computer and Information Sciences*.

Sattar, Y., & Chhabra, L. (2024 Jan). Electrocardiogram. In *StatPearls*. StatPearls Publishing., Available from https://www.ncbi.nlm.nih.gov/books/NBK549803/

Schaffers, H., Komninos, N., Pallot, M., Trousse, B., Nilsson, M., & Oliveira, A. (2011, May). Smart cities and the future internet: Towards cooperation frameworks for open innovation. In The Future Internet Assembly (pp. 431–446). Springer, Berlin.

Sen, A. Ganesh, A. Bhan and S. Dixit, "Deep Learning based diagnosis of sickle cell anemia in human RBC", 2021 2nd International Conference on Intelligent Engineering and Management (ICIEM), London, United Kingdom. pp. 526-529.

Sen, B., Ganesh, A., Bhan, A., Dixit, S., & Goyal, A. "Machine learning based Diagnosis and Classification of Sickle Cell Anemia in Human RBC", *2021 Third International Conference on Intelligent Communication Technologies and Virtual Mobile Networks (ICICV)*, pp. 753-758, févr. 2021. DOI: 10.1109/ICICV50876.2021.9388610

Shakoor, M. T., Rahman, K., Rayta, S. N., & Chakrabarty, A. (2017, July). Agricultural production output prediction using supervised machine learning techniques. In 2017 1st international conference on next generation computing applications (NextComp) (pp. 182-187). IEEE.

Sharanbasappa, S., & Parvathi, C. (2018). Health monitoring system using wireless sensor network. *International Journal of Engineering Research and Applications*.

Sharma, M., Sharma, B., Gupta, A. K., & Pandey, D. (2023). Recent developments of image processing to improve explosive detection methodologies and spectroscopic imaging techniques for explosive and drug detection. *Multimedia Tools and Applications*, *82*(5), 6849–6865. DOI: 10.1007/s11042-022-13578-5

Sharma, M., Singh, H., Singh, S., Gupta, A., Goyal, S., & Kakkar, R. (2020). A novel approach of object detection using point feature matching technique for colored images. In *Proceedings of ICRIC 2019: Recent Innovations in Computing* (pp. 561-576). Springer International Publishing.

Shashanka, M., Shen, M.-Y., & Wang, J. (2016). "User and entity behavior analytics for enterprise security," 2016 IEEE International Conference on Big Data (Big Data), Washington, DC, USA.

Shivade, A. (2024). "Sickle Cell Detection Using CnnFrom Microscopic Blood Images" [JETIR]. *Journal of Emerging Technologies and Innovative Research*, *11*(3), 910–916.

Shwetha, M. S. & Pooja, M. R. (2024). The Impact of Smart Irrigation on Agricultural Productivity: A Study of Farmer Adoption and Challenges. 2024 3rd International Conference on Automation, Computing and Renewable Systems (ICACRS). IEEE.

Singh, A., & Kumar, R. (2022). Challenges in IoT data analytics: A review. *IEEE Access : Practical Innovations, Open Solutions*, *10*, 12345–12359. DOI: 10.1109/ACCESS.2022.3142573

Skopik, F., Höld, G., Landauer, M., & Kuhn, W. (2023). Behavior-Based Anomaly Detection in Log Data of Physical Access Control Systems. *IEEE Transactions on Dependable and Secure Computing*, *20*(4), 3158–3175.

Slipenchuk, P., & Epishkina, A. V. (2019). *Practical User and Entity Behavior Analytics Methods for Fraud Detection Systems in Online Banking: A Survey*. Biologically Inspired Cognitive Architectures.

Sund-Levander, M., & Grodzinsky, E. (2013). Assessment of body temperature measurement options. *British Journal of Nursing (Mark Allen Publishing)*, *22*(16), 942–950. DOI: 10.12968/bjon.2013.22.16.942 PMID: 24037397

Susana, E., Ramli, K., Murfi, H., & Apriantoro, N. H. (2022). Non-invasive classification of blood glucose level for early detection diabetes based on photoplethysmography signal. *Information (Basel)*, *13*(2), 59. DOI: 10.3390/info13020059

Tang, B., Chen, Z., Hefferman, G., Wei, T., He, H., & Yang, Q. (2015, October.) A hierarchical distributed fog computing architecture for big data analysis in smart cities. In Proceedings of the ASE Big Data & Social Informatics 2015 (p. 28).

Tang, B., Hu, Q., & Lin, D. "Reducing False Positives of User-to-Entity First-Access Alerts for User Behavior Analytics," *2017 IEEE International Conference on Data Mining Workshops (ICDMW)*, New Orleans, LA, USA, 2017.

Tang, L., Sun, Z., Idnay, B., Nestor, J. G., Soroush, A., Elias, P. A., Xu, Z., Ding, Y., Durrett, G., Rousseau, J. F., Weng, C., & Peng, Y. (2023). Evaluating large language models on medical evidence summarization. *NPJ Digital Medicine*, *6*(1), 158. DOI: 10.1038/s41746-023-00896-7 PMID: 37620423

Theerthagiri, P., Ruby, A. U., & Vidya, J. (2022). Diagnosis and classification of the diabetes using machine learning algorithms. *SN Computer Science*, *4*(1), 72. DOI: 10.1007/s42979-022-01485-3

Thilagam, K., Beno, A., Lakshmi, M. V., Wilfred, C. B., George, S. M., Karthikeyan, M., Peroumal, V., Ramesh, C., & Karunakaran, P. (2022). Secure IoT Healthcare Architecture with Deep Learning-Based Access Control System. *Journal of Nanomaterials*, *2022*(1). DOI: 10.1155/2022/2638613

Tian, Z., Gao, X., Su, S., Qiu, J., Du, X., & Guizani, M. (2019). Evaluating reputation management schemes of internet of vehicles based on evolutionary game theory. *IEEE Transactions on Vehicular Technology*, *68*(6), 5971–5980.

Tian, Z., Shi, W., Wang, Y., Zhu, C., Du, X., Su, S., Sun, Y., & Guizani, N. (2019). Real time lateral movement detection based on evidence reasoning network for edge computing environment. *IEEE Transactions on Industrial Informatics*, *15*(7), 4285–4294.

Tian, Z., Su, S., Shi, W., Du, X., Guizani, M., & Yu, X. (2019). A data-driven method for future internet route decision modeling. *Future Generation Computer Systems*, *95*, 212–220. DOI: 10.1016/j.future.2018.12.054

Tsai, C.-W., Lai, C.-F., Chao, H.-C., & Vasilakos, A. (2015). Big data analytics: A survey. *Journal of Big Data*, *2*(1), 21. DOI: 10.1186/s40537-015-0030-3 PMID: 26191487

Tyagi, A., Semwal, S., & Shah, G. (2012). A review of EEG sensors used for data acquisition. [IJCA]. *Jisuanji Yingyong*, •••, 13–17.

Vashishth, T. K., Sharma, V., Sharma, K. K., Kumar, B., Chaudhary, S., & Panwar, R. (2024). Enhancing biomedical signal processing with machine learning: A comprehensive review. Digital Transformation in Healthcare, 5.

Vashist, S. K. (2019). Continuous Glucose Monitoring Systems: A Review. *Diagnostics (Basel)*, *9*(1), 6. PMID: 30626128

Veerapandian, M., & Karuppiah, A. (2021). IoT-based Continuous Glucose Monitoring System: A Review. *Journal of Diabetes Science and Technology*, *15*(5), 1073–1082.

Vicent, M., Simon, K., & Yonasi, S. (2022). An algorithm to detect overlapping red blood cells for sickle cell disease diagnosis. *IET Image Processing*, *16*(6), 1669–1677.

Vijay, K. Garg, CHAPTER 1 - An Overview of Wireless Systems, Editor(s): Vijay K. Garg, In The Morgan Kaufmann Series in Networking, Wireless Communications & Networking, Morgan Kaufmann, 2007, Pages 1-21, ISSN 18759351, ISBN 9780123735805, https://doi.org/DOI: 10.1016/B978-012373580-5/50035-1

Waddell, W. J., & Bates, R. G. (1969). Intracellular pH. [PubMed] [CrossRef] [Google Scholar]. *Physiological Reviews*, *49*(2), 285–329. DOI: 10.1152/physrev.1969.49.2.285 PMID: 4889321

Wai, K. T., Aung, N. P., & Htay, L. L. (2019). Internet of things (iot) based healthcare monitoring system using nodemcu and arduino uno. [ijtsrd]. *Published in International Journal of Trend in Scientific Research and Development*, *3*(5), 755–759.

Wang, Q., Li, B., Xiao, T., Zhu, J., Li, C., Wong, D. F., & Chao, L. S. (2019). Learning deep transformer models for machine translation. arXiv preprint arXiv:1906.01787. DOI: 10.18653/v1/P19-1176

Wang, C., Wen, W., Zhang, H., Ni, J., Jiang, J., Cheng, Y., & Ge, Z. (2021). Anxiety, depression, and stress prevalence among college students during the COVID-19 pandemic: A systematic review and meta-analysis. *Journal of American College Health*, *•••*, 1–8. DOI: 10.1080/07448481.2021.1960849 PMID: 34469261

Warsi, M. F., Chauhan, U., Gupta, S. N., & Tiwari, P. (2022). A comparative analysis of melanoma detection methods based on computer aided diagnose system. *Materials Today: Proceedings*, *57*, 1962–1968. DOI: 10.1016/j.matpr.2021.10.137

Warsi, M. F., Khanam, R., Chauhan, U., & Kamya, S. (2022). Melanoma classification by 3D colour-texture feature and neural network with improved computational complexity using PCA. *International Journal of Medical Engineering and Informatics*, *14*(4), 369–378. DOI: 10.1504/IJMEI.2022.123929

Warsi, M. F., Khanam, R., Kamya, S., & Suárez-Araujo, C. P. (2019). An efficient 3D color-texture feature and neural network technique for melanoma detection. *Informatics in Medicine Unlocked*, *17*, 100176. DOI: 10.1016/j.imu.2019.100176

Wei, H., Sun, J., Shan, W., Xiao, W., Wang, B., Ma, X., Hu, W., Wang, X., & Xia, Y. (2022). Environmental chemical exposure dynamics and machine learning-based prediction of diabetes mellitus. *The Science of the Total Environment, 806*, 150674. DOI: 10.1016/j.scitotenv.2021.150674 PMID: 34597539

Yadav, P., & Rao, R. (2024). Trends in AI-driven IoT applications: A comprehensive review. *Artificial Intelligence Review, 57*(3), 121-142. https://doi.org/ miniDOI: 10.1007/s10462-024-10231-44o

Yamashita, R., Nishio, M., Do, R. K. G., & Togashi, K. (2018). Convolutional neural networks: An overview and application in radiology. *Insights Into Imaging, 9*(4), 611–629. DOI: 10.1007/s13244-018-0639-9 PMID: 29934920

Yeruva, S., Varalakshmi, M. S., Gowtham, B. P., Chandana, Y. H., & Prasad, P. K. (2021). Identification of sickle cell anemia using deep neural networks. *Emerging Science Journal, 5*(2), 200–210. DOI: 10.28991/esj-2021-01270

Yin, Z.. (2017, January). Health-CPS: Healthcare cyber-physical system assisted by cloud and big data. *IEEE Systems Journal, 11*(1), 88–95. DOI: 10.1109/JSYST.2015.2460747

Yousef, R., & Jazzar, M. (2021). Measuring the effectiveness of user and entity behavior analytics for the prevention of insider threats. *Journal of Xi'an University of Architecture & Technology, 13*, 10.

Zanella, A., Bui, N., Castellani, A., Vangelista, L., & Zorzi, M. (2014). Internet of Things for smart cities. *IEEE Internet of Things Journal, 1*(1), 22–32. DOI: 10.1109/JIOT.2014.2306328

Zhang, M., Li, X., Xu, M., & Li, Q. (2017). Image segmentation and classification for sickle cell disease using deformable U-Net. arXiv preprint arXiv:1710.08149.

Zhang, L., & Wu, H. (2024). The impact of 5G on IoT and machine learning: A review. *IEEE Wireless Communications, 31*(1), 55–64. DOI: 10.1109/MWC.2024.1234567

Zhou, H., Myrzashova, R., & Zheng, R. (2020). Diabetes prediction model based on an enhanced deep neural network. *EURASIP Journal on Wireless Communications and Networking, 2020*(1), 1–13. DOI: 10.1186/s13638-020-01765-7

Zhou, J., & Yang, J. (2020). Machine learning for Internet of Things: A survey. *IEEE Internet of Things Journal, 7*(2), 1245–1258. DOI: 10.1109/JIOT.2019.2942438

Zhu, F., Zhang, C., Zheng, Z., & Farouk, A. (2021). Practical Network Coding Technologies and Softwarization in Wireless Networks. *IEEE Internet of Things Journal, 8*(7), 5211–5218. DOI: 10.1109/JIOT.2021.3056580

Zou, Q., Qu, K., Luo, Y., Yin, D., Ju, Y., & Tang, H. (2018). Predicting diabetes mellitus with machine learning techniques. *Frontiers in Genetics*, *9*, 515. DOI: 10.3389/fgene.2018.00515 PMID: 30459809

About the Contributors

Nikhil Kumar Marriwala holds a Post-doc, PhD, M-Tech and B-Tech., in Engineering & Technology and currently serves as an Assistant Professor in the Department of Electronics and Communication Engineering at the University Institute of Engineering and Technology, Kurukshetra University, Kurukshetra. He earned his Postdoc from Amity University, Dubai and PhD from the National Institute of Technology (NIT), Kurukshetra, specializing in Electronics and Communication Engineering. His academic journey includes a post-graduation (M-Tech) in Electronics and Communication Engineering from the Institute of Advanced Studies in Education (IASE) University, along with a B-Tech in Electronics and Instrumentation from MMEC, Mullana, Kurukshetra University, Kurukshetra. With over 21 years of teaching experience at both graduate and postgraduate levels, Dr. Marriwala has significantly contributed to the academic field. As a mentor, he has supervised the successful completion of One PhD student and more than 33 M-Tech dissertations. Also he currently guides 2 students pursuing PhDs. Additionally, he has authored over 10 books with prestigious publishers like Pearson and Wiley, published over 35 papers in reputed international journals, and presented 30 papers in international/national conferences. Dr. Marriwala holds 8 patents, including 2 Indian patents and 6 international patents, showcasing his innovative research contributions. His involvement in academic leadership roles is extensive, having chaired special sessions at over 22 international/national conferences and delivered keynote addresses at 9 international conferences. Furthermore, he has organized multiple international and national conferences, demonstrating his organizational prowess. Dr. Marriwala is also deeply engaged in fostering academic collaborations and knowledge dissemination. He has delivered over 70 invited talks/guest lectures at leading universities and colleges across India. Moreover, he holds additional responsibilities as the Training and Placement Officer at UIET, Kurukshetra University, Kurukshetra, and serves as the Single Point of Contact (SPOC) for various academic initiatives, including the SWAYAM NPTEL Local

Chapter and Infosys campus connect program. He is the editor of more than 07 book proceedings with Springer and guest editor for the special session in Journal Measurement and Sensors, Elsevier. He is also the reviewer for many reputed journals. His contributions to academia have been widely recognized, with awards such as the NPTEL Enthusiasts Award and the "Career Guru of the Month" award. Dr. Marriwala has also been acknowledged by Elsevier for his contribution to open science and research addressing the United Nations Sustainable Development Goals. Dr. Marriwala's research interests span across various domains, including Wireless Communications, Software Defined Radios, Cognitive Radios, Soft Computing, Wireless Sensor Networks, Fuzzy System Design, Advanced Microprocessors, Internet of Things, Augmented Reality, Virtual Reality, and Blockchain. His dedication to academia, innovative research, and leadership in the field make Dr. Nikhil Kumar Marriwala a distinguished figure in the realm of Engineering and Technology.

Shruti Jain is an Associate Dean (Innovation) and Professor in the Department of Electronics and Communication Engineering at the Jaypee University of Information Technology, Waknaghat, H.P., India. She has received her Doctor of Science (D.Sc.) in Electronics and Communication Engineering. She has teaching experience of around 19 years. She has filed fourteen patents, of which six have been granted and eight have been published. She has published more than 30 book chapters and 150 research papers in reputed indexed journals (with IF ~ 73) and international conferences. She has also published 18 books. She has completed two government-sponsored projects. She has guided 08 Ph.D. students and now has 06 registered students. She has also guided 15 M.Tech. scholars and more than 115 B.Tech. undergrads. She has organized 14 conferences of IEEE and Springer as Conference General Chair. Her research interests are image and signal processing, soft computing, the Internet of Things, pattern recognition, bio-inspired computing, and computer-aided design of FPGA and VLSI circuits. She is a Joint Secretary of the IEEE Delhi Section, a Subcommittee member of IEEE India Council WIE, a senior member of IEEE, a life member and Executive member of the Biomedical Engineering Society of India, and a member of IAENG. She is a member of the editorial board of many reputed journals. She is also a reviewer of many journals and a member of the TPC of different conferences. She was awarded the Nation Builder Award in 2018-19 and enlisted in the 2% of scientists in the world rankings of 2021, 2023, and 2024 published by Elsevier, data compiled by Stanford University.

Vinod Kumar Shukla is currently working with Amity University, Dubai, U.A.E., as Associate Professor and Head of Academics for the Engineering Architecture and Interior Design department. He has more than 15 years of experience. He has completed his PhD in "Semantic Web and Ontology" and is an active member of IEEE. He has appeared in the prestigious Stanford's list, USA of top 2% of scientists for in 2022. He has authored 100+ research publications in journals, book chapters and Conferences, and have 500+ plus Scopus citations. He has edited books in the field of Data Science, Artificial Intelligence, Blockchain, Industry 4.0 and Healthcare, and People Analytics. He is the recipient of various awards such as the "Global Academic Excellence Award- 2021", "Faculty Achievement Award" under the category of research publication in continuous two years 2021, 2022, "Best Paper Award" in the International Conference on Machine Intelligence and Data Science Application- 2020". His research area includes cyber security, the Internet of Things, and Blockchain. Currently, he is working on the books and exploring the transition of technologies and their possible impact from Industry 4.0 to Industry 5.0.

Dinesh Kumar completed B.Tech. from IIT Madras and Ph.D. from IIT Delhi and is Professor at RMIT University, Melbourne, Australia. He is a Fellow of Australasian Institute of Digital Health. He has published over 400 papers, authored 8 books, and is on a range of Australian and international committees for Biomedical Engineering. His passion is for affordable diagnostics and making a difference for his students. His work has been cited over 8400 times, and he has also had multiple successes with technology translation. He is Member of Therapeutics Goods Administration (TGA), Ministry of Health (Australia) for medical devices. He is also on the editorial boards for IEEE Transactions of Neural Systems and Rehabilitation Engineering and Biomedical Signals and Controls. He has been Chair of large number of conferences and given over 50 keynotes speeches.

***

Hina Bansal is an inspirational teacher and researcher with 16+ years of experience specializing in Bioinformatics/Computational Biology, working as an Assistant Professor in the centre for Bioinformatics and Computational Biology, Amity Institute of Biotechnology, Amity University, Noida since January 2008. Her research interest includes Network pharmacology, functional Genomics and Genome informatics, NGS, functional Proteomics, Molecular docking and simulation, Python, Artificial intelligence, and Machine learning. She has more than forty research publications in reputable peer reviewed journals, book, and book chapters. She has presented numerous papers in various national and international conferences. She has been an active member in organising several workshops and conferences. She is a dynamic reviewer for various peer reviewed journals including BMC Computational Biology and Scientific Reports. She is very proficient in programming languages like C, C++, Java and Python. With her perseverance, academic excellence, research capabilities, and leadership abilities, Dr. Hina a very potential candidate.

Anuj Kumar Gupta is working as a Professor in the CSE Dept. at CGC College of Engineering. He has a Ph.D. in Computer Science & Engineering. He has a vast academic & administrative experience of 20+ years. He has guided many PG & PhD research scholars. He has published more than 90 research papers in reputed international & national journals and conferences. He has filed more than 10 patents and published 4 books. He is a member of the Computer Society of India & ISTE.

Shiv Narain Gupta received B. Tech. degree in Electronics and Communication Engineering from Uttar Pradesh Technical University in 2006, M.Tech degree in Digital Communication from Ambedkar Institute of Technology, Delhi in 2009 and Ph.D. degree from Jaypee Institute of Information Technology (JIIT), Noida in 2023. His research areas are analog integrated circuits and analog signal processing applications.

Shruti Jain has received PhD degree from Jaypee University of Information Technology, Waknaghat, Solan. She has a teaching experience of around 13 years and before joining JUIT, she worked as Assistant Professor in Haryana Engineering College, Jagadhari, Ambala College of Engineering, Ambala. She has specialization in Biomedical Signal Processing, Computer- Aided design of FPGA and VLSI circuits, combinatorial optimization. She has published more than 50 papers in reputed journals and 30 papers in International conferences. She is a senior member of IEEE, life member of Biomedical Engineering Society of India and member of IAENG. She is currently working as Associate Professor in the Department of Electronics and Communication Engineering, JUIT Waknaghat.

Firas Tayseer Mohammad Ayasrah is an esteemed scholar and educator specializing in Educational Technology and its applications in teaching and learning. He holds a PhD in Educational Technologies and serves as an Assistant Professor at Al Ain University, UAE. With extensive academic experience, he has taught undergraduate and graduate courses in educational technology, instructional design, and digital learning. His research focuses on Artificial Intelligence (AI) in education, digital learning environments, and immersive technologies such as virtual and augmented reality. He explores the integration of AI in instructional systems, its impact on science education, and its applications in higher education. Additionally, his work addresses online learning, educational data analytics, and innovative teaching methodologies. He has published his research findings in reputable international journals and actively participates in research projects exploring AI-driven educational solutions. His contributions aim to enhance technology-enhanced learning, digital pedagogy, and intelligent educational systems, shaping the future of education in the digital age.

Jitendra Mohan obtained his B.Tech. degree from S. R. T. M. University, Nanded. He got his M.Tech degree from Aligarh Muslim University and Ph.D. degree from Uttarakhand Technical University. He is currently working as Professor in the Department of Electronics and Communication Engineering at Jaypee Institute of Information Technology, Noida (India). His main areas of interest are current-mode circuits and analog signal processing applications. He has guided 03 PhD, 03 Master's Dissertation and 55 projects. He has more than 85 International Journal and conference papers.

Basab Nath is currently serving as an Assistant Professor in the Department of Computer Science and Engineering at IILM University, Greater Noida, India. He holds a Ph.D. in Computer Science and Engineering and has over 6.5 of experience in academia and research. His research interests primarily focus on Natural Language Processing (NLP), Machine Translation, Artificial Intelligence (AI), and Machine Learning (ML). Dr. Nath has published extensively in SCI and Scopus-indexed journals, with notable contributions in the areas of multilingual neural machine translation, deep learning for healthcare applications, and AI-driven recommendation systems. He has also participated in multiple AI/ML hackathons and is actively engaged in developing AI-based solutions for real-world problems, including cervical cancer detection and mood-based music recommendation systems. In addition to his research, Dr. Nath has delivered workshops and training sessions on Power BI, Google Sheets, and AI tools for management and hospital management students. He is also actively involved in Project-Based Learning (PBL) curriculum development, emphasizing interdisciplinary project integration and real-world application of AI technologies. Dr. Nath is a dedicated academician and researcher, committed to bridging the gap between theoretical knowledge and practical implementation, while contributing to the advancement of AI and ML in various domains.

Harshal Patil is a distinguished educator and researcher in Computer Science and Engineering, specializing in Information Security. He currently serves as Professor and Head of the Department of Computing and Security at IILM University. With over 14 years of teaching experience, he has made significant contributions to higher education and research. He has an impressive research portfolio, with over 80+ published research papers and 12 patents to his credit. He is also the author of seven books, further solidifying his expertise in the field. As a Certified Cyber Security Intervention Officer, he actively contributes to cybersecurity by assisting victims of cybercrime. His work reflects a commitment to innovation, academic excellence, and the practical application of cybersecurity principles.

Pooja M R, is currently working as Professor in the Department of Computer Science & Engineering. She has more than 40 research publications in peer reviewed international journals and international conferences. Her research interest includes Machine Learning and Artificial Intelligence, Analytics and Health informatics. She has received appreciations for her multidisciplinary research with substantial contributions in the field of health informatics and Artificial Intelligence. She is nominated as Bentham Ambassador from INDIA in recognition of her research in Medical Informatics. In recognition of her research, she has been selected as Editorial Board Member for various peer reviewed journals and also is a member of the Technical Program Committee of various international conferences. She has delivered talks at various international technical platforms and is an invited speaker at various conferences and workshops. She is a member of various international professional Bodies.

M. Preethi is currently working as an Assistant Professor in the Department of Information Technology at Sri Ramakrishna Engineering College, Coimbatore..

Manmohan Rauthan is working as Head of the department and professor in HNB Garhwal University in computer science and engineering department with 30 years of teaching experience. He has done M.Tech in 1987 from Roorkee University and has done his Ph.D. from Kumaon University in 2013. He has written a several research paper as well as 5 books in computer science. He is a core member of research committees, visiting committees.

Jasminder Kaur Sandhu is an Associate Professor and Head – Department of Machine Learning & Data Science at the School of Computer Science and Engineering, IILM University. Previously, she served as an Associate Professor and PhD Coordinator – CSE at Chandigarh University for nearly two years. With 15 years of teaching and research experience, she holds a Doctorate in Computer Science & Engineering from Thapar University, Patiala. She has an extensive research portfolio, with 94 publications in SCI and Scopus-indexed journals, along with three edited books published by international publishers such as Wiley and IGI. Her research interests span Machine Learning, Ensemble Modelling, Artificial Intelligence, Soft Computing, Dependability Evaluation, Quality of Service, Wireless Sensor Networks, and Ad-Hoc Networks. She is also an active reviewer for prestigious journals, including the International Journal of Machine Learning and Cybernetics (Springer), Computational and Mathematical Methods (Wiley), IEEE Access, Journal of Network and Computer Applications (Elsevier), and Archives of

Computational Methods (Springer). Beyond research, Dr. Sandhu has played a key role in academic accreditations, serving as a criteria coordinator for NAAC, NBA, and ABET. She possesses deep expertise in curriculum design, Bloom's Taxonomy, and research enhancement policies.

Anita Venugopal received her Ph.D. in Computer Science and Mathematics. She is currently working as Assistant Prof. at Dhofar University, Oman. Her research interest includes Artificial Intelligence, Database systems, Machine learning system, Pattern recognition, Neural network and Information Science. She has published number of research papers in various referred International/ National Journals and Conferences. She is having more than 28 years of experience in teaching. She has taught relevant areas of Computer Science, GUI Programming, Database, Multimedia and Web Technology at different levels.

P. William is working as Dean, Research & Development at Sanjivani College of Engineering affiliated to SPPU, Pune. He is the Post Doctoral Fellow from Amity University, Dubai and adjunct faculty of Victorian Institute of Technology, Australia. He is a member of IEEE, QCFI, ISTE and various other professional bodies. His research includes innovation and development of cutting-edge solutions in the fields of natural language processing, artificial intelligence, deep learning, machine learning, soft computing, cybersecurity, and cloud computing. He has published 135+ papers in Scopus indexed journals and Conferences. He has 30+ patents published with grants in his credit. He has authored and edited 10+ books with renowned publishers of global recognition. He has been associated with numerous Multi-National Companies and various Educational Groups for his expertise in research, corporate training and consulting where he has contributed to the advancement of knowledge and practice in his domain. A focused professional with experience of consulting in Research, Innovation and Development. He served as a Chairperson and Auditor in multiple committees of national recognition.

Index

N

O

P

R

S

U

W

www.ingramcontent.com/pod-product-compliance
Lightning Source LLC
LaVergne TN
LVHW081334300926
849161LV00008B/1974